ANNUAL EDITIONS

Developing World 10/11
Twentieth Edition

EDITOR

Robert J. Griffiths
University of North Carolina

Robert J. Griffiths is Associate Professor of Political Science at the University of North Carolina at Greensboro. His teaching and research interests are in the field of comparative and international politics with a focus on Africa. He teaches courses on the politics of the non-western world, African politics, international law and organization, international security, and international political economy. His recent publications include "Democratizing South African Civil-Military Relations: A Blueprint for Post-Conflict Reform?" in *War and Peace in Africa: History, Nationalism, and the State,* edited by Toyin Falola and Raphael C. Njoku (forthcoming 2009) and "Parliamentary Oversight of Defense in South Africa" in *Legislative Oversight and Budgeting: A World Perspective,* Rick Stapenhurst, Riccardo Pelizzo, David Olson, & Lisa von Trapp edited by World Bank Institute Development Studies (2008).

McGraw Hill

Connect
Learn
Succeed™

ANNUAL EDITIONS: DEVELOPING WORLD, TWENTIETH EDITION

Published by McGraw-Hill, a business unit of The McGraw-Hill Companies, Inc., 1221 Avenue
of the Americas, New York, NY 10020. Copyright © 2010 by The McGraw-Hill Companies, Inc.
All rights reserved. Previous edition(s) 1989–2009. No part of this publication may be reproduced
or distributed in any form or by any means, or stored in a database or retrieval system, without the
prior written consent of The McGraw-Hill Companies, Inc., including, but not limited to, in any
network or other electronic storage or transmission, or broadcast for distance learning.

Some ancillaries, including electronic and print components, may not be available to customers
outside the United States.

Annual Editions® is a registered trademark of the McGraw-Hill Companies, Inc.

Annual Editions is published by the **Contemporary Learning Series** group within the
McGraw-Hill Higher Education division.

1 2 3 4 5 6 7 8 9 0 QPD/QPD 0 9

ISBN 978–0–07–812781–6
MHID 0–07–812781–5
ISSN 1096–4215

Managing Editor: *Larry Loeppke*
Senior Managing Editor: *Faye Schilling*
Developmental Editor: *Debra Henricks*
Editorial Coordinator: *Mary Foust*
Editorial Assistant: *Cindy Hedley*
Production Service Assistant: *Rita Hingtgen*
Permissions Coordinator: *Lenny J. Behnke*
Senior Marketing Manager: *Julie Keck*
Marketing Communications Specialist: *Mary Klein*
Marketing Coordinator: *Alice Link*
Project Manager: *Joyce Watters*
Design Specialist: *Tara McDermott*
Senior Production Supervisor: *Laura Fuller*
Cover Graphics: *Kristine Jubeck*

Compositor: Laserwords Private Limited
Cover Image: Department of Defense (both)

Library of Congress Cataloging-in-Publication Data
Main entry under title: Annual Editions: Developing World. 2010/2011.
1. Developing World—Periodicals. I. Griffiths, Robert J., *comp*. II. Title: Developing World.
658'.05

Editors/Academic Advisory Board

Members of the Academic Advisory Board are instrumental in the final selection of articles for each edition of ANNUAL EDITIONS. Their review of articles for content, level, and appropriateness provides critical direction to the editors and staff. We think that you will find their careful consideration well reflected in this volume.

ANNUAL EDITIONS: Developing World 10/11
20th Edition

EDITOR

Robert J. Griffiths
University of North Carolina

ACADEMIC ADVISORY BOARD MEMBERS

Preface

In publishing ANNUAL EDITIONS we recognize the enormous role played by the magazines, newspapers, and journals of the public press in providing current, first-rate educational information in a broad spectrum of interest areas. Many of these articles are appropriate for students, researchers, and professionals seeking accurate, current material to help bridge the gap between principles and theories and the real world. These articles, however, become more useful for study when those of lasting value are carefully collected, organized, indexed, and reproduced in a low-cost format, which provides easy and permanent access when the material is needed. That is the role played by ANNUAL EDITIONS.

The developing world continues to play an increasingly important role in world affairs.

It is home to the vast majority of the world's population and it has an increasingly significant impact on the international economy. From the standpoint of international security, developing countries are not only sites of frequent conflicts and humanitarian crises, but also a source of continuing concern related to international terrorism. Developing countries also play a critical role in the efforts involved to protect the global environment.

The developing world demonstrates considerable ethnic, cultural, political, and economic diversity, thus making generalizations about such a diverse group of countries difficult. Increasing differentiation among developing countries further complicates our comprehension of the challenges of modernization, development, and globalization that they face. A combination of internal and external factors shape the current circumstances throughout the developing world, and issues of peace and security, international trade and finance, debt, poverty, the environment, human rights, and gender illustrate the complexity of these challenges as well as the effects of globalization and the growing interdependence between nations. The ways in which these issues interrelate suggest the need for greater understanding of the connections between developing and industrialized countries. There continues to be significant debate about the best way to address the challenges faced by the developing world.

The developing world competes for attention on an international agenda that is often dominated by relations between the industrialized nations. Moreover, the domestic concerns of the industrial countries frequently overshadow the plight of the developing world. The twentieth edition of *Annual Editions: Developing World* seeks to provide students with an understanding of the diversity and complexity of the developing world and to acquaint them with the challenges that these nations confront. I remain convinced of the need for greater awareness of the problems that confront the developing world and that the international community must make a commitment to effectively address these issues, especially in the era of globalization. I hope that this volume contributes to students' knowledge and understanding of current trends and their implications and serves as a catalyst for further discussion.

Fifty percent of the articles in this edition are new. I chose articles that I hope are both interesting and informative and that can serve as a basis for further student research and discussion. The units deal with what I regard as the major issues facing the developing world. In addition, I have attempted to suggest the similarities and differences between developing countries, the nature of their relationships with the industrialized nations, and the different perspectives that exist regarding the causes of and approaches to meet the issues.

I would again like to thank McGraw-Hill for the opportunity to put together a reader on a subject that is the focus of my teaching and research. I would also like to thank those who have sent in the response forms with their comments and suggestions. I have tried to take these into account in preparing the current volume. No book on a topic as broad as the developing world can be completely comprehensive. There certainly are additional and alternative readings that might be included. Any suggestions for improvement are welcome. Please complete and return the postage-paid article rating form at the end of the book with your comments.

Robert J. Griffiths
Editor

Contents

UNIT 1
Understanding the Developing World

The concepts in bold italics are developed in the article. For further expansion, please refer to the Topic Guide.

UNIT 2
Political Economy and the Developing World

Unit Overview

30

The concepts in bold italics are developed in the article. For further expansion, please refer to the Topic Guide.

UNIT 3
Conflict and Instability

The concepts in bold italics are developed in the article. For further expansion, please refer to the Topic Guide.

The concepts in bold italics are developed in the article. For further expansion, please refer to the Topic Guide.

UNIT 4
Political Change in the Developing World

The concepts in bold italics are developed in the article. For further expansion, please refer to the Topic Guide.

UNIT 5
Population, Resources, Environment, and Health

The concepts in bold italics are developed in the article. For further expansion, please refer to the Topic Guide.

UNIT 6
Women and Development

The concepts in bold italics are developed in the article. For further expansion, please refer to the Topic Guide.

The concepts in bold italics are developed in the article. For further expansion, please refer to the Topic Guide.

Correlation Guide

The *Annual Editions* series provides students with convenient, inexpensive access to current, carefully selected articles from the public press. **Annual Editions: Developing World 10/11** is an easy-to-use reader that presents articles on important topics such as *democracy, foreign aid, human rights,* and many more. For more information on *Annual Editions* and other *McGraw-Hill Contemporary Learning Series* titles, visit www.mhcls.com.

This convenient guide matches the units in **Annual Editions: Developing World 10/11** with the corresponding chapters in two of our best-selling McGraw-Hill Political Science textbooks by Rourke/Boyer and Rourke.

Annual Editions: Developing World 10/11	International Politics on the World Stage, Brief, 8/e by Rourke/Boyer	International Politics on the World Stage, 12/e by Rourke
Unit 1: Understanding the Developing World	**Chapter 1:** Thinking and Caring about World Politics **Chapter 2:** The Evolution of World Politics **Chapter 4:** Nationalism: The Traditional Orientation **Chapter 5:** Globalism: The Alternative Orientation	**Chapter 1:** Thinking and Caring about World Politics **Chapter 2:** The Evolution of World Politics **Chapter 4:** Nationalism: The Traditional Orientation **Chapter 5:** Globalism: The Alternative Orientation
Unit 2: Political Economy and the Developing World	**Chapter 3:** Levels of Analysis and Foreign Policy **Chapter 5:** Globalism: The Alternative Orientation **Chapter 11:** International Economics: The Alternative Road	**Chapter 3:** Levels of Analysis and Foreign Policy **Chapter 5:** Globalism: The Alternative Orientation **Chapter 12:** National Economic Competition: The Traditional Road **Chapter 13:** International Economic Cooperation: The Alternative Road
Unit 3: Conflict and Instability	**Chapter 9:** Pursuing Security	**Chapter 8:** National Power and Statecraft: The Traditional Approach **Chapter 10:** National Security: The Traditional Road **Chapter 11:** International Security: The Alternative Road
Unit 4: Political Change in the Developing World	**Chapter 6:** Power, Statecraft, and the National State: The Traditional Structure **Chapter 7:** Intergovernmental Organizations: Alternative Governance	**Chapter 6:** National States: The Traditional Structure **Chapter 7:** Intergovernmental Organization: Alternative Governance
Unit 5: Population, Resources, Environment, and Health	**Chapter 8:** International Law and Human Rights **Chapter 10:** National Economic Competition: The Traditional Road **Chapter 11:** International Economics: The Alternative Road **Chapter 12:** Preserving and Enhancing the Biosphere	**Chapter 12:** National Economic Competition: The Traditional Road **Chapter 14:** Preserving and Enhancing Human Rights and Dignity **Chapter 15:** Preserving and Enhancing the Biosphere
Unit 6: Women and Development	**Chapter 8:** International Law and Human Rights	**Chapter 14:** Preserving and Enhancing Human Rights and Dignity

Topic Guide

This topic guide suggests how the selections in this book relate to the subjects covered in your course. You may want to use the topics listed on these pages to search the Web more easily.

On the following pages a number of websites have been gathered specifically for this book. They are arranged to reflect the units of this Annual Editions reader. You can link to these sites by going to *http://www.mhcls.com*.

All the articles that relate to each topic are listed below the bold-faced term.

Internet References

The following Internet sites have been selected to support the articles found in this reader. These sites were available at the time of publication. However, because websites often change their structure and content, the information listed may no longer be available. We invite you to visit http://www.mhcls.com for easy access to these sites.

Annual Editions: Developing World 10/11

General Sources

Foreign Policy in Focus (FPIF): Progressive Response Index
http://fpif.org/progresp/index_body.html

This index is produced weekly by FPIF, a "think tank without walls," which is an international network of analysts and activists dedicated to "making the U.S. a more responsible global leader and partner by advancing citizen movements and agendas." This index lists volume and issue numbers, dates, and topics covered by the articles.

People & Planet
http://www.peopleandplanet.org

People & Planet is an organization of student groups at universities and colleges across the United Kingdom. Organized in 1969 by students at Oxford University, it is now an independent pressure group campaigning on world poverty, human rights, and the environment.

United Nations System Web Locator
http://www.unsystem.org

This is the website for all the organizations in the United Nations family. According to its brief overview, the United Nations, an organization of sovereign nations, provides the machinery to help find solutions to international problems or disputes and to deal with pressing concerns that face people everywhere, including the problems of the developing world, through the UN Development Program at *http://www.undp.org* and UNAIDS at *http://www.unaids.org*.

United States Census Bureau: International Summary Demographic Data
http://www.census.gov/ipc/www/idb/

The International Data Base (IDB) is a computerized data bank containing statistical tables of demographic and socioeconomic data for all countries of the world.

World Health Organization (WHO)
http://www.who.ch

The WHO's objective, according to its website, is the attainment by all peoples of the highest possible level of health. Health, as defined in the WHO constitution, is a state of complete physical, mental, and social well-being and not merely the absence of disease or infirmity.

UNIT 1: Understanding the Developing World

Africa Index on Africa
http://www.afrika.no/index/

A complete reference source on Africa is available on this website.

African Studies WWW (U. Penn)
http://www.sas.upenn.edu/African_Studies/AS.html

The African Studies Center at the University of Pennsylvania supports this ongoing project that lists online resources related to African Studies.

UNIT 2: International Political Economy

Center for Third World Organizing
http://www.ctwo.org/

The Center for Third World Organizing (CTWO, pronounced "C-2") is a racial justice organization dedicated to building a social justice movement led by people of color. CTWO is a 20-year-old training and resource center that promotes and sustains direct action organizing in communities of color in the United States.

ENTERWeb
http://www.enterweb.org

ENTERWeb is an annotated meta-index and information clearinghouse on enterprise development, business, finance, international trade, and the economy in this age of cyberspace and globalization. The main focus is on micro-, small-, and medium-scale enterprises, cooperatives, and community economic development both in developed and developing countries.

International Monetary Fund (IMF)
http://www.imf.org

The IMF was created to promote international monetary cooperation, to facilitate the expansion and balanced growth of international trade, to promote exchange stability, to assist in the establishment of a multilateral system of payments, to make its general resources temporarily available under adequate safeguards to its members experiencing balance of payments difficulties, and to shorten the duration and lessen the degree of disequilibrium in the international balances of payments of members.

TWN (Third World Network)
http://www.twnside.org.sg/

The Third World Network is an independent, nonprofit international network of organizations and individuals involved in issues relating to development, the Third World, and North-South issues.

U.S. Agency for International Development (USAID)
http://www.usaid.gov

USAID is an independent government agency that provides economic development and humanitarian assistance to advance U.S. economic and political interests overseas.

The World Bank
http://www.worldbank.org

The International Bank for Reconstruction and Development, frequently called the World Bank, was established in July 1944

Internet References

at the UN Monetary and Financial Conference in Bretton Woods, New Hampshire. The World Bank's goal is to reduce poverty and improve living standards by promoting sustainable growth and investment in people. The bank provides loans, technical assistance, and policy guidance to developing country members to achieve this objective.

UNIT 3: Conflict and Instability

The Carter Center
http://www.cartercenter.org

The Carter Center is dedicated to fighting disease, hunger, poverty, conflict, and oppression through collaborative initiatives in the areas of democratization and development, global health, and urban revitalization.

Center for Strategic and International Studies (CSIS)
http://www.csis.org/

For four decades, the Center for Strategic and International Studies (CSIS) has been dedicated to providing world leaders with strategic insights on, and policy solutions to, current and emerging global issues.

Conflict Research Consortium
http://conflict.colorado.edu/

The site offers links to conflict- and peace-related Internet sites.

Institute for Security Studies
http://www.iss.co.za

This site is South Africa's premier source for information related to African security studies.

PeaceNet
http://www.igc.org/peacenet/

PeaceNet promotes dialogue and sharing of information to encourage appropriate dispute resolution, highlights the work of practitioners and organizations, and is a proving ground for ideas and proposals across the range of disciplines within the conflict resolution field.

Refugees International
http://www.refintl.org

Refugees International provides early warning in crises of mass exodus. It seeks to serve as the advocate of the unrepresented—the refugee. In recent years, Refugees International has moved from its initial focus on Indochinese refugees to global coverage, conducting almost 30 emergency missions in the last 4 years.

UNIT 4: Political Change

Latin American Network Information Center—LANIC
http://www.lanic.utexas.edu

According to Latin Trade, LANIC is "a good clearinghouse for Internet-accessible information on Latin America."

ReliefWeb
http://www.reliefweb.int/w/rwb.nsf

ReliefWeb is the UN's Department of Humanitarian Affairs clearinghouse for international humanitarian emergencies.

World Trade Organization (WTO)
http://www.wto.org

The WTO is promoted as the only international body dealing with the rules of trade between nations. At its heart are the WTO agreements, the legal ground rules for international commerce and for trade policy.

UNIT 5: Population, Resources, Environment and Health

Earth Pledge Foundation
http://www.earthpledge.org

The Earth Pledge Foundation promotes the principles and practices of sustainable development—the need to balance the desire for economic growth with the necessity of environmental protection.

EnviroLink
http://envirolink.org

EnviroLink is committed to promoting a sustainable society by connecting individuals and organizations through the use of the World Wide Web.

Greenpeace
http://www.greenpeace.org

Greenpeace is an international NGO (nongovernmental organization) that is devoted to environmental protection.

Linkages on Environmental Issues and Development
http://www.iisd.ca/linkages/

Linkages is a site provided by the International Institute for Sustainable Development. It is designed to be an electronic clearinghouse for information on past and upcoming international meetings related to both environmental issues and economic development in the developing world.

Population Action International
http://www.populationaction.org

According to its mission statement, Population Action International is dedicated to advancing policies and programs that slow population growth in order to enhance the quality of life for all people.

The Worldwatch Institute
http://www.worldwatch.org

The Worldwatch Institute advocates environmental protection and sustainable development.

UNIT 6: Women and Development

WIDNET: Women in Development NETwork
http://www.focusintl.com/widnet.htm

This site provides a wealth of information about women in development, including the Beijing '95 Conference, WIDNET statistics, and women's studies.

Women Watch/Regional and Country Information
http://www.un.org/womenwatch/

The UN Internet Gateway on the Advancement and Empowerment of Women provides a rich mine of information.

UNIT 1

Understanding the Developing World

Unit Selections

Key Points to Consider

- How has the emphasis of development changed?

- In what ways does democracy contribute to development?

- What is the ideology of development?

- What are the criticisms of the Millennium Villages Project?

- Why is the influence of the West declining?

- What constitutes the Western model of development?

- Is the Western model of development transferable to the developing world?

- What accounts for the increase in religious activism?

Student Website
www.mhcls.com

Internet References

Africa Index on Africa
http://www.afrika.no/index/
African Studies WWW (U. Penn)
http://www.sas.upenn.edu/African_Studies/AS.html

The diversity of the countries that make up the developing world has made it difficult to characterize and understand these countries and their role in international affairs. The task has become even more difficult as further differentiation among developing countries has occurred. "Developing world" is a catch-all term that lacks precision and explanatory power. It is used to describe societies that are desperately poor as well as those rich in resources. The term also refers to societies ranging from traditional to modern and from authoritarian to democratic. To complicate things even further, there is also debate over what actually constitutes development. For some, it is economic growth or progress towards democracy, while for others it involves greater empowerment and dignity. There are also differing views on why progress toward development has been uneven. The West tends to see the problem as stemming from poor governance, institutional weakness, and failure to embrace free-market principles. Critics from the developing world cite the legacy of colonialism and the nature of the international political and economic structures as the reasons for the lack of development. Not only are there differing views on the causes of lagging development, but there is also considerable debate on how best to tackle these issues. The Millennium Development Goals (MDGs) seek to eradicate extreme poverty and hunger and address issues of education, health, gender, and the environment. Progress in this effort so far has been uneven. This has contributed to the debate on the best way to achieve development. Critics maintain that the top-down ideology of development epitomized in the MDGs focuses attention at the macro level of development and impedes the emergence of local, grassroots solutions. The emphasis of development has shifted as well; it now extends beyond the traditional focus on poverty reduction to include issues like civil and political rights, human security, and environmental sustainability. Reflecting this broader emphasis is a growing list of actors that includes non-governmental organizations and philanthropic organizations involved in development efforts. In any case, lumping together the 120-plus nations that make up the developing world obscures the disparities in size, population, resources, forms of government, level of industrialization, distribution of wealth, ethnicity, and a host of other indicators that makes it difficult to categorize and generalize about this large, diverse group of countries.

Despite their diversity, most nations of the developing world share some characteristics. Many developing countries have large populations, with annual growth rates that often exceed 2 percent. Although there has been some improvement, poverty continues to be widespread in both rural and urban areas, with rural areas often containing the poorest of the poor . While the majority of the developing world's inhabitants continue to live in the countryside, there is a massive rural-to-urban migration under way, cities are growing rapidly, and some developing countries are approaching urbanization rates similar to those of industrialized countries. Wealth is unevenly distributed, making education, employment opportunities, and access to health care luxuries that only a few enjoy. Corruption and mismanagement

© Connie Coleman/Getty Images

are too common. With very few exceptions, these nations share a colonial past that has affected them both politically and economically. A critical perspective from the developing world charges that the neocolonial structure of the international economy and the West's political, military, and cultural links with the developing world amount to continued domination.

The roots of the diverging views between the rich and the poor nations on development emerged shortly after the beginning of the independence era. The neocolonial viewpoint encouraged efforts to alter the international economic order during the 1970s. While the New International Economic Order (NIEO) succumbed to neoliberalism in the 1980s, developing countries still frequently seek solidarity in their interactions with the West. The efforts to extract concessions from the industrialized countries in the negotiations on the Doha Trade Round illustrated this effort. Moreover, developing countries still view Western prescriptions for development skeptically and chafe under the Washington Consensus, which dictates the terms for the access to funds from international financial institutions and foreign aid. Furthermore, some critics suggest that Western development models result in inequitable development and give rise to cultural imperialism. In contrast to the developing world's criticism of the West, industrial countries continue to maintain the importance of institution-building and following the Western model that emphasizes a market-oriented approach to development. As the developing world comes to play a more prominent role in economic, security, and environmental issues, the West's ability to dictate the terms on which development occurs will diminish.

There is a clear difference of opinion between the industrialized countries and the developed world on issues ranging from economic development to governance. Ultimately the development process will be shaped primarily by the countries experiencing it. The industrialized countries can, however, continue to contribute to this process although it may require re-evaluation of policies on trade and technology transfer, along with more emphasis on innovative and effective aid.

The New Face of Development

"As the traditional development challenge of reducing poverty is increasingly met, a new challenge for the twenty-first century emerges: that of ensuring a livable, peaceful, and prosperous world."

CAROL LANCASTER

A number of trends in international development that were already emerging at the end of the last millennium—including the introduction of new actors and technologies, the increasing role of private investment, and the remarkable reduction in poverty in countries such as China and India—have become even more apparent as we approach the end of the current decade. These trends go to the core of what development is, how it is achieved, and who is involved in promoting it. In combination, they suggest that international development in the future will likely be very different from what it has been in the past.

The world first turned its attention to the challenge of international development in the decades immediately after World War II, as the cold war began and decolonization got under way. How, the international community asked itself, could growth be accelerated and poverty reduced in newly independent, less developed nations? Wealthy countries increasingly engaged in promoting economic progress in developing countries (primarily through foreign aid), and also established professional agencies, both bilateral and multilateral, to allocate and manage development assistance. The motives for the developed countries' actions, of course, were not purely altruistic. They sought to promote their national interests (such as the containment of Soviet influence); to ensure that decolonization proceeded smoothly; to preserve spheres of influence in former colonies; to expand their own exports; and to secure sources of raw materials abroad.

During the 40 years between 1960 and 2000, the international aid and development regime depended on rich countries' providing concessional economic assistance. They provided such assistance either directly to recipient governments, or indirectly, through international institutions. The aid was targeted toward agreed-upon projects like roads, government-provided agricultural services, primary education, and health care. Rich countries' trade and investment policies were understood to be an important part of the development equation, but they tended to be much less prominent than development aid itself, since trade and investment usually involved powerful domestic interests

within rich countries, a circumstance that constrained their use for development purposes.

Over the same period, the ways in which aid was used to promote development underwent an evolution. In the 1960s, the primary emphasis was on encouraging economic growth by providing funds for infrastructure and other projects meant to expand national production. In the 1970s, the main focus was direct action to alleviate poverty, with aid devoted to projects that would meet the basic needs of the poor in developing countries (including basic education, primary health care, and development of small farms). In the 1980s, the emphasis was on fostering growth through budgetary support for economic reforms and "structural adjustment."

The 1990s turned out to be a transition decade for development. With the end of the cold war and the breakup of the Soviet Union, many of the former communist bloc countries began a transition to free markets and democratic governance. Aid-giving governments turned their attention, and their aid, to furthering this transition. A wave of democratization washed over other parts of the world as well, including sub-Saharan Africa, and democracy became increasingly linked with development in the minds of many development practitioners. Democracy, it was now argued, was a key facilitator of development, and thus foreign aid was increasingly used to promote political development.

At the same time, rising concerns over transnational problems, such as environmental deterioration and infectious diseases (especially HIV/AIDS), expanded the development discourse. Conflict prevention and mitigation became part of the broadening framework of international development as civil conflicts erupted in a number of countries, especially in Africa, and it became obvious that economic progress required peaceful conditions. Finally, the development dialogue renewed its emphasis on poverty reduction, partly because of the "associational revolution"—an explosion of civil society organizations, in both rich and poor countries. Many of these organizations were interested in bettering the human condition.

The continued evolution of information technologies will empower the poor, probably in ways we cannot foresee.

And so, between the postwar period and the year 2000, much changed. In particular, the notion of development expanded to include a much wider range of issues. Yet the core focus remained poverty reduction, and the primary instrument for achieving it remained government-based economic assistance.

An Elastic Idea

Today, international development has become an even more elastic concept, as ideas about what constitutes development, how it is best achieved, and who should be part of the process continue to evolve. Starting from the early years of the international development era a half-century ago, development was thought of as a means to improve the material conditions of life. That is, public and private investment would promote growth, which in turn would eventually reduce or even eliminate poverty. This basic concept remains at the heart of development, but there have been some important additions.

"Human development" is now part of the equation, meaning that education, health, life expectancy, and other indicators of well-being are given greater attention. Political rights are also considered a key aspect of development, in part to ensure that the poor and excluded have a political voice. Some have incorporated "human security," as well, including security against economic deprivation and against physical violence, actual or threatened. "Sustainable development," or economic progress that does not affect the environment too harshly, is another element in the welter of ideas that currently define development. Some in recent years have defined development as the freedom to choose a fulfilling life.

This trend is likely to continue. Development will have at its core the reduction of severe poverty as long as that problem endures; but it will also continue to evolve to reflect changing global beliefs about the basic requirements of a decent human life and about how to meet those requirements.

Western economists have always believed that the driver of development is private investment—on the theory that because it increases productivity, production, growth, incomes, and jobs, it will ultimately eliminate poverty. Others, however, have taken the view that the market is unable to create equitable development and that state intervention is necessary to direct and hasten economic progress. This state-versus-market tension was evident during the cold war, with the socialist and capitalist models doing battle. The same philosophical difference is part of the debate between those who emphasize macroeconomic growth (for example, through structural adjustment) and those who emphasize direct interventions to reduce poverty. From an institutional perspective, this tension has been reflected in the often differing approaches of the World Bank and nongovernmental organizations (NGOs) toward promoting development.

In recent years, something of a consensus has emerged. It is now broadly accepted that private investment and well functioning markets are essential to sustaining long-term growth, and that the state cannot do it alone. But it is also generally recognized that without a well-functioning state, markets cannot produce sustained growth and reduce poverty.

When the era of international development began, the major actors were states, along with international institutions like the World Bank. Rich states shaped world trade policies and the special trade arrangements (for example, the Generalized System of Preferences) that affected the trade of poor countries. Not much foreign investment in poor countries was carried out, and even then it was sometimes unwelcome. Essentially, the governments of rich countries provided aid to the governments of poor countries. It was, in the language of telecommunications, a "one-to-one" world.

This has changed. Governments still play a major role but they are joined by civil society organizations, both in developed and developing countries. These groups deliver services, funded both by governments and through private giving, and advocate for more action to improve the lives of the poor. Growing numbers of corporations are investing large amounts in poor countries. They are also funding development activities on their own, often in public-private partnerships that also involve governments of rich countries and NGOs. These activities are part of corporate social responsibility programs, or even part of businesses' marketing strategies.

The scale of global philanthropy has grown over time, and the number of philanthropic organizations funding development activities has also grown. The Gates Foundation is the most prominent of the new foundations but there are many others. Countless so-called social entrepreneurs have come on the scene as well. These are individuals in developed and developing countries who create NGOs to tackle development problems—as well as "venture philanthropists" who create enterprises with double and triple bottom lines, enterprises that aim to do good while doing well. (An example would be an equity fund that combines investing with providing technical assistance to small enterprises that have few alternatives for capital or training.)

These actors have created a "many-to-many" development space that promises to grow in the coming decades. Also contributing to many-to-many development is the growing flow of remittances from immigrants working in rich countries to their families in poor countries. Indeed, the flow of remittances exceeds the global total of foreign aid by a considerable amount.

The Technology Revolution

All these trends have been facilitated by new information technologies. We are living, in fact, in the midst of several technology revolutions—information technology, biotechnology, nano-technology, and materials technology. All of these hold the promise of radically changing not only our lives but also the lives of the poor in developing countries.

Information technology is already connecting many inhabitants of developing nations to the internet, as computers become increasingly affordable in poor countries. Cell phones are being used for banking, medical investigations, market updates, and obtaining all manner of otherwise out-of-reach information (as well as for political networking). The continued evolution of information technologies will empower the poor, probably in ways we cannot foresee. It has already provided new means for financial support to reach the poor through NGOs operating in developing countries, as wealthy people contribute through internet portals. This innovation cuts out middlemen and encourages direct giving. The internet has also facilitated the transfer of remittances from rich to poor countries. And it permits the poor to network as never before, an opportunity that will surely be seized even more in the future as cell phones come to resemble computers and become more affordable for all.

The biological revolution promises gains in medicine and agriculture, though these are not without controversy. The benefits have not yet reached a large enough scale to have a major impact on the lives of the poor, but this seems only a matter of time. Nanotechnology fosters miniaturization that, among other things, will make more powerful and cheaper cell phones possible. And advances in materials technology could lead to the production of commodities especially designed for difficult environments, an encouraging prospect for the poor living in those environments.

The Third World's End

During much of the past 40 years, people spoke and wrote about the "Third World"—the many developing countries that were an arena of competition between the United States and the Soviet Union. The Soviet Union, of course, is gone. But so is any semblance of shared poverty among the 150 or so countries comprising Asia, Africa, and Latin America. China has provided the most dramatic example of a poor country achieving rapid growth through manufacturing and exporting. In the past 25 years, China's development has lifted a quarter of a billion people out of poverty. This is a degree of economic progress, even with all of its accompanying problems, that is historically unprecedented. China is in fact now a major source of trade, aid, and investment for countries in Africa, Latin America, and elsewhere in Asia.

Economic progress in India—the other country with large-scale poverty and a population in excess of a billion—is increasingly evident as well. There, development is based to a large extent on the export of services. Poverty has fallen somewhat in Latin America, too, as many economies there diversify and grow. This means that the world's hard-core poverty and development problem is now concentrated in sub-Saharan Africa.

In many countries in sub-Saharan Africa, little economic progress has been achieved since independence. The difficulties standing in the way of the region's advancement include a difficult climate and the heavy disease load that comes with being located in the tropics. Also, many sub-Saharan nations are small and landlocked. Others are resource-rich but have found these resources to be a curse (Nigeria with its oil; Sierra Leone with its diamonds; the Democratic Republic of Congo [DRC] with its copper, cobalt, and other minerals).

One discerns a real opportunity—for the first time in history—to eradicate severe poverty worldwide.

Governments in these countries have long exhibited incompetence and corruption, and their resources have made it possible for them to provide little accountability to their citizens. Discontent has often led to violent conflict, which has been further stoked by competition for the control of resources. Civil conflicts in the DRC, Sierra Leone, and elsewhere have killed large numbers of people, created even more refugees and displaced persons, and destroyed national assets. Nigeria continues to teeter on the brink of a political abyss, the DRC continues to be plagued by internal war, and Somalia is still a collapsed state—with predictable effects on development.

But not all the news out of Africa is gloomy. Economic growth in India and China has increased demand, and thus prices, for the raw materials that many African countries export. Economic management in Africa, at least in most places, is better than it has been in several decades. Democratic development—or political openness, anyway—is greater than it has been during much of the period since independence.

Corruption, on the other hand, remains a major problem in many African countries. Additionally, China's extraordinary success in producing cheap manufactured goods appears to have left African countries—which lack the cheap, productive labor that China has—with few opportunities to attract the investment that might lead them into world manufacturing markets. In short, Africa is experiencing some new economic opportunities but also some new challenges.

Global Challenges

Beginning in the 1990s, major powers began to take greater note of global and transnational problems when they calculated their foreign policy and foreign aid policies. For much of that decade, the focus of this set of concerns, known as global public goods, was the environment—pollution, loss of plant and animal species, and loss of the ozone layer. While these transnational concerns (other than the ozone layer) have not abated, two more have joined them: infectious disease (above all HIV/AIDS) and climate change (which was not yet such a prominent concern in the 1990s).

The Bush administration has promised an extraordinary amount of aid to fight HIV/AIDS worldwide—$30 billion over the coming five years. Concern over this disease has risen in the United States as its global impact has become ever more evident, above all in Africa. The American religious right—long skeptical of the appropriateness and efficacy of foreign aid—has embraced fighting HIV/AIDS as the duty of Christians to aid those, especially women and children, who are suffering through no fault of their own. Although allocations of assistance so far have not kept pace with pledges, it is possible that fighting this disease will become the largest element in US foreign aid in the future.

But the next US president will also need to confront the issue of climate change, the reality and probable impact of which can no longer be ignored. That impact, incidentally, is expected to be particularly damaging to many of the world's poor countries. It seems likely, given that the governments of rich countries only have so much money to spend on development, that some development money will be shifted over the coming decades to fund activities intended to combat global warming—perhaps some of it as incentive payments to encourage governments to reduce greenhouse gas emissions.

Beyond climate change, two other trends may produce major development challenges in decades to come: the continuing growth of the world's population and the economic growth in China, India, and elsewhere. Global population is expected to continue expanding over the coming years—with nearly all of the growth taking place in the world's poor countries. Increased population will mean additional greenhouse gas emissions, as well as additional pressure on supplies of food, water, and energy. Economic growth, though it is hoped for and expected, will exacerbate those pressures, especially as demand for superior foods—meats instead of grains—increases. (A widely observed growth pattern is that as people's incomes rise they demand more protein in their diets in the form of meat and fish. But producing one pound of beef requires eight pounds of grain, and this increases pressures on food production systems.)

As for water, pressures on supply are already evident in Africa, the Middle East, northern China, and the Indian subcontinent. Where adequate water supplies cannot be procured, threats to human health and well-being emerge, along with threats to peace, stability, and income growth. Severe tensions over water already exist in the Middle East, and such situations are likely to become more common as population continues to increase. Meanwhile, a growing world population will use more fossil fuels, which will not only lead to progressively higher petroleum prices but will also exacerbate global warming.

These trends suggest that the combination of worldwide population growth and income growth needs to be managed carefully if the planet is to remain livable for our children and grandchildren. This challenge may prove the greatest of the twenty-first century.

An additional problem affecting development worldwide will be movements of people. The populations of many rich countries, and China as well, are growing at or below the replacement rate (with the United States, for reasons that are not entirely clear, a notable exception). The average age of people in these countries is rising, and this means that the dependency ratio is rising as well—each worker is in effect supporting more people. Unsurprisingly, the demand for additional workers is growing in these economies, and immigration from poorer countries to richer ones—from China to Japan, from North Africa and sub-Saharan Africa to Europe, and from Latin America to the United States—has exploded. Much of this immigration is illegal.

This movement of people has delivered benefits both to host countries and to countries of origin. It allows necessary work to be carried out in host countries while immigrants are able to send home remittances that finance consumption and investment there. This seems like a win-win arrangement—except that some citizens of the host countries experience the arrangement as a threat to their identities and ways of life. Even in the United States, where national identity is based on the idea of republican democracy rather than ethnicity, religion, or language, tensions surrounding immigration are increasingly evident.

Such tensions, in the United States and also in Japan and Europe, threaten sometimes to erupt into social strife (as indeed has occurred in recent years in France). It is not clear what will happen as the irresistible force of immigration continues to collide with the immovable object of host-country resistance, but certainly if the remittance economy and access to labor are constrained, international development will suffer a setback.

After Poverty

Since the end of the cold war, because we no longer live in a bipolar world, we have lacked a certain clarity that allowed us to order our international relations and forge domestic consensus on urgent problems. Today's world has a single major power—and many complex problems that are beyond that power's ability to resolve. International development is one of them.

Nevertheless, within this complex and fluid world, one discerns a real opportunity—for the first time in history—to eradicate severe poverty worldwide. The resources and know-how are available and much progress has already been made, especially in China and, increasingly, in India. It will not be easy to "make poverty history" over the coming decades. A great deal needs to be achieved in education, investment, and governance, and in addition we must address the issue of migrations of people away from areas of the world with too few resources to sustain a minimally acceptable standard of living. The obstacles may be insuperable in some cases. But the opportunities are there.

Meanwhile, as the traditional development challenge of reducing poverty is increasingly met, a new development challenge for the twenty-first century emerges: that of ensuring a livable, peaceful, and prosperous world. This will require addressing the global problems that arise when growing populations and rising incomes collide with limited resources.

CAROL LANCASTER is an associate professor at Georgetown University's Walsh School of Foreign Service and director of the university's Mortara Center for International Studies. A former deputy administrator of the US Agency for International Development, she is author of the forthcoming *George Bush's Foreign Aid: Revolution or Chaos?* (Center for Global Development, 2008).

How Development Leads to Democracy
What We Know about Modernization

Ronald Inglehart and Christian Welzel

In the last several years, a democratic boom has given way to a democratic recession. Between 1985 and 1995, scores of countries made the transition to democracy, bringing widespread euphoria about democracy's future. But more recently, democracy has retreated in Bangladesh, Nigeria, the Philippines, Russia, Thailand, and Venezuela, and the Bush administration's attempts to establish democracy in Afghanistan and Iraq seem to have left both countries in chaos. These developments, along with the growing power of China and Russia, have led many observers to argue that democracy has reached its high-water mark and is no longer on the rise.

That conclusion is mistaken. The underlying conditions of societies around the world point to a more complicated reality. The bad news is that it is unrealistic to assume that democratic institutions can be set up easily, almost anywhere, at any time. Although the outlook is never hopeless, democracy is most likely to emerge and survive when certain social and cultural conditions are in place. The Bush administration ignored this reality when it attempted to implant democracy in Iraq without first establishing internal security and overlooked cultural conditions that endangered the effort.

The good news, however, is that the conditions conducive to democracy can and do emerge—and the process of "modernization," according to abundant empirical evidence, advances them. Modernization is a syndrome of social changes linked to industrialization. Once set in motion, it tends to penetrate all aspects of life, bringing occupational specialization, urbanization, rising educational levels, rising life expectancy, and rapid economic growth. These create a self-reinforcing process that transforms social life and political institutions, bringing rising mass participation in politics and—in the long run—making the establishment of democratic political institutions increasingly likely. Today, we have a clearer idea than ever before of why and how this process of democratization happens.

The long-term trend toward democracy has always come in surges and declines. At the start of the twentieth century, only a handful of democracies existed, and even they fell short of being full democracies by today's standards. There was a major increase in the number of democracies following World War I, another surge following World War II, and a third surge at the end of the Cold War. Each of these surges was followed by a

decline, although the number of democracies never fell back to the original base line. By the start of the twenty-first century, about 90 states could be considered democratic.

Although many of these democracies are flawed, the overall trend is striking: in the long run, modernization brings democracy. This means that the economic resurgence of China and Russia has a positive aspect: underlying changes are occurring that make the emergence of increasingly liberal and democratic political systems likely in the coming years. It also means that there is no reason to panic about the fact that democracy currently appears to be on the defensive. The dynamics of modernization and democratization are becoming increasingly clear, and it is likely that they will continue to function.

The Great Debate

The concept of modernization has a long history. During the nineteenth and twentieth centuries, a Marxist theory of modernization proclaimed that the abolition of private property would put an end to exploitation, inequality, and conflict. A competing capitalist version held that economic development would lead to rising living standards and democracy. These two visions of modernization competed fiercely throughout much of the Cold War. By the 1970s, however, communism began to stagnate, and neither economic development nor democratization was apparent in many poor countries. Neither version of utopia seemed to be unfolding, and critics pronounced modernization theory dead.

Since the end of the Cold War, however, the concept of modernization has taken on new life, and a new version of modernization theory has emerged, with clear implications for our understanding of where global economic development is likely to lead. Stripped of the oversimplifications of its early versions, the new concept of modernization sheds light on ongoing cultural changes, such as the rise of gender equality the recent wave of democratization, and the democratic peace theory.

For most of human history, technological progress was extremely slow and new developments in food production were offset by population increases—trapping agrarian economies in a steady-state equilibrium with no growth in living standards. History was seen as either cyclic or in long-term decline from a past golden age. The situation began to change with the Industrial Revolution and the advent of sustained economic growth—which led to both the capitalist and the communist visions of modernization. Although the ideologies competed fiercely, they were both committed to economic growth and social progress and brought mass participation in politics. And each side believed that the developing nations of the Third World would follow its path to modernization.

At the height of the Cold War, a version of modernization theory emerged in the United States that portrayed underdevelopment as a direct consequence of a country's psychological and cultural traits. Underdevelopment was said to reflect irrational traditional religious and communal values that discouraged achievement. The rich Western democracies, the theory went, could instill modern values and bring progress to "backward" nations through economic, cultural, and military assistance. By the 1970s, however, it had become clear that assistance had not brought much progress toward prosperity or democracy—eroding confidence in this version of modernization theory, which was increasingly criticized as ethnocentric and patronizing. It came under heavy criticism from "dependency theorists," who argued that trade with rich countries exploits poor ones, locking them into positions of structural dependence. The elites in developing countries welcomed such thinking, since it implied that poverty had nothing to do with internal problems or the corruption of local leaders; it was the fault of global capitalism. By the 1980s, dependency theory was in vogue. Third World nations, the thinking went, could escape from global exploitation only by withdrawing from global markets and adopting import-substitution policies.

More recently, it has become apparent that import-substitution strategies have failed: the countries least involved in global trade, such as Cuba, Myanmar (also called Burma), and North Korea, have not been the most successful—they have actually grown the least. Export-oriented strategies have been far more effective in promoting sustained economic growth and, eventually, democratization. The pendulum, accordingly, has swung back, and a new version of modernization theory has gained credibility. The rapid economic development of East Asia, and the subsequent democratization of South Korea and Taiwan, seem to confirm its basic claims: producing for the world market enables economic growth; investing the returns in human capital and upgrading the work force to produce high-tech goods brings higher returns and enlarges the educated middle class; once the middle class becomes large and articulate enough, it presses for liberal democracy—the most effective political system for advanced industrial societies. Nevertheless, even today, if one mentions modernization at a conference on economic development, one is likely to hear a reiteration of dependency theory's critique of the "backward nations" version of modernization theory, as if that were all there is to modernization theory—and as if no new evidence had emerged since the 1970s.

The New Modernization

In retrospect, it is obvious that the early versions of modernization theory were wrong on several points. Today, virtually nobody expects a revolution of the proletariat that will abolish private property, ushering in a new era free from exploitation and conflict. Nor does anyone expect that industrialization will automatically lead to democratic institutions; communism and fascism also emerged from industrialization. Nonetheless, a massive body of evidence suggests that modernization theory's central premise was correct: economic development does tend to bring about important, roughly predictable changes in society, culture, and politics. But the earlier versions of modernization theory need to be corrected in several respects.

First, modernization is not linear. It does not move indefinitely in the same direction; instead, the process reaches inflection points. Empirical evidence indicates that each phase of modernization is associated with distinctive changes in people's worldviews. Industrialization leads to one major process of change, resulting in bureaucratization, hierarchy, centralization of authority, secularization, and a shift from traditional to secular-rational values. The rise of postindustrial society brings another set of cultural changes that move in a different direction: instead of bureaucratization and centralization, the new trend is toward an increasing emphasis on individual autonomy and self-expression values, which lead to a growing emancipation from authority.

Thus, other things being equal, high levels of economic development tend to make people more tolerant and trusting, bringing more emphasis on self-expression and more participation in decision-making. This process is not deterministic, and any forecasts can only be probabilistic, since economic factors are not the only influence; a given country's leaders and nation-specific events also shape what happens. Moreover, modernization is not irreversible. Severe economic collapse can reverse it, as happened during the Great Depression in Germany, Italy, Japan, and Spain and during the 1990s in most of the Soviet successor states. Similarly, if the current economic crisis becomes a twenty-first-century Great Depression, the world could face a new struggle against renewed xenophobia and authoritarianism.

Second, social and cultural change is path dependent: history matters. Although economic development tends to bring predictable changes in people's worldviews, a society's heritage—whether shaped by Protestantism, Catholicism, Islam, Confucianism, or communism—leaves a lasting imprint on its worldview. A society's value system reflects an interaction between the driving forces of modernization and the persisting influence of tradition. Although the classic modernization theorists in both the East and the West thought that religion and ethnic traditions would die out, they have proved to be highly resilient. Although the publics of industrializing societies are becoming richer and more educated, that is hardly creating a uniform global culture. Cultural heritages are remarkably enduring.

Third, modernization is not westernization, contrary to the earlier, ethnocentric version of the theory. The process of industrialization began in the West, but during the past few decades, East Asia has had the world's highest economic growth rates, and Japan leads the world in life expectancy and some other aspects of modernization. The United States is not the model for global cultural change, and industrializing societies in general are not becoming like the United States, as a popular version of modernization theory assumes. In fact, American society retains more traditional values than do most other high-income societies.

Fourth, modernization does not automatically lead to democracy. Rather, it, in the long run, brings social and cultural changes that make democratization increasingly probable. Simply attaining a high level of per capita GDP does not produce democracy: if it did, Kuwait and the United Arab Emirates would have become model democracies. (These countries have not gone through the modernization process described above.) But the emergence of postindustrial society brings certain social and cultural changes that are specifically conducive to democratization. Knowledge societies cannot function effectively without highly educated publics that have become increasingly accustomed to thinking for themselves. Furthermore, rising levels of economic security bring a growing emphasis on a syndrome of self-expression values—one that gives high priority to free choice and motivates political action. Beyond a certain point, accordingly, it becomes difficult to avoid democratization, because repressing mass demands for more open societies becomes increasingly costly and detrimental to economic effectiveness. Thus, in its advanced stages, modernization brings social and cultural changes that make the emergence and flourishing of democratic institutions increasingly likely.

The core idea of modernization theory is that economic and technological development bring a coherent set of social, cultural, and political changes. A large body of empirical evidence supports this idea. Economic development is, indeed, strongly linked to pervasive shifts in people's beliefs and motivations, and these shifts in turn change the role of religion, job motivations, human fertility rates, gender roles, and sexual norms. And they also bring growing mass demands for democratic institutions and for more responsive behavior on the part of elites. These changes together make democracy increasingly likely to emerge, while also making war less acceptable to publics.

Evaluating Values

New sources of empirical evidence provide valuable insights into how modernization changes worldviews and motivations. One important source is global surveys of mass values and attitudes. Between 1981 and 2007, the World Values Survey and the European Values Study carried out five waves of representative national surveys in scores of countries, covering almost 90 percent of the world's population. (For the data from the surveys, visit www.worldvaluessurvey.org.) The results show large cross-national differences in what people believe and value. In some countries, 95 percent of the people surveyed said that God was very important in their lives; in others, only 3 percent did. In some societies, 90 percent of the people surveyed said they believed that men have more of a right to a job than women do; in others, only 8 percent said they thought so. These cross-national differences are robust and enduring, and they are closely correlated with a society's level of economic development: people in low-income societies are much likelier to emphasize religion and traditional gender roles than are people in rich countries.

These values surveys demonstrate that the worldviews of people living in rich societies differ systematically from those of people living in low-income societies across a wide range of political, social, and religious norms. The differences run along two basic dimensions: traditional versus secular-rational values and survival versus self-expression values. (Each dimension reflects responses to scores of questions asked as part of the values surveys.)

The shift from traditional to secular-rational values is linked to the shift from agrarian to industrial societies. Traditional societies emphasize religion, respect for and obedience to authority, and national pride. These characteristics change as societies become more secular and rational. The shift from survival to self-expression values is linked to the rise of postindustrial societies. It reflects a cultural shift that occurs when younger generations emerge that have grown up taking survival for granted. Survival values give top priority to economic and physical security and conformist social norms. Self-expression values give high priority to freedom of expression, participation in decision-making, political activism, environmental protection, gender equality, and tolerance of ethnic minorities, foreigners, and gays and lesbians. A growing emphasis on these latter values engenders a culture of trust and tolerance in which people cherish individual freedom and self-expression and have activist political orientations. These attributes are crucial to democracy—and thus explain how economic growth, which takes societies from agrarian to industrial and then from industrial to postindustrial, leads to democratization. The unprecedented economic growth of the past 50 years has meant that an increasing share of the world's population has grown up taking survival for granted. Time-series data from the values surveys indicate that mass priorities have shifted from an overwhelming emphasis on economic and physical security to an emphasis on subjective well-being, self-expression, participation in decision-making, and a relatively trusting and tolerant outlook.

Both dimensions are closely linked to economic development: the value systems of high-income countries differ dramatically from those of low-income countries. Every nation that the World Bank defines as having a high income ranks relatively high on both dimensions—with a strong emphasis on both secular-rational and self-expression values. All the low-income and lower-middle-income countries rank relatively low on both dimensions. The upper-middle-income countries fall somewhere in between. To a remarkable degree, the values and beliefs of a given society reflect its level of economic developments—just as modernization theory predicts.

This strong connection between a society's value system and its per capita GDP suggests that economic development tends to produce roughly predictable changes in a society's beliefs and values, and time-series evidence supports this hypothesis. When one compares the positions of given countries in successive waves of the values surveys, one finds that almost all the countries that experienced rising per capita GDPs also experienced predictable shifts in their values.

The values survey evidence also shows, however, that cultural change is path dependent; a society's cultural heritage also shapes where it falls on the global cultural map. This map shows distinctive clusters of countries: Protestant Europe, Catholic Europe, ex-communist Europe, the English-speaking countries, Latin America, South Asia, the Islamic world, and Africa. The values emphasized by different societies fall into a remarkably coherent pattern that reflects both those societies' economic development and their religious and colonial heritage. Still, even if a society's cultural heritage continues to shape its prevailing values, economic development brings changes that have important consequences. Over time, it reshapes beliefs and values of all kinds—and it brings a growing mass demand for democratic institutions and for more responsive elite behavior. And over the quarter century covered by the values surveys, the people of most countries placed increasing emphasis on self-expression values. This cultural shift makes democracy increasingly likely to emerge where it does not yet exist and increasingly likely to become more effective and more direct where it does.

Development and Democracy

Fifty years ago, the sociologist Seymour Martin Lipset pointed out that rich countries are much more likely than poor countries to be democracies. Although this claim was contested for many years, it has held up against repeated tests. The causal direction of the relationship has also been questioned: Are rich countries more likely to be democratic because democracy makes countries rich, or is development conducive to democracy? Today, it seems clear that the causality runs mainly from economic development to democratization. During early industrialization, authoritarian states are just as likely to attain high rates of growth as are democracies. But beyond a certain level of economic development, democracy becomes increasingly likely to emerge and survive. Thus, among the scores of countries that democratized around 1990, most were middle-income countries: almost all the high-income countries already were democracies, and few low-income countries made the transition. Moreover, among the countries that democratized between 1970 and 1990, democracy has survived in every country that made the transition when it was at the economic level of Argentina today or higher; among the countries that made the transition when they were below this level, democracy had an average life expectancy of only eight years.

The strong correlation between development and democracy reflects the fact that economic development is conducive to democracy. The question of why, exactly, development leads to democracy has been debated intensely, but the answer is beginning to emerge. It does not result from some disembodied force that causes democratic institutions to emerge automatically when a country attains a certain level of GDP. Rather, economic development brings social and political changes only when it changes people's behavior. Consequently, economic development is conducive to democracy to the extent that it, first, creates a large, educated, and articulate middle class of people who are accustomed to thinking for themselves and, second, transforms people's values and motivations.

Today, it is more possible than ever before to measure what the key changes are and how far they have progressed in given countries. Multivariate analysis of the data from the values surveys makes it possible to sort out the relative impact of economic, social, and cultural changes, and the results point to the conclusion that economic development is conducive to democracy insofar as it brings specific structural changes (particularly the rise of a knowledge sector) and certain cultural changes (particularly the rise of self-expression values). Wars, depressions, institutional changes, elite decisions, and specific leaders also influence what happens, but structural and cultural change are major factors in the emergence and survival of democracy.

Modernization brings rising educational levels, moving the work force into occupations that require independent thinking and making people more articulate and better equipped to intervene in politics. As knowledge societies emerge, people become accustomed to using their own initiative and judgment on the job and are also increasingly likely to question rigid and hierarchical authority.

Modernization also makes people economically more secure, and self-expression values become increasingly widespread when a large share of the population grows up taking survival for granted. The desire for freedom and autonomy are universal aspirations. They may be subordinated to the need for subsistence and order when survival is precarious, but they take increasingly high priority as survival becomes more secure. The basic motivation for democracy—the human desire for free choice—starts to play an increasingly important role. People begin to place a growing emphasis on free choice in politics and begin to demand civil and political liberties and democratic institutions.

Effective Democracy

During the explosion of democracy that took place between 1985 and 1995, electoral democracy spread rapidly throughout the world. Strategic elite agreements played an important role in this process, facilitated by an international environment in which the end of the Cold War opened the way for democratization. Initially, there was a tendency to view any regime that held free and fair elections as a democracy. But many of the new democracies suffered from massive corruption and failed to apply the rule of law, which is what makes democracy effective. A growing number of observers today thus emphasize the inadequacy of "electoral demomcy," "hybrid democracy," "authoritarian democracy," and other forms of sham democracy in which mass preferences are something that political elites can largely ignore and in which they do not decisively influence government decisions. It is important, accordingly, to distinguish between effective and ineffective democracies.

The essence of democracy is that it empowers ordinary citizens. Whether a democracy is effective or not is based on not only the extent to which civil and political rights exist on paper but also the degree to which officials actually respect these rights. The first of these two components—the existence of rights on paper—is measured by Freedom House's annual rankings: if a country holds free elections, Freedom House tends to rate it as "free," giving it a score at or near the top of its scale. Thus, the new democracies of eastern Europe receive scores as high as those of the established democracies of western Europe, although in-depth analyses show that widespread corruption makes these new democracies far less effective in responding to their citizens' choices. Fortunately, the World Bank's governance scores measure the extent to which a country's democratic institutions are actually effective. Consequently, a rough index of effective democracy can be obtained by multiplying these two scores: formal democracy, as measured by Freedom House, and elite and institutional integrity, as measured by the World Bank.

Effective democracy is a considerably more demanding standard than electoral democracy. One can establish electoral democracy almost anywhere, but it will probably not last long if it does not transfer power from the elites to the people. Effective democracy is most likely to exist alongside a relatively developed infrastructure that includes not only economic resources but also widespread participatory habits and an emphasis on autonomy. Accordingly, it is closely linked to the degree to which a given public emphasizes self-expression values. Indeed, the correlation between a society's values and the nature of the country's political institutions is remarkably strong.

Virtually all the stable democracies show strong self-expression values. Most Latin American countries are underachievers, showing lower levels of effective democracy than their publics' values would predict. This suggests that these societies could support higher levels of democracy if the rule of law were strengthened there. Iran is also an underachiever—a theocratic regime that allows a much lower level of democracy than that to which its people aspire. Surprising as it may seem to those who focus only on elite-level politics, the Iranian public shows relatively strong support for democracy. Conversely, Cyprus, Estonia, Hungary, Poland, Latvia, and Lithuania are overachievers, showing higher levels of democracy than their publics' values would predicts—perhaps reflecting the incentives to democratize provided by membership in the European Union.

But do self-expression values lead to democracy, or does democracy cause self-expression values to emerge? The evidence indicates that these values lead to democracy. (For the full evidence for this claim, see our book *Modernization, Cultural Change, and Democracy.*) Democratic institutions do not need to be in place for self-expression values to emerge. Time-series evidence from the values surveys indicates that in the years preceding the wave of democratization in the late 1980s and early 1990s, self-expression values had already emerged through a process of an intergenerational change in values—not only in the Western democracies but also within many authoritarian societies. By 1990, the publics of East Germany and Czechoslovakia—which had been living under two of the most authoritarian regimes in the world—had developed high levels of self-expression values. The crucial factor was not the political system but the fact that these countries were among the most economically advanced countries in the communist world, with high levels of education and advanced social welfare systems. Thus, when the Soviet leader Mikhail Gorbachev renounced the Brezhnev Doctrine, removing the threat of Soviet military intervention, they moved swiftly toward democracy.

In recent decades, self-expression values have been spreading and getting stronger, making people more likely to directly intervene in politics. (Indeed, unprecedented numbers of people took part in the demonstrations that helped bring about the most recent wave of democratization.) Does this mean that authoritarian systems will inevitably crumble? No. A rising emphasis on self-expression values tends to erode the legitimacy of authoritarian systems, but as long as determined authoritarian elites control the army and the secret police, they can repress pro-democratic forces. Still, even repressive regimes find it costly to check these tendencies, for doing so tends to block the emergence of effective knowledge sectors.

Modern Strategy

This new understanding of modernization has broad implications for international relations. For one thing, it helps explain why advanced democracies do not fight one another. Recent research provides strong empirical support for the claim that they do not, which goes back to Adam Smith and Immanuel Kant. Since they emerged in the early nineteenth century, liberal democracies have fought a number of wars, but almost never against one another. This new version of modernization theory indicates that the democratic peace phenomenon is due more to cultural changes linked to modernization than to democracy per se.

In earlier periods of history, democracies fought one another frequently. But the prevailing norms among them have evolved over time, as is illustrated by the abolition of slavery, the gradual expansion of the franchise, and the movement toward gender equality in virtually all modern societies. Another cultural change that has occurred in modern societies—which tend to be democracies—is that war has become progressively less acceptable and people have become more likely to express this preference and try to affect policy accordingly. Evidence from the World Values Survey indicates that the publics of high-income countries have much lower levels of xenophobia than do the publics of low-income countries, and they are much less willing to fight for their country than are the publics of low-income countries. Moreover, economically developed democracies behave far more peacefully toward one another than do poor democracies, and economically developed democracies are far less prone to civil war than are poor democracies.

Modernization theory has both cautionary and encouraging implications for U.S. foreign policy. Iraq, of course, provides a cautionary lesson. Contrary to the appealing view that democracy can be readily established almost anywhere, modernization theory holds that democracy is much more likely to flourish under certain conditions than others. A number of factors made it unrealistic to expect that democracy would be easy to establish in Iraq, including deep ethnic cleavages that had been exacerbated by Saddam Hussein's regime. And after Saddam's defeat, allowing physical security to deteriorate was a particularly serious mistake. Interpersonal trust and tolerance flourish when people feel secure. Democracy is unlikely to survive in a society torn by distrust and intolerance, and Iraq currently manifests the highest level of xenophobia of any society for which data are available. A good indicator of xenophobia is the extent to which people say they would not want to have foreigners as neighbors. Across 80 countries, the median percentage of those surveyed who said this was 15 percent. Among Iraqi Kurds, 51 percent of those polled said they would prefer not to have foreigners as neighbors. Among Iraqi Arabs, 90 percent of those polled said they would not want foreigners as neighbors. In keeping with these conditions, Iraq (along with Pakistan and Zimbabwe) shows very low levels of both self-expression values and effective democracy.

Modernization theory also has positive implications for U.S. foreign policy. Supported by a large body of evidence, it points to the conclusion that economic development is a basic driver of democratic change—meaning that Washington should do what it can to encourage development. If it wants to bring democratic change to Cuba, for example, isolating it is counterproductive. The United States should lift the embargo, promote economic development, and foster social engagement with, and other connections to, the world. Nothing is certain, but empirical evidence suggests that a growing sense of security and a growing emphasis on self-expression values there would undermine the authoritarian regime.

Similarly, although many observers have been alarmed by the economic resurgence of China, this growth has positive implications for the long term. Beneath China's seemingly monolithic political structure, the social infrastructure of democratization is emerging, and it has progressed further than most observers realize. China is now approaching the level of mass emphasis on self-expression values at which Chile, Poland, South Korea, and Taiwan made their transitions to democracy. And, surprising as it may seem to observers who focus only on elite-level politics, Iran is also near this threshold. As long as the Chinese Communist Party and Iran's theocratic leaders control their countries' military and security forces, democratic institutions will not emerge at the national level. But growing mass pressures for liberalization are beginning to appear, and repressing them will bring growing costs in terms of economic inefficiency and low public morale. On the whole, increasing prosperity for China and Iran is in the United States' national interest.

More broadly, modernization theory implies that the United States should welcome and encourage economic development around the world. Although economic development requires difficult adjustments, its long-term effects encourage the emergence of more tolerant, less xenophobic, and ultimately more democratic societies.

RONALD INGLEHART is Professor of Political Science at the University of Michigan and Director of the World Values Survey. **CHRISTIAN WELZEL** is Professor of Political Science at Jacobs University Bremen, in Germany. They are the co-authors of *Modernization, Cultural Change, and Democracy*.

The Ideology of Development

The failed ideologies of the last century have come to an end. But a new one has risen to take their place. It is the ideology of Development—and it promises a solution to all the world's ills. But like Communism, Fascism, and the others before it, Developmentalism is a dangerous and deadly failure.

WILLIAM EASTERLY

A dark ideological specter is haunting the world. It is almost as deadly as the tired ideologies of the last century—communism, fascism, and socialism—that failed so miserably. It feeds some of the most dangerous trends of our time, including religious fundamentalism. It is the half-century-old ideology of Developmentalism. And it is thriving.

Like all ideologies, Development promises a comprehensive final answer to all of society's problems, from poverty and illiteracy to violence and despotic rulers. It shares the common ideological characteristic of suggesting there is only one correct answer, and it tolerates little dissent. It deduces this unique answer for everyone from a general theory that purports to apply to everyone, everywhere. There's no need to involve local actors who reap its costs and benefits. Development even has its own intelligentsia, made up of experts at the International Monetary Fund (IMF), World Bank, and United Nations.

The power of Developmentalism is disheartening, because the failure of all the previous ideologies might have laid the groundwork for the opposite of ideology—the freedom of individuals and societies to choose their destinies. Yet, since the fall of communism, the West has managed to snatch defeat from the jaws of victory, and with disastrous results. Development ideology is sparking a dangerous counterreaction. The "one correct answer" came to mean "free markets," and, for the poor world, it was defined as doing whatever the IMF and the World Bank tell you to do. But the reaction in Africa, Central Asia, Latin America, the Middle East, and Russia has been to fight against free markets. So, one of the best economic ideas of our time, the genius of free markets, was presented in one of the worst possible ways, with unelected outsiders imposing rigid doctrines on the xenophobic unwilling.

The backlash has been so severe that other failed ideologies are gaining new adherents throughout these regions. In Nicaragua, for instance, IMF and World Bank structural adjustments failed so conspicuously that the pitiful Sandinista regime of the 1980s now looks good by comparison. Its leader, Daniel Ortega,

is back in power. The IMF's actions during the Argentine financial crisis of 2001 now reverberate a half decade later with Hugo Chávez, Venezuela's illiberal leader, being welcomed with open arms in Buenos Aires. The heavy-handed directives of the World Bank and IMF in Bolivia provided the soil from which that country's neosocialist president, Evo Morales, sprung. The disappointing payoff following eight structural adjustment loans to Zimbabwe and $8 billion in foreign aid during the 1980s and 1990s helped Robert Mugabe launch a vicious counterattack on democracy. The IMF-World Bank-Jeffrey Sachs application of "shock therapy" to the former Soviet Union has created a lasting nostalgia for communism. In the Middle East, $154 billion in foreign aid between 1980 and 2001, 45 structural adjustment loans, and "expert" advice produced zero per capita GDP growth that helped create a breeding ground for Islamic fundamentalism.

This blowback against "globalization from above" has spread to every corner of the Earth. It now threatens to kill sensible, moderate steps toward the freer movement of goods, ideas, capital, and people.

Development's Politburo

The ideology of Development is not only about having experts design your free market for you; it is about having the experts design a comprehensive, technical plan to solve all the problems of the poor. These experts see poverty as a purely technological problem, to be solved by engineering and the natural sciences, ignoring messy social sciences such as economics, politics, and sociology.

Sachs, Columbia University's celebrity economist, is one of its main proprietors. He is now recycling his theories of overnight shock therapy, which failed so miserably in Russia, into promises of overnight global poverty reduction. "Africa's problems," he has said, "are . . . solvable with practical and proven technologies." His own plan features hundreds of expert interventions to solve every last problem of the poor—from green manure, breast-feeding education, and bicycles to solar-energy systems, school uniforms for aids orphans, and wind-mills. Not to mention such critical interventions as "counseling and information services for men to address their reproductive health needs." All this will be done, Sachs says, by "a united and effective United Nations country team, which coordinates in one place the work of the U.N. specialized agencies, the IMF, and the World Bank."

Under Developmentalism, an end to starvation, tyranny, and war are thrown in like a free toaster.

So the admirable concern of rich countries for the tragedies of world poverty is thus channeled into fattening the international aid bureaucracy, the self-appointed priesthood of Development. Like other ideologies, this thinking favors collective goals such as national poverty reduction, national economic growth, and the global Millennium Development Goals, over the aspirations of individuals. Bureaucrats who write poverty-reduction frame-works outrank individuals who actually reduce poverty by, say, starting a business. Just as Marxists favored world revolution and socialist internationalism, Development stresses world goals over the autonomy of societies to choose their own path. It favors doctrinaire abstractions such as "market-friendly poli-cies," "good investment climate," and "pro-poor globalization" over the freedom of individuals.

Development also shares another Marxist trait: It aspires to be scientific. Finding the one correct solution to poverty is seen as a scientific problem to be solved by the experts. They are always sure they know the answer, vehemently reject disagree-ment, and then later change their answers. In psychiatry, this is known as Borderline Personality Disorder. For the Development Experts, it's a way of life. The answer at first was aid-financed investment and industrialization in poor countries, then it was market-oriented government policy reform, then it was fixing institutional problems such as corruption, then it was globaliza-tion, then it was the Poverty Reduction Strategy to achieve the Millennium Development Goals.

One reason the answers keep changing is because, in real-ity, high-growth countries follow a bewildering variety of paths to development, and the countries with high growth rates are constantly changing from decade to decade. Who could be more different than successful developers such as China and Chile, Botswana and Singapore, Taiwan and Turkey, or Hong Kong and Vietnam? What about the many countries who tried to emulate these rising stars and failed? What about the former stars who have fallen on hard times, like the Ivory Coast, which was one of the fastest develop-ers of the 1960s and 1970s, only to become mired in a civil war? What about Mexico, which saw rapid growth until 1980 and has had slow growth ever since, despite embracing the experts' reforms?

The experts in Developmentalism's Politburo don't bother themselves with such questions. All the previous answers were right; they were just missing one more "necessary condition" that the experts have only just now added to the list. Like all ideologies, Development is at the same time too rigid to predict what will work in the messy real world and yet flexible enough to forever escape falsification by real-world events. The high church of Development, the World Bank, has guaranteed it can never be wrong by making statements such as, "different poli-cies can yield the same result, and the same policy can yield dif-ferent results, depending on country institutional contexts and underlying growth strategies." Of course, you still need experts to figure out the contexts and strategies.

Resistance Is Futile

Perhaps more hypocritical yet is Development's simple theory of historical inevitability. Poor societies are not just poor, the experts tell us, they are "developing" until they reach the final stage of history, or "development," in which poverty will soon end. Under this historiography, an end to starvation, tyranny, and war are thrown in like a free toaster on an infomercial. The experts judge all societies on a straight line, per capita income, with the superior countries showing the inferior countries the image of their own future. And the experts heap scorn on those who resist the inevitabilities on the path to development.

One of today's leading Developmentalists, *New York Times* columnist Thomas Friedman, can hardly conceal his mockery of those who resist the march of history, or "the flattening of the world." "When you are Mexico," Friedman has written, "and your claim to fame is that you are a low-wage manufacturing country, and some of your people are importing statuettes of your own patron saint from China, because China can make them and ship them all the way across the Pacific more cheaply than you can produce them . . . you have got a problem. [T]he only way for Mexico to thrive is with a strategy of reform . . . the more Mexico just sits there, the more it is going to get run over." Friedman seems blissfully unaware that poor Mexico, so far from God yet so close to American pundits, has already tried much harder than China to implement the experts' "strategy of reform."

The self-confidence of Developmentalists like Friedman is so strong that they impose themselves even on those who accept their strategies. This year, for instance, Ghana celebrated its 50th anniversary as the first black African nation to gain indepen-dence. Official international aid donors to Ghana told its alleg-edly independent government, in the words of the World Bank: "We Partners are here giving you our pledge to give our best to make lives easier for you in running your country." Among the things they will do to make your life easier is to run your country for you.

Unfortunately, Development ideology has a dismal record of helping any country actually develop. The regions where the ideology has been most influential, Latin America and Africa, have done the worst. Luckless Latins and Africans are left chas-ing yesterday's formulas for success while those who ignored the Developmentalists found homegrown paths to success. The nations that have been the most successful in the past 40 years did so in such a variety of different ways that it would be hard to argue that they discovered the "correct answer" from development ideology. In fact, they often conspicuously violated whatever it was the experts said at the time. The East Asian tigers, for instance, chose outward orientation on their own in the 1960s, when the experts' conventional wisdom was industrialization for the home market. The rapid growth of China over the past quarter century came when it was hardly a poster child for either the 1980s Washington Consensus or the 1990s institutionalism of democracy and cracking down on corruption.

What explains the appeal of development ideology despite its dismal track record? Ideologies usually arise in response to tragic situations in which people are hungry for clear and comprehensive solutions. The inequality of the Industrial Revolution bred Marxism, and the backwardness of Russia its Leninist offshoot. Germany's defeat and demoralization in World War I birthed Nazism. Economic hardship accompanied by threats to identity led to both Christian and Islamic fundamentalism. Similarly, development ideology appeals to those who want a definitive, complete answer to the tragedy of world poverty and inequality. It answers the question, "What is to be done?" to borrow the title of Lenin's 1902 tract. It stresses collective social outcomes that must be remedied by collective, top-down action by the intelligentsia, the revolutionary vanguard, the development expert. As Sachs explains, "I have . . . gradually come to understand through my scientific research and on the ground advisory work the awesome power in our generation's hands to end the massive suffering of the extreme poor . . . although introductory economics textbooks preach individualism and decentralized markets, our safety and prosperity depend at least as much on collective decisions."

Freeing the Poor

Few realize that Americans in 1776 had the same income level as the average African today. Yet, like all the present-day developed nations, the United States was lucky enough to escape poverty before there were Developmentalists. In the words of former IMF First Deputy Managing Director Anne Krueger, development in the rich nations "just happened." George Washington did not have to deal with aid partners, getting structurally adjusted by them, or preparing poverty-reduction strategy papers for them. Abraham Lincoln did not celebrate a government of the donors, by the donors, and for the donors. Today's developed nations were free to experiment with their own pragmatic paths toward more government accountability and freer markets. Individualism and decentralized markets were good enough to give rise to penicillin, air conditioning, high-yield corn, and the automobile—not to mention better living standards, lower mortality, and the iPod.

The opposite of ideology is freedom, the ability of societies to be unchained from foreign control. The only "answer" to poverty reduction is freedom from being told the answer. Free societies and individuals are not guaranteed to succeed. They will make bad choices. But at least they bear the cost of those mistakes, and learn from them. That stands in stark contrast to accountability-free Developmentalism. This process of learning from mistakes is what produced the repositories of common sense that make up mainstream economics. The opposite of Development ideology is not anything goes, but the pragmatic use of time-tested economic ideas—the benefits of specialization, comparative advantage, gains from trade, market-clearing prices, trade-offs, budget constraints—by individuals, firms, governments, and societies as they find their own success.

History proves just how much good can come from individuals who both bear the costs and reap the benefits of their own choices when they are free to make them. That includes local politicians, activists, and businesspeople who are groping their way toward greater freedom, contrary to the Developmentalists who oxymoronically impose freedom of choice on other people. Those who best understood the lessons of the 20th century were not the ideologues asking, "What is to be done?" They were those asking, "How can people be more free to find their own solutions?"

The ideology of Development should be packed up in crates and sent off to the Museum of Dead Ideologies, just down the hall from Communism, Socialism, and Fascism. It's time to recognize that the attempt to impose a rigid development ideology on the world's poor has failed miserably. Fortunately, many poor societies are forging their own path toward greater freedom and prosperity anyway. That is how true revolutions happen.

WILLIAM EASTERLY is professor of economics at New York University.

Africa's Village of Dreams

**A small Kenyan village is the laboratory for celebrity economist
Jeffrey Sachs's ambitious scheme to lift Africa out of poverty.
Can big money buy the continent's poorest people a better future?**

SAM RICH

S auri must be the luckiest village in Africa. The maize is taller, the water cleaner, and the schoolchildren better fed than almost anywhere else south of the Sahara.

Just two years ago, Sauri was an ordinary Kenyan village where poverty, hunger, and illness were facts of everyday life. Now it is an experiment, a prototype "Millennium Village." The idea is simple: Every year for five years, invest roughly $100 for each of the village's 5,000 inhabitants, and see what happens.

The Millennium Villages Project is the brainchild of economist Jeffrey Sachs, the principal architect of the transition from state-owned to market economies in Poland and Russia. His critics and supporters disagree about the success of those efforts, often referred to as "shock therapy," but his role in radical economic reform in the two countries vaulted him to fame. Now he has a new mission: to end poverty in Africa.

Africa has been drip-fed aid for decades, Sachs writes in his 2005 book The End of Poverty, but it has never received enough to make a difference. What money has trickled in has been wasted on overpriced consultants and misspent on humanitarian relief and food aid, not directed at the root causes of poverty. The average African, Sachs says, is caught in a "poverty trap." He farms a small plot for himself and his family, and simply doesn't have enough assets to make a profit. As the population grows, people have less and less land, and grow poorer. When the farmer has to pay school fees for his children or buy medication, he is forced to sell the few assets he has or else go into debt. But if he had some capital, he could invest in his farm, grow enough to harvest a surplus, sell it, and start making money.

It's not this diagnosis of Africa's problems that makes Sachs's theories contentious, but his proposed solution, which might be called shock aid—huge, sudden injections of money into poor areas. Over five years, $2.75 million is being invested in the single village of Sauri, and an equal amount will be sunk into each of another 11 Millennium Village sites that are being established in 10 African countries.

The project is structured around the Millennium Development Goals that the United Nations laid out in 2000 as part of an ambitious plan to reduce global poverty. The UN wants poor countries to meet these benchmarks in health, education, and other sectors by 2015. Halfway there, most countries appear unlikely to meet these targets. However, the first two Millennium Villages—Sauri, which was so designated in 2004, and Koraro, Ethiopia, where efforts were launched in 2005—are on track to surpass them.

Sachs has persuaded Western governments, local governments, businesses, and private donors such as Hollywood stars and international financiers to foot the bill. Under the auspices of the Earth Institute, the project he heads at Columbia University, he has gathered specialists in fields from HIV/AIDS research to soil science to work out master plans for these dozen villages.

Never before has so much money been invested in an African community as small as Sauri. If Sauri succeeds, it could usher in a new era for development in Africa. The hope of Sachs as well as those who head the United Nations Millennium Project, with which he has partnered, is that by 2015, when the Millennium Development Goals still seem far away, these villages will be seen as models whose success can be duplicated across Africa. But if Sauri fails, the West may become yet more disillusioned with aid, and perhaps even reduce what it presently contributes. This is a defining moment in the aid debate.

Last year I paid a visit to Sauri, this village on which so much appears to hang. I'd just finished reading The End of Poverty, and I'll admit I was skeptical about the soundness of spending vast amounts of money in a single small village. But most of all, I was looking for early indications of what this exhibit in the aid argument might show.

I was carried on a bicycle taxi through the dusty streets of Kisumu, Kenya, past vendors selling barbecued maize in front of shacks cobbled together from tin cans beaten flat and nailed onto wooden struts. Occasionally I could make out the faded logo of the U.S. Agency for International Development on the rusted shell of an old vegetable-oil can. As I neared my destination I caught a glimpse of Lake Victoria's shore, where vendors in stalls sell fried tilapia and chunks of boiled maize meal.

Inside a concrete compound at the headquarters of the Millennium Villages Project, development experts sat at computer monitors in glass-walled offices. As I entered, the receptionist at the front desk was on the phone: "You need notebooks? . . . How many? . . .Three hundred, is that all? Right, I'll order them for you tomorrow. You'll get them in a few days."

I've spent the last five years in Africa, where I've worked with outfits ranging from big international nongovernmental organizations to tiny one-man-band agencies, but I've never seen an order made as breezily as this. At most NGOs, the procurement even of stationery entails filling out forms in triplicate and long delays.

There was a tour leaving on the 30-mile trip to Sauri the next day. I imagined trekking around the model village with one of Sachs's celebrity protégés, perhaps Angelina Jolie or Bono, or maybe a millionaire altruist the likes of George Soros, so I was slightly disappointed to find myself at the appointed hour in a Toyota Land Cruiser beside a couple of unglamorous American professors on a brief visit to advise the project.

The air conditioning purred as our driver bumped the Toyota over potholes on the single-lane highway that runs inland from the Kenyan coast through the capital, Nairobi, toward Uganda. Sauri itself lies just off the road, some 200 miles from Nairobi, and the sight of tall, strong stalks of maize was the first indication that we'd arrived. Women in brightly colored headscarves and second-hand clothes imported from America and Europe sold homemade snacks and Coca-Cola from wooden shacks dotting the sides of the red-brown dirt road. The grass behind them was a lush green, giving way to a wall of maize plants beneath a sky heavy with the clouds that hang in the rainy season.

Our four-by-four negotiated footpaths through the maize fields and under acacias. The first stop was Sauri's health clinic, which provided stark reminders of the depth of Sauri's problems and the benefits money can bring. The nurse there told us that each household received mosquito nets at the start of the project, when a sample test of villagers revealed that more than 40 percent had malaria. Now that figure has dropped to 20 percent. Malaria, a debilitating and sometimes deadly disease, is being treated free of charge with Coartem, an expensive drug unavailable in most parts of Kenya. The clinic provides condoms and Depo-Provera contraceptive injections, and there are plans to introduce tests for HIV, thought to afflict one in four villagers, and to administer anti-retroviral therapy. Outside the clinic was a covered waiting area furnished with benches. It wasn't big enough to accommodate the burden of the clinic's success: a queue of 50 people waiting to see the facility's sole doctor. More than 200 patients arrive for treatment every day. Most walk from villages miles away.

Minutes later, we arrived at the green courtyard of Bar Sauri Primary School. The red-brick buildings with holes for doors and windows house classrooms for more than 600 children. One of the buildings lacked a roof. The teacher seemed embarrassed to tell us that it had blown off in a storm just days before. He knew roofs don't blow off schoolrooms where we come from.

But he was enthusiastic about the school's innovative feeding program. Ten percent of the village's harvest goes toward school lunches for the children, he said. In addition, the Mil-

lennium Villages Project buys fruit, meat, and fish to provide students with necessary vitamins and protein. The project has built upon Sauri's own school feeding program, established five years ago for students in the top year. Now the entire student body receives nourishing meals. Since Sauri began the program, its school ranking has risen from just inside the top 200 in the district into the top 10. Improved nutrition means that the students can concentrate better, and they're also healthier and more energetic. Sauri won everything at the regional sports day, the teacher told us. With a proud smile, he recalled, "And not one of our children fainted!"

The next stop was the information technology center. It was just a shack with a nice sign on the outside and a few books inside. One day, when the village is connected to the electricity grid, computers will be bought and Internet access provided. Bridging the digital divide may seem a low priority when Sauri has so many pressing problems. But textbooks are a rare commodity, and an Internet connection will allow students access to unlimited information; their parents will be able to obtain up-to-date reports on crop prices, pesticides, and fertilizers.

We returned to the Land Cruiser and set off to visit another ramshackle brick building with a crude dirt floor. Here, the dozen men and women who constitute the village's agriculture committee make decisions key to the success of the whole project. Improved harvests can support the school feeding program and provide income for farmers. Successful farming should enable the village to continue to grow after the five-year project finishes in 2009.

The project's major contribution to agriculture has been the purchase of fertilizer to increase maize production. Maize, which has been grown for as long as anyone can remember, is the main subsistence crop here, as it is in large parts of Africa. Synthetic fertilizers are far too expensive for the average farmer, but in Sauri the project spends $50,000 a year on them. The chairman of the committee said the maize harvest has increased two and a half times as a result. Now the question is how to store the surplus so that villagers can sell it in the dry season when prices are high.

At the tour's final stop, the professors stayed in the Land Cruiser to apply more sunscreen. Outside, I found a cement block with a tap jutting out of it. A water and sanitation expert at the site explained that this was an outlet for a filtered spring, and that purified drinking water is supplied to 50 taps around the village. In neighboring villages, long queues form by a single borehole that slops out murky water, which must be boiled over a charcoal stove before it is potable.

The tour over, the professors drove off, but I decided to stay. Clearly, the Millennium Villages Project has achieved some great things, but I didn't feel I'd seen the full picture. As the light fell, I walked toward the guesthouse by the main highway. A woman was handing out cobs of corn to some kids, and offered me one too. We sat on a bench to eat it and watched the steady stream of lorries roll by, carrying imported goods from the Kenyan port of Mombasa into Uganda, 40 miles up the road. The returning lorries moved faster: They were usually empty. None of them stopped in Sauri.

There are two schools of thought about development. The "macro" school, with its emphasis on national-level economic policy, aims at developing an entire society by changing government policies and encouraging investment. This is often called a top-down approach, because people at the top are making decisions for the benefit of those at the grass roots. This is the work of many economists and other academic specialists as well as organizations such as the World Bank and the International Monetary Fund.

Then there's the "micro" school, oriented toward community development, which advocates working with one group of people at a time, trying to solve particular problems by providing training and minimal investment. This bottom-up approach is the domain of most NGOs and charities.

Though these two schools have the same general objectives, their adherents rarely interact and seemingly speak different languages. What's interesting about the Millennium Villages Project is that it is essentially a micro project run by experts from the macro school, such as Sachs.

But Sachs is no ordinary economist. His charisma and fundraising ability are legendary. He convinced Bono, the lead singer of U2 and a well-known activist in his own right, to write the introduction to The End of Poverty. In it, Bono describes traveling with Sachs as the economist enthused about development. Bono modestly portrays himself as the smart, clean-cut geek hanging on the words of the wild-haired creative guy.

It was Sachs's influence and initiative that spawned the Millennium Villages Project. In 2004, after a visit to Sauri as a special adviser to Kofi Annan, then secretary-general of the UN, he wrote an open letter in which he outlined a plan of action for the village that he had developed with the Earth Institute and the UN Millennium Project. He called on donors to support the plan: "The rich world needs to wake from its slumber."

Even Sachs's harshest critic, New York University professor and former World Bank economist William Easterly, has described Sachs as "the economist as rock star." But Sachs's fan base doesn't rescue his theories, in Easterly's opinion. He points out that the idea of investing vast sums of money to close the poverty gap in Africa was tried in the 1950s and '60s, and failed. He says that Sachs's book peddles an "administrative central plan" in which the UN secretary-general "would supervise and coordinate thousands of international civil servants and technocratic experts to solve the problems of every poor village and city slum everywhere." The solutions Easterly favors instead include measures designed to improve accountability and reduce corruption, and specific investments aimed at tackling one problem at a time. In his eyes, Sachs is a utopian. Sachs dismisses Easterly as a "can't do" economist.

But economists aren't Sachs's only critics; others within the micro school he wants to win over are asking questions, too. They want to make sure communities such as Sauri are not simply passive recipients of handouts from donors and lectures from experts, but are actively involved in making decisions about their own development. This is what they mean when they talk about empowerment. Any development project can bring temporary benefits. The trick is to ensure that a community is not enjoying a honeymoon that ends when the project does, but is making changes on which it can continue to build. They want sustainability.

When I tried to ask questions on the tour about these issues, I received some evasive answers. Millennium Villages staffers and Sauri residents seemed reluctant to criticize the project. This is a common problem in areas that receive a good deal of aid: Workers on the project don't want to criticize their employers, and villagers don't want to bite the hand that's feeding them. Would the crop yields and health care in Sauri be better in 10 years' time? Did the villagers believe the changes the project had bought were valuable? Would they be able to keep them up when the money ran out, and did they want to? I decided to spend a few more days in Sauri and talk to the villagers themselves.

I crossed the highway and walked into the village to meet one of Sachs's graduate students, a researcher from Columbia University. When I caught up with him, he was wearing a yellow T-shirt that said "Jeff Sachs Is My Home Boy." I'd run into him earlier in the day, and he had offered to take me to the home of a Sauri resident, Ben Bunde.

When we arrived at Bunde's house, he and his friends were seated under a tree on wooden benches that seemed to grow from the soil in which they were planted. The group was hunched over bits of scrap paper densely covered in handwriting. They had decided to start up a publication called The Sauri Times, and the Millennium Villages Project had helped fund the first print run.

"There are so many stories to be told about Sauri," Bunde said. "The problem is which ones to tell."

When I asked him how Sauri had changed in the last two years, he leaned back, laughing, and said, "The girls have better haircuts now." There are more hair salons, he said, warming to his subject, and the girls are all getting braids. For the first time, people are selling French fries on the side of the highway. People are more generous, too. "A funeral is a big event in the village, with lots of food. In the old days we would get rice and beans, but now we get meat and soup too." There was so much excitement when the project started that mothers named their babies "Millennium."

I mentioned the elections that took place at the start of the project. Committees of about a dozen villagers for health, education, agriculture, and other key sectors were elected on the advice of project coordinators. The committees' role is to decide how the Millennium Villages money should be spent, and to empower Sauri as a result. But Bunde didn't seem to have confidence in the elections or the committees.

"Few people took part, and they didn't know who to vote for. . . . What would Sachs say if he knew about the witchcraft that took place before the elections? The Kalanya were scaring people to vote for them. In Kenya, we have the Kikuyu factor—the Kikuyu are the dominant tribe. Here in Sanri, we have the Kalanya factor. The Kalanya are the dominant clan. Kalanya elders head all the committees, and yet many of them are uneducated and illiterate. And yet here," he said, gesturing at the young journalists around him, "we have some clever, educated people."

Bunde argued that "clanism" was fostering nepotism and other forms of favoritism. As an example, he cited one of the buildings at the new clinic, which was so badly constructed that it has been condemned. And he hinted at other forms of corruption.

There were rumors that the clinic was charging patients from outside Sauri. Civil servants and police in neighboring villages were allegedly using their influence to get their children into Sauri's school.

There was fighting both within and between committees, he continued, and this had delayed development in the village. In the early days of the project, he said, Sachs had ceremoniously handed over the keys to a truck that was to be used to take goods to market and as an ambulance. But because of power struggles over it, the truck hadn't been used or seen in the village since.

Bunde said that there wasn't enough education of Sauri's people at the start of the project. After receiving free fertilizer and mosquito nets, some villagers sold them to people in the surrounding communities the very next day and then conspired to get more fertilizer and nets.

When I asked if he planned to put any of these stories in The Sauri Times, he shook his head. "No, we don't want the donors to pull out!"

In the end, Bunde questioned whether outside experts really understand the problems in Sauri. While life had improved in the years since the Millennium Village experiment began, Bunde wondered fearfully what will happen when the project ends, "because we have become so dependent." Change, he said, needs to be led from inside the village. "As we say here, only the wearer knows where the shoe pinches."

At breakfast the next morning in the courtyard of the guesthouse, I ran into one of the project coordinators, who agreed to chat with me if he could remain anonymous.

On the tour, our guide had emphasized that the elected committees make all the decisions about how Sauri is run and how aid money is spent. I asked the coordinator if there was tension between what the project's representatives wanted to do with the money and what the committees wanted.

"Yes," he said. "We provided the inputs like the fertilizers, and so the committees just sat back. There were mistakes made on entry to Sauri. There was not enough sensitization. . . . Now the problem is [that] the project is moving so fast, the committees can't keep up."

Lack of education, or "sensitization," both within the committees and in the village generally, has caused problems, the project coordinator observed. The villagers often disappoint their benefactors. When project officials want to implement a change, they advise the committees. But the committees sometimes move slowly, because there's not enough support for a particular proposal either within the committee or in the village as a whole. In the surrounding villages to which the project has been expanded, there has been more education, but he doubted that there has been enough.

The basic inputs of the project have also changed. In Sauri, he said, the amount of fertilizer given to farmers was based on plot size. But this scheme was contrary to traditional community practice because its effects were thought to exacerbate existing inequalities and were often divisive. At the new Millennium Villages Project sites, each farmer will be given the same amount of fertilizer.

From Sauri, I walked half a mile down some railway tracks to the neighboring village of Yala, passing the old, dilapidated train station. Even though only one train passes by a week, the station's colonial-era ornamental gardens are still tended with care.

The local government is based in Yala, and I wanted to find out how its members viewed the new Sauri. A hand-painted sign pointed to a small, spare room, where the paint peeled under a corrugated-iron roof. There I found Richard Odunga, a resident of Sauri and Yala's town clerk. His secretary sat next door in front of a typewriter.

Odunga owns a big plot, uses the fertilizer, and has sold a lot of maize. When I asked him if he'd been able to save money, he sighed. He has been forced to support family members who live outside of Sauri. They ask him for help with school fees and medication, and have drained all his maize profits.

He said relations between the local government and project organizers have been strained. "At first, there was no consultation with government. Later, they realized we were a stakeholder and they needed our assistance." Project leaders initially wanted to build not just a clinic but a hospital in Sauri, before the government pointed out that there was already a hospital just a few kilometers away. The project wanted help from government in electrifying Sauri and grading its roads. Two years on, work has started on the roads, but there is still no connection to the national power grid.

Odunga wondered what will remain after the project finishes. When I asked if the community had started contributing to the project yet, he said, "There is some cost sharing, but it's at a minimum level." Who will pay for the clinic after the project ends? he asked. But villagers will at least benefit from the training they've received: "Skills. That's the most important thing."

A couple of days later, I met a senior official working on the Millennium Villages Project for the UN who has a background in community development, as Sachs, he noted, does not. This official, too, would only talk if he were not identified.

The Millennium Villages Project, he said, "has made all the classic development mistakes. . . . If you give away tons of fertilizer, it's predictable that much of it will end up on the open market. If you put millions [of dollars] in a small place, you're going to have problems."

Encouraging farmers to grow maize is the wrong strategy, he argued. "It just means you move from being food insecure for 11 months of the year to food insecure for just nine months of the year."

Growing only maize year after year depletes the soil. It's also a high-risk strategy, he said, as the entire crop may fail. The price of maize has dropped dramatically around Sauri, he noted, as the village's crop yields have improved and supply has increased. Maize is a subsistence crop that has fed Sauri families for years, but, he contended, its price is too low to make it a cash crop. He is trying to push the project to spend more time touting vegetable crops that fetch good prices at market, such as onions, tomatoes, and cabbages.

In this official's opinion, the project could be more effective if it pushed for some macroeconomic changes, rather than concentrate all its efforts in the village. For instance, farmers in Kenya don't buy fertilizer because it costs three times as much as it does in Europe, he said. If the Kenyan government eased taxes and import duties on fertilizer, "a lot more farmers would buy it."

Many UN officials I spoke to criticized the Sauri project, but none would speak openly. It was clear that dissenting voices were not welcomed, as an e-mail I received from one made plain: "Unfortunately I'm already in a lot of trouble for talking about what every good scientist should be talking about. The current environment is one in which scientists can no longer speak openly and expect to keep their jobs."

The Millennium Villages Project is being launched in locations in Kenya, Ethiopia, Ghana, Malawi, Mali, Nigeria, Senegal, Tanzania, Rwanda, and Uganda. Each cluster of villages will be transformed thanks to the investment of nearly $3 million over five years. The sheer scale of investment in the Millennium Villages Project is difficult to convey. The sums involved are not just bigger than those for other community development projects in Africa; they are hundreds of times bigger.

But is this level of investment really plausible for all of Africa? In Kenya alone, aid from abroad would need to increase 10 times, from $100 million to $1 billion, to blanket the whole of the country with the amounts equivalent to what is spent in Millennium Villages.

Sachs says that if the West spent the 0.7 percent of its gross national product on aid set as a goal by the Monterrey Consensus in 2002, this could start to become a reality. This assumes that all the additional aid would go to Africa, and not, as is often the case, to projects in more developed countries such as those of the former Soviet bloc. Currently, only a few countries, such as Denmark, Sweden, and the Netherlands, are reaching the 0.7 percent mark; the United States gives about 0.2 percent of GNP in aid. It justifies its contribution by pointing out that it's still giving more in absolute terms than any other nation—in fact, it gives more than the world's next two biggest economies, Germany and Japan, put together.

The scale of the Millennium Villages Project makes it seem a different breed entirely from most micro programs, which go into a village with modest funds to achieve a specific goal. They may give a farmer a single cow bred in the West for its high milk yield, and train him to look after it. The farmer passes his first calves on to a neighbor and trains him, and gradually the benefits extend to the wider community. The idea is to create a cycle of development that doesn't require extra money. The progress in this kind of program may be slow, but it's much easier to pinpoint what's working and what's not, to figure out why, and to adapt as necessary.

Sauri has achieved more than such projects could ever reasonably hope to, but it's not yet a model village. Instead, Sauri remains Africa in microcosm. All the fundamental problems that exist in Africa still exist in Sauri; in some cases, these problems are magnified.

The village's political framework is confused. Sauri now has two governments in conflict with each other: the committees and the existing local government. The project's committees have introduced a new layer of bureaucracy, and their vastly superior resources have weakened the local government's power. Further, committees are accused of working against each other, and of being corrupt, slow, and unwieldy. Their representatives are said to have been chosen for their ethnic ties and standing in society, rather than their political acumen. As in many parts of Africa, it's unclear which decisions are made by government and which by donors.

Sauri faces the same economic challenges it always has. Most farmers are still growing subsistence crops and depleting their soils. They could instead be growing crops for market or investing in livestock. Low-cost improvements in farming techniques, such as the use of manure and other organic methods that are more sustainable in the long run, are only beginning to be promoted. Growth will be slow because taxation, bad roads, and a lack of electricity need to be addressed at a national level.

Villagers are clearly enjoying better health as a result of the project. The simple extension of a school feeding program has improved students' performance and could serve as a model for schools across Africa. The clinic has transformed health care: The incidence of malaria has decreased, family planning has increased, and soon anti-retroviral treatments will be available to people with HIV and AIDS. But when the project ends, the funds for the clinic and the doctor, the mosquito nets, and the anti-retrovirals will dry up. In three years, the Kenyan government will face the difficult choice between continuing to fund one model clinic in Sauri or cutting the budget considerably.

And Sauri still must contend with the divisions that are typical throughout Kenya: between ethnic groups, men and women, young and old. Witchcraft was employed to influence the outcome of the elections. The practice of wife inheritance remains common, indicative of a wider set of gender issues. These kinds of cultural problems can't be solved with handouts, but only with subtler interventions.

This is not to say that Sauri cannot change, or that investment in the village is wasted. But if Sauri is to become a useful model for development on a bigger scale, and not just another development expert's white elephant, Sachs and others working on the project must acknowledge that they are still learning about Africa. Sauri is not yet a success.

Lasting changes in Sauri will come about not through distribution of commodities, but through education for children and training for adults. To put it another way, give a man a mosquito net, and when it rips, he'll come and ask for another one. But show him how using a mosquito net benefits his health and how it will save him money on medication in the long run, and he might just go out and buy one for himself.

SAM RICH is a development consultant who has worked on community and international development projects in East Africa for nongovernmental organizations, governments, and the World Bank.

The Case against the West
America and Europe in the Asian Century

Kishore Mahbubani

There is a fundamental flaw in the West's strategic thinking. In all its analyses of global challenges, the West assumes that it is the source of the solutions to the world's key problems. In fact, however, the West is also a major source of these problems. Unless key Western policymakers learn to understand and deal with this reality, the world is headed for an even more troubled phase.

The West is understandably reluctant to accept that the era of its domination is ending and that the Asian century has come. No civilization cedes power easily, and the West's resistance to giving up control of key global institutions and processes is natural. Yet the West is engaging in an extraordinary act of self-deception by believing that it is open to change. In fact, the West has become the most powerful force preventing the emergence of a new wave of history, clinging to its privileged position in key global forums, such as the UN Security Council, the International Monetary Fund, the World Bank, and the G-8 (the group of highly industrialized states), and refusing to contemplate how the West will have to adjust to the Asian century.

Partly as a result of its growing insecurity, the West has also become increasingly incompetent in its handling of key global problems. Many Western commentators can readily identify specific failures, such as the Bush administration's botched invasion and occupation of Iraq. But few can see that this reflects a deeper structural problem: the West's inability to see that the world has entered a new era.

Apart from representing a specific failure of policy execution, the war in Iraq has also highlighted the gap between the reality and what the West had expected would happen after the invasion. Arguably, the United States and the United Kingdom intended only to free the Iraqi people from a despotic ruler and to rid the world of a dangerous man, Saddam Hussein. Even if George W. Bush and Tony Blair had no malevolent intentions, however, their approaches were trapped in the Western mindset of believing that their interventions could lead only to good, not harm or disaster. This led them to believe that the invading U.S. troops would be welcomed with roses thrown at their feet by happy Iraqis. But the twentieth century showed that no country welcomes foreign invaders. The notion that any Islamic nation would approve of Western military boots on its soil was ridiculous. Even in the early twentieth century, the British

invasion and occupation of Iraq was met with armed resistance. In 1920, Winston Churchill, then British secretary for war and air, quelled the rebellion of Kurds and Arabs in British-occupied Iraq by authorizing his troops to use chemical weapons. "I am strongly in favor of using poisoned gas against uncivilized tribes," Churchill said. The world has moved on from this era, but many Western officials have not abandoned the old assumption that an army of Christian soldiers can successfully invade, occupy, and transform an Islamic society.

Many Western leaders often begin their speeches by remarking on how perilous the world is becoming. Speaking after the August 2006 discovery of a plot to blow up transatlantic flights originating from London, President Bush said, "The American people need to know we live in a dangerous world." But even as Western leaders speak of such threats, they seem incapable of conceding that the West itself could be the fundamental source of these dangers. After all, the West includes the best-managed states in the world, the most economically developed, those with the strongest democratic institutions. But one cannot assume that a government that rules competently at home will be equally good at addressing challenges abroad. In fact, the converse is more likely to be true. Although the Western mind is obsessed with the Islamist terrorist threat, the West is mishandling the two immediate and pressing challenges of Afghanistan and Iraq. And despite the grave threat of nuclear terrorism, the Western custodians of the nonproliferation regime have allowed that regime to weaken significantly. The challenge posed by Iran's efforts to enrich uranium has been aggravated by the incompetence of the United States and the European Union. On the economic front, for the first time since World War II, the demise of a round of global trade negotiations, the Doha Round, seems imminent. Finally, the danger of global warming, too, is being mismanaged.

Yet Westerners seldom look inward to understand the deeper reasons these global problems are being mismanaged. Are there domestic structural reasons that explain this? Have Western democracies been hijacked by competitive populism and structural short-termism, preventing them from addressing long-term challenges from a broader global perspective?

Fortunately, some Asian states may now be capable of taking on more responsibilities, as they have been strengthened by implementing Western principles. In September 2005, Robert

Zoellick, then U.S. deputy secretary of state, called on China to become a "responsible stakeholder" in the international system. China has responded positively, as have other Asian states. In recent decades, Asians have been among the greatest beneficiaries of the open multilateral order created by the United States and the other victors of World War II, and few today want to destabilize it. The number of Asians seeking a comfortable middle-class existence has never been higher. For centuries, the Chinese and the Indians could only dream of such an accomplishment; now it is within the reach of around half a billion people in China and India. Their ideal is to achieve what the United States and Europe did. They want to replicate, not dominate, the West. The universalization of the Western dream represents a moment of triumph for the West. And so the West should welcome the fact that the Asian states are becoming competent at handling regional and global challenges.

The Middle East Mess

Western Policies have been most harmful in the Middle East. The Middle East is also the most dangerous region in the world. Trouble there affects not just seven million Israelis, around four million Palestinians, and 200 million Arabs; it also affects more than a billion Muslims worldwide. Every time there is a major flare-up in the Middle East, such as the U.S. invasion of Iraq or the Israeli bombing of Lebanon, Islamic communities around the world become concerned, distressed, and angered. And few of them doubt the problems origin: the West.

The invasion and occupation of Iraq, for example, was a multidimensional error. The theory and practice of international law legitimizes the use of force only when it is an act of self-defense or is authorized by the UN Security Council. The U.S.-led invasion of Iraq could not be justified on either count. The United States and the United Kingdom sought the Security Council's authorization to invade Iraq, but the council denied it. It was therefore clear to the international community that the subsequent war was illegal and that it would do huge damage to international law.

This has created an enormous problem, partly because until this point both the United States and the United Kingdom had been among the primary custodians of international law. American and British minds, such as James Brierly, Philip Jessup, Hersch Lauterpacht, and Hans Morgenthau, developed the conceptual infrastructure underlying international law, and American and British leaders provided the political will to have it accepted in practice. But neither the United States nor the United Kingdom will admit that the invasion and the occupation of Iraq were illegal or give up their historical roles as the chief caretakers of international law. Since 2003, both nations have frequently called for Iran and North Korea to implement UN Security Council resolutions. But how can the violators of UN principles also be their enforcers?

One rare benefit of the Iraq war may be that it has awakened a new fear of Iran among the Sunni Arab states. Egypt, Jordan, and Saudi Arabia, among others, do not want to deal with two adversaries and so are inclined to make peace with Israel. Saudi Arabia's King Abdullah used the opportunity of the special Arab League summit meeting in March 2007 to relaunch his long-standing proposal for a two-state solution to the Israeli-Palestinian conflict. Unfortunately, the Bush administration did not seize the opportunity—or revive the Taba accords that President Bill Clinton had worked out in January 2001, even though they could provide a basis for a lasting settlement and the Saudis were prepared to back them. In its early days, the Bush administration appeared ready to support a two-state solution. It was the first U.S. administration to vote in favor of a UN Security Council resolution calling for the creation of a Palestinian state, and it announced in March 2002 that it would try to achieve such a result by 2005. But here it is 2008, and little progress has been made.

The United States has made the already complicated Israeli-Palestinian conflict even more of a mess. Many extremist voices in Tel Aviv and Washington believe that time will always be on Israel's side. The pro-Israel lobby's stranglehold on the U.S. Congress, the political cowardice of U.S. politicians when it comes to creating a Palestinian state, and the sustained track record of U.S. aid to Israel support this view. But no great power forever sacrifices its larger national interests in favor of the interests of a small state. If Israel fails to accept the Taba accords, it will inevitably come to grief. If and when it does, Western incompetence will be seen as a major cause.

Never Say Never

Nuclear nonproliferation is another area in which the West, especially the United States, has made matters worse. The West has long been obsessed with the danger of the proliferation of weapons of mass destruction, particularly nuclear weapons. It pushed successfully for the near-universal ratification of the Biological and Toxin Weapons Convention, the Chemical Weapons Convention, and the Nuclear Nonproliferation Treaty (NPT).

But the West has squandered many of those gains. Today, the NPT is legally alive but spiritually dead. The NPT was inherently problematic since it divided the world into nuclear haves (the states that had tested a nuclear device by 1967) and nuclear have-nots (those that had not). But for two decades it was reasonably effective in preventing horizontal proliferation (the spread of nuclear weapons to other states). Unfortunately, the NPT has done nothing to prevent vertical proliferation, namely, the increase in the numbers and sophistication of nuclear weapons among the existing nuclear weapons states. During the Cold War, the United States and the Soviet Union agreed to work together to limit proliferation. The governments of several countries that could have developed nuclear weapons, such as Argentina, Brazil, Germany, Japan, and South Korea, restrained themselves because they believed the NPT reflected a fair bargain between China, France, the Soviet Union, the United Kingdom, and the United States (the five official nuclear weapons states and five permanent members of the UN Security Council) and the rest of the world. Both sides agreed that the world would be safer if the five nuclear states took steps to reduce their arsenals and worked toward the eventual goal of universal disarmament and the other states refrained from acquiring nuclear weapons at all.

So what went wrong? The first problem was that the NPT's principal progenitor, the United States, decided to walk away from the postwar rule-based order it had created, thus eroding the infrastructure on which the NPT's enforcement depends. During the time I was Singapore's ambassador to the UN, between 1984 and 1989, Jeane Kirkpatrick, the U.S. ambassador to the UN, treated the organization with contempt. She infamously said, "What takes place in the Security Council more closely resembles a mugging than either a political debate or an effort at problem-solving." She saw the postwar order as a set of constraints, not as a set of rules that the world should follow and the United States should help preserve. This undermined the NPT, because with no teeth of its own, no self-regulating or sanctioning mechanisms, and a clause allowing signatories to ignore obligations in the name of "supreme national interest," the treaty could only really be enforced by the UN Security Council. And once the United States began tearing holes in the fabric of the overall system, it created openings for violations of the NPT and its principles. Finally, by going to war with Iraq without UN authorization, the United States lost its moral authority to ask, for example, Iran to abide by Security Council resolutions.

Another problem has been the United States'—and other nuclear weapons states'—direct assault on the treaty. The NPT is fundamentally a social contract between the five nuclear weapons states and the rest of the world, based partly on the understanding that the nuclear powers will eventually give up their weapons. Instead, during the Cold War, the United States and the Soviet Union increased both the quantity and the sophistication of their nuclear weapons: the United States' nuclear stockpile peaked in 1966 at 31,700 warheads, and the Soviet Union's peaked in 1986 at 40,723. In fact, the United States and the Soviet Union developed their nuclear stockpiles so much that they actually ran out of militarily or economically significant targets. The numbers have declined dramatically since then, but even the current number of nuclear weapons held by the United States and Russia can wreak enormous damage on human civilization.

The nuclear states' decision to ignore Israel's nuclear weapons program was especially damaging to their authority. No nuclear weapons state has ever publicly acknowledged Israel's possession of nuclear weapons. Their silence has created a loophole in the NPT and delegitimized it in the eyes of Muslim nations. The consequences have been profound. When the West sermonizes that the world will become a more dangerous place when Iran acquires nuclear weapons, the Muslim world now shrugs.

India and Pakistan were already shrugging by 1998, when they tested their first nuclear weapons. When the international community responded by condemning the tests and applying sanctions on India, virtually all Indians saw through the hypocrisy and double standards of their critics. By not respecting their own obligations under the NPT, the five nuclear states had robbed their condemnations of any moral legitimacy; criticisms from Australia and Canada, which have also remained silent about Israel's bomb, similarly had no moral authority. The near-unanimous rejection of the NPT by the Indian establishment, which is otherwise very conscious of international opinion, showed how dead the treaty already was.

The world has lost its trust in the five nuclear weapons states and now sees them as the NPT's primary violators.

From time to time, common sense has entered discussions on nuclear weapons. President Ronald Reagan said more categorically than any U.S. president that the world would be better off without nuclear weapons. Last year, with the NPT in its death throes and the growing threat of loose nuclear weapons falling into the hands of terrorists forefront in everyone's mind, former Secretary of State George Shultz, former Defense Secretary William Perry, former Secretary of State Henry Kissinger, and former Senator Sam Nunn warned in *The Wall Street Journal* that the world was "now on the precipice of a new and dangerous nuclear era." They argued, "Unless urgent new actions are taken, the U.S. soon will be compelled to enter a new nuclear era that will be more precarious, psychologically disorienting, and economically even more costly than was Cold War deterrence." But these calls may have come too late. The world has lost its trust in the five nuclear weapons states and now sees them as the NPT's primary violators rather than its custodians. Those states' private cynicism about their obligations to the NPT has become public knowledge.

Contrary to what the West wants the rest of the world to believe, the nuclear weapons states, especially the United States and Russia, which continue to maintain thousands of nuclear weapons, are the biggest source of nuclear proliferation. Mohamed ElBaradei, the director general of the International Atomic Energy Agency, warned in *The Economist* in 2003, "The very existence of nuclear weapons gives rise to the pursuit of them. They are seen as a source of global influence, and are valued for their perceived deterrent effect. And as long as some countries possess them (or are protected by them in alliances) and others do not, this asymmetry breeds chronic global insecurity." Despite the Cold War, the second half of the twentieth century seemed to be moving the world toward a more civilized order. As the twenty-first century unfurls, the world seems to be sliding backward.

Irresponsible Stakeholders

After leading the world toward a period of spectacular economic growth in the second half of the twentieth century by promoting global free trade, the West has recently been faltering in its global economic leadership. Believing that low trade barriers and increasing trade interdependence would result in higher standards of living for all, European and U.S. economists and policymakers pushed for global economic liberalization. As a result, global trade grew from seven percent of the world's GDP in 1940 to 30 percent in 2005.

But a seismic shift has taken place in Western attitudes since the end of the Cold War. Suddenly, the United States and Europe no longer have a vested interest in the success of the East Asian economies, which they see less as allies and more as competitors. That change in Western interests was reflected in the fact that the West provided little real help to East Asia during the Asian financial crisis of 1997–98. The entry of China into the global marketplace, especially after its admission to the World Trade Organization, has made a huge difference in both economic and psychological terms. Many Europeans have lost confidence in their ability to compete with the Asians. And many Americans have lost confidence in the virtues of competition.

There are some knotty issues that need to be resolved in the current global trade talks, but fundamentally the negotiations are stalled because the conviction of the Western "champions" of free trade that free trade is good has begun to waver. When Americans and Europeans start to perceive themselves as losers in international trade, they also lose their drive to push for further trade liberalization. Unfortunately, on this front at least, neither China nor India (nor Brazil nor South Africa nor any other major developing country) is ready to take over the West's mantle. China, for example, is afraid that any effort to seek leadership in this area will stoke U.S. fears that it is striving for global hegemony. Hence, China is lying low. So, too, are the United States and Europe. Hence, the trade talks are stalled. The end of the West's promotion of global trade liberalization could well mean the end of the most spectacular economic growth the world has ever seen. Few in the West seem to be reflecting on the consequences of walking away from one of the West's most successful policies, which is what it will be doing if it allows the Doha Round to fail.

At the same time that the Western governments are relinquishing their stewardship of the global economy, they are also failing to take the lead on battling global warming. The awarding of the Nobel Peace Prize to former U.S. Vice President Al Gore, a longtime environmentalist, and the UN's Intergovernmental Panel on Climate Change confirms there is international consensus that global warning is a real threat. The most assertive advocates for tackling this problem come from the U.S. and European scientific communities, but the greatest resistance to any effective action is coming from the U.S. government. This has left the rest of the world confused and puzzled. Most people believe that the greenhouse effect is caused mostly by the flow of current emissions. Current emissions do aggravate the problem, but the fundamental cause is the stock of emissions that has accumulated since the Industrial Revolution. Finding a just and equitable solution to the problem of greenhouse gas emissions must begin with assigning responsibility both for the current flow and for the stock of greenhouse gases already accumulated. And on both counts the Western nations should bear a greater burden.

The West has to learn to share power and responsibility for the management of global issues with the rest of the world.

When it comes to addressing any problem pertaining to the global commons, such as the environment, it seems only fair that the wealthier members of the international community should shoulder more responsibility. This is a natural principle of justice. It is also fair in this particular case given the developed countries' primary role in releasing harmful gases into the atmosphere. R. K. Pachauri, chair of the Intergovernmental Panel on Climate Change, argued last year, "China and India are certainly increasing their share, but they are not increasing their per capita emissions anywhere close to the levels that you have in the developed world." Since 1850, China has contributed less than 8 percent of the world's total emissions of carbon dioxide, whereas the United States is responsible for 29 percent and western Europe is responsible for 27 percent. Today, India's per capita greenhouse gas emissions are equivalent to only 4 percent of those of the United States and 12 percent of those of the European Union. Still, the Western governments are not clearly acknowledging their responsibilities and are allowing many of their citizens to believe that China and India are the fundamental obstacles to any solution to global warming.

Washington might become more responsible on this front if a Democratic president replaces Bush in 2009. But people in the West will have to make some real concessions if they are to reduce significantly their per capita share of global emissions. A cap-and-trade program may do the trick. Western countries will probably have to make economic sacrifices. One option might be, as the journalist Thomas Friedman has suggested, to impose a dollar-per-gallon tax on Americans' gasoline consumption. Gore has proposed a carbon tax. So far, however, few U.S. politicians have dared to make such suggestions publicly.

Temptations of the East

The Middle East, nuclear proliferation, stalled trade liberalization, and global warming are all challenges that the West is essentially failing to address. And this failure suggests that a systemic problem is emerging in the West's stewardship of the international order—one that Western minds are reluctant to analyze or confront openly. After having enjoyed centuries of global domination, the West has to learn to share power and responsibility for the management of global issues with the rest of the world. It has to forgo outdated organizations, such as the Organization for Economic Cooperation and Development, and outdated processes, such as the G-8, and deal with organizations and processes with a broader scope and broader representation. It was always unnatural for the 12 percent of the world population that lived in the West to enjoy so much global power. Understandably, the other 88 percent of the world population increasingly wants also to drive the bus of world history.

First and foremost, the West needs to acknowledge that sharing the power it has accumulated in global forums would serve its interests. Restructuring international institutions to reflect the current world order will be complicated by the absence of natural leaders to do the job. The West has become part of the problem, and the Asian countries are not yet ready to step in. On the other hand, the world does not need to invent any new principles to improve global governance; the concepts of domestic good governance can and should be applied to the international community. The Western principles of democracy, the rule of law, and social justice are among the world's best bets. The ancient virtues of partnership and pragmatism can complement them.

Democracy, the foundation of government in the West, is based on the premise that each human being in a society is an equal stakeholder in the domestic order. Thus, governments are selected on the basis of "one person, one vote." This has produced long-term stability and order in Western societies. In order to produce long-term stability and order worldwide, democracy should be the cornerstone of global society, and the planet's 6.6 billion inhabitants should become equal stakeholders. To inject the spirit of democracy into global governance and global decision-making, one must turn to institutions with universal representation, especially the UN. UN institutions such as the World Health Organization and the World Meteorological Organization enjoy widespread legitimacy because of their universal membership, which means their decisions are generally accepted by all the countries of the world.

The problem today is that although many Western actors are willing to work with specialized UN agencies, they are reluctant to strengthen the UN's core institution, the UN General Assembly, from which all these specialized agencies come. The UN General Assembly is the most representative body on the planet, and yet many Western countries are deeply skeptical of it. They are right to point out its imperfections. But they overlook the fact that this imperfect assembly enjoys legitimacy in the eyes of the people of this imperfect world. Moreover, the General Assembly has at times shown more common sense and prudence than some of the most sophisticated Western democracies. Of course, it takes time to persuade all of the UN's members to march in the same direction, but consensus building is precisely what gives legitimacy to the result. Most countries in the world respect and abide by most UN decisions because they believe in the authority of the UN. Used well, the body can be a powerful vehicle for making critical decisions on global governance.

The world today is run not through the General Assembly but through the Security Council, which is effectively run by the five permanent member states. If this model were adopted in the United States, the U.S. Congress would be replaced by a selective council comprised of only the representatives from the country's five most powerful states. Would the populations of the other 45 states not deem any such proposal absurd? The West must cease its efforts to prolong its undemocratic management of the global order and find ways to effectively engage the majority of the world's population in global decision-making.

Another fundamental principle that should underpin the global order is the rule of law. This hallowed Western principle insists that no person, regardless of his or her status, is above the law. Ironically, while being exemplary in implementing the rule of law at home, the United States is a leading international outlaw in its refusal to recognize the constraints of international law. Many Americans live comfortably with this contradiction while expecting other countries to abide by widely accepted treaties. Americans react with horror when Iran tries to walk away from the NPT. Yet they are surprised that the world is equally shocked when Washington abandons a universally accepted treaty such as the Comprehensive Test Ban Treaty.

The Bush administration's decision to exempt the United States from the provisions of international law on human rights is even more damaging. For over half a century, since Eleanor Roosevelt led the fight for the adoption of the Universal Declaration of Human Rights, the United States was the global champion of human rights. This was the result of a strong ideological conviction that it was the United States' God-given duty to create a more civilized world. It also made for a good ideological weapon during the Cold War: the free United States was fighting the unfree Soviet Union. But the Bush administration has stunned the world by walking away from universally accepted human rights conventions, especially those on torture. And much as the U.S. electorate could not be expected to tolerate an attorney general who broke his own laws from time to time, how can the global body politic be expected to respect a custodian of international law that violates these very rules?

Finally, on social justice, Westerns nations have slackened. Social justice is the cornerstone of order and stability in modern Western societies and the rest of the world. People accept inequality as long as some kind of social safety net exists to help the dispossessed. Most western European governments took this principle to heart after World War II and introduced welfare provisions as a way to ward off Marxist revolutions seeking to create socialist societies. Today, many Westerners believe that they are spreading social justice globally with their massive foreign aid to the developing world. Indeed, each year, the members of the Organization for Economic Cooperation and Development, according to the organization's own estimates, give approximately $104 billion to the developing world. But the story of Western aid to the developing world is essentially a myth. Western countries have put significant amounts of money into their overseas development assistance budgets, but these funds' primary purpose is to serve the immediate and short-term security and national interests of the donors rather than the long-term interests of the recipients.

Some Asian countries are now ready to join the West in becoming responsible custodians of the global order.

The experience of Asia shows that where Western aid has failed to do the job, domestic good governance can succeed. This is likely to be Asia's greatest contribution to world history. The success of Asia will inspire other societies on different continents to emulate it. In addition, Asia's march to modernity can help produce a more stable world order. Some Asian countries are now ready to join the West in becoming responsible custodians of the global order; as the biggest beneficiaries of the current system, they have powerful incentives to do so. The West is not welcoming Asia's progress, and its short-term interests in preserving its privileged position in various global institutions are trumping its long-term interests in creating a more just and stable world order. Unfortunately, the West has gone from being the world's primary problem solver to being its single biggest liability.

KISHORE MAHBUBANI is Dean of the Lee Kuan Yew School of Public Policy at the National University of Singapore. This essay is adapted from his latest book, *The New Asian Hemisphere: The Irresistible Shift of Global Power to the East* (Public Affairs, 2008).

Development as Poison
Rethinking the Western Model of Modernity

Stephen A. Marglin

A t the beginning of Annie Hall, Woody Allen tells a story about two women returning from a vacation in New York's Catskill Mountains. They meet a friend and immediately start complaining: "The food was terrible," the first woman says, "I think they were trying to poison us." The second adds, "Yes, and the portions were so small." That is my take on development: the portions are small, and they are poisonous. This is not to make light of the very real gains that have come with development. In the past three decades, infant and child mortality have fallen by 66 percent in Indonesia and Peru, by 75 percent in Iran and Turkey, and by 80 percent in Arab oil-producing states. In most parts of the world, children not only have a greater probability of surviving into adulthood, they also have more to eat than their parents did—not to mention better access to schools and doctors and a prospect of work lives of considerably less drudgery.

Nonetheless, for those most in need, the portions are indeed small. Malnutrition and hunger persist alongside the tremendous riches that have come with development and globalization. In South Asia almost a quarter of the population is undernourished and in sub-Saharan Africa, more than a third. The outrage of anti-globalization protestors in Seattle, Genoa, Washington, and Prague was directed against the meagerness of the portions, and rightly so.

But more disturbing than the meagerness of development's portions is its deadliness. Whereas other critics highlight the distributional issues that compromise development, my emphasis is rather on the terms of the project itself, which involve the destruction of indigenous cultures and communities. This result is more than a side-effect of development; it is central to the underlying values and assumptions of the entire Western development enterprise.

The White Man's Burden

Along with the technologies of production, healthcare, and education, development has spread the culture of the modern West all over the world, and thereby undermined other ways of seeing, understanding, and being. By culture I mean something more than artistic sensibility or intellectual refinement. "Culture" is used here the way anthropologists understand the term, to mean the totality of patterns of behavior and belief that characterize a specific society. Outside the modern West, culture is sustained through community, the set of connections that bind people to one another economically, socially, politically, and spiritually. Traditional communities are not simply about shared spaces, but about shared participation and experience in producing and exchanging goods and services, in governing, entertaining and mourning, and in the physical, moral, and spiritual life of the community. The culture of the modern West, which values the market as the primary organizing principle of life, undermines these traditional communities just as it has undermined community in the West itself over the last 400 years.

The West thinks it does the world a favor by exporting its culture along with the technologies that the non-Western world wants and needs. This is not a recent idea. A century ago, Rudyard Kipling, the poet laureate of British imperialism, captured this sentiment in the phrase "White Man's burden," which portrayed imperialism as an altruistic effort to bring the benefits of Western rule to uncivilized peoples. Political imperialism died in the wake of World War II, but cultural imperialism is still alive and well. Neither practitioners nor theorists speak today of the white man's burden—no development expert of the 21st century hankers after clubs or golf courses that exclude local folk from membership. Expatriate development experts now work with local people, but their collaborators are themselves formed for the most part by Western culture and values and have more in common with the West than they do with their own people. Foreign advisers—along with their local collaborators—are still missionaries, missionaries for progress as the West defines the term. As our forbears saw imperialism, so we see development.

There are in fact two views of development and its relationship to culture, as seen from the vantage point of the modern West. In one, culture is only a thin veneer over a common, universal behavior based on rational calculation and maximization of individual self interest. On this view, which is probably the view of most economists, the Indian subsistence-oriented peasant is no less calculating, no less competitive, than the US commercial farmer.

Cultural imperialism is still alive and well. . . . Foreign advisers ... are still missionaries, missionaries for progress as the West defines the term. As our forebears saw imperialism, so we see development.

There is a second approach which, far from minimizing cultural differences, emphasizes them. Cultures, implicitly or explicitly, are ranked along with income and wealth on a linear scale. As the West is richer, Western culture is more progressive, more developed. Indeed, the process of development is seen as the transformation of backward, traditional, cultural practices into modern practice, the practice of the West, the better to facilitate the growth of production and income.

What these two views share is confidence in the cultural superiority of the modern West. The first, in the guise of denying culture, attributes to other cultures Western values and practices. The second, in the guise of affirming culture, posits an inclined plane of history (to use a favorite phrase of the Indian political psychologist Ashis Nandy) along which the rest of the world is, and ought to be, struggling to catch up with us. Both agree on the need for "development." In the first view, the Other is a miniature adult, and development means the tender nurturing by the market to form the miniature Indian or African into a full-size Westerner. In the second, the Other is a child who needs structural transformation and cultural improvement to become an adult.

Both conceptions of development make sense in the context of individual people precisely because there is an agreed-upon standard of adult behavior against which progress can be measured. Or at least there was until two decades ago when the psychologist Carol Gilligan challenged the conventional wisdom of a single standard of individual development. Gilligan's book *In A Different Voice* argued that the prevailing standards of personal development were male standards. According to these standards, personal development was measured by progress from intuitive, inarticulate, cooperative, contextual, and personal modes of behavior toward rational, principled, competitive, universal, and impersonal modes of behavior, that is, from "weak" modes generally regarded as feminine and based on experience to "strong" modes regarded as masculine and based on algorithm.

Drawing from Gilligan's study, it becomes clear that on an international level, the development of nation-states is seen the same way. What appear to be universally agreed upon guidelines to which developing societies must conform are actually impositions of Western standards through cultural imperialism. Gilligan did for the study of personal development what must be done for economic development: allowing for difference. Just as the development of individuals should be seen as the flowering of that which is special and unique within each of us—a process by which an acorn becomes an oak rather than being obliged to become a maple—so the development of peoples should be conceived as the flowering of what is special and unique within each culture. This is not to argue for a cultural relativism in which all beliefs and practices sanctioned by some culture are equally valid on a moral, aesthetic, or practical plane. But it is to reject the universality claimed by Western beliefs and practices.

Of course, some might ask what the loss of a culture here or there matters if it is the price of material progress, but there are two flaws to this argument. First, cultural destruction is not necessarily a corollary of the technologies that extend life and improve its quality. Western technology can be decoupled from the entailments of Western culture. Second, if I am wrong about this, I would ask, as Jesus does in the account of Saint Mark, "[W]hat shall it profit a man, if he shall gain the whole world, and lose his own soul?" For all the material progress that the West has achieved, it has paid a high price through the weakening to the breaking point of communal ties. We in the West have much to learn, and the cultures that are being destroyed in the name of progress are perhaps the best resource we have for restoring balance to our own lives. The advantage of taking a critical stance with respect to our own culture is that we become more ready to enter into a genuine dialogue with other ways of being and believing.

The Culture of the Modern West

Culture is in the last analysis a set of assumptions, often unconsciously held, about people and how they relate to one another. The assumptions of modern Western culture can be described under five headings: individualism, self interest, the privileging of "rationality," unlimited wants, and the rise of the moral and legal claims of the nation-state on the individual.

Individualism is the notion that society can and should be understood as a collection of autonomous individuals, that groups—with the exception of the nation-state—have no normative significance as groups; that all behavior, policy, and even ethical judgment should be reduced to their effects on individuals. All individuals play the game of life on equal terms, even if they start with different amounts of physical strength, intellectual capacity, or capital assets. The playing field is level even if the players are not equal. These individuals are taken as given in many important ways rather than as works in progress. For example, preferences are accepted as given and cover everything from views about the relative merits of different flavors of ice cream to views about the relative merits of prostitution, casual sex, sex among friends, and sex within committed relationships. In an excess of democratic zeal, the children of the 20th century have extended the notion of radical subjectivism to the whole domain of preferences: one set of "preferences" is as good as another.

Self-interest is the idea that individuals make choices to further their own benefit. There is no room here for duty, right, or obligation, and that is a good thing, too. Adam Smith's best remembered contribution to economics, for better or worse, is the idea of a harmony that emerges from the pursuit of self-interest. It should be noted that while individualism is a prior condition for self-interest—there is no place for self-interest

Insurance

Spending on Insurance Premiums

Region	Percent of Global Premium Market
North America	**37.32**
Canada	1.91
United States	35.41
Latin America	**1.67**
Brazil	0.51
Mexico	0.4
Europe	**31.93**
France	4.99
Germany	5.06
UK	9.7
Asia	**26.46**
China	0.79
India	0.41
Japan	20.62
Africa	**1.03**
South Africa	0.87
Oceania	**1.59**
Australia	1.46

http://www.internationalinsurance.org

without the self—the converse does not hold. Individualism does not necessarily imply self-interest.

The third assumption is that one kind of knowledge is superior to others. The modern West privileges the algorithmic over the experiential, elevating knowledge that can be logically deduced from what are regarded as self-evident first principles over what is learned from intuition and authority, from touch and feel. In the stronger form of this ideology, the algorithmic is not only privileged but recognized as the sole legitimate form of knowledge. Other knowledge is mere belief, becoming legitimate only when verified by algorithmic methods.

Fourth is unlimited wants. It is human nature that we always want more than we have and that there is, consequently, never enough. The possibilities of abundance are always one step beyond our reach. Despite the enormous growth in production and consumption, we are as much in thrall to the economy as our parents, grandparents, and great-grandparents. Most US families find one income inadequate for their needs, not only at the bottom of the distribution—where falling real wages have eroded the standard of living over the past 25 years—but also in the middle and upper ranges of the distribution. Economics, which encapsulates in stark form the assumptions of the modern West, is frequently defined as the study of the allocation of limited resources among unlimited wants.

Finally, the assumption of modern Western culture is that the nation-state is the preeminent social grouping and moral authority. Worn out by fratricidal wars of religion, early mod-

ern Europe moved firmly in the direction of making one's relationship to God a private matter—a taste or preference among many. Language, shared commitments, and a defined territory would, it was hoped, be a less divisive basis for social identity than religion had proven to be.

An Economical Society

Each of these dimensions of modern Western culture is in tension with its opposite. Organic or holistic conceptions of society exist side by side with individualism. Altruism and fairness are opposed to self interest. Experiential knowledge exists, whether we recognize it or not, alongside algorithmic knowledge. Measuring who we are by what we have has been continually resisted by the small voice within that calls us to be our better selves. The modern nation-state claims, but does not receive, unconditional loyalty.

So the sway of modern Western culture is partial and incomplete even within the geographical boundaries of the West. And a good thing too, since no society organized on the principles outlined above could last five minutes, much less the 400 years that modernity has been in the ascendant. But make no mistake—modernity is the dominant culture in the West and increasingly so throughout the world. One has only to examine the assumptions that underlie contemporary economic thought—both stated and unstated—to confirm this assessment. Economics is simply the formalization of the assumptions of modern Western culture. That both teachers and students of economics accept these assumptions uncritically speaks volumes about the extent to which they hold sway.

It is not surprising then that a culture characterized in this way is a culture in which the market is the organizing principle of social life. Note my choice of words, "the market" and "social life," not markets and economic life. Markets have been with us since time out of mind, but the market, the idea of markets as a system for organizing production and exchange, is a distinctly modern invention, which grew in tandem with the cultural assumption of the self-interested, algorithmic individual who pursues wants without limit, an individual who owes allegiance only to the nation-state.

There is no sense in trying to resolve the chicken-egg problem of which came first. Suffice it to say that we can hardly have the market without the assumptions that justify a market system—and the market system can function acceptably only when the assumptions of the modern West are widely shared. Conversely, once these assumptions are prevalent, markets appear to be a "natural" way to organize life.

Markets and Communities

If people and society were as the culture of the modern West assumes, then market and community would occupy separate ideological spaces, and would co-exist or not as people chose. However, contrary to the assumptions of individualism, the individual does not encounter society as a fully formed human being. We are constantly being shaped by our experiences, and in a society organized in terms of markets, we are formed by our experiences in the market. Markets organize not only the production and distribution of things; they also organize the production of people.

The rise of the market system is thus bound up with the loss of community. Economists do not deny this, but rather put a market friendly spin on the destruction of community: impersonal markets accomplish more efficiently what the connections of social solidarity, reciprocity, and other redistributive institutions do in the absence of markets. Take fire insurance, for example. I pay a premium of, say, US$200 per year, and if my barn burns down, the insurance company pays me US$60,000 to rebuild it. A simple market transaction replaces the more cumbersome method of gathering my neighbors for a barn-raising, as rural US communities used to do. For the economist, it is a virtue that the more efficient institution drives out the less efficient. In terms of building barns with a minimal expenditure of resources, insurance may indeed be more efficient than gathering the community each time somebody's barn burns down. But in terms of maintaining the community, insurance is woefully lacking. Barn-raisings foster mutual interdependence: I rely on my neighbors economically—as well as in other ways—and they rely on me. Markets substitute impersonal relationships mediated by goods and services for the personal relationships of reciprocity and the like.

Why does community suffer if it is not reinforced by mutual economic dependence? Does not the relaxation of economic ties rather free up energy for other ways of connecting, as the English economist Dennis Robertson once suggested early in the 20th century? In a reflective mood toward the end of his life, Sir Dennis asked, "What does the economist economize?" His answer: "[T]hat scarce resource Love, which we know, just as well as anybody else, to be the most precious thing in the world." By using the impersonal relationships of markets to do the work of fulfilling our material needs, we economize on our higher faculties of affection, our capacity for reciprocity and personal obligation—love, in Robertsonian shorthand—which can then be devoted to higher ends.

In the end, his protests to the contrary notwithstanding, Sir Dennis knew more about banking than about love. Robertson made the mistake of thinking that love, like a loaf of bread, gets used up as it is used. Not all goods are "private" goods like bread. There are also "public" or "collective" goods which are not consumed when used by one person. A lighthouse is the canonical example: my use of the light does not diminish its availability to you. Love is a *hyper* public good: it actually increases by being used and indeed may shrink to nothing if left unused for any length of time.

Economics is simply the formalization of the assumptions of modern Western culture. That both teachers and students of economics accept these assumptions uncritically speaks volumes about the extent to which they hold sway.

If love is not scarce in the way that bread is, it is not sensible to design social institutions to economize on it. On the contrary, it makes sense to design social institutions to draw out and develop the community's stock of love. It is only when we focus on barns rather than on the people raising barns that insurance appears to be a more effective way of coping with disaster than is a community-wide barn-raising. The Amish, who are descendants of 18th century immigrants to the United States, are perhaps unique in the United States for their attention to fostering community; they forbid insurance precisely because they understand that the market relationship between an individual and the insurance company undermines the mutual dependence of the individuals that forms the basis of the community. For the Amish, barn-raisings are not exercises in nostalgia, but the cement which holds the community together.

Indeed, community cannot be viewed as just another good subject to the dynamics of market supply and demand that people can choose or not as they please, according to the same market test that applies to brands of soda or flavors of ice cream. Rather, the maintenance of community must be a collective responsibility for two reasons. The first is the so-called "free rider" problem. To return to the insurance example, my decision to purchase fire insurance rather than participate in the give and take of barn raising with my neighbors has the side effect—the "externality" in economics jargon—of lessening my involvement with the community. If I am the only one to act this way, this effect may be small with no harm done. But when all of us opt for insurance and leave caring for the community to others, there will be no others to care, and the community will disintegrate. In the case of insurance, I buy insurance because it is more convenient, and—acting in isolation—I can reasonably say to myself that my action hardly undermines the community. But when we all do so, the cement of mutual obligation is weakened to the point that it no longer supports the community.

The free rider problem is well understood by economists, and the assumption that such problems are absent is part of the standard fine print in the warranty that economists provide for the market. A second, deeper, problem cannot so easily be translated into the language of economics. The market creates more subtle externalities that include effects on beliefs, values, and behaviors—a class of externalities which are ignored in the standard framework of economics in which individual "preferences" are assumed to be unchanging. An Amishman's decision to insure his barn undermines the mutual dependence of the Amish not only by making him less dependent on the community, but also by subverting the beliefs that sustain this dependence. For once interdependence is undermined, the community is no longer valued; the process of undermining interdependence is self-validating.

Thus, the existence of such externalities means that community survival cannot be left to the spontaneous initiatives of its members acting in accord with the individual maximizing model. Furthermore, this problem is magnified when the externalities involve feedback from actions to values, beliefs, and then to behavior. If a community is to survive, it must structure the interactions of its members to strengthen ways of being and knowing which support community. It will have to constrain the market when the market undermines community.

A Different Development

There are two lessons here. The first is that there should be mechanisms for local communities to decide, as the Amish routinely do, which innovations in organization and technology are compatible with the core values the community wishes to preserve. This does not mean the blind preservation of whatever has been sanctioned by time and the existing distribution of power. Nor does it mean an idyllic, conflict-free path to the future. But recognizing the value as well as the fragility of community would be a giant step forward in giving people a real opportunity to make their portions less meager and avoiding the poison.

The second lesson is for practitioners and theorists of development. What many Westerners see simply as liberating people from superstition, ignorance, and the oppression of tradition, is fostering values, behaviors, and beliefs that are highly problematic for our own culture. Only arrogance and a supreme failure of the imagination cause us to see them as universal rather than as the product of a particular history. Again, this is not to argue that "anything goes." It is instead a call for sensitivity, for entering into a dialogue that involves listening instead of dictating—not so that we can better implement our own agenda, but so that we can genuinely learn that which modernity has made us forget.

STEPHEN A. MARGLIN is Walter S. Barker Professor of Economics at Harvard University.

UNIT 2

Political Economy and the Developing World

Unit Selections

Key Points to Consider

- In what ways are emerging markets playing a growing role in the global economy?

- How will the global economic crisis affect developing countries?

- Why might the global economic crisis trigger greater government intervention in developing country economies?

- How are the developing countries disadvantaged by international trade?

- How have cotton subsidies affected the poor cotton-producing countries?

- What triggered the global food crisis?

- What needs to be done to address the food crisis?

- Why have NGOs taken on greater responsibility for humanitarian aid and development?

- Why is NGO activity controversial?

- What are the criticisms of microcredit?

- What is the reason behind the optimistic belief that there will be a dramatic increase in Africa's agricultural production?

Student Website

www.mhcls.com

Internet References

Center for Third World Organizing
   http://www.ctwo.org/
ENTERWeb
   http://www.enterweb.org
International Monetary Fund (IMF)
   http://www.imf.org

TWN (Third World Network)
   http://www.twnside.org.sg/
U.S. Agency for International Development (USAID)
   http://www.usaid.gov
The World Bank
   http://www.worldbank.org

Economic issues are one of the most pressing concerns of the developing world. Economic growth and stability are essential to tackle the various problems confronting developing countries. Even though the developing world is beginning to play a larger role in the global economy, many countries still continue to struggle to achieve consistent economic growth. Although there is some indication that the number of people below the poverty line is decreasing worldwide, over a billion people still live on less than a dollar a day. Economic inequality between the industrial countries and much of the developing world persists. This is especially true of the poorest countries that have become further marginalized due to their limited participation in the global economy. Substantial inequality within developing countries is also obvious. The elite's access to education, capital, and technology has significantly widened the gap between the rich and the poor. Since their incorporation into the international economic system during colonialism, the majority of developing countries have been primarily suppliers of raw materials, agricultural products, and inexpensive labor. Dependence on commodity exports means that developing countries have had to deal with fluctuating, and frequently declining, prices for their exports. At the same time, prices for imports have remained constant or have increased. At best, this decline in terms of trade has made development planning difficult; at worst, it has led to economic stagnation and decline. Although industrialization in China and India boosted demand for primary products over the past few years, the recent global economic decline has resulted in falling demand and lower prices for commodities. Clearly, dependence on export of raw materials and agricultural goods is not an ideal long-term strategy for economic success.

With a few exceptions, most of the developing nations have had limited success in breaking out of this dilemma through the process of diversifying their economies. Efforts at industrialization and export of light manufactured goods have led to competition with the less efficient industries of the industrialized world. The response of industrialized countries has often been protectionism and demands for trade reciprocity, which can overwhelm the markets of the developing countries. The World Trade Organization (WTO) was established to standardize trade regulations and increase international trade, but critics charge that the WTO continues to be dominated by the wealthy industrial countries. Developing world countries also assert that they are often shut out of trade negotiations, that they must accept deals dictated by the wealthy countries, and that they lack sufficient resources to effectively participate in the wide range of forums and negotiations that take place around the world. Moreover, developing countries charge that the industrialized countries are selective in their efforts to dismantle trade barriers and emphasize only those trade issues that reflect their interests. Delegates from poor countries walked out of the 2003 WTO ministerial meeting in Cancún, Mexico protesting the rich countries' reluctance to eliminate agricultural subsidies and their efforts to dominate the agenda. Neither the 2005 Hong Kong WTO ministerial meeting nor the 2006 talks in Geneva made much progress on a forming a comprehensive international trade agreement. Further talks in 2007 and 2008 also failed to produce an agreement,

© Royalty-Free/CORBIS

largely due to disagreement over agricultural trade. It seems increasingly unlikely that the Doha Round will produce a broad agreement further liberalizing trade.

The economic situation in the developing world, however, is not entirely attributable to colonial legacy and protectionism on the part of industrialized countries. Developing countries have sometimes constructed their own trade barriers. Evidence suggests that developing countries would benefit from dismantling their trade barriers even if the industrialized countries do not reciprocate. Industrialization schemes involving heavy government direction were often ill-conceived or have resulted in corruption and mismanagement. Industrialized countries frequently point to these inefficiencies in calling for market-oriented reforms, but the emphasis on privatization does not adequately recognize the role of the state in developing countries' economies; and privatization may result in foreign control of important sectors of the economy, as well as a loss of jobs. Debt has further compounded economic problems for many developing countries.

During the 1970s, developing countries' prior economic performance and the availability of petrodollars encouraged extensive commercial lending. The worldwide recession in the early 1980s left many developing countries unable to meet their debt obligations. The commercial banks weathered the crisis, and some actually showed a profit. Commercial lending declined as an aftermath of the debt crisis, and international financial institutions became the lenders of last resort for many developing countries. Access to the World Bank and International Monetary Fund became conditional on the adoption of structural adjustment programs that involved steps such as reduced public expenditures, devaluation of currencies, and export promotion, all geared to debt reduction. The consequences of these programs have been painful for developing countries, resulting in declining public services, higher prices, and greater reliance on primary production. The poorest countries in particular struggled with heavy debt burdens, and the IMF and World Bank came under increasing criticism for their programs in these countries. Although these institutions have made efforts to shift the emphasis to poverty reduction, some critics charge that the reforms are superficial, that the international financial institutions lack accountability, and that the developing countries do not have adequate influence in decisionmaking. Eliminating the debt of the world's poorest countries was a major focus of the G-8 summit in July 2005 but whether the promised debt relief will have the desired effect remains to be seen. The recent global economic crisis will certainly have an impact on trade, aid, and investment. Plans to increase the IMF's reserves will thrust the Fund into the effort to deal with the financial crisis and is sure to re-open questions about the IMF's policies and the lack of developing country influence in its decision making. Coming on the heels of the global food crisis that began in 2005, the twin problems of high food prices and global recession will hit the developing world particularly hard.

Globalization has produced differing views regarding the benefits and costs of this trend for the developing world. Advocates claim that closer economic integration, especially through trade and financial liberalization, increases economic prosperity in developing countries and encourages good governance, transparency, and accountability. Critics respond that globalization favors the powerful nations and through the international financial institutions, imposes difficult and perhaps counterproductive policies on the struggling economies. They also charge that globalization undermines workers' rights and causes environmental degradation. Moreover, most of the benefits of globalization have gone to those countries that are already growing—leaving the poorest even further behind. Partly due to the realization that the poverty in the developing world contributes to the despair and resentment that leads some to terrorism, there has been increased focus on foreign aid. Although the recently renewed emphasis on aid is likely to run into the reality that in a global financial crisis aid levels will decline, attention has been focused on how aid can be used more effectively. While aid has often been criticized, it does produce benefits. Those benefits, however, could be enhanced by more effective implementation. NGOs have become increasingly important players in this effort to improve effectiveness but this has also raised questions about NGO motivations and efficacy.

Industrial Revolution 2.0

In the corner offices of New York and Tokyo, business leaders cling to the notion that their designs, technologies, and brands are cutting edge. Increasingly, however, that just isn't so. In industries ranging from steel and cement to automobiles and electronics, "Third World companies" are poised to overtake their Western rivals. Get ready for the biggest firms you've never heard of to become household names.

Antoine van Agtmael

For a few minutes, I held the future in my hand. The third-generation cell phone in my palm made a BlackBerry look like a Model T Ford. Looking down at the color video screen, I could see the person on the other end of the line. The gadget, which fit easily into my pocket, could check local traffic, broadcast breaking television news, and play interactive computer games across continents. Internet and e-mail access were a foregone conclusion. So were downloading music and watching video clips.

None of this would be all that surprising were it not for where I was standing. I wasn't visiting Apple Computers in Cupertino, California, or Nokia headquarters outside Helsinki. It was January 2005, and I was in Taiwan, standing in the research lab of High Tech Computer Corporation (HTC). The innovative Taiwanese company employs 1,100 research engineers, invented the iPAQ pocket organizer (which it sold to Hewlett-Packard), and developed a series of advanced handheld phones for companies such as Palm, Verizon, and Vodafone. All around me were young, smart, ambitious engineers. They represented the cream of the crop of Taiwanese universities with, in some cases, years of experience in international firms. They were hard at work testing everything from sound quality in a sophisticated acoustics studio to the scratch resistance of newly developed synthetic materials.

I was being shown not just the prototype of a new smart phone but the prototype of a new kind of company—savvy, global, and, most important, well ahead of its nearest competitors in the United States and Europe. My experience in Taiwan is not that unusual. From Asia to Latin America, companies that many still regard as "Third World" makers of cheap Electronics or producers of raw materials are emerging as competitive firms capable of attaining world-class status. Only a decade ago, the attention of the international business community was focused on a new economy backed by hot tech firms in California and

Tokyo. But the reality of the current global dynamic is that, more likely than not, the next Microsoft or General Electric will come from the "new economies" of Asia, Latin America, and Eastern Europe, not the United States, Europe, or Japan.

Today, emerging-market countries account for 85 percent of the world's population but generate just 20 percent of global gross national product. By 2035, however, the combined economies of emerging markets will be larger than (and by the middle of this century, nearly double) the economies of the United States, Western Europe, or Japan. The reality of globalization—which is only slowly and reluctantly sinking in—is that outsourcing means more than having "cheap labor" toil away in mines, factories, and call centers on behalf of Western corporations. Yet in the West, business leaders and government officials cling to the notion that their companies lead the world in technology, design, and marketing prowess.

Just as the Industrial Revolution turned American companies from imitators to innovators, emerging-market multinationals will do the same.

Increasingly, that just isn't so. South Korea's Samsung is now a better recognized brand than is Japan's Sony. Its research and development budget is larger than that of America's Intel. And its 2005 profits exceeded those of Dell, Motorola, Nokia, and Philips, Mexico's CEMEX is now the largest cement company in the United States, the second largest in the United Kingdom, and the third largest in the world. The gas reserves of Russian giant Gazprom are larger than those of all the major oil companies combined, and its market capitalization—or total stock value—is larger than that of Microsoft. South Korean engineers are helping U.S. steel companies modernize their outdated plants. New proprietary drugs are being developed in Indian and Slovenian labs, where researchers are no longer content to turn out high volumes of low-cost generics for sale in the United States and Europe. New inventions in consumer electronics and wireless technology are moving from Asia to the United States and Europe, not just the other way around.

The growth in emerging-market companies has been nothing short of astounding. In 1988, there were just 20 companies in emerging markets' with sales topping $1 billion. Last year, there were 270, including at least 38 with sales exceeding $10 billion. In 1981, the total value of all stocks listed on stock exchanges in emerging markets was $80 billion. That was less than the market capitalization of the largest emerging-market firm, Samsung, in 2005. Over the past quarter century, the total market capitalization of emerging markets as a group has risen to more than $5 trillion. Twenty-five years ago, portfolio investors had invested less than a few hundred-million dollars in emerging-market firms. Today, annual portfolio investment flows of more than $60 billion constitute the leading edge of a trend. Fifty-eight of the Fortune 500 top global corporations are from emerging markets, and many of them are more profitable than their peers in the West. The era of emerging-market companies being nothing more than unsophisticated makers of low-cost, low-tech products has ended.

Lifting the Veil

Most people are blissfully unaware that companies from emerging markets already play a major part in their lives by making much of what they eat, drink, and wear. One reason that these new multinationals have flown below the radar of so many executives, as well as the general public, is that companies such as Taiwan-based Yue Yuen and Hon Hai remain deliberately hidden in the shadows. Even though Yue Yuen produces the actual shoes for Nike and Hon Hai makes much of what can be found inside Dell computers, Apple iPods, and Sony PlayStations, the bigger brands continue to control the distribution and marketing. When will they remove their veil? These firms' prevailing invisibility—a conscious stealth strategy in some cases—does not mean that they are powerless, less profitable, or that they will be content to have a low profile forever. It won't be long before the biggest companies you have never heard of become household names.

Companies like Samsung, LG, and Hyundai, all based in South Korea, began by making products efficiently and cheaply. Now, they have recognized brand names, a high-quality image, world-class technology, and appealing designs. China's Haier, the country's leading producer of household appliances, is following in their footsteps. In fact, it is already better known than GE, Sony, or Toyota by hundreds of millions of consumers in China, India, and other emerging markets. Firms such as Haier have not relied on big brand names to reach consumers in the United States and Europe. Instead, they used niche products such as small refrigerators and wine coolers to get their lines into big-box stores such as Walmart. And as time goes on, more

emerging-market firms will overtake the long-established Western companies that they now supply.

That has already happened in a number of industries ranging from semiconductors to beer. Samsung now holds the No. 1 global market position not only in semiconductors used in hard disks and flash memory cards but also in flat-screen monitors used for computers and televisions. In 2004, China's Lenovo purchased IBM's ThinkPad brand. In a wholly different industry, Brazilian investment bankers merged domestic beer companies in 1999 and then swapped shares with Europe's largest beer giant, Interbrew, to form a new entity that is now managed by a Brazilian CEO. Meanwhile, Corona beer, produced by Mexico's Modelo, is now the leading imported beer brand in the United States. Elsewhere, the global supply chain is turning upside-down, with Western companies selling components and services to multinationals from emerging markets. GE, for instance, sells jet engines to Brazilian plane manufacturer Embraer. Other smart firms will soon follow suit. Just as the rise of the United States after the Industrial Revolution turned American companies from imitators into innovators, emerging-market multinationals will increasingly do the same.

For many of these firms, the road to success included weathering global financial crises. These economic shocks squeezed out many emerging-market companies. The ensuing Darwinian struggle for survival left only battle-hardened firms still standing. As newcomers, emerging multinationals had to fight for shelf space against preconceived notions of inferior product quality (a bias that wasn't always without justification). When the financial crises were over, a few world-class companies had carved out leading roles. Today, more than 25 emerging-market multinationals have attained a leading global market share in their respective industries. Fifteen command the No. 1 market share—and they are no longer limited to a narrow slice of low-tech industries. The truth is, emerging multinationals now maintain dominant market positions in some of the world's fastest-growing industries. Consider Samsung, which is the global market leader in flash memory cards used in iPods, cameras, and mobile phones. The memory card market was worth $370 million in 2000. This year, it is valued at $13 billion. In fact, more than half of all emerging-market companies of world-class status operate in capital-intensive or technology-oriented industries, where high rates of spending on research and development are required to remain competitive.

Nothing to Lose

But the road to success has not been easy. Emerging-market multinationals did not succeed simply by following textbook practices and solutions. Contrary to popular belief, it is unconventional thinking, adaptability, a global mind-set, and disciplined ambition—not natural resources or the advantage of lowcost labor—that have been the crucial ingredients for their success. As newcomers, emerging-market firms could only wrestle away market share from deeply entrenched incumbents through audacious solutions. Their success hinged upon novel thinking that was widely ridiculed by competitors from the rich world. In many cases, emerging multinationals became

---

From Small-Time to Prime-Time

A growing number of companies in emerging markets now enjoy the No. 1 global market share for their products. Here's a look at some of the industries they dominate.

Company	Industry	Country
Samsung Electronics	Flat-screen televisions	South Korea
Aracruz Celulose	Market pulp for paper products	Brazil
Sasol	Synthetic fuels	South Africa
TSMC	Logic semiconductors	Taiwan
Yue Yuen	Athletic and casual shoes	Hong Kong
MISC	Liquified natural gas shipping	Malaysia
Embraer	Regional jet aircraft	Brazil
Gazprom	Natural gas	Russia
Hon Hai	Electronics manufacturing by contract	Taiwan
Tenaris	Oil pipes	Argentina

---

successful only by following the opposite of tried and true textbook policies. Two of the best examples are Taiwan's HTC and Argentina's Tenaris.

By the 1990s, Taiwanese companies had carved out a leading position in notebook computers and various PC accessories. But they were way behind on smaller, more cutting-edge personal digital assistants (PDAS) and smart phones. Until 1997, that is, when a group of Taiwanese engineers got together and decided that the future was elsewhere. Instead of making knockoff organizers or cheap cell phones, the engineers at HTC designed the stylish iPAQ, the first PDA to challenge Palm's unrivaled position. The iPAQ had elements that Palm and other manufacturers had studiously avoided—a Microsoft operating system, an Intel chip, and a Sony screen, all technologies that mobile companies had hitherto considered inferior. But HTC recognized that wireless technology would soon turn PDAS into pocket PCs, combining cell phones with e-mail and Internet access. That insight helped them land a contract to become the primary manufacturer of the Treo PDA and inspired them to embark on a leapfrogging Effort by designing a whole series of versatile handhelds and smart phones that eventually became the chief Windows-based competitors of BlackBerry.

A similarly innovative approach was taken in Argentina by oil-pipe manufacturer Siderca. Realizing that government protection had led to technological mediocrity and a poor global image, Siderca CEO Paolo Rocca decided that global oil giants wanted more than top-quality pipes. They wanted suppliers that could react quickly to their needs anywhere in the world, able to deliver a pipe to a remote oil well in the middle of Nigeria on short notice. Siderca already had loose alliances with companies in Brazil, Italy, Japan, Mexico, and Romania. Rocca transformed this ad hoc group of companies into a well-oiled machine that was able to integrate researchers from far-flung subsidiaries to invent sophisticated pipes that were increasingly in demand for deep-ocean and arctic drilling operations. He also introduced high-tech systems that enabled the company to deliver its pipes "just in time" to the major oil companies, a feat that took leading, rich-world players such as Mannesmann several years to match. When Rocca was finished, the small "club" of traditional Western oil-pipe makers had lost its stranglehold on the market.

Emerging markets now control the bulk of the world's foreign exchange reserves and energy resources.

Other examples abound. Take Aracruz, in Brazil. The company used eucalyptus trees to make market pulp, even though it had generally been looked down upon before as "filler pulp" while the "real" pulp was made from slow-growing pine trees. In Mexico, CEMEX began a global acquisition spree by taking over two Spanish cement producers after it was locked out of the U.S. market by anti-dumping laws. The company's CEO, Lorenzo Zambrano, says, "For Spaniards, the idea of a Mexican company coming to Spain and changing top management was unthinkable."

Superior execution and an obsession with quality are now hallmarks of virtually all of the world-class companies based in emerging markets. That has helped feed a mind-set in which emerging multi-nationals are no longer content with being viewed as leading Chinese, Korean, Mexican, or Taiwanese companies. They aspire to be global, and this aspiration is rapidly becoming a reality.

Back to the Future?

Those who recall the Cold War may be forgiven for entertaining a sense of déjà vu. The launch of Sputnik in 1957 prompted anxieties that the West was falling behind. Two decades later, the overwhelming success of Japanese firms Toyota and Sony resulted in alarmed cries that "the Japanese are winning." Similar calls, proclaiming that the Chinese and the Indians are winning, can be heard today. But those who speak of winners and losers are regarding the global economy as a zero-sum game. There is ample reason to believe that is not the case—not based on naive internationalism, but on the well-justified belief that, in the current global economic order, both sides can come out ahead.

Many emerging multinationals are already owned by shareholders from all over the world. Foreign shareholders own 52 percent of Samsung, 71 percent of CEMEX, 57 percent of Hon Hai, and 54 percent of India-based Infosys. As a group, emerging multinationals can claim about 50 percent of their ownership as being foreign. Emerging multinationals are also becoming significant employers in the United States and Europe, as well as attractive prospective employers for business school graduates and scientists. More than 30,000 people in the United States and Europe work for CEMEX, many more than the company employs in Mexico. Its management meetings are conducted in English, because more than half of the firm's employees do not speak Spanish. Hyundai just opened a plant in Alabama, creating 2,000 American jobs; its regional suppliers employ an additional 5,500 workers. Haier makes most of its refrigerators for the U.S. market at a plant in North Carolina.

Of course, the road ahead for these emerging-market winners will not be without setbacks. Motorola's Razr cell phone has already helped the firm recover much of the ground it lost to Samsung. CEMEX's aggressive acquisition strategy may have worked, but the takeover bids of other emerging multinationals have failed, including Haier's bid to buy Maytag. Others have fallen flat, such as the Taiwanese company BenQ's failure to turn around Germany's Siemens Mobile. The very fact that the Latin and Asian financial crises are receding in memory and that new public offerings by Chinese and Russian companies are often oversubscribed could tempt these emerging competitors to rest on their laurels. An unexpected crisis or decline in China's growth could deliver a blow to the economy that many

consider the anchor of the developing world. And a growing list of innovative companies—such as Amazon, Apple, Google, Qualcomm, and Toyota, with its new hybrid car in Japan—reveals that the rich world's creativity is far from dead.

Still, the larger trends are clear. In recent years, it has become apparent that the dominance of the United States as a superpower is resulting in its deepening dependence on foreign money, foreign resources, foreign professionals, and, increasingly, foreign technology. Only 25 years ago, most sophisticated investors scoffed at the notion of investing even a tiny portion of respectable retirement funds or endowments in developing-world companies. Just as the conventional wisdom then wrongly depicted emerging markets as "Third World," today it is all too common to underestimate the leading companies from these markets. Emerging markets now control the bulk of the world's foreign exchange reserves and energy resources. They are growing faster than the United States and many European countries (and have been for decades). Most have budget and trade surpluses, and a few are even recognized as major economic powers.

Standing inside a research lab in China, South Korea, or Taiwan, it is painfully clear just how stymieing Western protectionism has been for Western companies. Such measures led to a false sense of security, a reluctance to streamline, and a lack of innovative thinking in industries ranging from steel and automobiles, to electronics and cement. As Western firms spent the 1980s and 90s protecting themselves from foreign exports, emerging multinationals built campuses of bright, young software engineers in India and incredibly efficient mining operations in Brazil and Chile. Instead of denying the new reality, the West must formulate a creative response to this global shift of power. That task is now the central economic challenge of our time.

ANTOINE VAN AGTMAEL, known for coining the term "emerging markets," is founder and chief investment officer of Emerging Markets Management L.L.C. He is the author of *The Emerging Markets Century: How a New Breed of World Class Companies is Taking over the World* (New York: Free Press, 2007).

The Toxins Trickle Downwards

A downturn that began in the rich world is hurting those who can least afford it.

"Poor countries are innocent," says Ngozi Okonjo-Iweala, the Nigerian managing director of the World Bank. They did not contribute one jot to the global credit crunch, and their banks and firms have few links to global capital markets. For a while, it seemed as if the rich world's mess might even pass them by. The oil-price fall of 2008 benefited oil-importing developing countries to the tune of 2% of their national incomes. As recently as January, the IMF thought emerging and developing countries would grow 3.3% this year, compared with a predicted fall of 2% for rich economies.

But innocence, it seems, will not protect anyone. A financial crisis that began in New York and London and spread to manufacturing in rich, then industrialising countries, has now hit the "bottom billion": the poorest people in 60-odd countries who have seen only halting gains from globalisation, but will feel its reverse, perhaps precipitously.

Many live in sub-Saharan Africa, where the IMF has just cut its forecast for growth this year to 3.3% from an original 6.7%. The figure may fall further. Dominique Strauss-Kahn, the IMF's managing director, told a conference in Tanzania that millions could be thrown back into poverty by the crisis. Piling on gloom, he saw a "threat of civil unrest, perhaps even of war" as a result.

The poor are being hit not by the financial tsunami itself but by second-order waves of trouble. So the impact has been delayed—but it may also be prolonged.

The global meltdown affects poor countries in three ways. First, capital: as investors in the West rebuild balance sheets, private capital flows dry up, hurting marginal borrowers like the poor. According to the Institute of International Finance, a think-tank in Washington, DC, net private capital flows to poor countries will slump from almost $1 trillion in 2007 to $165 billion in 2009. The main victims are big emerging markets in East Asia and eastern Europe. But African countries have been turning to private capital too. In 2007 they raised $6.5 billion in international bonds, trivial in global terms but not to Africa. In 2008, they raised nothing.

For the poor, the other kind of external capital is aid. Britain's Overseas Development Institute reckons that official aid may fall by about a fifth, or $20 billion, this year, after being more or less flat in 2005-07. The fall is partly a product of the recession in donor countries (some give a certain share of their GDP as aid) and partly a result of currency changes which make aid in pounds and euros worth less in local terms. Italy and Ireland are cutting their aid effort. Others are "front-loading" it (borrowing from future years to keep steady now), so aid could fall further after 2009.

As capital flows dry up, investment is being slashed. Arcelor-Mittal has mothballed an iron-ore project in Liberia. Malawi is losing a uranium project that the government had hoped would account for a tenth of national income. The World Bank estimates that new private activity in infrastructure was 40% lower in August-November of 2008 than a year before.

The second effect of the meltdown is the dive in commodity prices (see figure 1). Most poor states still rely on commodities for big shares of their foreign exchange and tax revenues. Cocoa generates a fifth of Côte d'Ivoire's revenues, for instance.

For such places, price volatility has been a curse. The drop in oil and commodity prices in 2008 benefited oil- and food-importers. But this followed a sharp price rise and, for many, relief has come too late. The food crisis of 2007-08 increased the number of people suffering from malnutrition by 44m. Farmers and oil exporters benefited then. No longer.

Now, falling export earnings are exacerbating poor countries' woes. In theory, the poorest should be cushioned from declining world trade. Even so, the latest data look dire. American imports from middle-income countries fell 3% in the year to November 2008. But imports from poor countries fell 6%; those from sub-Saharan Africa, 12%. The African Development Bank says African current accounts, in surplus by 3.8% of GDP in 2007, will be 6% in the red this year.

The fall in commodity prices puts further pressure on budgets, already hit by declining aid (which can substitute for taxes). African budgets have swung from a healthy surplus of 3% of GDP in 2007 to a forecast deficit of the same amount in 2009. This leaves no room for economic stimulus. On one estimate, only one-quarter of vulnerable countries have any scope to raise their budget deficits and boost spending—in contrast with the West.

The third area where the meltdown is being felt is labour. Those poor countries that do make things for export are suffering from the fall in world trade. India lost 500,000 export jobs in the last quarter of 2008, for example. Many countries also export workers who send back remittances. These were worth $300 billion in 2008, more than aid. Some countries depend

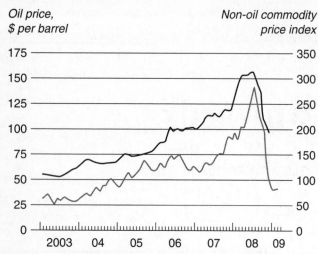

Figure 1 **Big dippers** Oil price and commodities.
Sources: DEC Prospects Group; World Bank

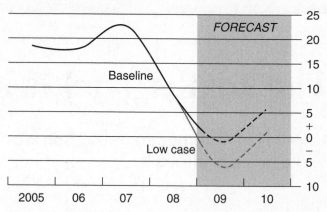

Figure 2 **Fewer happy returns** Remittance flows to developing countries.
Sources: World Bank

on them. They account for 45% of GDP in Tajikistan, 38% in Moldova and 24% in Lebanon and Guyana. Remittances had been rising fast in 2005-07; now they are falling (see figure 2). Malaysia recently revoked work visas for 55,000 Bangladeshis in order to boost job prospects for locals. Countries which send workers to Russia are doubly hit: many work in the crisis-affected oil industry and send money back in fast-depreciating roubles.

The overall picture is dire. As capital inflows and export earnings vanish, poor countries face a mountain of debt: $2.5 trillion-3 trillion of emerging-market debt falls due in 2009—as much as the American and European budget deficits, plus Europe's bank bail-out costs. The World Bank puts emerging markets' financing shortfall between $270 billion and $700 billion.

Tragically, these problems follow a decade of growth that has lifted millions out of poverty. According to Martin Ravallion of the World Bank, roughly one person in six in emerging markets had raised themselves above the $2-a-day poverty line in 2005, though they still got less than $3 a day. Many may now slip back. Mr Ravallion thinks that 65m people will fall below the $2-a-day poverty line this year, 12m more than he had expected a month ago; 53m will fall below the level of absolute poverty, which is $1.25 a day—compared with 46m expected last month.

The consequence will be dreadful. The World Bank reckons that between 200,000 and 400,000 more children will die every year between now and 2015 than would have perished without the crisis. Progress towards a richer, more equitable world has been set back years.

The Poor Man's Burden

Eighty years ago, a depression changed the way we think about poverty. It took decades for the world to recover and to remember that if people are given freedom, they will prosper. Now, in the wake of another massive meltdown, the fear that shocked us into depending on government to fix poverty is spreading once again—and threatening to undo many of the gains we've made.

WILLIAM EASTERLY

Will Richard Fuld, the disgraced CEO of the now defunct Lehman Brothers, go down in history as the father of Bolivian socialism? If we learn the wrong lessons from the global financial Crash of 2008, he very well could.

That's because the crash arrived at a crucial moment in the global fight to reduce poverty. For Bolivia—and so many other countries like it—the crash represents much more than a temporary downturn; it could mean the end of one of the greatest openings for prosperity in decades. Amid today's gloom, it is easy to forget we have just witnessed half a century of the greatest mass escape from poverty in human history. The proportion of the world's population living in extreme poverty in 2008 (those earning less than a $1 a day) was a fifth of what it was in 1960. In 2008, the income of the average citizen of the world was nearly three times higher than it was in 1960. But those tremendous gains are now in peril. For this crash hit many poor countries from Asia to Africa to Latin America that are still experimenting with political and economic freedom—but have yet to fully embrace it and experience its benefits. For decades, these countries have struggled tremendously to realize the potential of individual creativity as opposed to the smothering hand of the state. And it even seemed that the power of individual liberty might be winning.

It wasn't happening because experts had handed out some blueprint for achieving economic growth to governments and then down to their people. What happened instead was a Revolution from Below—poor people taking initiative without experts telling them what to do. We saw such surprising success stories as the family grocer in Kenya who became a supermarket giant, the Nigerian women who got rich making tie-dyed garments, the Chinese schoolteacher who became a millionaire exporting socks, and the Congolese entrepreneur who started a wildly successful cellphone business in the midst of his country's civil

war. Perhaps not coincidentally, the share of countries enjoying greater levels of economic and political freedom steadily and simultaneously shot upward.

Then came the crash.

Today, global economic calamity risks aborting that hopeful Revolution from Below. As India's Prime Minister Manmohan Singh warned late last fall, "It would be a great pity if this growing support for open policies in the developing world is weakened" because of the crash. Singh understands that the risk of a backlash against individual freedom is far more dangerous than the direct damage to poor countries caused by a global recession, falling commodity prices, or shrinking capital flows. We're already seeing this dangerous trend in Latin America. In Bolivia, President Evo Morales has openly crowed about the failure of Fuld's Lehman Brothers and other Wall Street giants: The capitalist "models in place are not a good solution for humanity . . . because [they are] based on injustice and inequality." Socialism, he said, will be the solution—in Bolivia, the state "regulates the national economy, and not the free market." The leaders of Argentina, Bolivia, Brazil, Ecuador, Nicaragua, Honduras, Paraguay, Venezuela, and even tiny Dominica to varying degrees align with these anticapitalist pretensions, all seemingly vindicated by the Crash of 2008. And it's not confined to Latin America: Vladimir Putin blamed the U.S. financial system for his own populist mismanagement of Russia's even more catastrophic crisis. A spreading fire of statism would find plenty of kindling already stacked in the Middle East, the former Soviet Union, Africa, and Asia. And there are many Western "development" experts who would eagerly fan the flames with their woolly, paternalistic thinking.

To Jeffrey Sachs, perhaps the foremost of these experts, the crash is an opportunity to gain support for the hopelessly utopian Millennium Development Goals of reducing poverty, achieving gender equality, and improving the general state of the planet through a centrally planned, government-led Big Push. "The US could find $700 billion for a bailout of its corrupt and errant banks but couldn't find a small fraction of that for the world's poor and dying," he wrote in September. "The laggards in the struggle for the [goals] are not the poor countries . . . the laggards are the rich world." To Sachs and his acolytes, poor people can't prosper without Western-country plans—and the crash only serves to turn Western governments inward. Therefore, progress on poverty is bound to suffer. To governments of poor countries that have failed to give their people the freedom needed to prosper, the neglect of Western governments is an easy excuse. So the gospel of Sachs and his disciples, though terribly condescending and wrong-headed, could attract many converts in the coming months.

A Depressing History

At least we've been here before—and we have a chance to avoid the philosophical traps we fell into after the last calamity that did so much harm to our economic system. But so far, there have been strikingly similar reactions to the crashes of 1929 and 2008. In both cases, when stocks registered some of their largest percentage declines on record, highly leveraged firms and individuals who had placed large bets using complex financial securities that few understood lost everything. The failure of gigantic financial firms spread panic. Complaints about the greedy and reckless rich escalated; a shift toward protectionism and government interventionism appeared inevitable even where free markets once reigned supreme. Authoritarian populists abroad mocked the U.S. system. The catastrophe seemed to threaten democratic capitalism everywhere.

So far, there have been strikingly similar reactions to the crashes of 1929 and 2008.

The difference is today we know that after a long and scary Great Depression, democratic capitalism did survive. And the U.S. economy returned to exactly the same long-run trend path it was on before the Depression.

We also know that, for another important part of the world, democratic capitalism did not hold up so well. In many ways, that failure stemmed from a misguided overreaction on the part of a new, influential field of economics that was highly skeptical of capitalism, was deeply traumatized by economic calamity, and considered much of the world "underdeveloped." Born in the aftermath of the Depression, "development economics" grew on a foundation of bizarre misconceptions and dangerous assumptions.

This approach to poor-country development, promulgated by the economists who took up its cause in the 1950s, had four unfortunate lasting consequences, the effects of which we're still reckoning with today in the midst of the latest big crash.

First, seeing Depression-style unemployment in every part of the world led these economists to assume that poor countries simply had too many people who were literally producing nothing. A U.N. report in 1951, produced by a group of economists, including future Nobel laureate Arthur Lewis, estimated that fully half of the farming population of Egypt produced

nothing. The insulting assumption that poor people had "zero" productivity led these economists to think that individual freedoms for the poor should not be the foundation for wealth creation, as they had been during the Industrial Revolution, when the state had played a secondary, supportive role. And because governments seemed to successfully take on a larger role during the Depression, development economists assumed that granting extensive powers to the state was the surest path to progress. A 1947 U.N. report on development gave equivalent approval to state action in democratic capitalist countries like Chile, enslaved Soviet satellites like Poland, African colonies of the British and French, and apartheid South Africa, ignoring the vast differences in individual liberty between these places.

Second, these thinkers lost faith in bottom-up economic development that was "spontaneous, as in the classical capitalist pattern" (as a later history put it), preferring instead development "consciously achieved through state planning." After all, the Five-Year Plans of the 1930s Soviet Union had avoided the Depression, at an appalling but then ignored cost in lives and human rights. This thinking was so universal that Gunnar Myrdal (who would later win a Nobel Prize in economics) claimed in 1956: "Special advisors to underdeveloped countries who have taken the time and trouble to acquaint themselves with the problem . . . all recommend central planning as the first condition of progress."

Third, these economists grew to believe that the most important factor in reducing poverty was the amount of money invested in the tools to do so. After all, if there were simply too many people, they reasoned, the binding constraint on growth must be the lack of physical equipment. As a result, this line of economic philosophy would forever stress the volume of investment over the efficiency of using those resources; would be stubbornly indifferent as to whether it was the state or individuals who made the investments; would always stress the total amount of aid required to finance investment as the crucial ingredient in escaping poverty; and would ignore the role of a dynamic financial system in allocating investment resources to those private uses where they would get the highest return.

Fourth, the collapse of international trade during the Depression made development economists skeptical about trade as an engine of growth. So in Africa, for example, they pushed for heavy taxes on export crops like cocoa to finance domestic industrialization. In Latin America, Raúl Prebisch pushed import-substituting industrialization instead of export-led growth. This strategy was supposed to help developing countries in Africa and Latin America escape a presumed "poverty trap." But the only "trap" it kept them out of was the greatest global trade boom in history following World War II, which fueled record growth in Asia, Europe, and the United States.

By the 1980s, the state-led plans had clearly failed. The wreckage of unsuccessful state enterprises, bankrupt state banks, and inefficient hothouse industries behind protectionist walls—all of which culminated in African and Latin American debt crises that destroyed growth—became too obvious to ignore. These factors, plus East Asia's rise to power in global markets, finally fueled a counterrevolution in development thinking that favored free markets and individual liberty. By the new millennium, the long record of failure of the top-down development experts triggered a well-deserved collapse of confidence in top-downplanning. It had taken nearly 50 years for the world to recognize the damage that the state-led, expert-directed, anti-freedom agenda had done to the world's poor. Today, the only remaining holdouts among the top-down experts are so utopian that they are safely insulated from reality.

A 5(0)-Year Plan

Today, just when we were getting over the long, toxic legacy of the Depression and its misguided emphasis on statist plans to fight poverty, this financial crash threatens to take us back to the bad old days. To avoid such a return, we must keep some principles in mind.

First, we must not fall into the trap of protectionism—neither unilaterally nor multilaterally, neither in rich countries nor poor. Protectionism will just make the recession spread further and deeper, as it did during the Depression.

Second, when changing financial regulations to repair the excesses of the past several years, don't strangle the financial system altogether. You can't have a Revolution from Below without it. This lesson is especially salient as Washington bails out Wall Street banks and failing industries and intervenes in the U.S. financial sector to an unprecedented degree. This bailout might turn out to be the bitter medicine that saves "finance capitalism" from a stronger form of anticapitalism, but in developing countries, open economies are still an open question.

Third, keep slashing away at the enormous red tape that is left over from previous harebrained attempts at state direction of the economy. Learn from the combined dismal track record of state-owned enterprises but also from the unexpected success stories: Private entrepreneurs are far better than the government at picking industries that can be winners in the global economy. Although fierce opposition will be inevitable, to adopt these policies would be to turn the bad hand we've been dealt into an outright losing one.

Fourth, don't look to economists to create "development strategies," and don't back up such experts with external coercion like IMF and World Bank conditions on loans. Such efforts will be either a waste of local politicians' time or positively harmful. Jeffrey Sachs alone can take partial credit for the rise of two xenophobic rulers hostile to individual liberty—Evo Morales and Vladimir Putin—after his expert advice backfired in Bolivia and Russia. If like-minded experts couldn't get it done in the 50 years after the Great Depression, they can't do it in the next 50 years. Nothing in the current crash changes these common-sense principles.

Driving the Right Way

In the coming months and years, the world's economists, politicians, and average consumers could find it incredibly easy to fall again for the wrongheaded policies of the past century. But if we are truly to continue the miraculous exodus from poverty that was under way before this traumatic crash, we ought to keep in mind stories like that of Chung Ju-yung.

The son of North Korean peasant farmers, Chung had to leave school at 14 to support his family. He held jobs as a railway construction laborer, a dockworker, a bookkeeper, and a deliveryman for a rice shop in Seoul. At 22, he took over the rice shop, but it failed. He then started A-Do Service garage, but that failed, too. In 1946, at age 31, Chung tried once again to start an auto repair service in Seoul. At last, his enterprise succeeded, largely through the contracts he won to repair U.S. Army vehicles. As his success continued, Chung diversified into construction, and his company kept growing rapidly. In 1968, he started manufacturing cars.

He named his company Hyundai. It became one of the largest companies contributing to South Korea's rise. His first effort to export cars to the United States in 1986 brought ridicule because of the cars' poor quality. The Asian crisis of 1997-98 led to a partial breakup of the Hyundai Group, but the Hyundai Motor Company continues to thrive. Chung died in 2001, but his dreams for the U.S. market came true. By 2008, Hyundai cars had received awards in the United States for the highest level of quality from *Consumer Reports*.

However terrifying the latest crash may be, let's never forget that it is the Chungs of the world that will end poverty—not the Depression-inspired regression into statism.

Want to Know More?

William Easterly's most recent book, *The White Man's Burden: Why the West's Efforts to Aid the Rest Have Done So Much Ill and So Little Good* (New York: Oxford University Press, 2006), criticizes Western approaches to global poverty. In **"The Ideology of Development"** (*Foreign Policy* July/August 2007), Easterly warns of the dangers of "Developmentalism."

Easterly's chief economic adversaries, Jeffrey Sachs and Paul Collier, take a more aid-oriented approach. Sachs's *Common Wealth: Economics for a Crowded Planet* (New York: Penguin Press, 2008) and Collier's *The Bottom Billion: Why the Poorest Countries Are Failing and What Can Be Done About It* (New York: Oxford University Press, 2008) offer policy solutions for the world's most pressing problems.

For a look at one of the earliest and most prescient (and now forgotten) economists to advocate the potential of free markets as a tool for development, read S. Herbert Frankel's *Some Conceptual Aspects of International Economic Development of Underdeveloped Territories* (Princeton: Princeton University, 1952). For a more well-known early critique of development, see P.T. Bauer's *Dissent on Development* (Cambridge: Harvard University Press, 1976).

WILLIAM EASTERLY is professor of economics at New York University.

Social Justice and Global Trade

JOSEPH STIGLITZ

The history of recent trade meetings—from Seattle to Daha to Cancun to Hong Kong—shows that something is wrong with the global trading system. Behind the discontent are some facts and theories.

The facts: Current economic arrangements disadvantage the poor. Tariff levels by the advanced industrial countries against the developing countries are four times higher than against the developed countries. The last round of trade negotiations, the Uruguay Round, actually left the poorest countries worse off. While the developing countries were forced to open up their markets and eliminate subsidies, the advanced developed countries continued to subsidize agriculture and kept trade barriers against those products which are central to the economies of the developing world.

Indeed, the tariff structures are designed to make it more difficult for developing countries to move up the value-added chain—to transition, for instance, from producing raw agricultural produce to processed foods. As tariffs have come down, America has increasingly resorted to the use of nontariff barriers as the new forms of protectionism. Trade agreements do not eliminate protectionist sentiments or the willingness of governments to attempt to protect producer and worker interests.

The theories: Trade liberalization leads to economic growth, benefiting all. This is the prevalent mantra. Political leaders champion liberalization. Those who oppose it are cast as behind the times, trying to roll back history.

Yet the fact that so many seem to have been hurt so much by globalization seems to belie their claims. Or more accurately, it has shown that the process of "liberalization"—the details of the trade agreements—make a great deal of difference.

That Mexico has done so poorly under NAFTA has not helped the case for liberalization. If there ever was a free trade agreement that should have promoted growth, that was it, for it opened up to Mexico the largest market of the world. But growth in the decade since has been slower than in the decades before 1980, and the poorest in the country, the corn farmers, have been particularly hurt by subsidized American corn.

The fact of the matter is that the economics of trade liberalization are far more complicated than political leaders have portrayed them. There are some circumstances in which trade liberalization brings enormous benefits—when there are good risk markets, when there is full employment, when an economy is mature. But none of these conditions are satisfied in developing countries. With full employment, a worker who loses his job to new imports quickly finds another; and the movement from low-productivity protected sectors to high-productivity export sectors leads to growth and increased wages. But if there is high unemployment, a worker who loses his job may remain unemployed. A move from a low-productivity, protected sector to the unemployment pool does not increase growth, but it does increase poverty. Liberalization can expose countries to enormous risks, and poor countries—and especially the poor people in those countries—are ill equipped to cope with those risks.

Perhaps most importantly, successful development means going stagnant traditional sectors with low productivity to more modern sectors with faster increases in productivity. But without protection, developing countries cannot compete in the modern sector. They are condemned to remain in the low growth part of the global economy. South Korea understood this. Thirty-five years ago, those who advocated free trade essentially told Korea to stick with rice farming. But Korea knew that even if it were successful in improving productivity in rice farming, it would be a poor country. It had to industrialize.

What are we to make of the oft-quoted studies that show that countries that have liberalized more have grown faster? Put aside the numerous statistical problems that plague almost all such "cross-country" studies. Most of the studies that claim that liberalization leads to growth do no such thing. They show that countries that have traded more have grown more. Studies that focus directly on liberalization—that is, what happens when countries take away trade barriers—present a less convincing picture that liberalization is good for growth.

But we know which countries around the world have grown the fastest: they are the countries of East Asia, and their growth was based on export-driven trade. They did not pursue policies of unfettered liberalization. Indeed, they actively intervened in markets to encourage exports, and only took away trade barriers as their exports grew. They avoided the pitfall described earlier of individuals moving from low-productivity sectors into zero productivity unemployment by maintaining their economies at close to full employment.

The point is that no country approaches liberalization as an abstract concept that it might or might not buy in to for the good of the world. Every country wants to know: For a country with its unemployment rate, with its characteristics, with its financial markets, will liberalization lead to faster growth?

If the economics are nuanced, the politics are simple. Trade negotiations provide a field day for special interests. Their agenda is also straightforward: Exporters want others' markets opened up; those threatened by competition do not. Trade negotiators pay little attention to principles (though they work hard to clothe their position under the guise of principle). They pay attention to campaign contributions and votes.

In the most recent trade talks, for example, enormous attention has been focused on developed countries' protection of their agricultural sectors—protections that exist because of the power of vested agricultural interests there. Such protectionism has become emblematic of the hypocrisy of the West in preaching free trade yet practicing something quite different. Some 25,000 rich American cotton farmers, reliant on government subsidies for cotton, divide among themselves some $3 billion to $4 billion a year, leading to higher production and lower prices. The damage that these subsidies wreak on some 10 million cotton farmers eking out a subsistence living in sub-Saharan Africa is enormous. Yet the United States seems willing to put the interests of 25,000 American cotton farmers above that of the global trading system and the well-being of millions in the developing world. It is understandable if those in the developing world respond with anger.

The anger is increased by America's almost cynical attitude in "marketing" its offers. For instance, at the Hong Kong meeting, U.S. trade officials reportedly offered to eliminate import restrictions on cotton but refused to do anything about subsidies. The cotton subsidies actually allow the U.S. to export cotton. When a country can export a particular commodity, it does little good to allow imports of that commodity. America, to great fanfare, has made an offer worth essentially zero to the developing countries and berated them for not taking it up on its "generous" offer.

At home, the Bush administration might be working harder to provide greater access to low-cost drugs. In trade negotiations, though, it takes the side of drug companies, arguing for stronger intellectual property protection, even if the protection of pharmaceutical-company patents means unnecessary deaths for hundreds of thousands of people who cannot afford the monopoly prices but could be treated if generic medicines were made available.

The international community has announced its commitment to helping the developing countries reduce poverty by half by 2015. There have been enormous efforts at increasing aid and debt relief. But developing countries do not want just a hand out; they want a hand up. They need and want enhanced opportunities for earning a living. That is what a true development round would provide.

In short, trade liberalization should be "asymmetric," but it needs to be asymmetric in a precisely opposite way to its present configuration. Today, liberalization discriminates against developing countries. It needs to discriminate in their favor. Europe has shown the way by opening up its economy to the poorest countries of the world in an initiative called Everything But Arms. Partly because of complicated regulations ("rules of origin"), however, the amount of increased trade that this policy has led to has been very disappointing thus far. Because agriculture is still highly subsidized and restricted, some call the policy "Everything But Farms." There is a need for this initiative to be broadened. Doing this would help the poor enormously and cost the rich little. In fact, the advanced industrial countries as a whole would be better off, and special interests in these countries would suffer.

There is, in fact, abroad agenda of trade liberalization (going well beyond agriculture) that would help the developing countries. But trade is too important to be left to trade ministers. If the global trade regime is to reflect common shared values, then negotiations over the terms of that trade regime cannot be left to ministers who, at least in most countries, are more beholden to corporate and special interests than almost any other ministry. In the last round, trade ministers negotiated over the terms of the intellectual property agreement. This is a subject of enormous concern to almost everyone in today's society. With excessively strong intellectual property rights, one can have monopolies raising prices and Stirling innovation. Poor countries will not have access to life-saving medicines. That was why both the Office of Science and Technology Policy and the Council of Economic Advisers opposed the TRIPS (intellectual property) provisions of the Uruguay Round. It reflected the interests of America's drug and entertainment industries, not the most important producers of knowledge, those in academia. And it certainly did not reflect the interests of users, either in the developed or less-developed countries. But the negotiations were conducted in secret, in Geneva. The U.S. trade representative (like most other trade ministers) was not an expert in intellectual property; he received his short course from the drug companies, and he quickly learned how to espouse their views. The agreement reflected this one-sided perspective.

Several reforms in the structure of trade talks are likely to lead to better outcomes. The first is that the basic way in which trade talks are approached should be changed. Now, it is a clear negotiation. Each country seeks to get the best deal for its firms. This stands in marked contrast to how legislation in all other arenas of public policy is approached. Typically, we ask what our objectives are, and how we can best achieve them. Around those themes, of course, there are negotiations. There are often large differences in views both about what should be the objectives and how best to achieve them. If we began trade talks from this position of debate and inquiry, we could arrive at a picture of what a true development round look like.

Thinking of the task of the WTO as creating a legal framework reflecting principles of fairness, social justice and efficiency—akin to how we think about domestic rules and regulations governing economic behavior—helps us think about what other reforms are needed. We simply need to think about how we attempt to improve the quality of domestic democratic processes and legislation by increasing, for instance, transparency and other governance reforms.

Transparency is essential so there can be more open debate about the merits of various proposals and a chance to put a check on the abuses special interests. Clearly, had there been more transparency and open debate, the excesses in intellectual property protection of the Uruguay Round might have been avoided.

As more and more countries have demanded a voice in trade negotiations, there is often nostalgia for the old system in which four partners (the U.S., EU, Canada and Japan) could hammer out a deal. There are complaints that the current system with so many members is simply unworkable. We have learned how to deal with this problem in other contexts, however, using the principles of representation. We must form a governing council with representatives of various "groups"—a group of the least developed countries, of the agricultural exporting countries, etc. Each representative makes sure that the concerns of his or her constituency are heard. Such a system would be far better than the current "green room" procedures wherein certain countries are put together (in the green room) to negotiate a whole or part of the deal.

Finally, trade talks need to have more focus. Issues like intellectual property should never heven have been part of the Uruguay Round. There already was an international institution dealing with matters of intellectual property. It is not only that trade ministers are ill-equipped to understand what is at issue, and they are therefore subject to undue influence from the special interests that have long held sway over trade ministries. Broadening the agenda also puts developing countries at a particular disadvantage, because they do not have the resources to engage on a broad front of issues.

The most important changes are, however, not institutional changes, but changes in mindset. There should be an effort on the part of each of the countries to think about what kind of international rules and regulations would contribute to a global trading system that would be fair and efficient, and that would promote development.

Fifteen years ago, there was a great deal of optimism about the benefits which globalization and trade would bring to all countries. It has brought enormous benefits to some countries; but not to all. Some have even been made worse off. Development is hard enough. An unfair trade regime makes it even more difficult. Reforming the WTO would not guarantee that we would get a fair and efficient global trade regime, but it would enhance the chances that trade and globalization come closer to living up to their potential for enhancing the welfare of everyone.

Mr. Stiglitz is a professor of economics at Columbia University. In 2001, he was awarded the Nobel Prize in economics.

From *Far Eastern Economic Review,* March 2006, pp. 18–21. Copyright © 2006 by Far Eastern Economic Review (Dow Jones & Company, Inc). Reprinted by permission via the Copyright Clearance Center.

Cotton: The Huge Moral Issue

World cotton prices have dropped to an historic low: the reason being the immoral continuation of EU and US trade subsidies that allow non-competitive and inefficient farming to continue. While the recent WTO meeting in Hong Kong failed to resolve the issue, the livelihoods of West Africa's 12 million cotton farmers will soon be destroyed if subsidies are not slashed. This is a huge moral issue.

KATE ESHELBY

Seydou, dressed in a ripped T-shirt that hangs off his shoulders, looked at me blankly as I questioned him about the effects of US subsidies on his only source of income, cotton farming. "I don't know about cotton in the US but I know cotton prices have fallen here in Burkina Faso," he lamented.

The farmers working in the cotton fields of Burkina Faso, often in remote locations, have little knowledge of the intricacies of world markets. What they do know is that the price they receive for their cotton harvests—essential for basic necessities such as medicines and school fees—is dropping fast.

The end of cotton farming in Burkina Faso and other cotton producing West African countries is rapidly approaching. World cotton prices have dropped to an historic low: the reason being the immoral continuation of EU and US trade subsidies that allow non-competitive and inefficient farming to continue.

Cotton subsidies in richer countries cause over production, artificially distorting world markets. And who suffers? The poor countries, whose economies are wholly dependent on the cotton trade.

In Burkina Faso, a former French colony in West Africa, cotton is the country's main cash crop. It is the primary source of foreign income, making up one-third of export earnings, and the lifeblood for the majority of farmers. Here cotton is grown on small, family-owned farms, seldom bigger than five hectares. One farmer, called Yacouba, explains: "I also grow maize and groundnuts on the farm, to feed my family, but cotton is my only source of cash."

In contrast, US cotton operations are enormous and yet, unlike Burkina Faso, cotton is a minimal proportion of its GDP. Ironically, the US subsidies are concentrated on the biggest, and richest, farms. One such farm based in Arkansas has 40,000 acres of cotton and receives subsidies equivalent to the average income of 25,000 people in Burkina Faso.

The benefits of subsidies only reach a small number of people in the US and other Western countries, whereas two million people in Burkina Faso, one of the world's poorest countries with few other natural resources, depend on cotton for survival.

The farms in Burkina Faso are very productive, it is cheaper and more economical to grow cotton there than in the US. "I have to take out loans each year to buy enough insecticides and fertilisers for my cotton," says Yacouba. "They are very expensive so we have to work hard to ensure we get a good harvest. Each year I worry whether I will earn enough to pay back the loans." Burkinabe farmers are forced to be efficient, also prevailing against climatic uncertainties and limited infrastructure—all this, with no support from subsidies.

Fields are prepared by plough and both seed planting and picking are done by hand, which explains why cotton is also vital for providing jobs—being very labour intensive. Yacouba explains: "My family works on the farm throughout the year, but during harvesting we bring in extra help." Pickers are dotted around the fields surrounding him, plucking the cotton balls from the shoulder-high plants. Some of the women have children tied to their backs and the sacks of cotton are steadily placed under the shade of a giant baobab tree. This scene is in stark contrast to the US where huge, computerised harvesters pick the cotton and aerial spraying administers the chemicals required.

The meeting (in mid-December 2005) of the World Trade Organisation (WTO) in Hong Kong was to address this farcical situation as part of the Doha "development" talks. But nothing much came out of it. Burkina Faso is still resting its hopes on cotton subsidies being eliminated, or at least reduced, in order to save its fundamental crop from demise. The Doha negotiations, launched in 2001, are intended to show that trade could benefit the world's poor. But subsidies are a global injustice, and create major imbalances in world trade—it is argued they should only be available for products that are not exported, and targeted towards family and small-scale farmers.

The US gives approximately $3.4bn a year in subsidies to its 25,000 cotton farmers; this is more than the entire GDP of Burkina Faso. Subsidies dramatically increased in the US after the 2002 Farm Act and as a result US cotton production has recently reached historic highs. It is now the world's second largest cotton producer, after China, and the biggest exporter—an easy achievement because US cotton prices no longer bear any relation to production costs.

Current world cotton prices are in decline due to global over-production, fuelled by agricultural subsidies. EU and US taxpayers and consumers pay farmers billions of dollars to over-produce for a stagnant market. These surpluses are then dumped overseas, often in developing countries, destroying their markets and driving down world prices.

The livelihoods of West Africa's 12 million cotton farmers will soon be destroyed if subsidies are not slashed. This is a huge moral issue. It is simple—Burkina Faso cannot compete against heavily subsidised exports.

In March 2004, a WTO panel ruled that the majority of US cotton subsidies were illegal. The WTO agreements state that "domestic support should have no, or at most minimal trade-distorting effects on production." The US tried to appeal against this decision but it was overruled.

If Africa took just 1% more in world trade, it would earn $70bn more annually—three times what it now receives in aid. In 2003, Burkina Faso received $10m in US aid, but lost $13.7m in cotton export earnings, as a result of US subsidies. No country ever grew rich on charity, it is trade that holds the key to generating wealth. Fair trade would give the Burkinabe cotton farmers a decent opportunity to make a living by selling their produce, at a decent price, to the richer world; enabling them to work their way out of poverty.

The US was legally required to eliminate all trade-distorting subsidies by 21 September 2005, according to a WTO ruling. President George Bush keeps saying he will cut subsidies, but actions are louder than words. The delay is partly due to a long-standing arm wrestle between the US and the EU, neither of whom will budge. The British prime minister, Tony Blair, does seem to want to abolish EU subsidies, but the French argue that subsidies are not even negotiable. Despite four years of haggling, negotiators are still at loggerheads. Numerous reports have been compiled, many meetings held and yet scant progress has been made—and things are only getting worse for the Burkinabe cotton farmers.

"Both the US and EU brag about their boldness, but the actual reform they propose is minuscule, tiny fractions of their massive farm support. The negotiations have recently moved into the finger-pointing phase in which rich countries criticise the inadequacy of each other's proposals. Meanwhile, poor countries await something real," says Issaka Ouandago, from Oxfam's office in Burkina Faso.

Oxfam has been supporting the struggle of African cotton farmers in their campaign known as the "Big Noise", and are hoping to gather a petition of one million signatures against cotton subsidies. "We can only hope the US reform their subsidy programmes and stop dumping cheap cotton onto the world market," Ouandago continues. "Despite their WTO commitments to reduce trade-distorting subsidies, the EU and US have used loopholes and creative accounting to continue. Such practices are undermining the fragile national economics of countries that depend on cotton."

The rich countries have to come forward with more, otherwise the Doha Round will achieve nothing, as the meeting in Hong Kong proved—although developing countries have less political power, they are still capable of blocking the negotiations if they don't get what they want. In the last WTO meeting, held in Geneva, July 2004, negotiations on US cotton subsidies were supposed to be kept separate from broader agricultural negotiations—this did not happen. It was a blow for Burkina Faso and other West Africa countries who produce mainly cotton and are less interested in other commodities. A subcommittee on cotton was set up to "review" the situation, but the EU and US have not taken this committee seriously.

With the emergence of the G20 alliance, some developing countries, such as India and Brazil, are now powerful enough to resist pressures, but African countries have previously never been centre stage. West African cotton producers are, however, becoming far stronger as a group. "We have become more united to make our voice heard. Our aim is to gather all African cotton producers together," explains Yao, a member of the National Union of Cotton Producers in Burkina Faso.

The only reason Burkinabe cotton farmers are still surviving is that producer prices have been maintained at a minimum level-175 CFA per kg of cotton seed is the minimum price the farmers need to break even, prices never go below this, despite being above current world prices.

In recent years, the Burkinabe cotton companies used their profits from previous harvests to support the farmers; these savings are now depleted. The full effects of world prices have, therefore, not yet been felt by the farmers, the worst is to come—once the prices are forced to drop below this minimum, the farmers can no longer survive.

Leaving the house of Seydou, I wonder about his fate. A pile of bright-white cotton sits drying in the glaring sun, in front of his mud house. Inside the walls are bare, except for a single cross; a bundle of clothes hang from a rope and a pile of maize is stacked in the corner. "I cannot afford to buy things because cotton prices keep fluctuating," he says. "I know cotton grows well here but prices are down so I cannot send my youngest son to school. This makes me sad. I know his only chance of a good future is school."

In Burkina Faso, cotton is the country's biggest interest and essential to its economy, so it prays that cotton is addressed more seriously and given the attention it deserves. As the sun sets, the workers leave the fields, holding sacks of cotton above their heads. A donkey cart trundles by, carrying a mound of cotton—kicking up a trail of red earth. Their livelihoods depend on the decisions made at the WTO.

From *New African*, January 2006, pp. 26–28. Copyright © 2006 by IC Publications Ltd. Reprinted by permission.

Across Globe, Empty Bellies Bring Rising Anger

Marc Lacey

Hunger bashed in the front gate of Haiti's presidential palace. Hunger poured onto the streets, burning tires and taking on soldiers and the police. Hunger sent the country's prime minister packing.

Haiti's hunger, that burn in the belly that so many here feel, has become fiercer than ever in recent days as global food prices spiral out of reach, spiking as much as 45 percent since the end of 2006 and turning Haitian staples like beans, corn and rice into closely guarded treasures.

Saint Louis Meriska's children ate two spoonfuls of rice apiece as their only meal recently and then went without any food the following day. His eyes downcast, his own stomach empty, the unemployed father said forlornly, "They look at me and say, 'Papa, I'm hungry,' and I have to look away. It's humiliating and it makes you angry."

That anger is palpable across the globe. The food crisis is not only being felt among the poor but is also eroding the gains of the working and middle classes, sowing volatile levels of discontent and putting new pressures on fragile governments.

In Cairo, the military is being put to work baking bread as rising food prices threaten to become the spark that ignites wider anger at a repressive government. In Burkina Faso and other parts of sub-Saharan Africa, food riots are breaking out as never before. In reasonably prosperous Malaysia, the ruling coalition was nearly ousted by voters who cited food and fuel price increases as their main concerns.

"It's the worst crisis of its kind in more than 30 years," said Jeffrey D. Sachs, the economist and special adviser to the United Nations secretary general, Ban Ki-moon. "It's a big deal and it's obviously threatening a lot of governments. There are a number of governments on the ropes, and I think there's more political fallout to come."

Indeed, as it roils developing nations, the spike in commodity prices—the biggest since the Nixon administration—has pitted the globe's poorer south against the relatively wealthy north, adding to demands for reform of rich nations' farm and environmental policies. But experts say there are few quick fixes to a crisis tied to so many factors, from strong demand for food from emerging economies like China's to rising oil prices to the diversion of food resources to make biofuels.

There are no scripts on how to handle the crisis, either. In Asia, governments are putting in place measures to limit hoarding of rice after some shoppers panicked at price increases and bought up everything they could.

Even in Thailand, which produces 10 million more tons of rice than it consumes and is the world's largest rice exporter, supermarkets have placed signs limiting the amount of rice shoppers are allowed to purchase.

But there is also plenty of nervousness and confusion about how best to proceed and just how bad the impact may ultimately be, particularly as already strapped governments struggle to keep up their food subsidies.

'Scandalous Storm'

"This is a perfect storm," President Elías Antonio Saca of El Salvador said Wednesday at the World Economic Forum on Latin America in Cancún, Mexico. "How long can we withstand the situation? We have to feed our people, and commodities are becoming scarce. This scandalous storm might become a hurricane that could upset not only our economies but also the stability of our countries."

In Asia, if Prime Minister Abdullah Ahmad Badawi of Malaysia steps down, which is looking increasingly likely amid postelection turmoil within his party, he may be that region's first high-profile political casualty of fuel and food price inflation.

In Indonesia, fearing protests, the government recently revised its 2008 budget, increasing the amount it will spend on food subsidies by about $280 million.

"The biggest concern is food riots," said H.S. Dillon, a former adviser to Indonesia's Ministry of Agriculture. Referring to small but widespread protests touched off by a rise in soybean prices in January, he said, "It has happened in the past and can happen again."

Last month in Senegal, one of Africa's oldest and most stable democracies, police in riot gear beat and used tear gas against people protesting high food prices and later raided a television station that broadcast images of the event. Many Senegalese have expressed anger at President Abdoulaye Wade for spending lavishly on roads and five-star hotels for an Islamic summit meeting last month while many people are unable to afford rice or fish.

"Why are these riots happening?" asked Arif Husain, senior food security analyst at the World Food Program, which has issued urgent appeals for donations. "The human instinct is to survive, and people are going to do no matter what to survive. And if you're hungry you get angry quicker."

Leaders who ignore the rage do so at their own risk. President René Préval of Haiti appeared to taunt the populace as the chorus of complaints about la vie chère—the expensive life—grew. He said if Haitians could afford cellphones, which many do carry, they should be able to feed their families. "If there is a protest against the rising prices," he said, "come get me at the palace and I will demonstrate with you."

When they came, filled with rage and by the thousands, he huddled inside and his presidential guards, with United Nations peacekeeping troops, rebuffed them. Within days, opposition lawmakers had voted out Mr. Préval's prime minister, Jacques-Édouard Alexis, forcing him to reconstitute his government. Fragile in even the best of times, Haiti's population and politics are now both simmering.

"Why were we surprised?" asked Patrick Élie, a Haitian political activist who followed the food riots in Africa earlier in the year and feared they might come to Haiti. "When something is coming your way all the way from Burkina Faso you should see it coming. What we had was like a can of gasoline that the government left for someone to light a match to it."

Dwindling Menus

The rising prices are altering menus, and not for the better. In India, people are scrimping on milk for their children. Daily bowls of dal are getting thinner, as a bag of lentils is stretched across a few more meals.

Maninder Chand, an auto-rickshaw driver in New Delhi, said his family had given up eating meat altogether for the last several weeks.

Another rickshaw driver, Ravinder Kumar Gupta, said his wife had stopped seasoning their daily lentils, their chief source of protein, with the usual onion and spices because the price of cooking oil was now out of reach. These days, they eat bowls of watery, tasteless dal, seasoned only with salt.

Down Cairo's Hafziyah Street, peddlers selling food from behind wood carts bark out their prices. But few customers can afford their fish or chicken, which bake in the hot sun. Food prices have doubled in two months.

Ahmed Abul Gheit, 25, sat on a cheap, stained wooden chair by his own pile of rotting tomatoes. "We can't even find food," he said, looking over at his friend Sobhy Abdullah, 50. Then raising his hands toward the sky, as if in prayer, he said, "May God take the guy I have in mind."

Mr. Abdullah nodded, knowing full well that the "guy" was President Hosni Mubarak.

The government's ability to address the crisis is limited, however. It already spends more on subsidies, including gasoline and bread, than on education and health combined.

"If all the people rise, then the government will resolve this," said Raisa Fikry, 50, whose husband receives a pension equal to about $83 a month, as she shopped for vegetables. "But everyone has to rise together. People get scared. But we will all have to rise together."

It is the kind of talk that has prompted the government to treat its economic woes as a security threat, dispatching riot forces with a strict warning that anyone who takes to the streets will be dealt with harshly.

Niger does not need to be reminded that hungry citizens overthrow governments. The country's first postcolonial president, Hamani Diori, was toppled amid allegations of rampant corruption in 1974 as millions starved during a drought.

More recently, in 2005, it was mass protests in Niamey, the Nigerien capital, that made the government sit up and take notice of that year's food crisis, which was caused by a complex mix of poor rains, locust infestation and market manipulation by traders.

"As a result of that experience the government created a cabinet-level ministry to deal with the high cost of living," said Moustapha Kadi, an activist who helped organize marches in 2005. "So when prices went up this year the government acted quickly to remove tariffs on rice, which everyone eats. That quick action has kept people from taking to the streets."

The Poor Eat Mud

In Haiti, where three-quarters of the population earns less than $2 a day and one in five children is chronically malnourished, the one business booming amid all the gloom is the selling of patties made of mud, oil and sugar, typically consumed only by the most destitute.

"It's salty and it has butter and you don't know you're eating dirt," said Olwich Louis Jeune, 24, who has taken to eating them more often in recent months. "It makes your stomach quiet down."

But the grumbling in Haiti these days is no longer confined to the stomach. It is now spray-painted on walls of the capital and shouted by demonstrators.

In recent days, Mr. Préval has patched together a response, using international aid money and price reductions by importers to cut the price of a sack of rice by about 15 percent. He has also trimmed the salaries of some top officials. But those are considered temporary measures.

Real solutions will take years. Haiti, its agriculture industry in shambles, needs to better feed itself. Outside investment is the key, although that requires stability, not the sort of widespread looting and violence that the Haitian food riots have fostered.

Meanwhile, most of the poorest of the poor suffer silently, too weak for activism or too busy raising the next generation of hungry. In the sprawling slum of Haiti's Cité Soleil, Placide Simone, 29, offered one of her five offspring to a stranger. "Take one," she said, cradling a listless baby and motioning toward four rail-thin toddlers, none of whom had eaten that day. "You pick. Just feed them."

Reporting was contributed by Lydia Polgreen from Niamey, Niger, Michael Slackman from Cairo, Somini Sengupta from New Delhi, Thomas Fuller from Bangkok and Peter Gelling from Jakarta, Indonesia.

The Politics of Hunger

How Illusion and Greed Fan the Food Crisis.

Paul Collier

After many years of stability, world food prices have jumped 83 percent since 2005—prompting warnings of a food crisis throughout much of the world earlier this year. In the United States and Europe, the increase in food prices is already yesterday's news; consumers in the developed world now have more pressing concerns, such as the rising price of energy and the falling price of houses. But in the developing world, a food shock of this magnitude is a major political event. To the typical household in poor countries, food is the equivalent of energy in the United States, and people expect their government to do something when prices rise. Already, there have been food riots in some 30 countries; in Haiti, they brought down the prime minister. And for some consumers in the world's poorest countries, the true anguish of high food prices is only just beginning. If global food prices remain high, the consequences will be grim both ethically and politically.

Politicians and policymakers do, in fact, have it in their power to bring food prices down. But so far, their responses have been less than encouraging: beggar-thy-neighbor restrictions, pressure for yet larger farm subsidies, and a retreat into romanticism. In the first case, neighbors have been beggared by the imposition of export restrictions by the governments of food-exporting countries. This has had the immaculately dysfunctional consequence of further elevating world prices while reducing the incentives for the key producers to invest in the agricultural sector. In the second case, the subsidy hunters have, unsurprisingly, turned the crisis into an opportunity; for example, Michel Barnier, the French agricultural minister, took it as a chance to urge the European Commission to reverse its incipient subsidy-slashing reforms of the Common Agricultural Policy. And finally, the romantics have portrayed the food crisis as demonstrating the failure of scientific commercial agriculture, which they have long found distasteful. In its place they advocate the return to organic small-scale farming—counting on abandoned technologies to feed a prospective world population of nine billion.

The real challenge is not the technical difficulty of returning the world to cheap food but the political difficulty of confronting the lobbying interests and illusions on which current policies rest. Feeding the world will involve three politically challenging steps. First, contrary to the romantics, the world needs more commercial agriculture, not less. The Brazilian model of high-productivity large farms could readily be extended to areas where land is underused. Second, and again contrary to the romantics, the world needs more science: the European ban and the consequential African ban on genetically modified (GM) crops are slowing the pace of agricultural productivity growth in the face of accelerating growth in demand. Ending such restrictions could be part of a deal, a mutual de-escalation of folly, that would achieve the third step: in return for Europe's lifting its self-damaging ban on GM products, the United States should lift its self-damaging subsidies supporting domestic biofuel.

Supply-Side Solutions

Typically, in trying to find a solution to a problem, people look to its causes—or, yet more fatuously, to its "root" cause. But there need be no logical connection between the cause of a problem and appropriate or even just feasible solutions to it. Such is the case with the food crisis. The root cause of high food prices is the spectacular economic growth of Asia. Asia accounts for half the world's population, and because its people are still poor, they devote much of their budgets to food. As Asian incomes rise, the world demand for food increases. And not only are Asians eating more, but they are also eating better: carbohydrates are being replaced by protein. And because it takes six kilograms of grain to produce one kilogram of beef, the switch to a protein-heavy diet further drives up demand for grain.

The two key parameters in shaping demand are income elasticity and price elasticity. The income elasticity of demand for food is generally around 0.5, meaning that if income rises by, say, 20 percent, the demand for food rises by 10 percent. (The price elasticity of demand for food is only around 0.1: that is, people simply have to eat, and they do not eat much less in response to higher prices.) Thus, if the supply of food were fixed, in order to choke off an increase in demand of 10 percent after a 20 percent rise in income, the price of food would need to double. In other words, modest increases in global income will drive prices up alarmingly unless matched by increases in supply.

In recent years, the increase in demand resulting from gradually increasing incomes in Asia has instead been matched with several supply shocks, such as the prolonged drought in Australia. These shocks will only become more common with the climatic volatility that accompanies climate change. Accordingly, against a backdrop of relentlessly rising demand, supply will fluctuate more sharply as well.

Because food looms so large in the budgets of the poor, high world food prices have a severely regressive effect in their toll. Still, by no means are all of the world's poor adversely affected by expensive food. Most poor people who are farmers are largely self-sufficient. They may buy and sell food, but the rural markets in which they trade are often not well integrated into global markets and so are largely detached from the surge in prices. Where poor farmers are integrated into global markets, they are likely to benefit. But even the good news for farmers needs to be qualified. Although most poor farmers will gain most of the time, they will lose precisely when they are hardest hit: when their crops fail. The World Food Program is designed to act as the supplier of last resort to such localities. Yet its budget, set in dollars rather than bushels, buys much less when food prices surge. Paradoxically, then, the world's insurance program against localized famine is itself acutely vulnerable to global food shortages. Thus, high global food prices are good news for farmers but only in good times.

The unambiguous losers when it comes to high food prices are the urban poor. Most of the developing world's large cities are ports, and, barring government controls, the price of their food is set on the global market. Crowded in slums, the urban poor cannot grow their own food; they have no choice but to buy it. Being poor, they would inevitably be squeezed by an increase in prices, but by a cruel implication of the laws of necessity, poor people spend a far larger proportion of their budgets on food, typically around a half, in contrast to only around a tenth for high-income groups. (Hungry slum dwellers are unlikely to accept their fate quietly. For centuries, sudden hunger in slums has provoked the same response: riots. This is the classic political base for populist politics, such as Peronism in Argentina, and the food crisis may provoke its ugly resurgence.)

At the end of the food chain comes the real crunch: among the urban poor, those most likely to go hungry are children. If young children remain malnourished for more than two years, the consequence is stunted growth—and stunted growth is not merely a physical condition. Stunted people are not just shorter than they would have been; their mental potential is impaired as well. Stunted growth is irreversible. It lasts a lifetime, and indeed, some studies find that it is passed down through the generations. And so although high food prices are yesterday's news in most of the developed world, if they remain high for the next few years, their consequences will be tomorrow's nightmare for the developing world.

In short, global food prices must be brought down, and they must be brought down fast, because their adverse consequences are so persistent. The question is how. There is nothing to be done about the root cause of the crisis—the increasing demand for food. The solution must come from dramatically increasing world food supply. That supply has been growing for decades, more than keeping up with population growth, but it now must be accelerated, with production increasing much more rapidly than it has in recent decades. This must happen in the short term, to bring prices down from today's levels, and in the medium and long terms, since any immediate increase in supply will soon be overtaken by increased demand.

Fortunately, policymakers have the power to do all of this: by changing regulation, they can quickly generate an increase in supply; by encouraging organizational changes, they can raise the growth of production in the medium term; and by encouraging innovations in technology, they can sustain this higher growth indefinitely. But currently, each of these steps is blocked by a giant of romantic populism: all three must be confronted and slain.

The First Giant of Romantic Populism

The first giant that must be slain is the middle- and upper-class love affair with peasant agriculture. With the near-total urbanization of these classes in both the United States and Europe, rural simplicity has acquired a strange allure. Peasant life is prized as organic in both its literal and its metaphoric sense. (Prince Charles is one of its leading apostles.) In its literal sense, organic agricultural production is now a premium product, a luxury brand. (Indeed, Prince Charles has his own such brand, Duchy Originals.) In its metaphoric sense, it represents the antithesis of the large, hierarchical, pressured organizations in which the middle classes now work. (Prince Charles has built a model peasant village, in traditional architectural style.) Peasants, like pandas, are to be preserved.

Peasants, like pandas, show little inclination to reproduce themselves.

But distressingly, peasants, like pandas, show little inclination to reproduce themselves. Given the chance, peasants seek local wage jobs, and their offspring head to the cities. This is because at low-income levels, rural bliss is precarious, isolated, and tedious. The peasant life forces millions of ordinary people into the role of entrepreneur, a role for which most are ill suited. In successful economies, entrepreneurship is a minority pursuit; most people opt for wage employment so that others can have the worry and grind of running a business. And reluctant peasants are right: their mode of production is ill suited to modern agricultural production, in which scale is helpful. In modern agriculture, technology is fast-evolving, investment is lumpy, the private provision of transportation infrastructure is necessary to counter the lack of its public provision, consumer food fashions are fast-changing and best met by integrated marketing chains, and regulatory standards are rising toward the holy grail of the traceability of produce back to its source. Far from being the answer to global poverty, organic self-sufficiency is a luxury lifestyle. It is appropriate for burnt-out investment bankers, not for hungry families.

Large organizations are better suited to cope with investment, marketing chains, and regulation. Yet for years, global development agencies have been leery of commercial agriculture, basing their agricultural strategies instead on raising peasant production. This neglect is all the more striking given the standard account of how economic development started in Europe: the English enclosure movement, which was enabled by legislative changes, is commonly supposed to have launched development by permitting large farms that could achieve higher productivity. Although current research qualifies the conventional account, reducing the estimates of productivity gains to the range of 10–20 percent, to ignore commercial agriculture as a force for rural development and enhanced food supply is surely ideological.

Innovation, especially, is hard to generate through peasant farming. Innovators create benefits for the local economy, and to the extent that these benefits are not fully captured by the innovators, innovation will be too slow. Large organizations can internalize the effects that in peasant agriculture are localized externalities—that is, benefits of actions that are not reflected in costs or profits—and so not adequately taken into account in decision-making. In the European agricultural revolution, innovations occurred on small farms as well as large, and today many peasant farmers, especially those who are better off and better educated, are keen to innovate. But agricultural innovation is highly sensitive to local conditions, especially in Africa, where the soils are complex and variable. One solution is to have an extensive network of publicly funded research stations with advisers who reach out to small farmers. But in Africa, this model has largely broken down, an instance of more widespread malfunctioning of the public sector. In eighteenth-century Great Britain, the innovations in small-holder agriculture were often led by networks among the gentry, who corresponded with one another on the consequences of agricultural experimentation. But such processes are far from automatic (they did not occur, for example, in continental Europe). Commercial agriculture is the best way of making innovation quicker and easier.

Over time, African peasant agriculture has fallen further and further behind the advancing commercial productivity frontier, and based on present trends, the region's food imports are projected to double over the next quarter century. Indeed, even with prices as high as they currently are, the United Nations Food and Agriculture Organization is worried that African peasants are likely to reduce production because they cannot afford the increased cost of fertilizer inputs. There are partial solutions to such problems through subsidies and credit schemes, but it should be noted that large-scale commercial agriculture simply does not face this particular problem: if output prices rise by more than input prices, production will be expanded.

A model of successful commercial agriculture is, indeed, staring the world in the face. In Brazil, large, technologically sophisticated agricultural companies have demonstrated how successfully food can be mass-produced. To give one remarkable example, the time between harvesting one crop and planting the next—the downtime for land—has been reduced to an astounding 30 minutes. Some have criticized the Brazilian model for displacing peoples and destroying rain forest, which has indeed happened in places where commercialism has gone unregulated. But in much of the poor world, the land is not primal forest; it is just badly farmed. Another benefit of the Brazilian model is that it can bring innovation to small farmers as well. In the "out-growing," or "contract farming," model, small farmers supply a central business. Depending on the details of crop production, sometimes this can be more efficient than wage employment.

There are many areas of the world that have good land that could be used far more productively if properly managed by large companies. Indeed, large companies, some of them Brazilian, are queuing up to manage those lands. Yet over the past 40 years, African governments have worked to scale back large commercial agriculture. At the heart of the matter is a reluctance to let land rights be marketable, and the source of this reluctance is probably the lack of economic dynamism in Africa's cities. As a result, land is still the all-important asset (there has been little investment in others). In more successful economies, land has become a minor asset, and thus the rights of ownership, although initially assigned based on political considerations, are simply extensions of the rights over other assets; as a result, they can be acquired commercially. A further consequence of a lack of urban dynamism is that jobs are scarce, and so the prospect of mass landlessness evokes political fears: the poor are safer on the land, where they are less able to cause trouble.

Commercial agriculture is not perfect. Global agribusiness is probably overly concentrated, and a sudden switch to an unregulated land market would probably have ugly consequences. But allowing commercial organizations to replace peasant agriculture gradually would raise global food supply in the medium term.

The War on Science

The second giant of romantic populism is the European fear of scientific agriculture. This has been manipulated by the agricultural lobby in Europe into yet another form of protectionism: the ban on GM crops. GM crops were introduced globally in 1996 and already are grown on around ten percent of the world's crop area, some 300 million acres. But due to the ban, virtually none of this is in Europe or Africa.

Robert Paarlberg, of Wellesley College, brilliantly anatomizes the politics of the ban in his new book, *Starved for Science*. After their creation, GM foods, already so disastrously named, were described as "Frankenfoods"—sounding like a scientific experiment on consumers. Just as problematic was the fact that genetic modification had grown out of research conducted by American corporations and so provoked predictable and deep-seated hostility from the European left. Although Monsanto, the main innovator in GM-seed technology, has undertaken never to market a seed that is incapable of reproducing itself, skeptics propagated a widespread belief that farmers will be trapped into annual purchases of "terminator" seeds from a monopoly supplier. Thus were laid the political foundations for a winning coalition: onto the base of national agricultural protectionism was added the anti-Americanism of the left and the paranoia of health-conscious consumers who, in the wake of the mad cow disease outbreak in the United Kingdom in the 1990s, no longer trusted their governments' assurances. In the 12 years since the ban was introduced, in 1996, the scientific case for lifting it has become progressively more robust, but the political coalition against GM foods has only expanded.

The GM-crop ban has had three adverse effects. Most obviously, it has retarded productivity growth in European agriculture. Prior to 1996, grain yields in Europe tracked those in the United States. Since 1996, they have fallen behind by 1–2 percent a year. European grain production could be increased by around 15 percent were the ban lifted. Europe is a major cereal producer, so this is a large loss. More subtly, because Europe is out of the market for GM-crop technology, the pace of research has slowed. GM-crop research takes a very long time to come to fruition, and its core benefit, the permanent reduction in food prices, cannot fully be captured through patents. Hence, there is a strong case for supplementing private research with public money. European governments should be funding this research, but instead research is entirely reliant on the private sector. And since private money for research depends on the prospect of sales, the European ban has also reduced private research.

However, the worst consequence of the European GM-crop ban is that it has terrified African governments into themselves banning GM crops, the only exception being South Africa. They fear that if they chose to grow GM crops, they would be permanently shut out of European markets. Now, because most of Africa has banned GM crops, there has been no market for discoveries pertinent to the crops that Africa grows, and so little research—which in turn has led to the critique that GM crops are irrelevant for Africa.

Africa cannot afford this self-denial; it needs all the help it can possibly get from genetic modification. For the past four decades, African agricultural productivity per acre has stagnated; raising production has depended on expanding the area under cultivation. But with Africa's population still growing rapidly, this option is running out, especially in light of global warming. Climate forecasts suggest that in the coming years, most of Africa will get hotter, the semiarid parts will get drier, and rainfall variability on the continent will increase, leading to more droughts. It seems likely that in southern Africa, the staple food, maize, will at some point become nonviable. Whereas for other regions the challenge of climate change is primarily about mitigating carbon emissions, in Africa it is primarily about agricultural adaptation.

It has become commonplace to say that Africa needs a green revolution. Unfortunately, the reality is that the green revolution in the twentieth century was based on chemical fertilizers, and even when fertilizer was cheap, Africa did not adopt it. With the rise in fertilizer costs, as a byproduct of high-energy prices, any African green revolution will perforce not be chemical. To counter the effects of Africa's rising population and deteriorating climate, African agriculture needs a biological revolution. This is what GM crops offer, if only sufficient money is put into research. There has as yet been little work on the crops of key importance to the region, such as cassava and yams. GM-crop research is still in its infancy, still on the first generation: single-gene transfer. A gene that gives one crop an advantage is identified, isolated, and added to another crop. But even this stage offers the credible prospect of vital gains. In a new scientific review, Jennifer Thomson, of the Department of Molecular and Cell Biology at the University of Cape Town, considers the potential of GM technology for Africa. Maize, she reports, can be made more drought-resistant, buying Africa time in the struggle against climatic deterioration. Grain can be made radically more resistant to fungi, reducing the need for chemicals and cutting losses due to storage. For example, stem borer beetles cause storage losses in the range of 15–40 percent of the African maize crop; a new GM variety is resistant.

It is important to recognize that genetic modification, like commercialization, is not a magic fix for African agriculture: there is no such fix. But without it, the task of keeping Africa's food production abreast of its population growth looks daunting. Although Africa's coastal cities can be fed from global supplies, the vast African interior cannot be fed in this way other than in emergencies. Lifting the ban on GM crops, both in Africa and in Europe, is the policy that could hold down global food prices in the long term.

The final giant of romantic populism is the American fantasy that the United States can escape dependence on Arab oil by growing its own fuel—making ethanol or other biofuels, largely from corn. There is a good case for growing fuel. But there is not a good case for generating it from American grain: the conversion of grain into ethanol uses almost as much energy as it produces. This has not stopped the American agricultural lobby from gouging out grotesquely inefficient subsidies from the government; as a result, around a third of American grain has rapidly been diverted into energy. This switch demonstrates both the superb responsiveness of the market to price signals and the shameful power of subsidy-hunting lobbying groups. If the United States wants to run off of agrofuel instead of oil, then Brazilian sugar cane is the answer; it is a far more efficient source of energy than American grain. The killer evidence of political capture is the response of the U.S. government to this potential lifeline: it has actually restricted imports of Brazilian ethanol to protect American production. The sane goal of reducing dependence on Arab oil has been sacrificed to the self-serving goal of pumping yet more tax dollars into American agriculture.

Inevitably, the huge loss of grain for food caused by its diversion into ethanol has had an impact on world grain prices. Just how large an impact is controversial. An initial claim by the Bush administration was that it had raised prices by only three percent, but a study by the World Bank suggests that the effect has been much larger. If the subsidy were lifted, there would probably be a swift impact on prices: not only would the supply of grain for food increase, but the change would shift speculative expectations. This is the policy that could bring prices down in the short term.

Striking a Deal

The three policies—expanding large commercial farms, ending the GM-crop ban, and doing away with the U.S. subsidies on ethanol—fit together both economically and politically. Lifting the ethanol subsidies would probably puncture the present ballooning of prices. The expansion of commercial farms could, over the next decade, raise world output by a further few percentage points. Both measures would buy the time needed for GM crops to deliver on their potential (the time between starting research and the mass application of its results is around 15 years). Moreover, the expansion of commercial farming in Africa would encourage global GM-crop research on Africa-suited crops, and innovations would find a ready market not so sensitive to political interference. It would also facilitate the localized adaptation of new varieties. It is not by chance that the only African country in which GM crops have not been banned is South Africa, where the organization of agriculture is predominantly commercial.

Politically, the three policies are also complementary. Homegrown energy, keeping out "Frankenfoods," and preserving the peasant way of life are all classic populist programs: they sound instantly appealing but actually do harm. They must be countered by messages of equal potency.

One such message concerns the scope for international reciprocity. Although Americans are attracted to homegrown fuel, they are infuriated by the European ban on GM crops. They see the ban for what it is: a standard piece of anti-American protectionism. Europeans, for their part, cling to the illusory comfort of the ban on high-tech crops, but they are infuriated by the American subsidies on ethanol. They see the subsidies for what they are: a greedy deflection from the core task of reducing U.S. energy profligacy. Over the past half century, the United States and Europe have learned how to cooperate. The General Agreement on Tariffs and Trade was fundamentally a deal between the United States and Europe that virtually eliminated tariffs on manufactured goods. NATO is a partnership in security. The Organization for Economic Cooperation and Development is a partnership in economic governance. Compared to the difficulties of reaching agreement in these areas, the difficulties of reaching a deal on the mutual de-escalation of recent environmental follies is scarcely daunting: the United States would agree to scrap its ethanol subsidies in return for Europe's lifting the ban on GM crops. Each side can find this deal infuriating and yet attractive. It should be politically feasible to present this to voters as better than the status quo.

The romantic hostility to scientific and commercial agriculture must be countered.

How might the romantic hostility toward commercial and scientific agriculture be countered politically? The answer is to educate the vast community of concern for the poorest countries on the bitter realities of the food crisis. In both the United States and Europe, millions of decent citizens are appalled by global hunger. Each time a famine makes it to television screens, the popular response is overwhelming, and there is a large overlap between the constituency that responds to such crises and the constituency attracted by the idea of preserving organic peasant lifestyles. The cohabitation of these concerns needs to be challenged. Many people will need to agonize over their priorities. Some will decide that the vision articulated by Prince Charles is the more important one: a historical lifestyle must be preserved regardless of the consequences. But however attractive that vision, these people must come face-to-face with the prospect of mass malnutrition and stunted children and realize that the vital matter for public policy is to increase food supplies. Commercial agriculture may be irredeemably unromantic, but if it fills the stomachs of the poor, then it should be encouraged.

American environmentalists will also need to do some painful rethinking. The people most attracted to achieving energy self-sufficiency through the production of ethanol are potentially the constituency that could save the United States from its ruinous energy policies. The United States indeed needs to reduce its dependence on imported oil, but growing corn for biofuel is not the answer. Americans are quite simply too profligate when it comes to their use of energy; Europeans, themselves pretty profligate, use only half the energy per capita and yet sustain a high-income lifestyle. The U.S. tax system needs to be shifted from burdening work to discouraging energy consumption.

The mark of a good politician is the ability to guide citizens away from populism.

The mark of a good politician is the ability to guide citizens away from populism. Unless countered, populism will block the policies needed to address the food crisis. For the citizens of the United States and Europe, the continuation of high food prices will be an inconvenience, but not sufficiently so to slay the three giants on which the current strain of romantic populism rests. Properly informed, many citizens will rethink their priorities, but politicians will need to deliver these messages and forge new alliances. If food prices are not brought down fast and then kept down, slum children will go hungry, and their future lives will be impaired. Shattering a few romantic illusions is a small price to pay.

PAUL COLLIER is Professor of Economics and Director of the Center for the Study of African Economies at Oxford University and the author of *The Bottom Billion: Why the Poorest Countries Are Failing and What Can Be Done About It.*

The New Colonialists

Only a motley group of aid agencies, international charities, and philanthropists stands between some of the world's most dysfunctional states and collapse. But for all the good these organizations do, their largesse often erodes governments' ability to stand up on their own. The result: a vicious cycle of dependence and too many voices calling the shots.

MICHAEL A. COHEN, MARIA FIGUEROA KÜPÇÜ, AND PARAG KHANNA

Even on their best days, the world's failed states are difficult to mistake for anything but tragic examples of countries gone wrong. A few routinely make the headlines—Somalia, Iraq, Congo. But alongside their brand of extreme state dysfunction exists an entirely separate, easily missed class of states teetering on the edge. In dozens of countries, corrupt or feeble governments are proving themselves dangerously incapable of carrying out the most basic responsibilities of statehood. These countries—nations such as Botswana, Cambodia, Georgia, and Kenya—might appear to be recovering, even thriving, developing countries, but like their failed-state cousins, they are increasingly unable, and perhaps unwilling, to fulfill the functions that have long defined what it means to be a state.

What—or who—is keeping these countries from falling into the abyss? Not so long ago, former colonial masters and superpower patrons propped them up. Today, however, the thin line that separates weak states from truly failed ones is manned by a hodgepodge of international charities, aid agencies, philanthropists, and foreign advisors. This armada of nonstate actors has become a powerful global force, replacing traditional donors' and governments' influence in poverty-stricken, war-torn world capitals. And as a measure of that influence, they are increasingly taking over key state functions, providing for the health, welfare, and safety of citizens. These private actors have become the "new colonialists" of the 21st century.

In much the same way European empires once dictated policies across their colonial holdings, the new colonialists—among them international development groups such as Oxfam, humanitarian nongovernmental organizations (NGOs) like Doctors Without Borders, faith-based organizations such as Mercy Corps, and megaphilanthropies like the Bill & Melinda Gates Foundation—direct development strategies and craft government policies for their hosts. But though the new colonialists are the glue holding society together in many weak states, their presence often deepens the dependency of these states on outsiders. They unquestionably fill vital roles, providing lifesaving healthcare, educating children, and distributing food in countries where the government can't or won't. But, as a consequence, many of these states are failing to develop the skills necessary to run their countries effectively, while others fall back on a global safety net to escape their own accountability. Have the new colonialists gone too far in attempting to manage responsibilities that should be those of governments alone? And given the dependency they have nurtured, can the world afford to let them one day walk away?

A Shift of Money and Power

Dependency is not a new phenomenon in the world's most destitute places. But as wealthy governments have lost their appetite for the development game, the new colonialists have filled the breach. In 1970, seven of every 10 dollars given by the United States to the developing world came from official development assistance (ODA). Today, ODA is a mere 15 percent of such flows, with the other 85 percent coming from private capital flows, remittances, and NGO contributions. Nor is this trend strictly an American phenomenon. In 2006, total aid to the developing world from countries of the Organisation for Economic Co-operation and Development (OECD) amounted to $325 billion. Just a third of that sum came from governments.

The expanding budgets of humanitarian NGOs are indicative of the power shift taking place. During the 1990s, the amount of aid flowing through NGOs in Africa, rather than governments, more than tripled. Spending by the international relief and development organization CARE has jumped 65 percent since 1999, to $607 million last year. Save the Children's budget has tripled since 1998; Doctors Without Borders' budget has doubled since 2001; and Mercy Corps' expenditures have risen nearly 700 percent in a decade.

The shift is equally apparent on the receiving end. When aid reaches developing countries, it increasingly bypasses the host governments altogether, often going straight into the coffers of the new colonialists on the ground. In 2003, the USAID Office of U.S. Foreign Disaster Assistance distributed two thirds of its budget through NGOs rather than affected governments. Between 1980 and 2003, the amount of aid from OECD countries channeled through NGOs grew from $47 million to more than $4 billion. One reason for the shift is the growing reluctance of rich countries to route aid through corrupt foreign officials. That has created an increasing reliance on new colonialists to deliver assistance—and produce results.

But the new colonialists are doing far more than simply carrying out the mandates of wealthy benefactors back home. They often tackle challenges that donors and developing-country governments either ignore or have failed to address properly. International Alert, a London-based peace-building organization, monitors corruption in natural-resource management in unstable countries such as the Democratic Republic of the Congo and serves as an early warning system to Western governments about impending conflicts. The Gates Foundation, which has spent more in the past decade on neglected-disease research than all the world's governments combined, has been so dissatisfied with existing international health indexes that it is funding the development of brand-new metrics for ranking developing-world health systems.

Seeing jobs that need to be done, the new colonialists simply roll up their sleeves and go to work, with or without the cooperation of states. That can be good for the family whose house needs rebuilding or the young mother who needs vaccinations for her child. But it can be a blow to the authority of an already weak government. And it may do nothing to ensure that a state will be able to provide for its citizens in the future.

The Power behind the Throne

The responsibilities the new colonialists assume are diverse—improving public health, implementing environmental initiatives, funding small businesses, providing military training, even promoting democracy. But whatever the task, the result is generally the same: the slow and steady erosion of the host state's responsibility and the empowerment of the new colonialists themselves.

The extent of the new colonialists' influence is perhaps best illustrated in Afghanistan. The government possesses only the most rudimentary control over its territory, and President Hamid Karzai has made little progress in combating corruption and narcotics trafficking. The result is a shell of a government, unable to provide basic services or assert its authority. Today, 80 percent of all Afghan services, such as healthcare and education, are delivered by international and local NGOs. According to its own estimates, the Afghan government administers only a third of the several billion dollars of aid flowing into the country each year. The rest is managed directly by private contractors, development agencies, and humanitarian aid groups. Major donors such as Britain only briefly include the Afghan government in their aid agendas: Although 80 percent of Britain's $200 million in annual aid to Afghanistan is dedicated to state ministries, as soon as the money arrives, it is swiftly handed over to NGOs like Oxfam or CARE for the actual construction of schools and hospitals. The transfers simply reflect many donors' lack of confidence in Afghan ministries to distribute funds competently and implement aid mandates on their own.

Many of the gains that Afghanistan has made since the fall of the Taliban can undoubtedly be attributed to the efforts and largesse of the many thousands of NGOs that have set up shop in Kabul. But not everyone is thankful for their labor. Karzai has derided the wasteful overlap, cronyism, and unaccountability among foreign NGOs in Afghanistan as "NGOism," just another "ism," after communism and Talibanism, in his country's unfortunate history. In 2005, Ramazan Bashardost, a parliamentary candidate in Kabul, sailed to electoral victory by running on an anti-NGO platform, threatening to expel nearly 2,000 NGOs that he claimed were corrupt, for-profit ventures providing little service to the country.

Many NGOs understandably resent such criticism, particularly as it lumps together a diverse lot—private contractors, international aid agencies, local NGOs—and ignores the important contributions some have made. But none of these groups is anxious to perform so well that it works itself out a job. No matter how well-intentioned, these new colonialists need weak states as much as weak states need them.

None of the new colonialists is anxious to perform so well that it works itself out of a job. They need weak states as much as weak states need them.

This kind of perverse dependency is on display in Georgia, where new colonialists have come to wield an inordinate amount of influence since the country emerged from Soviet rule. Today, its pro-Western president is supported by a steady dose of financial and political aid from abroad, and many state functions are financed or managed by outside help. In advance of the country's Rose Revolution, foreign political consultants advised the opposition's campaign strategy. The American consulting firm Booz Allen Hamilton has been hired to help rebuild state ministries from the ground up, recruiting new staff and retraining bureaucrats. These foreign technocrat-consultants participate in the day-to-day decision-making on critical national matters, such as political reform and intelligence sharing. But in Georgia, as well as other countries where these consultants operate, as they help mold state functions and prioritize development policies, they also write the complex grant applications that their home governments consider—grants that effectively extend their own positions of influence. The result is a vicious cycle of dependency as new colonialists vie for the contracts that will keep them in business.

That isn't to say that the new colonialists don't get results—many do. And in few areas are the efforts of the new colonialists more impressive than in the public-health arena. When Cambodia emerged from more than a decade of civil war in 1991, the public healthcare system was nonexistent. Since 1999, the government has outsourced much of the country's healthcare to international NGOs such as HealthNet and Save the Children. Today, it is estimated that 1 in 10 Cambodians receives Healthcare from such groups, which run hundreds of hospitals and clinics throughout the country and often provide far better care than government institutions. So reliable are these NGOs in providing quality care that it is difficult to imagine the government taking over responsibilities anytime soon—if ever.

Many aid organizations will say that their ultimate goal is to ensure their services are no longer needed. But aid organizations and humanitarian groups need dysfunction to maintain their relevance. Indeed, their institutional survival depends on it. Although aid groups occasionally have pulled out of countries because of security concerns or to protest the manipulation of aid, it is difficult to find examples where these groups have pulled up stakes because the needs they seek to address are no more. And as these groups deepen their presence in weak states, they often bleed the country of local talent. The salaries they offer are not only better and the work more effective, but there are often no comparable opportunities for well-educated locals in their country's civil service or private sector. The new colonialists may depend on this talent to ensure their legitimacy and local expertise, but it further weakens the host government's ability to attract their own best and brightest, ensuring that they remain reliant on new colonialists for know-how and results.

An Unbroken Cycle

There is no single global clearinghouse that coordinates, or even tracks, how these actors behave around the world. If new colonialists only pay lip service to local ownership and democracy, there is little to suggest that the cycle of mutual dependence will ever be broken. And if that is the case, the new-colonialist crutch may enable corrupt governments to continue to avoid their responsibilities in perpetuity.

Of course, there is another disturbing possibility that many observers do not like to countenance: Without the new colonialists, today's weak states could be tomorrow's basket cases. It speaks to the ubiquity of the new colonialists that this prospect seems remote. Nor can most weak states successfully resist their influence. When Cyclone Nargis struck Burma in May, the governing military junta initially resisted outside assistance. But state incapacity, corruption, and incompetence often make a defiant stance impossible. After several weeks, the regime's leaders had little choice but to accept the help of aid workers who were clamoring to gain access to the people in greatest need.

How then should the international community respond to the increasing influence of the new colonialists? Some observers argue that the market should take the lead in solving development challenges. Unfortunately, new investment often avoids failing states, and aid groups can rightly say that they do the work no one else is willing to do. Other observers think it is time to restore the centrality of the United Nations, at least as a coordinating force among these actors. But globalization resists the centralization of power, and the United Nations lacks the support of member states to take on such ambitious and expensive goals.

The fundamental challenge in this messy new landscape will be to establish a system of accountability. To earn a place at the table of global governance, the new colonialists will have to keep their promises not only to their donors and benefactors but to the citizens of failing states themselves. Competition among aid groups might actually serve to improve this accountability in the future. In many ways, the new colonialists are building a genuine global constituency, and, for better or worse, they may be the first—and last—line of defense for states sliding toward failure.

Want to Know More?

In *Global Development 2.0: Can Philanthropists, the Public, and the Poor Make Poverty History?* (Washington: Brookings Institution Press, 2008), economists and NGO experts debate whether the incredible proliferation of development players can work together to improve life for the world's poor. Ann Florini argues that only collective action by civil society, national governments, and private enterprise can tackle the challenges of the 21st century in *The Coming Democracy: New Rules for Running a New World* (Washington: Island Press, 2003). For an influential analysis of the rise of global civil society, see Jessica T. Mathews's "**Power Shift**" (*Foreign Affairs*, January/ February 1997).

Several organizations produce rankings on the performance of global development players. The Hudson Institute's **Index of Global Philanthropy** tracks the scale of private giving to the developing world with case studies of its effectiveness. The One World Trust, established by a group of British parliamentarians, assesses the operations of some of the world's most powerful NGOs in the **2007 Global Accountability Report.**

Sebastian Mallaby exposes the often contentious relations between NGOs and international aid agencies—and the poor who get lost in the shuffle—in **"NGOs: Fighting Poverty, Hurting the Poor"** (*Foreign Policy*, September/October 2004). Erika Check reports on the fight to get lifesaving medicines to the world's poor and the growing influence of the Gates Foundation on global publichealth priorities in **"Quest for the Cure"** (*Foreign Policy*, July/August 2006).

For links to relevant Web sites, access to the *FP* Archive, and a comprehensive index of related *Foreign Policy* articles, go to ForeignPolicy.com.

MICHAEL A. COHEN, MARIA FIGUEROA KÜPÇÜ, and PARAG KHANNA are senior research fellows at the New America Foundation.

Reprinted in entirety by McGraw-Hill with permission from *Foreign Policy,* July/August 2008, pp. 74–79. www.foreignpolicy.com. © 2008 Washingtonpost.Newsweek Interactive, LLC.

Power to the People

Why it's the poor-not the experts-who can best solve the food crisis.

Eric Werker

Every nongovernmental organization has a mission statement. For example, CARE, one of the world's largest
and best-funded NGOs, explains its mission as serving "individuals and families in the poorest communities in the
world. Drawing strength from our global diversity, resources
and experience, we promote innovative solutions and are advocates for global responsibility." Indeed, CARE has teams of
experts with years of experience in more than 70 countries,
and its efforts to tackle the "underlying causes of poverty" are
impressive. Implicit in its mission statement, like those of most
NGOs, is the notion that CARE is exceptionally knowledgeable
about how to meet the needs of the world's poor. But does it
know best?

Take one of the most confounding global problems today:
the skyrocketing cost of food. Prices for staple crops such as
rice and wheat have more than doubled since 2006, putting an
enormous strain on the 1.2 billion people living on a dollar a
day or less. In 2004, a typical poor farmer in Udaipur, India, was
already spending more than half his daily dollar of income on
food—and that was before grain prices went through the roof.

NGOs and relief agencies are on the front lines of this global
crisis, distributing food and other forms of assistance to the
hardest-hit victims. But food handouts may be the last thing that
poor countries need right now. In many of the worst-stricken
places, agriculture is the top employer. High food prices are
offering a rare opportunity for farmers in these countries to
make a tidy profit. Dumping imported food on the market will
cut into many farmers' incomes and thus might do more harm
than good. Low-wage work programs could help people avoid
hunger, but they might also take farmers away from their fields
just when farming is becoming lucrative.

Priorities, moreover, vary from person to person and from
place to place. A West African farmer might choose to forgo
next season's seeds and fertilizer to put food on the table today.
A garbage collector in Jakarta might sacrifice trips to the doctor
to keep from going hungry. Mexican parents might keep their
kids home from school as the cost of education gets priced out
of the family budget. Aid agencies can't always predict what the
poor value most.

The first step in truly addressing the food crisis, therefore,
is abandoning the idea that the donor knows best. Instead of

more advice or another bag of rice, the poor should be given
relief vouchers. The basic premise is simple: Give poor people
a choice about what type of assistance they receive. Vouchers,
backed by major donor countries, could be distributed to needy
recipients in the areas hardest hit by the food crisis. The recipients could then redeem the vouchers in exchange for approved
goods (such as food or fertilizer) or services (such as healthcare
or job training). Relief vouchers would allow families to meet
their most pressing needs without harming the very markets that
can bring about permanent solutions. At the same time, they
would give firms and NGOs an incentive to provide a wider
array of services.

Relief vouchers could also save NGOs millions of dollars
that victims never see. Figuring out what people need is hard
enough during a natural disaster, when a helicopter flyover can
reveal the physical damage. But the effects of the food crisis are
much harder to diagnose. Each NGO must conduct household
surveys, hire experts, meet with local government officials and
foreign donors, and then write grant applications and raise funds
before it can ever help its first victim. Meanwhile, monitoring
these efforts eats up precious resources. With vouchers, agencies would simply follow the invisible hand of the market—in
this case, the market for relief.

Relief vouchers would solve another problem: accountability. Most NGOs today answer only to the donors who fund their
operations, not to their actual clients—the poor. Most major
donors do their utmost to make sure their money is spent as
promised. But even donors whose hearts are in the right place
cannot anticipate the exact needs of so many different communities. With no mechanism for the poor to communicate their
priorities, nonprofits and their donors are only accountable to
themselves. A system of relief vouchers would change that.

Such a radical shift in accountability will have major rami-
fications. The development world is littered with projects that
keep getting funded long after they are no longer useful. Under
a voucher system, if an NGO delivered a product that no one
needed, or failed to deliver what it promised, beneficiaries
would stop coming to it for relief. This is why nonprofits working for vouchers wouldn't have to waste funds on expensive
evaluations. After all, Pepsi does not have to prove whether its
soda makes its customers better off. Products that people aren't

willing to buy typically don't survive long. It is time to expose the nonprofit sector to the same market feedback.

If that scares some NGOs, it shouldn't. Too often, they must cater to the whims of donors when they would prefer to serve those in need. Without financial support, they would never be able to conduct their important work. But if a significant share of NGOs' financing came through voucher redemption, they would be able to focus their attention on the poor without worrying as much about pleasing large foundations and government agencies, which often have their own agendas.

Vouchers, of course, aren't a silver bullet. Corruption and fraud will be a concern. Moreover, some needs are best delivered at the community level, such as clean water, or at the national level, such as public-health campaigns. And in countries with well-developed national safety nets, such as South Africa, there may be no need to bypass functioning institutions by introducing vouchers. In some cases, relief vouchers would be impractical.

Aid workers are fortunate if they can even reach those in need in a failed state like Somalia or a dictatorship like Burma.

Voucher schemes have already shown promise. Catholic Relief Services pioneered their use in 2000 by setting up "seed fairs" for farmers. In Ethiopia in 2004, the organization successfully introduced livestock vouchers for sheep, goats, and even veterinary services. The Red Cross distributed vouchers to vulnerable families in the West Bank in 2002 and 2003; the program was only discontinued for political reasons. Governments have long used other types of vouchers on larger scales: for schools, in many developing countries, and in the form of food stamps in the United States. Vouchers, in short, can work—and it's time to extend their logic to a much wider array of problems. It's time to give the poor the power of choice.

ERIC WERKER is assistant professor at Harvard Business School.

Reprinted in entirety by McGraw-Hill with permission from *Foreign Policy,* November/December 2008, pp. 78–79. www.foreignpolicy.com. © 2008 Washingtonpost.Newsweek Interactive, LLC.

The Micromagic of Microcredit

Karol Boudreaux and Tyler Cowen

Microcredit has star power. In 2006, the Nobel Committee called it "an important liberating force" and awarded the Nobel Peace Prize to Muhammad Yunus, the "godfather of microcredit." The actress Natalie Portman is a believer too; she advocates support for the Village Banking Campaign on its MySpace page. The end of poverty is "just a mouse click away," she promises. A button on the site swiftly redirects you to paypal.com, where you can make a contribution to microcredit initiatives.

After decades of failure, the world's aid organizations seem to think they have at last found a winning idea. The United Nations declared 2005 the "International Year of Microcredit." Secretary-General Kofi Annan declared that providing microloans to help poor people launch small businesses recognizes that they "are the solution, not the problem. It is a way to build on their ideas, energy, and vision. It is a way to grow productive enterprises, and so allow communities to prosper."

Many investors agree. Hundreds of millions of dollars are flowing into microfinance from international financial institutions, foundations, governments, and, most important, private investors—who increasingly see microfinance as a potentially profitable business venture. Private investment through special "microfinance investment vehicles" alone nearly doubled in 2005, from $513 million to $981 million.

On the charitable side, part of microcredit's appeal lies in the fact that the lending institutions can fund themselves once they are launched. Pierre Omidyar, the founder of eBay, explains that you can begin by investing $60 billion in the world's poorest people, "and then you're done!"

But can microcredit achieve the massive changes its proponents claim? Is it the solution to poverty in the developing world, or something more modest—a way to empower the poor, particularly poor women, with some control over their lives and their assets?

On trips to Africa and India we have talked to lenders, borrowers, and other poor people to try to understand the role microcredit plays in their lives. We met people like Stadile Menthe in Botswana. Menthe is, in many ways, the classic borrower. A single mother with little formal education, she borrowed money to expand the small grocery store she runs on a dusty road on the outskirts of Botswana's capital city, Gaborone. Menthe's store has done well, and she has expanded into the lucrative business of selling phone cards. In fact, she's been successful enough that she has built two rental homes next to her store. She has diversified her income and made a better life for herself and her daughter. But how many borrowers are like Menthe? In our judgment, she is the exception, not the norm. Yes, microcredit is mostly a good thing. Very often it helps keep borrowers from even greater catastrophes, but only rarely does it enable them to climb out of poverty.

The modern story of microcredit began 30 years ago, when Yunus—then an economics professor at Chittagong University in southeastern Bangladesh—set out to apply his theories to improving the lives of the poor in the nearby village of Jobra. He began in 1976 by lending $27 to a group of 42 villagers, who used the money to develop informal businesses, such as making soap or weaving baskets to sell at the local market. After the success of the first experiment, Yunus founded Grameen Bank. Today, the bank claims more than five million "members" and a loan repayment rate of 98 percent. It has lent out some $6.5 billion.

At the outset, Yunus set a goal that half of the borrowers would be women. He explained, "The banking system not only rejects poor people, it rejects women. . . . Not even one percent of their borrowers are women." He soon discovered that women were good credit risks, and good at managing family finances. Today, more than 95 percent of Grameen Bank's borrowers are women. The UN estimates that women make up 76 percent of microcredit customers around the world, varying from nearly 90 percent in Asia to less than a third in the Middle East.

While 70 percent of microcredit borrowers are in Asia, the institution has spread around the world; Latin America and sub-Saharan Africa account for 14 and 10 percent of the number of borrowers, respectively. Some of the biggest microfinance institutions include Grameen Bank, ACCION International, and Pro Mujer of Bolivia.

The average loan size varies, usually in proportion to the income level of the home country. In Rwanda, a typical loan might be $50 to $200; in Romania, it is more likely to be $2,500 to $5,000. Often there is no explicit collateral. Instead, the banks lend to small groups of about five people, relying on peer pressure for repayment. At mandatory weekly meetings, if one borrower cannot make her payment, the rest of the group must come up with the cash.

The achievements of microcredit, however, are not quite what they seem. There is, for example, a puzzling fact at the heart of the enterprise. Most microcredit banks charge interest rates of 50 to 100 percent on an annualized basis (loans, typically, must be paid off within weeks or months). That's not as scandalous as it sounds—local moneylenders demand much higher rates. The puzzle is a matter of basic economics: How can people in new businesses growing at perhaps 20 percent annually afford to pay interest at rates as high as 100 percent?

The answer is that, for the most part, they can't. By and large, the loans serve more modest ends—laudable, but not world changing.

Microcredit does not always lead to the creation of small businesses. Many microlenders refuse to lend money for start-ups; they insist that a business already be in place. This suggests that the business was sustainable to begin with, without a micro-loan. Sometimes lenders help businesses to grow, but often what they really finance is spending and consumption.

That is not to say that the poor are out shopping for jewelry and fancy clothes. In Hyderabad, India, as in many other places, we saw that loans are often used to pay for a child's doctor visit. In the Tanzanian capital of Dar es Salaam, Joel Mwakitalu, who runs the Small Enterprise Foundation, a local microlender, told us that 60 percent of his loans are used to send kids to school; 40 percent are for investments. A study of microcredit in Indonesia found that 30 percent of the borrowed money was spent on some form of consumption.

Sometimes consumption and investment are one and the same, such as when parents send their children to school. Indian borrowers often buy mopeds and motorbikes—they are fun to ride but also a way of getting to work. Cell phones are used to call friends but also to run businesses.

For better or worse, microborrowing often entails a kind of bait and switch. The borrower claims that the money is for a business, but uses it for other purposes. In effect, the cash allows a poor entrepreneur to maintain her business without having to sacrifice the life or education of her child. In that sense, the money is for the business, but most of all it is for the child. Such lifesaving uses for the funds are obviously desirable, but it is also a sad reality that many microcredit loans help borrowers to survive or tread water more than they help them get ahead. This sounds unglamorous and even disappointing, but the alternative—such as no doctor's visit for a child or no school for a year—is much worse.

Commentators often seem to assume that the experience of borrowing and lending is completely new for the poor. But moneylenders have offered money to the world's poor for millennia, albeit at extortionate rates of interest. A typical money-lender is a single individual, well-known in his neighborhood or village, who borrows money from his wealthier connections and in turn lends those funds to individuals in need, typically people he knows personally. But that personal connection is rarely good for a break; a moneylender may charge 200 to 400 percent interest on an annualized basis. He will insist on col-lateral (a television, for instance), and resort to intimidation and sometimes violence if he is not repaid on time. The money-lender operates informally, off the books, and usually outside the law.

So compared to the alternative, microcredit is often a very good deal indeed. Microcredit critics often miss this point. For instance, Aneel Karnani, who teaches at the University of Michigan's business school, argues that microfinance "misses its mark." Karnani says that in some cases microcredit can make life for the planet's bottom billion even worse by reducing their cash flow. Karnani cites the high interest rates that microlenders charge and points out that "if poor clients cannot earn a greater return on their investment than the interest they must pay, they will become poorer as a result of microcredit, not wealthier." But the real question has never been credit vs. no credit; rather, it is moneylender vs. modern microcredit. Credit can bring some problems, but microcredit is easing debt burdens more than it is increasing them.

At microlender SERO Lease and Finance in Tanzania, bor-rower Margaret Makingi Marwa told us that she prefers working with a microfinance institution to working with a moneylender. Moneylenders demand quick repayment at high interest rates. At SERO, Marwa can take six months or a year to pay off her lease contract. Given that her income can vary and that she may not have money at hand every month, she prefers to have a longer-term loan.

Moneylenders do offer some advantages, especially in rural areas. Most important, they come up with cash on the spot. If your child needs to go to the doctor right now, the moneylender is usually only a short walk away. Even under the best of cir-cumstances, a microcredit loan can take several days to process, and the recipient will be required to deal with many documents, not to mention weekly meetings.

There is, however, an upside to this "bureaucracy." In reality, it is the moneylender who is the "micro" operator. Microcredit is a more formal, institutionalized business relationship. It represents a move up toward a larger scale of trade and busi-ness organization. Microcredit borrowers gain valuable expe-rience in working within a formal institution. They learn what to expect from lenders and fellow borrowers, and they learn what is expected of themselves. This experience will be a help should they ever graduate to commercial credit or have other dealings with the formal financial world.

The comparison to moneylending brings up another impor-tant feature of microcredit. Though its users avoid the kind of intimidation employed by moneylenders, microcredit could not work without similar incentives. The lender does not demand collateral, but if you can't pay your share of the group loan, your fellow borrowers will come and take your TV. That enforcement process can lead to abuses, but it is a gentler form of intimida-tion than is exercised by the moneylender. If nothing else, the group members know that at the next meeting any one of them might be the one unable to repay her share of the loan.

If borrowers are using microcredit for consumption and not only to improve a small business, how do they repay? Most borrowers are self-employed and work in the informal sector of the economy. Their incomes are often erratic; small, unexpected expenses can make repayment impossible in any given week or month. In the countryside, farmers have seasonal incomes and little cash for long periods of time.

Borrowers manage, at least in part, by relying on family members and friends to help out. In some cases, the help comes in the form of remittances from abroad. Remittances that cross national borders now total more than $300 billion yearly. A recent study in Tanzania found that microcredit borrowers get 34 percent of their income from friends and family, some of whom live abroad, but others of whom live in the city and have jobs in the formal sector. That's the most effective kind of foreign aid, targeted directly at the poor and provided by those who understand their needs.

Here again, microcredit does something that traditional banks do not. A commercial bank typically will not lend to people who work in the informal sector, precisely because their erratic incomes make them risky bets. The loan officer at a commercial bank does not care that your brother in Doha is sending money each month to help you out. But a microcredit institution cares only that you come to your weekly meeting with a small sum in hand for repayment. Because of microcredit, families can leverage one person's ability to find work elsewhere to benefit the entire group.

Sometimes microcredit leads to more savings rather than more debt. That sounds paradoxical, but borrowing in one asset can be a path toward (more efficient) saving in other assets.

To better understand this puzzle, we must set aside some of our preconceptions about how saving operates in poor countries, most of all in rural areas. Westerners typically save in the form of money or money-denominated assets such as stocks and bonds. But in poor communities, money is often an ineffective medium for savings; if you want to know how much net saving is going on, don't look at money. Banks may be a daylong bus ride away or may be plagued, as in Ghana, by fraud. A cash hoard kept at home can be lost, stolen, taken by the taxman, damaged by floods, or even eaten by rats. It creates other kinds of problems as well. Needy friends and relatives knock on the door and ask for aid. In small communities it is often very hard, even impossible, to say no, especially if you have the cash on hand.

People who have even extremely modest wealth are also asked to perform more community service, or to pay more to finance community rituals and festivals. In rural Guerrero State, in Mexico, for example, one of us (Cowen) found that most people who saved cash did not manage to hold on to it for more than a few weeks or even days. A dollar saved translates into perhaps a quarter of that wealth kept. It is as if cash savings faces an implicit "tax rate" of 75 percent.

Under these kinds of conditions, a cow (or a goat or pig) is a much better medium for saving. It is sturdier than paper money. Friends and relatives can't ask for small pieces of it. If you own a cow, it yields milk, it can plow the fields, it produces dung that can be used as fuel or fertilizer, and in a pinch it can be slaughtered and turned into saleable meat or simply eaten. With a small loan, people in rural areas can buy that cow and use cash that might otherwise be diverted to less useful purposes to pay back the microcredit institution. So even when microcredit looks like indebtedness, savings are going up rather than down.

Microcredit *is* making people's lives better around the world. But for the most part, it is not pulling them out of poverty. It is hard to find entrepreneurs who start with these tiny loans and graduate to run commercial empires. Bangladesh, where Grameen Bank was born, is still a desperately poor country. The more modest truth is that microcredit may help some people, perhaps earning $2 a day, to earn something like $2.50 a day. That may not sound dramatic, but when you are earning $2 a day it is a big step forward. And progress is not the natural state of humankind; microcredit is important even when it does nothing more than stave off decline.

With microcredit, life becomes more bearable and easier to manage. The improvements may not show up as an explicit return on investment, but the benefits are very real. If a poor family is able to keep a child in school, send someone to a clinic, or build up more secure savings, its well-being improves, if only marginally. This is a big part of the reason why poor people are demanding greater access to microcredit loans. And microcredit, unlike many charitable services, is capable of paying for itself—which explains why the private sector is increasingly involved. The future of microcredit lies in the commercial sector, not in unsustainable aid programs. Count this as another benefit.

If this portrait sounds a little underwhelming, don't blame microcredit. The real issue is that we so often underestimate the severity and inertia of global poverty. Natalie Portman may not be right when she says that an end to poverty is "just a mouse click away," but she's right to be supportive of a tool that helps soften some of poverty's worst blows for many millions of desperate people

---

KAROL BOUDREAUX is a senior research fellow at the Mercatus Center at George Mason University. **TYLER COWEN** is a professor of economies at George Mason University and author of *Discover Your Inner Economist: Use Incentives to Fall in Love, Survive Your Next Meeting, and Motivate Your Dentist* (2007).

Reprinted with permission from *The Wilson Quarterly,* Winter 2008. Copyright © 2008 by Karol Boudreaux and Tyler Cowen. Reprinted by permission.

The Coming Revolution in Africa

Even as headlines bring grim news of misery, disease, and death in Africa, an agricultural transformation is lifting tens of millions of people out of poverty. A rising generation of small farmers promises not only to put food on the African table but to fundamentally change the continent's economic and political life.

G. Pascal Zachary

The heat is deadening. After a morning picking cotton on the side of a hill, Souley Madi, wearing a knock-off Nike T-shirt and thongs made from discarded tires, staggers down a steep slope, a heavy bag of cotton bolls on his back. Reaching his small compound 10 minutes later, he greets his two wives. The older one nurses a baby while preparing a lunch of maize and cassava. The second wife, visibly pregnant, rises from a seat under a shade tree, responding to Madi's instructions. He wants to impress his foreign visitor, so he prepares to introduce his latest agro-business brainstorm.

Ducks.

A few words from Madi, and wife number two dashes out of sight. When she reappears, some three dozen baby ducks waddle behind her. Madi beams, scoops up a duck, then hands it to me. He asks me to guess how much it will sell for at maturity.

I guess too low. Three dollars, Madi says. He is the first to raise ducks in the parched village of Badjengo, in the far north of Cameroon, about 45 minutes from the provincial capital of Garoua. Madi is a shrewd risk taker. Despite the challenging climate of Africa's rain-sparse savanna belt, Madi's ducks thrive, thanks partly to the diligent care provided by his new wife.

Madi, who is 41, sells nearly all of the ducks he raises, saving only a few for his family to eat. The birds are big sellers around local holidays, when Cameroonians in Europe and the United States send cash to relatives back home. Madi uses part of his duck money—about $100—to buy inventory for a small grocery store he maintains on the side of a main road. The store, a shack really, is secured by a heavy Chinese-made padlock. When people want to shop, they must first find Madi and coax him to open (he's got too few customers to justify an employee). From the sale of cotton, dry goods, and the ducks, Madi has accumulated a cash hoard he hides in his sleeping hut.

Having finished high school, Madi is better educated than most of his fellow farmers, and he embodies an important rule in rural Africa: The more educated the farmer, the more effective his practices and the higher his income. Madi won't allow his two school-age children to skip class in favor of fieldwork. "They should study instead," he says.

Short and stocky, Madi sits down on a low wooden bench and begins to eat roasted corn. He tells me through a translator how he—a Muslim—took a second wife, not for status or love, but to help him take advantage of the farm boom. He complains that prices, especially for cotton, should be higher. Yet he says he's never had more money saved.

To Americans, bombarded with dire images of Africa—starving Africans, diseased Africans, Africans fleeing disasters or fleeing other Africans trying to kill them—Madi may seem like a character from a novel. But he is no fiction. Despite the horrors of Darfur, the persistence of HIV/AIDS, and the failure to end famines and civil wars in a handful of countries, the vast majority of sub-Saharan Africans neither live in war zones nor struggle with an active disease or famine. Extreme poverty is relatively rare in rural Africa, and there is a growing entrepreneurial spirit among farmers that defies the usual image of Africans as passive victims. They are foot soldiers in an agrarian revolution that never makes the news. In 25 visits to the region since 2000, I have met many Souley Madis, and have come to believe that they are the key to understanding Africa's present and reshaping its future.

After decades of mistreatment, abuse, and exploitation, African farmers—still overwhelmingly smallholders working family-tilled plots of land—are awakening from a long slumber. Because farmers are the majority (about 60 percent) of all sub-Saharan Africans, farming holds the key to reducing poverty and helping to spread prosperity. Over the longer term, prosperous African farmers could become the backbone of a social and political transformation. They are the sort of canny and independent tillers of the land Thomas Jefferson envisioned as the foundation for American democracy. In a region where elites often seem more committed to enjoying the trappings of success abroad than creating success at home, farmers have a real stake in improving their turf. Life will still be hard for them, but in the years ahead they can be expected to demand better government policies and more effective services. As their incomes and aspirations rise, they could someday even form their own political parties, in much the way that farmers in the American Midwest and Western Europe did in the past. At a minimum, African governments seem likely to increasingly promote trade and development policies that advance rural interests.

Improved livelihoods for farmers alone won't reverse Africa's marginalization in the global economy or solve the region's many vexing problems. But among people concerned about Africa—and certainly among those in multinational organizations who must grapple with humanitarian disasters on the continent—the unfolding rural revival holds out new hope. Having once dismissed agriculture as an obstacle or an irrelevance, African leaders and officials in multinational organizations recently have come around to a new view, nicely summarized by Stephen Lewis, a former United Nations official who concentrated on African affairs. "Agricultural productivity," Lewis declared in 2005, "is indispensable to progress on all other fronts."

The potential for advances through agriculture is large. African farmers today are creating wealth on a scale unimagined a decade ago. They are likely to continue prospering into the foreseeable future. Helped by low costs of land and labor and by rising prices for farm products, African farmers are defying pessimists by increasing their output. They are cultivating land once abandoned or neglected; forging profitable links with local, regional, and international buyers; and reviving crops that flourished in the pre-1960 colonial era, when Africa provided a remarkable 10 percent of the world's tradable food. Today, that share is less than one percent.

"The boom in African agriculture is the most important, neglected development in the region, and it has years to run," says Andrew Mwenda, a leading commentator on African political economy.

The evidence of a farm boom is widespread. In southern Uganda, hundreds of farmers have begun growing apples for the first time, displacing imports and earning an astonishing 35 cents each. Brokers ferry the fruit from the countryside to the capital, Kampala, where it fetches almost twice as much. Cotton production in Zambia has increased 10-fold in 10 years, bringing new income to 120,000 farmers and their families, nearly one million people in all. Floral exports from Ethiopia are growing so rapidly that flowers threaten to surpass coffee as the country's leading cash earner. In Kenya, tens of thousands of small farmers who live within an hour of the Nairobi airport grow French beans and other vegetables, which are packaged, bar-coded, and air-shipped to Europe's grocers. Exports of vegetables, fruits, and flowers, largely from eastern and southern Africa, now exceed $2 billion a year, up from virtually zero a quarter-century ago.

Skeptics still insist that farmers in the region will be badly handicapped, in the long run, by climate change, overpopulation, new pandemics, and the vagaries of global commodity prices. Corruption, poor governance, and civil strife are all added to the list of supposedly insurmountable obstacles. But similar challenges haven't stopped Asian and Latin American farmers from advancing. Even people who see future gains for African farmers agree, however, that food shortages and famines will persist, at least within isolated or war-torn areas.

But while Malthusian nightmares dominate international discussions of Africa, food production in the most heavily peopled areas is outstripping population growth. In Nigeria, with the largest population of any African country, food production has grown faster than population for 20 years. In other West African countries, including Ghana, Niger, Mali, Burkina Faso, and Benin, crop output has risen by more than four percent annually, far exceeding the rate of population growth. Farm labor productivity in these countries is now so high that in some cases it matches the levels in parts of Asia.

"The driver of agriculture is primarily urbanization," observes Steve Wiggins, a farm expert at London's Overseas Development Institute. As more people leave the African countryside, there is more land for remaining farmers, and more paying customers in the city. The growth in food production is so impressive, Wiggins argues, that a "green revolution" is already under way in densely populated West Africa.

The growing international demand for food is also helping Africa's small farmers. The global ethanol boom has raised corn prices, and coffee is selling at a 10-year high, for instance. Multinational corporations are becoming more closely involved in African agriculture, moving away from plantation-based cultivation and opting instead to enter into contracts with thousands, even hundreds of thousands, of individual farmers. China and India, hungry to satisfy the appetites of expanding middle classes, view Africa as a potential breadbasket. Finally, African governments are generally more supportive of farmers than in the past. Even African elites, long disdainful of village life, are embracing farming, trying to profit from the boom—and raising the status of this once-scorned activity.

While Malthusian nightmares dominate international discussions of Africa, food production in the most heavily peopled areas is outstripping population growth.

No one model explains the surge in African agriculture. Diverse sources of success befit an Africa that, across the board, defies easy generalizations. One recent study finds 15 different farming "systems" in sub-Saharan Africa. At the level of the single African farm, diversity abounds too. Most individual farmers juggle as many as 10 crops. Outcomes among small farmers also vary. The top 25 percent of smallholders are believed to produce four to five times as much food as the bottom 25 percent. Just as in America not everyone is rich, in Africa not everyone is poor.

African farmers do share much in common. "A man with a hoe" remains an accurate description of nearly all who till the soil. Mechanization is rare. Less than one percent of land is worked by tractors. Only 10 percent is worked by draft animals. Nearly 90 percent is worked by hand, from initial plowing to planting, weeding, and harvesting. Irrigation is also rare; only one percent of sub-Saharan cropland receives irrigation water. Unpredictable weather, often drought and sometimes too much rain, bedevils farmers in many areas. Relatively little fertilizer is used; globally, farmers apply nine times as much per acre as Africans do. "Much of the food produced in Africa is lost" after harvest, according to one estimate, because of inaccessible markets, poor storage methods, and an absence of processing facilities. Finally, use of improved seed varieties is very limited by global standards.

But these sobering characteristics feature a silver lining: The potential for gains is large. Some ways farmers can move ahead are simple. One is to plant crops in straight lines. In Uganda, for instance, it was long the practice of many farmers to sow seeds haphazardly; they have been taught in recent years to plant in regularly spaced rows that vastly improve yields. When so simple a change delivers such great benefits, the importance of human choice is clear. In discussions of African affairs, the central role of the power of the individual and the desire of ordinary people to do better is often lost in a haze of dubious statistics, gloomy futuristic scenarios, and impossible calls for improved ethics, leadership, and institutions.

To glimpse a different picture of Africa, imagine traveling on a journey, not to Joseph Conrad's "heart of darkness," but to an uncharted, elusive, almost mythical part of the world's poorest region, where hope, personal responsibility, and new incentives are reshaping the lives of ordinary people, turning Conradian imagery on its head.

The first stop on our journey is the village of Bukhulu in eastern Uganda. From Kampala, I take an old van jammed with 15 people and rumble along dirt roads so pockmarked that pieces of the vehicle fly off during the journey without eliciting any reaction from the driver. The next morning, from the provincial center of Mbale, I hitch a ride through the foothills of towering Mount Elgon with an agricultural extension officer who works for a South African company that pays Ugandan farmers to grow cotton for export. On the final leg of the journey, I switch to a bicycle taxi. Balanced precariously on a makeshift rear seat, the man in front cycling leisurely, I pass cornfields brimming with ripening ears nearly ready to harvest. The ride costs a dime.

I am here to visit one of my favorite farmers, Ken Sakwa, who is in the forefront of a significant yet little-noticed back-to-the-land trend. The movement is powered by city dwellers who either can't earn enough money in the cities or are earning so much that they want to plow their savings into agro-businesses. Doomsayers constantly point to Africa's urbanization as a relentless scourge, stripping the countryside of talent, but quietly,

some Africans are going back to "the bush." Sakwa, 37, is one of them. He spent a decade in Uganda's mushrooming capital, doing odd jobs for cash. He enjoyed the excitement of city life but survived only because of the goodwill of relatives. Ultimately, he exhausted that goodwill. "I was a parasite," he admits.

Five years ago, Sakwa decided to claim the vacant farm of his deceased father in Bukhulu, the village of his birth. None of his brothers and sisters wanted the land, so he got it all. His wife in Kampala refused to join him. He divorced her and went back alone.

"I knew I'd achieve if I went back to my father's land," he recalls. "I felt ambition inside me."

Farmers in Bukhulu mainly grow cotton, corn, peanuts, and beans. Even the largest farms encompass no more than a dozen acres. In his first year back, Sakwa grew corn and beans on one acre, opening the ground alone, with a small hand hoe. "I worked like an animal," he recalls. Even before his first harvest, he looked for a wife. A few months after his return, he met Jessica in a nearby village. He decided to court her when he learned her parents were farmers.

"I wanted a wife who could help on the farm and would be happy doing so," Sakwa says. He married Jessica and, with her considerable help, he prospered. In his second year in Bukhulu, he tilled two acres of land, hiring a tractor to assist in plowing. From an American aid project, he and some neighbors learned to plant crops in straight lines. By the third year Sakwa mastered basic farming, "doing much, much better." When his old Kampala friends visit him, they ask, "How is this poor village man getting all this money?"

Accumulation is only part of Sakwa's story. How he spends his profits is significant. One early purchase was a mobile phone, which allows him to keep abreast of local markets and negotiate better prices for his crops. That a farmer who lives without electricity or running water should be able to receive phone calls from anywhere in the world is perhaps the most radical change in African material life in decades. Though wireless service came late to the region, nearly one in five sub-Saharan Africans now owns a cell phone, and the World Bank estimates that the region's wireless phone market is the "fastest-growing in the world." One morning, after he plants cottonseeds in a small field, Sakwa receives a call from the headmaster at his daughter's boarding school (yes, he can afford that too!). The headmaster asks for 500 pounds of beans. Sakwa, who has the beans bagged for sale, wants 15 cents a pound. "Will you accept?" he asks.

The headmaster wants to pay less. Sakwa refuses. "I can hold my beans until I get a fair price," he says.

A few days later, the headmaster calls back and agrees to the price.

One day, I walk with the Sakwas to one of their fields. The ground is wet from recent rains. We cut through a path separating the land of different farmers and soon meet a family harvesting beans. A husband and wife and their two children are haphazardly tossing uprooted beans on a

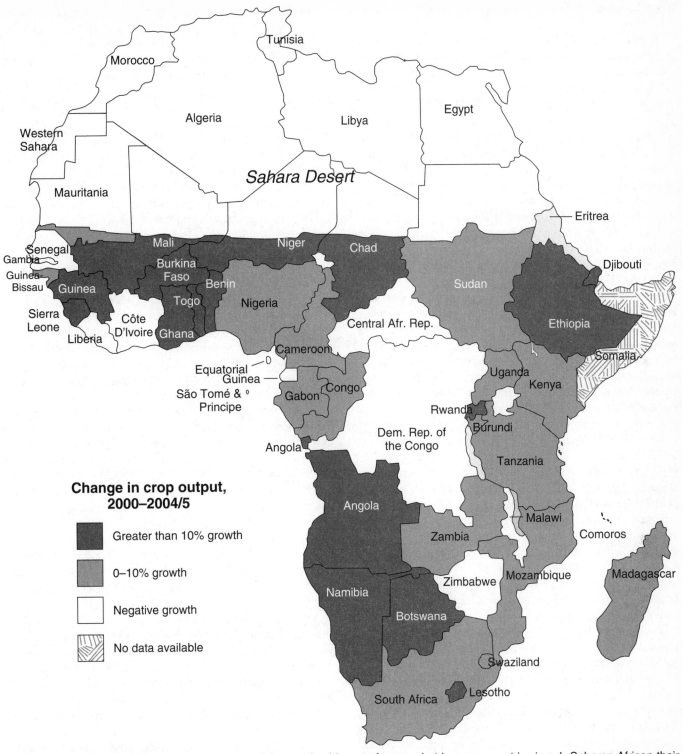

Change in crop output, 2000–2004/5

- Greater than 10% growth
- 0–10% growth
- Negative growth
- No data available

Violence, drought, and other disruptions can deal devastating blows to farmers, but in many countries in sub-Saharan African their output is expanding. The World Bank reports that many African economies "appear to have turned the corner and moved to a path of faster and steadier economic growth."

wooden cart. Sakwa greets them and stops to explain that they will fit more on the cart if they make neat piles. The man acts as if he's received a revelation. Sakwa starts rearranging the beans to make sure the man grasps his advice. The man begins to shift the beans around, and his wife flashes Sakwa a big smile, thanking him.

We turn off the path, slice through another field, and come upon a patch of peanuts. Ever the innovator, Sakwa is experimenting with different types in order to see which grow best. He pulls a few samples from the ground to show me. Just as I begin to chew on a peanut, Jessica screams in the distance.

Sakwa races off toward his wife. I follow. When we reach her, she cries out, "Someone has stolen the beans!"

The plants have been ripped from the field. "They must have come in the night," Sakwa says. He has been forced to hire a neighbor to guard this field in the daytime. He tells the man he will harvest the corn soon.

One of Sakwa's innovations isn't agricultural but commercial. In order to expand output and raise his income, he leases land from his neighbors and hires them as casual laborers, enriching them as well as himself.

Land sales are virtually impossible in rural Africa, but informal leases are becoming more common. There are no formal land titles in Sakwa's village, nor in nearly every other African village, so his claim to his father's land is grounded in the community's knowledge of Sakwa and his lineage. Until recently, no one ever bought or sold rural land in Uganda, but with the rise of small-scale commercial farming the value of farmland can now be "monetized," in rough terms, by estimating profit from cash crops grown over a period of years. Land is coming to be viewed as a commodity. Informal land deals are flexible, but because they are not supported by unassailable titles, there is always a possibility of costly disputes. Sakwa recently experienced such a problem when he leased a half-acre of very productive land from a neighbor for nearly $800. But one of the man's brothers, who didn't get any money in the deal, has sued Sakwa in court. He wants to be paid.

Sakwa and his friend Francis Nakiwuza are the most active acquirers of land in Bukhulu, having each leased four different plots over the past three years. The lawsuit worries them. One day Nakiwuza and I sit in Sakwa's living room as he sifts through his business records, which he stores in a worn leather briefcase stowed under his bed. He keeps records on each of his "gardens," listing the costs and income.

One reason for disputes: poorly drawn contracts. The lease for his newest plot, written in Sakwa's own hand, boils down to a single sentence in which a neighbor agrees to permit Sakwa to use "my swampy land of 61 strides in length and 32 strides in width" for about $200.

The contract lacks any surveyor information and isn't registered with any government agency or court. "We trust people," Sakwa says.

The rudimentary contract partly reflects the inexperience of the parties involved. Desiring land is new to Sakwa, and he dreams of obtaining more. He wants to double his current holding of 10 acres. "I want to make 20 acres," he says. "That will make my life good."

Across the table sits Nakiwuza. He wants more land too, and brings news of a neighbor who needs to raise money. The man was caught in a sex act with a young girl. In years past, there would have been no legal consequences. But today men caught abusing underage women can go to prison or pay a large fine. For this man, the only way to avoid prison is to raise money by leasing land.

Ken Sakwa's friends in Kampala ask, "How is this poor village man getting all this money?"

Sakwa is sorry for the man but happy that either he or Nakiwuza will get to expand his acreage. "Why shouldn't the stronger farmers have more land?" Nakiwuza asks. Often, the land they lease had been sitting idle. "We are using the land well," he says. "Others did nothing with it. Now they have our money, and we have crops to sell."

Ken Sakwa is Africa's future writ small. Gilbert Bukenya is the future writ large. He is the vice president of Uganda and a rarity among African politicians: He is passionate about the value of farming, is himself an innovative farmer, and publicly encourages farmers to work smarter. One of Bukenya's greatest achievements has been to encourage a can-do spirit in Uganda's farmers and a sense of pride among other Ugandans in what their farming compatriots produce.

I met Bukenya one balmy afternoon at his home on the shores of Lake Victoria, where he experiments with fruits, vegetables, and dairy cattle. "By farming smarter, Ugandans not only grow more, they earn more money," he tells me. Bukenya is an advocate of food self-sufficiency, pointing to the example of rice. Ugandans pay tens of millions of dollars annually for rice imported from overseas—sub-Saharan Africa as a whole imports nearly $2 billion worth. In order to expand the output of homegrown rice, Bukenya promoted a new African variety that grows in uplands (as opposed to paddies) and requires less water. Then he argued for the imposition of a 75 percent duty on foreign rice. The measure passed Parliament and brought rapid benefits: A few of the country's largest rice importers invested in milling plants, thus becoming customers of local farmers. The new mills created jobs and lowered the cost of bringing domestic rice to market, so that consumers now pay more or less the same for rice as always.

Since foreign rice exporters—notably the United States, Thailand, and Pakistan—subsidize their growers, Bukenya thinks it only fair that Uganda defend its own rice farmers, even though he realizes that some import-substitution schemes fail. (And rice is only one of the African crops hampered by U.S. and European farm subsidies and trade barriers.)

Fresh from his rice success, Bukenya is now promoting the benefits of raising livestock. One September morning I find him lecturing before a classroom full of ordinary farmers, about 50 of them, gathered in a school about an hour from Kampala. Wearing a loose-fitting shirt and sandals, Bukenya jokes easily with his audience, speaking in a local language. The classroom has no electricity, a concrete floor, and exposed wooden rafters. Bukenya recalls how his mother earned the money to send him to school from sales of a beer she concocted. Switching to a prepared talk, he preaches a simple lesson: "Make money daily." One way they can do that, he tells the small crowd, is by keeping a milk cow or egg-laying chickens. Only a few of the farmers do anything like this now, and Bukenya spends a good deal of time explaining how they can get started.

Then he criticizes the country's traditional big-horned Ankole cattle. These animals are beautiful and beloved but provide very little milk, he says, "no matter how hard you squeeze." He prefers European Friesian cows. "Five of them will produce the same as 50 Ankoles," he says.

Bukenya asks one of the women in the audience to stand up. He praises the bananas she grows and notes the high output of her Friesian cows. "You are a model for the others," he says. The woman smiles. Then, spreading out his arms and looking across the room, he says, "Everybody must be a model."

That kind of exhortation might seem hokey to Americans, but in an African context Bukenya's words are incendiary. It is the mental attitude of African farmers, as much as their lack of money, that holds them back, Bukenya argues. For ordinary farmers to be called heroes, or even recognized at all, by a senior political leader is unprecedented. And Bukenya's message makes perfect sense. Surprisingly, few farmers in Uganda or other parts of Africa keep livestock. In some locales, that's because of the extreme heat; disease is another limitation. Yet many farmers don't raise animals (at least productive ones) even when conditions for doing so are favorable, because of the irrational pull of tradition and a lack of knowledge. But teaching skills to farmers isn't enough, Bukenya says. "You have to instill confidence in them that by working harder, they will benefit."

The potential for breeding (as Souley Madi knows) is large. Two government ministers in Uganda have recently launched poultry operations. Uganda's farm output is soaring, having helped push total exports in 2006 to nearly $1 billion, double the value of 2002. Much of the growth came in agriculture: Exports of coffee, cotton, fish, fruits, and tea doubled. Corn exports nearly tripled. Cocoa quadrupled. Sesame seed exports are up nearly 10-fold. Says Bukenya, "We are doing very well, but we can run even faster."

The beginnings of a profarmer political movement represents a watershed in African history. During the 1960s and '70s, in the first decades after independence from European colonial rule, African political leaders blatantly exploited farmers as part of a calculated effort to speed economic development and make food cheaper for Africa's then-tiny urban elite. They essentially nationalized cash crops, such as cotton and coffee, forcing farmers to sell everything they grew to government "marketing boards" at fixed prices, often well below the going rate. That destroyed the incentive to produce. Worse, the boards were corrupt and inefficient, and they did little or nothing to introduce farmers to new growing techniques, crop varieties, or customers. Meanwhile, the industrial schemes financed by the agricultural "surplus" virtually all flopped.

It is the mental attitude of African farmers, as much as their lack of money, that holds them back.

By the 1990s, African countries were importing large amounts of food, at great cost and sometimes under absurd circumstances. Fresh tomatoes rotted in Ghana's fields, while canned tomatoes from Italy dominated grocery sales. The story was similar elsewhere, with the exception of South Africa. A lack of canneries and other means of preserving fresh fruit and vegetables meant that a third or more of African output spoiled.

The reliance on imported food, and the demoralization of farmers, drove many Africans from the bush to the city. But the situation also spawned a backlash. Change came in two forms. First, international aid agencies, which during the 1980s and '90s had essentially abandoned support for agriculture and encouraged Africans to develop light industry and services, began to realize the folly of their approach. As the World Bank admitted in late 2007, "Agriculture has been vastly underused for development."

African leaders also reversed course, albeit by fits and starts, liberalizing agriculture and permitting multinational corporations to begin buying cash crops such as coffee and cotton directly from smallholders, who were eager to sell to these private buyers after being underpaid or even stiffed by government agencies. In Uganda, once called the "pearl of Africa" by Winston Churchill because of its enormous agricultural output and excellent climate, thriving colonial-era agro-businesses were destroyed by the predations of government after independence in 1962. When a rebel leader named Yoweri Museveni assumed power in the mid-1980s, he took steps to reverse course, including a gradual dismantling of the socialized structure that made every farmer a de facto employee of the state. But the farmers, having been burned, did not respond quickly. They remembered the worthless IOUs dispensed by the government.

Besides, telling farmers to grow more is not enough; even giving them the freedom to sell to whomever they wish is not enough. Farmers need cash buyers. Without willing customers, paradoxically, growing more food can grievously hurt farmers—it raises costs and saddles them with worthless surpluses.

Incredibly, this commonplace escaped farm experts in Africa for half a century. They have learned the hard way that food shortages and famines often result not from a scarcity of food but from too much food. When farmers can't convert their surplus into cash, they stop growing extra. No less a farm expert than Norman Borlaug, celebrated for launching the "green revolution" in Latin America and Asia, made a sobering error in Ethiopia five years ago (for which he later apologized). Having helped introduce higher-yielding grains to Ethiopian farmers, he witnessed a huge growth in output. But because no one thought about who would purchase the expanded supplies of grain, in a bumper harvest the surplus rotted and the farmers, who had borrowed money to obtain seed and other "inputs," suffered badly.

Now farm experts are beginning to change their views, putting the customer ahead of production. In 2004, the U.S. Agency for International Development (USAID) became the first aid donor to pledge to organize its spending around the principle that the end customer is the prime mover in African agriculture. Given a ready buyer who is offering a fair price, African farmers will defy stereotypes of their inherent conservatism and backwardness. "They move like lightning when money is on the table," says David Barry, a British coffee buyer based in Kampala. "Cash is king."

USAID realized that expanding farm output only makes sense when farmers respond to the right signals from buyers about which products are in demand. Part of the answer was for the agency to pay the costs of training farmers to grow those crops, and in higher-quality forms and greater volumes, that the private buyers sought. It also directly assisted private agro-firms, paying part of their costs for training farmers.

A method known as "contract farming" has become a crucial instrument of African empowerment. Buyers agree to purchase everything a farmer grows—coffee, cotton, even fish—freeing him from the specter of rotting crops and allowing him to produce as much as possible. And because the buyers—some of them domestic companies, others multinationals—profit, they have a stake in farmer productivity and an incentive to provide such things as training and discounted seed.

A wonderful example of this virtuous circle has unfolded in Uganda. The country's largest provider of cooking oil, Mukwano, had long sold only palm oil imported from Southeast Asia. As an experiment, the company hired Ugandan farmers to grow sunflower seeds, which were then crushed into oil locally. In two years, Mukwano enlisted 100,000 farmers, hiring an experienced trainer from India, C. P. Chowdry, to organize farmers into groups, train leaders, distribute seeds, and collect the harvest.

Even though Mukwano is the only seller of the particular seed variety needed, and so sets the price, sunflowers are attractive to farmers because they require little tending or water, can be "intercropped" with corn or cotton, and are harvested three times a year. During the planting season, the company broadcasts a weekly radio program that gives advice on how to manage the crop. The effort is wildly popular among farmers. When I visited Uganda's sunflower belt on the eve of planting season, I witnessed one farmer, Isaac Aggrey, ask Chowdry for seeds. In the previous season, Aggrey had earned a whopping $300 from three acres of sunflowers, putting enough cash in his pocket to buy a motorbike. When Chowdry told him, "The seeds are gone," Aggrey became distraught. Chowdry reminded him that he had warned that this could happen. "Next time, set aside the money and buy as soon as we put the seeds on sale," he said sternly.

About the same time aid donors recognized the necessity of helping farmers grow more of what buyers want, the mentality of agricultural experts underwent a sea change. For nearly half a century, starting in the 1960s, there seemed to be an inverse correlation between the application of agricultural expertise by national and international aid agencies and the productivity of African farming: the greater the number of experts, the worse Africa's agricultural performance.

Disdainful of the market, these agricultural specialists preferred to obsess over arcane questions about soil quality, seed varieties, and some mythical ideal of crop diversity. In classic butt-covering mode, they blamed "market failures" and Africa's geography for farmer's low incomes and their vulnerability to famine and food shortages.

Then, about five years ago, a few brave specialists suddenly realized that under their very noses some of Africa's most significant farm sectors were booming—and booming without any help from the legions of agricultural scientists and bureaucrats in

Africa. In West Africa, corn production doubled between 1980 and 2000. Harvests of the lowly cassava—a starchy root that provides food insurance for many people—steadily expanded. In East Africa, sales of fresh flowers soared. Once-moribund cash crops, such as cotton, saw a large expansion, first in West Africa and then in Tanzania, Uganda, and Zambia. The list of improbable winners went on and on.

Even as a steady diet of stories about "urgent" food crises in Africa dominated public discussion, these successes became impossible to ignore. In 2004, the International Food and Policy Research Institute (IFPRI) published a series of papers titled "Successes in African Agriculture." The papers both reflected and provoked a revolution in thinking about African farming. They also ended a long conspiracy of silence among aid agencies and professional Africanists. For decades the "food mafia," led by the World Food Program and the UN's Food and Agriculture Organization, had refused to acknowledge any good news about African farming out of fear that evidence of bright spots would reduce the flow of charitable donations to the UN's massive "famine" bureaucracy, designed to feed the hungry.

The IFPRI report shattered the convenient consensus among experts, donors, and African governments that farmers south of the Sahara were doomed, perpetual victims who could never feed themselves and hence must permanently proffer the begging bowl. Now, because of IFPRI (itself a junior member of the "mafia"), some African agricultural successes could not be denied. That raised a logical question: If some African farmers can succeed, why can't even more?

The sea change in serious thinking about African farming is now of more than academic interest. In nation after nation, farming is commercially viable, expanding, diversifying, and generating profits at all levels of society. Though doomsayers continue to see a bleak outlook for African farmers (the new specter is climate change), even elites are catching farm fever, recognizing that record prices for many foodstuffs, along with growing domestic markets and the possibility of expanding farm acreage in most African countries, means a brightening future.

Not coincidentally, the World Bank devotes its newest *World Development Report* to the status of agriculture globally, and the authors highlight Africa's recent gains and future potential. What a turnaround. As recently as five years ago, economists at the World Bank were telling me that farm production mattered little since Africans could always import the food they needed. They would explain that Africans should exploit their "comparative advantage" in labor costs by building world-class manufacturing or service industries and allow others, "low-cost producers" elsewhere in the world, to deliver the necessary foodstuffs to African cities.

Today, Africans have a much greater appreciation of the value of food self-sufficiency. Africa never spawned the industries the World Bank favored, and in the face of the withering onslaught from rapidly industrializing China and India, it isn't likely to. Yet Africans are some of the world's lowest-cost producers of food. And the absence of large plantations (except in parts of Kenya, Ivory Coast, and southern Africa) is beneficial. International buyers of major African crops from Europe, Asia, and the United States have told me repeatedly that small farmers

A Wish List for Africa's Farmers

Bigger Cities: Often presented as a bane of African life, urbanization increases the demand for food and helps farmers and local agro-businesses strengthen their links to world markets.

Land and Legal Reform: Vast amounts of African farmland lie fallow or underused. In some countries, such as Kenya, Malawi, and Zambia, land locked up in large plantations created by colonial-era land grabs could be more productively employed if put in the hands of small farmers. But poor people also control a great deal of fallow land. Legal reforms are needed to allow efficient farmers to buy or lease land more easily.

More Technology and Infrastructure: Sub-Saharan Africa has the world's lowest utilization rates for irrigation, fertilizer, and genetically modified crops (which are illegal everywhere except South Africa). The continent lacks canneries, mills, and other ordinary food-processing facilities; even storage facilities are rare. Small improvements could make a big difference.

Better Farm Policy: Even successful agricultural country in the world—from the United States and France to Brazil and China—has relied on government intervention and incentives to assist farmers. Poor though they are, African governments can do much more to help growers—for example, by imposing tariffs on imported food and offering modest subsidies for fertilizer and other farm productivity enhancers.

Agricultural Airpower: For decades, poor or non-existent roads have crippled African farmers. Reformers should be bold. Think planes, not roads. Impossible? Just a dozen years ago, there were virtually no mobile phones in Africa. Today, nearly one in five Africans owns one. Just as the mobile phone by passed the vastly expensive challenge of upgrading dysfunctional African land-line systems, a big push into rural-based aviation, aimed at moving crops from the bush to African cities and beyond, would leapfrog the problem of bad roads.

Globalization: African farm exports have increased, along with farm prices, but the continent's farmers mostly serve local markets. They are still hampered by the trade barriers and farm subsidies in wealthy countries that hurt growers throughout the developing world. Such obstacles should be reduced. Over the longer term, rising worldwide demand for crop-based fuels such as ethanol and Asia's growing appetite for food will benefit African farmers. Because the continent has the world's lowerst growing costs, some food production is likely to migrate there from India and China.

—G. Pascal Zachary

The marriage of capitalism and agriculture is not a panacea for rural Africans. Uganda and Cameroon boast some of the best land in the sub-Saharan region. Many other African countries are doing well enough in farming that they can continue to raise output and incomes rapidly by working smarter, notwithstanding the challenges of climate change and poor soil. Yet a few parts of Africa live up to the nightmarish visions of the pessimists.

Malawi is one of those places. In this poor southern African country, Lorence Nyaka, a postal worker turned farmer, is fighting a losing battle.

On less than an acre of dry and dusty land, Nyaka, who is 51, tries to support his wife, Jesse, and 10 children, growing corn and cassava with only a hoe. Without fertilizers or irrigation, his yields are poor and he's totally dependent on uncertain rains.

Not long before I visited Nyaka, he lost a third of his land to his wife's brother, who had become old enough to collect his share of the family's inherited property. As he explained the situation, Nyaka slashed at a patch behind his house that was barely larger than a pool table. He was preparing furrows for corn seeds that he would plant at the onset of the rains, still months away.

Worse, thanks to disease, Nyaka has more mouths to feed. AIDS took the lives of Jesse's brother and his wife, so their four children now live with the Nyakas. That means less food for their own six children, but to Nyaka his obligation is clear. "If I don't help these children," he says, "they probably die."

In these parts, people are so crowded that there's little space for cattle or other domesticated animals. Nyaka does have six chickens, one of which stays, for safekeeping, in his bedroom.

"Our problem in Malawi is we do work hard, but we don't get enough food," Nyaka says. He and his family subsist on a diet of cassava and a fluffy corn dish called *nsima;* both provide calories but scant protein. There is nothing he can do, he says, to alter his routine except wait for the rains—and pray. His fatalism, however frustrating, is typical of poor farmers in these parts.

In truth, Nyaka's options are limited. Thomas Malthus, the English economist and demographer, is getting his revenge on Lorence Nyaka and hundreds of thousands others in Malawi, the most densely populated country in Africa, where 13 million people jam into a narrow strip of land. Two hundred years ago, Malthus described a world undone by too many people and too little food—a world much like Malawi today, where life expectancy is less than 40 years and food shortages are chronic. With about half its population under the age of 15, Malawi is expected to approach a population of 20 million by 2020.

While much of the world now worries about the effects of plunging birthrates and declining populations, in Africa overpopulation remains the most serious threat to well-being, and perhaps nowhere is the problem worse than in Malawi, a 550-mile-long wedge between much larger Zambia and Mozambique. "The challenge here is to enable the population to survive," says Stephen Carr, a specialist on rural development who has worked in Africa for 50 years.

Few Malawians use birth control, and any coercive action to cap family size is unthinkable. Nyaka says that whether he

in Africa, relying on their own land and family labor and using few costly inputs such as chemical fertilizers, are more efficient producers than plantations. Counterintuitively, Africa's attractiveness to global food buyers is growing precisely because its agriculture is dominated by small farmers. And there are plenty of them.

and his wife have more children "depends on God." Even in the midst of the AIDS pandemic—one in five Malawian adults is HIV positive—condom use is infrequent. Only one in two Malawians can read. The government seems confused, at best, over how to help farmers. "The distribution of the spoils of office takes precedence over the formal functions of the state, severely limiting the ability of public officials to make policies in the general interest," according to a 2006 study from a British think tank.

Carr, who advises the World Bank, says that migration "may be the only way to prevent a Malthusian meltdown." With aid from the World Bank, the Malawian government has started a resettlement scheme, bringing people from the country's overcrowded south to the north, but the effort helps relatively few. Another possibility is to encourage people to leave the country, just as migrants left Germany and Ireland during times of economic hardship. Land is plentiful in neighboring Mozambique, for example, and many people in both countries speak the same indigenous language and share customs. Zambia, another neighbor, needs more farm workers for its fertile land. Mobile Malawians could benefit both countries.

Time and again, of course, human ingenuity has provided an escape hatch, giving the lie to Malthus's central claim that population growth invariably outstrips food production. In Malawi, however, the chances are growing that his grim forecast is right on target.

While much of the world worries about declining birthrates, overpopulation is the most serious threat to Africa's well-being.

Even here, though, there is reason for hope, if only farmers can be roused to do more. Nyaka, for instance, lives within 200 yards of a working well. Water flows all day long. If he carried water to his land, he could bucket-irrigate vegetables during the long dry season. When I ask him why he won't irrigate in this manner, he creases his brow and shakes his head. The possibility is inconceivable.

Yet 30 miles away, outside the old colonial town of Zomba, nestled in the central highlands of Malawi, Philere Nkhoma, an inspired trainer in one of the Millennium Villages demonstration projects masterminded by Columbia University economist Jeffrey Sachs, is showing farmers the benefits of hand-irrigation. On the morning I visit, dozens of men are dripping water on row after row of vegetables in a "garden" the size of a football field. This method of babying high-value crops goes beyond watering. While Nkhoma chews on a piece of sugar cane, men feed spoonfuls of fertilizer to a row of cabbage plants. Nkhoma shouts encouragement to one farmer, addressing him as "brother" and complimenting him on his effort. "One secret of this thing," she says later, "you need to know how to speak to the people. You should make sure you're part of them."

Nkhoma's close involvement with hundreds of small farmers in central Malawi won't grab headlines, but it represents a radical new beginning for farmers, long ignored by the very people paid to help them. Malawi's "agricultural extension service has collapsed," according to a confidential British report. The gap is partly filled by aid projects such as the one that employs Nkhoma, whose own life story mirrors the shift in the status of farming in Africa. She's part of a new generation of urban Africans unafraid of getting their hands dirty. After more than 10 mostly frustrating years as a government farm adviser, she was chosen by a foreign donor to earn a bachelor's degree in agriculture. After graduation she joined the Sachs project, where she has wide latitude to innovate and the resources to carry out plans. "If you have an energetic extension worker, you only need to change the mindset of the people," she says. "When that happens, change can occur very quickly."

Indeed, last fall Malawi posted a record corn crop, far exceeding expectations and eliminating, at least for now, any threat of general famine in the country.

Men and women do not live by bread alone. I am reminded of this cliché on a cool September afternoon in Kampala, where I meet Ken Sakwa inside a fast-food restaurant called Nando's. Sakwa is in the capital alone, having traveled from his village in eastern Uganda in a rickety van. He looks fit, if a bit thinner than I recall him.

As we munch on grilled chicken and french fries, he recounts his latest achievements. In February he leased another piece of land, bringing his total acreage to 12, and he now regularly employs six of his neighbors to help him work his fields. In a sign of his standing in his community, village elders brokered a favorable settlement of his vexing dispute with the brother of a neighbor from whom he had leased land. Managing the resentments of less prosperous farmers in the village remains a burden. Sakwa tells me that lately he has been finding small bottles, stuffed with curious contents, near his house. He ignores them, though he knows they are meant as a form of juju, intended by his neighbors to put a hex on him. To smooth relations, Sakwa now lends money to people in need, but he admits, "I usually don't get paid back."

Sakwa's success is indeed striking. He has saved more than $10,000 out of his farm profits over the prior five years, and he's now constructing a large commercial building along the main road near his village. He plans to rent out about a dozen shops, then sell the building and bank his profits.

While we talk, one of Sakwa's cousins, a younger man who lives in the city, joins us. "My relatives in Kampala think I am rich now," Sakwa says. "But I feel I overwork myself." He normally works from dawn until dusk, and unlike many farmers he never drinks alcohol, sparing himself the expense of buying the local brew from the makeshift village pub.

I ask Sakwa whether he might make an exception today and share a Club beer with me. We have something to celebrate. His wife, Jessica, gave birth to twin daughters a few months before, and I imagine he must be proud. He says nothing. When his cousin steps away to the toilet, Sakwa whispers to me, "The children are sick."

He adds, "I am here to get medicine for them." Oh, no. Earlier, I told a friend of mine that Sakwa was traveling to Kampala for no apparent reason. She is from the same region and ethnic group as Sakwa and guessed that he must need "special" medicine that he is afraid to obtain near his village. I scoffed at her suggestion. I lean toward Sakwa and say softly, "Your newborn babies have AIDS."

Sakwa purses his lips and nods. Suddenly, his loss of weight seems ominous. His eyes look gaunt. "And you?" I ask.

"I tested positive. Jessica also."

I ask Sakwa if I can telephone my friend. She counsels people with the disease, helping them to get services and anti-retroviral drugs, often provided at no charge by foreign donors and the government. The ARVs are indeed remarkable, bringing many years of health to most who take them properly.

An hour later, I sit in an outdoor café with Sakwa and my friend. They immediately begin speaking in Gisu, the language of their ethnic group. "You can still be a successful farmer, even more successful," she tells Sakwa. "So long as you get treatment, you can still farm as well as you do now."

I wonder whether he believes her. She looks him in the eyes and says, this time in English, "Don't let the disease take away your success."

The woman, who is a few years younger than Sakwa, realizes that her sister attended school with him. She promises to help him and Jessica get treatment quickly.

Sakwa thanks us when he leaves. It is night in Kampala now, and I sit in the darkness. The electricity is out, and I clutch my Club beer, sipping at the bottle even though it is empty.

My friend orders me another beer, and a soda for herself. "It is good we can deal with what is," she says.

G. Pascal Zachary teaches journalism at Stanford University and is finishing a book on Africa for Scribner.

UNIT 3
Conflict and Instability

Unit Selections

Key Points to Consider

- What factors account for the worldwide decline in conflict?

- How do failed states threaten security and development?

- What accounts for the increase in violence in Afghanistan?

- What are the regional implications of the Iraq war?

- Why is Somalia the world's most dangerous place?

- What prompted the post-election violence in Kenya?

- Why has drug violence increased in Mexico?

- How has Colombia's rebel insurgency changed over time?

- What are the ways to enhance international peacekeeping?

Student Website
www.mhcls.com

Internet References

The Carter Center
  http://www.cartercenter.org
Center for Strategic and International Studies (CSIS)
  http://www.csis.org/
Conflict Research Consortium
  http://conflict.colorado.edu/
Institute for Security Studies
  http://www.iss.co.za
PeaceNet
  http://www.igc.org/peacenet/
Refugees International
  http://www.refintl.org

While evidence points to a decline in conflict worldwide, conflict and instability in the developing world remain major threats to international peace and security. Conflict stems from a combination of sources including ethnic and religious diversity, nationalism, the struggle for state control, and competition for resources. In some cases, colonial boundaries either encompass diverse groups or separate people from their ethnic kin, creating the circumstances that can lead to conflict. A state's diversity can increase tension among groups competing for scarce resources and opportunities. When some groups benefit or are perceived as enjoying privileges at the expense of others, ethnicity can offer a convenient vehicle for mobilization. Moreover, ethnic politics lends itself to manipulation both by regimes that are seeking to protect privileges, maintain order, or retain power and those that are challenging existing governments. In an atmosphere charged with ethnic and political tension, conflict and instability often arise as groups vie to gain control of the state apparatus in order to extract resources and allocate benefits. While ethnicity has played a role in many conflicts, competition over power and resources may sometimes be mistaken for ethnic warfare. Ethnic diversity and competition for resources combined with other factors, resulted in the war that raged in the Democratic Republic of Congo between 1998 and 2004. This was a prime example of the complex causes of conflicts. The war generated economic disruption, population migration, massive casualties, environmental degradation, and drew several other countries into the fighting. Weak and failing states also contribute to circumstances that give rise to conflict. States with limited capacity are unable to adequately address the poverty and deprivation that often leads to conflict. Failed states also encourage warlord behavior and may also offer a haven for terrorists and criminals. The spill-over from the conflict in these states can cause wider instability.

Early literature on modernization and development speculated that as developing societies progressed from traditional to modern, primary attachments such as ethnicity and religious affiliation would fade and be replaced by new forms of identification. Clearly, however, ethnicity and religion continue to remain potent forces. Ethnic politics and the emergence of religious radicalism demonstrate that such attachments have survived modernization. Inspired and encouraged initially by the establishment of the theocratic regime in Iran, radical Muslims have not only pushed for the establishment of governments based on Islamic law but have also engaged in a wider struggle with what they regard as the threat of western cultural dominance. Radical Islamic groups that advocate a more rigid and violent interpretation of Islam have engaged in high-profile terrorist attacks and continue to pose a threat, especially to the governments of Pakistan and Afghanistan. While these incidents encourage the tendency to equate Islam with terrorism and violence, it is a mistake to link the two. A deeper understanding of the various

© Historicus, Inc.

strands of Islamic thought is required to separate the legitimate challenges to repressive regimes and forge an alternative to western forms of political organization from the actions of radicals who pervert Islam and resort to terrorism.

There is no shortage of conflict around the world, although the causes may differ from region to region. Although United States involvement in Iraq is beginning to wind down, there is still concern that the Iraq war will inspire greater sectarian violence in the region. Meanwhile, the Taliban poses a renewed security threat in Afghanistan as well as an increasingly dangerous threat to the fragile government in Pakistan. The nuclear weapons programs of Iran and North Korea have heightened tensions in the United States and illustrate the growing problem of nuclear proliferation. Parts of Africa continue to be conflict-prone. Somalia remains the world's most prominent example of a failed state, and the chaos in the region has escalated once again. The tenuous peace in the Democratic Republic of Congo has been marred by sporadic fighting in the eastern part of the country. Disputed elections in Kenya unleashed ethnic violence that had been simmering just below the surface. It remains to be seen whether Zimbabwe's power-sharing agreement will halt the country's slide toward economic disaster. The killing in Darfur continues despite the deployment of a UN peacekeeping operation, highlighting the difficulties of effective international intervention. Colombian rebels have branched out into kidnapping and drug running. Accusations of connections between the FARC and Venezuelan president Hugo Chavez have heightened tensions in the region. Drug violence has also emerged as a serious threat to the Mexican government.

Although the number of conflicts may have declined worldwide, the threat to peace and stability in the developing world remains complicated, dangerous, and clearly has the potential to threaten international security.

The End of War?

Explaining 15 years of diminishing violence.

GREGG EASTERBROOK

Daily explosions in Iraq, massacres in Sudan, the Koreas staring at each other through artillery barrels, a Hobbesian war of all against all in eastern Congo—combat plagues human society as it has, perhaps, since our distant forebears realized that a tree limb could be used as a club. But here is something you would never guess from watching the news: War has entered a cycle of decline. Combat in Iraq and in a few other places is an exception to a significant global trend that has gone nearly unnoticed—namely that, for about 15 years, there have been steadily fewer armed conflicts worldwide. In fact, it is possible that a person's chance of dying because of war has, in the last decade or more, become the lowest in human history.

Five years ago, two academics—Monty Marshall, research director at the Center for Global Policy at George Mason University, and Ted Robert Gurr, a professor of government at the University of Maryland—spent months compiling all available data on the frequency and death toll of twentieth-century combat, expecting to find an ever-worsening ledger of blood and destruction. Instead, they found, after the terrible years of World Wars I and II, a global increase in war from the 1960s through the mid-'80s. But this was followed by a steady, nearly uninterrupted decline beginning in 1991. They also found a steady global rise since the mid-'80s in factors that reduce armed conflict—economic prosperity, free elections, stable central governments, better communication, more "peacemaking institutions," and increased international engagement. Marshall and Gurr, along with Deepa Khosla, published their results as a 2001 report, *Peace and Conflict,* for the Center for International Development and Conflict Management at the University of Maryland. At the time, I remember reading that report and thinking, "Wow, this is one of the hottest things I have ever held in my hands." I expected that evidence of a decline in war would trigger a sensation. Instead it received almost no notice.

"After the first report came out, we wanted to brief some United Nations officials, but everyone at the United Nations just laughed at us. They could not believe war was declining, because this went against political expectations,"

Marshall says. Of course, 2001 was the year of September 11. But, despite the battles in Afghanistan, the Philippines, and elsewhere that were ignited by Islamist terrorism and the West's response, a second edition of *Peace and Conflict,* published in 2003, showed the total number of wars and armed conflicts continued to decline. A third edition of the study, published last week, shows that, despite the invasion of Iraq and other outbreaks of fighting, the overall decline of war continues. This even as the global population keeps rising, which might be expected to lead to more war, not less.

In his prescient 1989 book, *Retreat from Doomsday,* Ohio State University political scientist John Mueller, in addition to predicting that the Soviet Union was about to collapse—the Berlin Wall fell just after the book was published—declared that great-nation war had become "obsolete" and might never occur again. One reason the Soviet Union was about to collapse, Mueller wrote, was that its leaders had structured Soviet society around the eighteenth-century assumption of endless great-power fighting, but great-power war had become archaic, and no society with war as its organizing principle can endure any longer. So far, this theory has been right on the money. It is worth noting that the first emerging great power of the new century, China, though prone to making threatening statements about Taiwan, spends relatively little on its military.

Last year Mueller published a follow-up book, *The Remnants of War,* which argues that fighting below the level of great-power conflict—small-state wars, civil wars, ethnic combat, and clashes among private armies—is also waning. *Retreat from Doomsday* and *The Remnants of War* are brilliantly original and urgent books. Combat is not an inevitable result of international discord and human malevolence, Mueller believes. War, rather, is "merely an idea"—and a really bad idea, like dueling or slavery. This bad idea "has been grafted onto human existence" and can be excised. Yes, the end of war has been predicted before, prominently by H.G. Wells in 1915, and horrible bloodshed followed. But could the predictions be right this time?

First, the numbers. The University of Maryland studies find the number of wars and armed conflicts worldwide peaked in 1991 at 51, which may represent the most wars happening simultaneously at any point in history. Since 1991, the number has fallen steadily. There were 26 armed conflicts in 2000 and 25 in 2002, even after the Al Qaeda attack on the United States and the U.S. counterattack against Afghanistan. By 2004, Marshall and Gurr's latest study shows, the number of armed conflicts in the world had declined to 20, even after the invasion of Iraq. All told, there were less than half as many wars in 2004 as there were in 1991.

Marshall and Gurr also have a second ranking, gauging the magnitude of fighting. This section of the report is more subjective. Everyone agrees that the worst moment for human conflict was World War II; but how to rank, say, the current separatist fighting in Indonesia versus, say, the Algerian war of independence is more speculative. Nevertheless, the *Peace and Conflict* studies name 1991 as the peak post-World War II year for totality of global fighting, giving that year a ranking of 179 on a scale that rates the extent and destructiveness of combat. By 2000, in spite of war in the Balkans and genocide in Rwanda, the number had fallen to 97; by 2002 to 81; and, at the end of 2004, it stood at 65. This suggests the extent and intensity of global combat is now less than half what it was 15 years ago.

How can war be in such decline when evening newscasts are filled with images of carnage? One reason fighting seems to be everywhere is that, with the ubiquity of 24-hour cable news and the Internet, we see many more images of conflict than before. A mere decade ago, the rebellion in Eritrea occurred with almost no world notice; the tirelessly globe-trotting Robert Kaplan wrote of meeting with Eritrean rebels who told him they hoped that at least spy satellites were trained on their region so that someone, somewhere, would know of their struggle. Today, fighting in Iraq, Sudan, and other places is elaborately reported on, with a wealth of visual details supplied by minicams and even camera-enabled cell phones. News organizations must prominently report fighting, of course. But the fact that we now see so many visuals of combat and conflict creates the impression that these problems are increasing: Actually, it is the reporting of the problems that is increasing, while the problems themselves are in decline. Television, especially, likes to emphasize war because pictures of fighting, soldiers, and military hardware are inherently more compelling to viewers than images of, say, water-purification projects. Reports of violence and destruction are rarely balanced with reports about the overwhelming majority of the Earth's population not being harmed.

Mueller calculates that about 200 million people were killed in the twentieth century by warfare, other violent conflicts, and government actions associated with war, such as the Holocaust. About twelve billion people lived during that century, meaning that a person of the twentieth century had a 1 to 2 percent chance of dying as the result of international war, ethnic fighting, or government-run genocide. A 1 to 2 percent chance, Mueller notes, is also an American's lifetime chance of dying in an automobile accident. The risk varies depending on where you live and who you are, of course; Mueller notes that, during the twentieth century, Armenians, Cambodians, Jews, kulaks, and some others had a far higher chance of death by war or government persecution than the global average. Yet, with war now in decline, for the moment men and women worldwide stand in more danger from cars and highways than from war and combat. World Health Organization statistics back this: In 2000, for example, 300,000 people died in combat or for war-related reasons (such as disease or malnutrition caused by war), while 1.2 million worldwide died in traffic accidents. That 300,000 people perished because of war in 2000 is a terrible toll, but it represents just .005 percent of those alive in that year.

This low global risk of death from war probably differs greatly from most of the world's past. In prehistory, tribal and small-group violence may have been endemic. Steven LeBlanc, a Harvard University archeologist, asserts in his 2003 book about the human past, *Constant Battles,* that warfare was a steady feature of primordial society. LeBlanc notes that, when the aboriginal societies of New Guinea were first observed by Europeans in the 1930s, one male in four died by violence; traditional New Guinean society was organized around endless tribal combat. Unremitting warfare characterized much of the history of Europe, the Middle East, and other regions; perhaps one-fifth of the German population died during the Thirty Years War, for instance. Now the world is in a period in which less than one ten-thousandth of its population dies from fighting in a year. The sheer number of people who are *not* being harmed by warfare is without precedent.

Next consider a wonderful fact: Global military spending is also in decline. Stated in current dollars, annual global military spending peaked in 1985, at $1.3 trillion, and has been falling since, to slightly over $1 trillion in 2004, according to the Center for Defense Information, a nonpartisan Washington research organization. Since the global population has risen by one-fifth during this period, military spending might have been expected to rise. Instead, relative to population growth, military spending has declined by a full third. In current dollars, the world spent $260 per capita on arms in 1985 and $167 in 2004.

The striking decline in global military spending has also received no attention from the press, which continues to promote the notion of a world staggering under the weight of instruments of destruction. Only a few nations, most prominently the United States, have increased their defense spending in the last decade. Today, the United States accounts for 44 percent of world military spending; if current trends continue, with many nations reducing defense spending while the United States continues to increase such spending as its military is restructured for new global anti-terrorism and peacekeeping roles, it is not out of the question that, in the future, the United States will spend more on arms and soldiers than the rest of the world combined.

Declining global military spending is exactly what one would expect to find if war itself were in decline. The peak year in global military spending came only shortly before the peak year for wars, 1991. There's an obvious chicken-or-egg question, whether military spending has fallen because wars are rarer or whether wars are rarer because military spending has fallen. Either way, both trend lines point in the right direction. This is an extremely favorable development, particularly for the world's poor—the less developing nations squander on arms, the more they can invest in improving daily lives of their citizens.

What is causing war to decline? The most powerful factor must be the end of the cold war, which has both lowered international tensions and withdrawn U.S. and Soviet support from proxy armies in the developing world. Fighting in poor nations is sustained by outside supplies of arms. To be sure, there remain significant stocks of small arms in the developing world—particularly millions of assault rifles. But, with international arms shipments waning and heavy weapons, such as artillery, becoming harder to obtain in many developing nations, factions in developing-world conflicts are more likely to sue for peace. For example, the long, violent conflict in Angola was sustained by a weird mix of Soviet, American, Cuban, and South African arms shipments to a potpourri of factions. When all these nations stopped supplying arms to the Angolan combatants, the leaders of the factions grudgingly came to the conference table.

During the cold war, Marshall notes, it was common for Westerners to say there was peace because no fighting affected the West. Actually, global conflict rose steadily during the cold war, but could be observed only in the developing world. After the cold war ended, many in the West wrung their hands about a supposed outbreak of "disorder" and ethnic hostilities. Actually, both problems went into decline following the cold war, but only then began to be noticed in the West, with confrontation with the Soviet empire no longer an issue.

Another reason for less war is the rise of peacekeeping. The world spends more every year on peacekeeping, and peacekeeping is turning out to be an excellent investment. Many thousands of U.N., NATO, American, and other soldiers and peacekeeping units now walk the streets in troubled parts of the world, at a cost of at least $3 billion annually. Peacekeeping has not been without its problems; peacekeepers have been accused of paying very young girls for sex in Bosnia and Africa, and NATO bears collective shame for refusing support to the Dutch peacekeeping unit that might have prevented the Srebrenica massacre of 1995. But, overall, peacekeeping is working. Dollar for dollar, it is far more effective at preventing fighting than purchasing complex weapons systems. A recent study from the notoriously gloomy RAND Corporation found that most U.N. peacekeeping efforts have been successful.

Peacekeeping is just one way in which the United Nations has made a significant contribution to the decline of war. American commentators love to disparage the organization in that big cereal-box building on the East River, and, of course, the United Nations has manifold faults. Yet we should not lose track of the fact that the global security system envisioned by the U.N. charter appears to be taking effect. Great-power military tensions are at the lowest level in centuries; wealthy nations are increasingly pressured by international diplomacy not to encourage war by client states; and much of the world respects U.N. guidance. Related to this, the rise in "international engagement," or the involvement of the world community in local disputes, increasingly mitigates against war.

The spread of democracy has made another significant contribution to the decline of war. In 1975, only one-third of the world's nations held true multiparty elections; today two-thirds do, and the proportion continues to rise. In the last two decades, some 80 countries have joined the democratic column, while hardly any moved in the opposite direction. Increasingly, developing-world leaders observe the simple fact that the free nations are the strongest and richest ones, and this creates a powerful argument for the expansion of freedom. Theorists at least as far back as Immanuel Kant have posited that democratic societies would be much less likely to make war than other kinds of states. So far, this has proved true: Democracy-against-democracy fighting has been extremely rare. Prosperity and democracy tend to be mutually reinforcing. Now prosperity is rising in most of the world, amplifying the trend toward freedom. As ever-more nations become democracies, ever-less war can be expected, which is exactly what is being observed.

For the great-power nations, the arrival of nuclear deterrence is an obvious factor in the decline of war. The atomic bomb debuted in 1945, and the last great-power fighting, between the United States and China, concluded not long after, in 1953. From 1871 to 1914, Europe enjoyed nearly half a century without war; the current 52-year great-power peace is the longest period without great-power war since the modern state system emerged. Of course, it is possible that nuclear deterrence will backfire and lead to a conflagration beyond imagination in its horrors. But, even at the height of the cold war, the United States and the Soviet Union never seriously contemplated a nuclear exchange. If it didn't happen then, it seems unlikely for the future.

In turn, lack of war among great nations sets an example for the developing world. When the leading nations routinely attacked neighbors or rivals, governments of emerging states dreamed of the day when they, too, could issue orders to armies of conquest. Now that the leading nations rarely use military force—and instead emphasize economic competition—developing countries imitate that model. This makes the global economy more turbulent, but reduces war.

In *The Remnants of War,* Mueller argues that most fighting in the world today happens because many developing nations lack "capable government" that can contain ethnic conflict or prevent terrorist groups, militias, and criminal gangs from operating. Through around 1500, he reminds us, Europe, too, lacked capable government: Criminal gangs and private armies roamed the countryside. As European governments became competent, and as police and courts grew more respected, legitimate government gradually vanquished thug elements from most of European life. Mueller thinks this same progression of events is beginning in much of the developing world. Government and civil institutions in India, for example, are becoming more professional and less corrupt—one reason why that highly populous nation is not falling apart, as so many predicted it would. Interstate war is in substantial decline; if civil wars, ethnic strife, and private army fighting also go into decline, war may be ungrafted from the human experience.

I s it possible to believe that war is declining, owing to the spread of enlightenment? This seems the riskiest claim. Human nature has let us down many times before. Some have argued that militarism as a philosophy was destroyed in World War II, when the states that were utterly dedicated to martial organization and violent conquest were not only beaten but reduced to rubble by free nations that initially wanted no part of the fight. World War II did represent the triumph of freedom over militarism. But memories are short: It is unrealistic to suppose that no nation will ever be seduced by militarism again.

Yet the last half-century has seen an increase in great nations acting in an enlightened manner toward one another. Prior to this period, the losing sides in wars were usually punished; consider the Versailles Treaty, whose punitive terms helped set in motion the Nazi takeover of Germany. After World War II, the victors did not punish Germany and Japan, which made reasonably smooth returns to prosperity and acceptance by the family of nations. Following the end of the cold war, the losers—the former Soviet Union and China—have seen their national conditions improve, if fitfully; their reentry into the family of nations has gone reasonably well and has been encouraged, if not actively aided, by their former adversaries. Not punishing the vanquished should diminish the odds of future war, since there are no generations who suffer from the victor's terms, become bitter, and want vengeance.

Antiwar sentiment is only about a century old in Western culture, and Mueller thinks its rise has not been given sufficient due. As recently as the Civil War in the United States and World War I in Europe, it was common to view war as inevitable and to be fatalistic about the power of government to order men to march to their deaths. A spooky number of thinkers even adulated war as a desirable condition. Kant, who loved democracy, nevertheless wrote that war is "sublime" and that "prolonged peace favors the predominance of a mere commercial spirit, and with it a debasing self-interest, cowardice and effeminacy." Alexis De Tocqueville said that war "enlarges the mind of a people." Igor Stravinsky called war "necessary for human progress." In 1895, Oliver Wendell Holmes Jr. told the graduating class of Harvard that one of the highest expressions of honor was "the faith . . . which leads a soldier to throw away his life in obedience to a blindly accepted duty."

Around the turn of the twentieth century, a counterview arose—that war is usually absurd. One of the bestselling books of late-nineteenth-century Europe, *Lay Down Your Arms!,* was an antiwar novel. Organized draft resistance in the United Kingdom during World War I was a new force in European politics. England slept during the '30s in part because public antiwar sentiment was intense. By the time the U.S. government abolished the draft at the end of the Vietnam War, there was strong feeling in the United States that families would no longer tolerate being compelled to give up their children for war. Today, that feeling has spread even to Russia, such a short time ago a totalitarian, militaristic state. As average family size has decreased across the Western world, families have invested more in each child; this should discourage militarism. Family size has started to decrease in the developing world, too, so the same dynamic may take effect in poor nations.

There is even a chance that the ascent of economics to its pinnacle position in modern life reduces war. Nations interconnected by trade may be less willing to fight each other: If China and the United States ever fought, both nations might see their economies collapse. It is true that, in the decades leading up to World War I, some thought rising trade would prevent war. But today's circumstances are very different from those of the fin de siècle. Before World War I, great powers still maintained the grand illusion that there could be war without general devastation; World Wars I and II were started by governments that thought they could come out ahead by fighting. Today, no major government appears to believe that war is the best path to nationalistic or monetary profit; trade seems much more promising.

The late economist Julian Simon proposed that, in a knowledge-based economy, people and their brainpower are more important than physical resources, and thus the lives of a country's citizens are worth more than any object that might be seized in war. Simon's was a highly optimistic view—he assumed governments are grounded in reason—and yet there is a chance this vision will be realized. Already, most Western nations have achieved a condition in which citizens' lives possess greater economic value than any place or thing an army might gain by combat. As knowledge-based economics spreads throughout the world, physical resources may mean steadily less, while life means steadily more. That's, well, enlightenment.

In his 1993 book, *A History of Warfare,* the military historian John Keegan recognized the early signs that combat and armed conflict had entered a cycle of decline. War "may well be ceasing to commend itself to human beings as a desirable or productive, let alone rational, means of reconciling their discontents," Keegan wrote. Now there are 15 years of positive developments supporting the idea. Fifteen years is not all that long. Many things could still go badly wrong; there could be ghastly surprises in store. But, for the moment, the trends have never been more auspicious: Swords really are being beaten into plowshares and spears into pruning hooks. The world ought to take notice.

Fixing a Broken World

The planet's most wretched places are not always the most dangerous.

In almost any discussion of world affairs, there is one thing on which doves and hawks invariably agree: much more needs to be done to shore up states that are failing, in a state of collapse, or so poor that they are heading in that direction.

For development-minded people, such benighted places are an obvious concern because of their desperate suffering; and for hard-nosed strategists, states that hardly work are places where terrorists could step into the vacuum. Indeed there is a certain convergence between these points of view: aid workers agree that security is essential to prosperity, and generals want economic development to boost security.

In America these days, defence planners say they worry more about weak states, even non-states, than about strong ones. "Ungoverned, undergoverned, misgoverned and contested areas" offer fertile grounds for terrorists and other nefarious groups, says the Pentagon's National Defence Strategy, issued last year. The penning of that document was overseen by the defence secretary, Robert Gates, who will remain in charge of defence policy under Barack Obama. Large chunks of its language could have been issued by bleeding-heart aid agencies or the United Nations: it speaks of the need to "build the capacity of fragile or vulnerable partners" and to address "local and regional conflicts" that exacerbate tensions and encourage drug-smuggling, gun-running and other illegality. To the chagrin of old-school sceptics, nation-building is now an integral part of American strategy.

Similarly, the European Union's declared security strategy sees state failure as an "alarming" phenomenon. It opines that: "Neighbours who are engaged in violent conflict, weak states where organised crime flourishes, dysfunctional societies or exploding population growth on its borders all pose problems for Europe."

A rather precise taxonomy is offered by Robert Cooper, a British diplomat and Eurocrat, in his book, "The Breaking of Nations". He splits the world into three zones: Hobbesian or "pre-modern" regions of chaos; areas ruled effectively by modern nation-states; and zones of "postmodern" co-operation where national sovereignty is being voluntarily dissolved, as in the European Union. In his view, chaos in critical parts of the world must be watched carefully. "It was not the well-organised Persian Empire that brought about the fall of Rome, but the barbarians," he writes.

Strategists have worried about failing states ever since the end of the cold war. At first, zones of war and chaos were seen primarily as threats to the people living within them, or not far away. But since the attacks on America in September 2001 such places have increasingly been seen as a threat to the entire world. Western intervention is now justified in the name of fighting terrorism, not just of altruism.

Take the case of Somalia: America sent troops there in 1992 to help the United Nations stave off a humanitarian catastrophe, but the armed chaos of Mogadishu soon drove it out. In recent years, America has again been active in that region, carrying out air strikes in Somalia against suspected jihadist camps. It supported Ethiopia's military invasion in 2006 to defeat the Islamist militias that had taken power in Mogadishu (arguably causing even more chaos) and is now backing an African peacekeeping mission for the same reasons. The waters off the Somali coast, moreover, have become one of the prime zones of piracy at sea, disrupting shipping through the Suez Canal. Even China has felt the need to send warships to the Gulf of Aden to protect its shipping.

Afghanistan, too, is often seen as a classic example of the perils of collapsing states: acute poverty and years of civil war led to the rise of the Taliban and allowed al-Qaeda to turn into a global menace. After the American-led intervention in 2001, both have rebated themselves across the border in Pakistan's lawless tribal regions, from where they wage a growing insurgency in southern Afghanistan, destabilise Pakistan and plot attacks against Western targets around the world.

Western intelligence agencies say that, with the recent improvement in security in Iraq (a totalitarian state that became a failed state only after the American-led invasion), the world's jihadists now prefer to head for Pakistan, Somalia or Yemen.

Misrule, violence, corruption, forced migration, poverty, illiteracy and disease can all reinforce each other. Conflict may impoverish populations, increase the availability of weapons and debilitate rulers. Weak governments, in turn, are less able to stop corruption and the production and smuggling of arms and drugs, which may in turn help finance warlords, insurgents and terrorists.

Instability breeds instability. The chronic weaknesses of civil institutions in Sierra Leone and Liberia contributed to the outbreak of devastating civil wars in both countries, fuelled by the profits from the illegal smuggling of "blood diamonds". Meanwhile war and genocide in Rwanda contributed to the collapse of the Democratic Republic of Congo in the 1990s. The chaos there, sustained in part by fighting over mineral resources, sucked in Rwanda, Burundi and Uganda. Chad and Sudan support rebels in each other's countries.

At the very least, there is evidence that economic growth in countries next to failing states can be badly damaged. And if a poorly functioning but important oil-producing state like Nigeria were to fall apart, the economic fallout would be global. Moreover, weak governments may lack the wherewithal to identify and contain a pandemic that could spread globally.

That said, the interplay of these factors is hard to describe, and the very definition of failed states and ungoverned spaces is anything but simple. Few states have completely failed, except perhaps for Somalia. And even here, the territory is not completely ungoverned. A part of the country, called Somaliland, is more or less autonomous and stable—and another bit, Puntland, is relatively calm, although it is the source of much piracy. The region to the south is dominated by warring clans, but even here some aspects of normal life, such as mobile telephone networks, manage to survive.

Lesser Breeds before the Law

One starting point in any analysis of failed countries is the theory of Max Weber, the father of social science. He defined the state as the agency which successfully monopolises the legitimate use of force. But what does legitimate mean? In some places, state power is exercised, brutally but effectively, by whoever is top dog in a perpetual contest between kleptocrats or warlords whose behaviour is lawless in every sense.

If definitions are elusive, what about degrees of state failure? Perhaps the most detailed study is the index of state weakness in developing countries drawn up by the Brookings Institution, a think-tank in Washington, DC. This synthesises 20 different indicators and identifies three "failed" states—Somalia, Afghanistan and the Democratic Republic of Congo—along with 24 other "critically weak" ones. One striking feature of such tables is that states fail in different ways. Among the ten worst performers, Iraq is comparatively wealthy and does well in social welfare, but is highly insecure; Zimbabwe is comparatively secure, but ruined economically and politically. The next ten-worst performers are even more mixed.

The collapse of states is as varied as the states themselves. Some were never functioning states at all, just lines drawn on maps by colonisers. Many African borders encompassed lots of ethnic groups and divided some of them. When the colonialists left, so did the bureaucracies that supported these entities, abandoning them to poverty, civil war or both. The cold war helped fuel many conflicts, for instance in Angola and Mozambique, where superpowers backed rival factions. Other parts of Africa, such as Somalia, fell apart after the withdrawal of superpower support.

The conflicts of Central America died down in the years following the end of the cold war. But the fighting in Colombia has dragged on, as the FARC guerrillas finance themselves through drugs and kidnapping. The end of Soviet communism freed or created many countries in Europe. Some prospered as they were absorbed into NATO and the European Union, while others fragmented bloodily, notably Yugoslavia. Enclaves of "frozen conflicts" remain on Russia's periphery—for example Abkhazia, South Ossetia and Transdniestria which survive as unrecognised statelets with the Kremlin's support.

Whichever way state collapse is assessed, it will always be an imperfect measure of priorities for policymakers. On a map of the world using the Brookings index of weak states, the epicentre is self-evidently sub-Saharan Africa, particularly around Congo, with blobs of red in Iraq, Afghanistan and Myanmar. But this overlaps only in part with, say, the ungoverned spaces that America's State Department regards as the nastiest havens for international terrorists, such as al-Qaeda.

On that list, Iraq and Afghanistan figure prominently—but in these countries, arguably, the problem is more one of national insurgencies than international terror. Once the tribes of western Iraq (whose grievances were local) had been induced to switch sides to the Americans, al-Qaeda was quickly evicted from that area. Al-Qaeda's senior leaders are sheltering in Pakistan, yet this ranks as only the 33rd-weakest state on the Brookings index.

One area of concern is the Sahel, a vast semi-arid area south of the Sahara desert. The Americans fear that in this region Islamist terrorists could begin co-operating with existing rebel outfits, such as the Tuareg, or with drug smugglers. The Pentagon has created a new Africa Command to help monitor the area more closely and train local government forces.

The State Department identifies other ungoverned spaces such as Yemen (30th on the Brookings index), parts of Colombia (47th), the seas between the Philippines (58th) and Indonesia (77th), bits of Lebanon (93rd) and the "tri-border area" between Brazil, Argentina and Paraguay (none ranked as particularly weak).

Conversely many of the most wretched places in the world—Congo, Burundi, Zimbabwe, Haiti, Myanmar and North Korea—are not known as havens for international terrorists. Attacks linked to al-Qaeda, moreover, have been conducted in well-run countries such as Britain and Spain. For American counter-terrorism officials, the biggest terrorist threat to the homeland is posed by European radicals who are able to travel to America more freely than, say, a Yemeni. Some scholars worry about social breakdown in poor mega-cities. But to regard the British Midlands and the *banlieues* of Paris as ungoverned spaces would be stretching a point.

The common denominator for al-Qaeda's activity is not state failure, but the fact that attacks are carried out by extremists claiming to act in the name of the world's Muslims. Their safe havens are not necessary geographical but social. Being based in a remote spot, far from government authorities, may be important for training, building *esprit de corps* and, in the view of intelligence agencies, trying to develop chemical and biological weapons.

But for al-Qaeda, remoteness alone is not enough. Terrorists need protection too, and that has to be secured from local populations as in Pakistan's tribal belt. International terrorists, moreover, need to be able to travel, communicate and transfer funds; they need to be within reach of functioning population centres. Stewart Patrick of the Council on Foreign Relations, an American think-tank, argues in a forthcoming book that international terrorists do not find the most failed states particularly attractive; they prefer "weak but moderately functional" states. The shell of state sovereignty protects them from outside intervention, but state weakness gives them space to operate autonomously.

Afghanistan's history is telling. Al-Qaeda was forged from the Arab volunteers who had fought with the Afghan *mujahideen* against the Soviet occupation of the country. With the end of the cold war and the fall of the communist government in Kabul, the country fell into civil war. Arab fighters largely pulled out in dismay.

Some went to Bosnia and Chechnya. Others intensified insurgencies back home in Egypt and Algeria. Osama bin Laden found shelter in Sudan under the protection of its Islamist regime. What took him back to Afghanistan was the rise of the Taliban. Afghanistan at that time was not an ungoverned space, but a state sponsor of terrorism; indeed, al-Qaeda arguably became a terrorist sponsor of a state.

Terrorism aside, what of other global plagues? Afghanistan is still the world's biggest source of the opium poppy, despite the presence of foreign troops. Next is Myanmar, also near the bottom of the pile. But Colombia, though not "critically" weak, is the biggest producer of cocaine. The cocaine routes pass through countries of all sorts; Mexico is among the top performers in the Brookings index, but is the main drugs highway to America. Similarly, piracy depends on geography. A non-existent state may allow pirates to flourish, but without the proximity of a shipping route they have no targets to prey on.

Measures of corruption, such as Transparency International's Corruption Perceptions Index, correlate strongly with the index of state weakness. But here too there are anomalies: Russia is ranked as a middling country in terms of state weakness, but does worse in the corruption index; Italy scores below some African countries.

When it comes to pandemics, there is no simple correlation between disease and dysfunctional states. The countries suffering most from HIV/AIDS are in southern Africa: apart from Zimbabwe, most governments in that region are quite well run. The states that have seen the most cases of the deadly H5N1 strain of bird flu are Indonesia, Vietnam, China and Egypt, none of them among the worst cases of misrule or non-rule.

Everybody agrees that more effective government around the world is desirable, especially for those living in or near broken countries. Failed states always cause misery, but only sometimes are they a global threat. Given that failures come in so many varieties, fixing them is bound to be more of an art than a science.

The Roots of Failure in Afghanistan

Improving the situation in Afghanistan remains as much a political and economic task as a military one.

THOMAS BARFIELD

Afghanistan has once again entered American political consciousness after a long period of neglect. Overshadowed for years by the war in Iraq, Afghanistan drew little press attention when things seemed to be going well, or at least not very badly, after US-led forces toppled the Taliban in 2001. By 2006, however, stability seemed to be slipping away. And by 2008, as the levels of fighting there exceeded the violence in Iraq, Afghanistan had become an issue in America's presidential campaign. While the two candidates agreed that the Bush administration had neglected Afghanistan, and both recommended sending more troops, neither provided an explanation for how initial US success there had been allowed to unravel and what needed to be done to fix the situation—if it could be fixed at all.

Shortly after September 11, 2001, events in Afghanistan had dominated news coverage in the United States, with pundits predicting the necessity of a protracted military campaign if America was to oust the well-entrenched Taliban regime. As the war began in October 2001, Mullah Muhammad Omar, the Taliban leader, played his "graveyard of empires" card, threatening that if the United States dared to enter Afghanistan it would meet the same fate that the Russians and British once suffered.

But the war ended far more quickly and decisively than either side expected. The Afghan Northern Alliance, with the help of American money, weapons, airpower, and a few score Special Operations troops, toppled the Taliban in less than 10 weeks, before regular US troops could even gear up to take part in the fighting. And much to the dismay of Mullah Omar and his ally Osama bin Laden, the Afghan people showed no sign of rising in rebellion against the Americans, even in the heartland of the ethnic Pashtuns, which had been the Taliban's base. Instead, Afghans seemed much more interested in what this new foreign force could do for them to reverse the destruction, abuses, and poverty wrought by a quarter century of war.

The United States and its allies had been expected to establish a robust military presence and, in one of the poorest countries on earth, make a substantial financial commitment to reestablish security and government institutions and to improve economic conditions. After all, the writ of Afghanistan's new central government barely extended beyond Kabul, regional militia commanders remained autonomous, and the country's infrastructure was practically nonexistent. Bin Laden, moreover, was still at large. He was regrouping his battered Al Qaeda in Pakistan's northwestern tribal areas, and Mullah Omar had moved the Taliban's headquarters to Quetta in Pakistani Baluchistan.

Long-term goals, however, quickly ran up against the short-term political reality that was driving US foreign policy in 2002—in particular, the Bush administration's desire to redeploy American assets from Afghanistan in preparation for the war on Saddam Hussein's Iraq that would begin a year later. US resources for Afghanistan were therefore limited, a gap left unfilled by UNAMA (the United Nations Assistance Mission in Afghanistan), which was supposed to coordinate the international community's projects in the country. Efforts in Afghanistan, rather than building a strong foundation for future stability, were deliberately limited to stopgap measures—just enough to keep immediate problems at bay, with the hope that the situation would improve on its own in the future.

But of course, the situation did not improve. Indeed, the deteriorating state of affairs in Afghanistan today can be traced to four factors that undermined attempts to bring long-term stability to the country in 2002. First was the failure to deploy enough troops to ensure security countrywide. Second was the reimposition of a highly centralized state structure that had failed Afghanistan in the past. Third was the failure to grasp the scale of Afghanistan's economic and infrastructure requirements and the political consequences of failing to meet them. And fourth was the assumption that Pakistan would act as an ally in bringing stability to Afghanistan and not retain its covert support for the Taliban.

These deficiencies were augmented by prioritizing process (establishing a constitution and holding elections) over substance (ensuring security, delivering services, and implementing the rule of law). Today the legacies of these failures have left Afghanistan insecure, unstable, and a source of growing alarm in the United States.

Military Shell Games

Following the defeat of the Taliban in late 2001, the United States was determined to maintain only a "light footprint" in Afghanistan. Initially it was so light as to be invisible. During

2002–2003, Washington committed only 7,000 troops to a country that is the size of France and that has a population of more than 30 million people. Most of these troops were tasked with tracking down the remnants of Al Qaeda and the Taliban in the south and east of Afghanistan as part of "Operation Enduring Freedom." The responsibility for securing Kabul, the capital, fell to a separate military command, the UN-mandated International Security Assistance Force (ISAF), initially comprised of 5,000 troops drawn from 40 nations. By comparison, NATO had deployed 54,000 troops to Bosnia in 1996 (a place one-twelfth the size and about one-sixth the population of Afghanistan), and New York City alone has more than 35,000 police officers.

Because the United States initially opposed the expansion of ISAF's mandate beyond Kabul, most regions outside the capital had no international military presence. By the time Washington came around to supporting ISAF expansion in 2003, allied support for sending additional troops to Afghanistan had waned. Countries that might have been willing to make substantial additional commitments in 2002 refused requests do so a year later, in part because the unity of the international coalition in Afghanistan was damaged by a split among the NATO allies over the Iraq War. Afghanistan got the worst of both worlds: The United States and Britain argued that they could send no more troops because of their commitments in Iraq, while France, Germany, and Turkey expressed their displeasure with America's Iraq policy by being less helpful in Afghanistan.

The international troop presence did not substantially increase until the run-up to the Afghan presidential election in October 2004. ISAF numbers doubled to 10,000 and US forces increased to 20,000. Some of this increase was absorbed by the deployment of new "Provincial Reconstruction Teams" designed to provide security for civilian groups and government officials delivering local aid. However, because most of these teams were manned by 60 to 90 soldiers and civilians, and were dispatched to parts of the country that were generally pro-government, their significance was more political than military.

The failure to extend ISAF beyond Kabul in 2002, and the focus by American troops on confronting an Al Qaeda enemy that had largely decamped to Pakistan, created a power vacuum. And because a national Afghan army and police force had not yet been trained (even by 2004 the national army of 9,000 could deploy only 4,500 troops), the new Afghan government lacked the capacity to extend its power much beyond the capital. As a result, former regional military leaders of the old Northern Alliance retained their political importance in the north and west even after their militias were officially demobilized. In the Pashtun east, American forces coped with their limited troop strength (and lack of familiarity with complex tribal divisions) by recruiting local militia allies to assist them. This was an easy short-term solution but highly divisive politically. (In a land where factionalism is rife, an alliance with one group is guaranteed to make an enemy of another, regardless of ideology.)

But at least there was an American presence in the east. In the Pashtun south, excluding a large airbase near Kandahar, the international presence was practically nonexistent before 2006. This allowed the Taliban to regroup unimpeded and to reestablish

themselves in the area from which they first arose. They also established a symbiotic and profitable relationship with influential drug dealers in the Helmand Valley, promising to protect the production and export of opium in exchange for a percentage of the proceeds. Since these profits amounted to billions of dollars, it is estimated that the Taliban take was between $60 million and $100 million annually, far more than the Kabul government had available to support its own administration in the region.

Despite the small number of international troops in Afghanistan, the situation appeared outwardly stable for a number of years. Predictions that the Afghans would surely mount an insurrection against the Americans, as they had against the British (twice) in the nineteenth century and the Soviets in the twentieth, did not materialize because the population viewed this intervention into their affairs as different from previous conflicts. Abuses of power during the civil war that followed the expulsion of the Soviets had so undermined the popularity of Afghan faction leaders (including the Taliban) that, despite Afghanistan's well earned history of xenophobia, foreign forces were seen as providing protection against the country's own discredited leadership. The international forces were accepted as a necessary evil needed to establish the conditions for their own withdrawal: security for Afghanistan's people and a government that could maintain stability on its own. No one was sure how long this would take—but popular support could not be expected to last indefinitely.

Leave It to Kabul

Afghanistan in 2001 was a classic failed state, one in which government institutions existed on paper but not in reality. There had been no national army or police since the civil war began in 1992. And though the country was not in danger of splitting up—its various leaders were seeking not independence but rather the largest share of power they could achieve—Afghanistan's regions had become autonomous. Yet, instead of recognizing these facts and working with them, UNAMA and the United States pushed to reestablish a highly centralized government of the type that had failed repeatedly in the past.

The United States pushed to reestablish a highly centralized government of the type that had failed repeatedly in the past.

Only the Soviets' invasion in 1979 had saved the unpopular regime of the People's Democratic Party of Afghanistan from collapse. During the civil war that followed the dissolution of that party in 1992, Afghanistan reverted to an older pattern of regional autonomy that even the Taliban could do little to change. Yet arriving UNAMA officials saw the lack of a strong centralized state as a symptom of Afghanistan's problems and moved to restore such a state. They used the constitutions of 1923 and 1964, though these documents were written to serve monarchs, as templates for the 2004 constitution. This charter made the government of Hamid Karzai responsible for everything from appointing provincial governors to paying local schoolteachers.

The enthusiasm for restoring a highly centralized government was largely confined to the international community and to the elite in Kabul that would run it. After 25 years of warfare, regions had become autonomous and more cognizant of their own interests. They were less willing to be dictated to by Kabul and wanted a direct choice in how they were to be governed at the local level. The international community saw assertions of such regional autonomy as signs of anarchy that needed to be curbed. Decentralization proponents were viewed as ethnic chauvinists and as supporters of warlords who would bring the country to ruin.

In fact, establishing governmental order and services by region, rather than centrally from Kabul, would likely have proved more effective and given people a larger stake in local administration. It also would have ameliorated some of the risks of a central government failure, since the consequences of such failure would not have been felt nationwide.

Even so, the prospect of state failure was dismissed by those who touted Karzai as a sure bet for success after he steered the country through a constitutional process and after his election as president in 2004. Karzai was skilled at dealing with the international community and he presented a positive face to the world, something Afghanistan badly needed because the government depended so greatly on international aid and military support. He did not, however, generate the same enthusiasm among Afghans, who saw him as a vacillating leader unwilling to confront and overcome enemies.

Karzai, rather than dismissing incompetent or crooked governors, merely transferred them from one province to another when complaints against them mounted. Powerful regional militia commanders such as Abdul Rashid Dostam and Atta Muhammad were left in place in the north, while Herat's Ishmael Khan was brought to Kabul as a cabinet minister. Taliban sympathizers continued to dominate the judiciary, making the task of bringing rule of law to the country all the more difficult. This strategy of appeasing the discredited leadership from the civil war period wedded Afghanistan to its failed past rather than charting a new future. While Karzai remained respected as a person, Afghans more and more saw his administration as corrupt, incompetent, and unable to meet the basic requirements of governance. In a system designed to operate only with firm direction from the top, this was a recipe for disaster.

Ephemeral Aid

Dependence on international aid is nothing new for Afghanistan. Since the mid–nineteenth century, central governments in Afghanistan have relied on foreign subsidies to help them finance their governments, equip their armies, and build infrastructure without taxing their own people. It was control of this revenue stream that gave Kabul-based governments their ability to centralize power through an elaborate system of patronage that rewarded allies and punished opponents. But the situation after 2001 put the Afghan government in a paradoxical position. Although more economic aid was poured into the country than ever before, the vast majority of it was distributed directly by foreign donors for projects that they themselves planned. This practice ended the central government's monopoly over such resources and crippled its ability to rule through patronage. More significantly, the amount of money pledged to Afghanistan, while seemingly large, could not begin to meet either the country's needs or the population's expectations.

Even before its wars began in 1978, Afghanistan had one of the least-educated and poorest populations in the world, with an infrastructure to match. Yet because the administration of George W. Bush had expressed its aversion to "nation building," it cast the American role in Afghanistan as one of "reconstruction." Never was a term a greater misnomer, since bringing the country back to prewar conditions would still leave it at the bottom of any development index. What the Afghans needed was construction and capacity building, not reconstruction to pitiful prewar levels. Yet the major projects planned for Afghanistan hardly began to meet the country's needs. For example, the critical 1,500-mile ring road that first linked the country's regions together in the 1960s was not an impressive divided highway, but a dangerously narrow two-lane road. Restoring it to a prewar condition would barely meet the engineering standards required of a rural farm-to-market road in the United States or Europe. Similarly, only slightly more than 10 percent of Afghanistan had been electrified before 1978—at a time when the population was half that of today.

Bringing the country back to prewar conditions would still leave it at the bottom of any development index.

While other nations may have recognized the need for nation building in Afghanistan, the amount of money available, even if well spent, would have been insufficient to do the job. At first glance this would not seem to be the case: Pledges to Afghanistan amounted to $10 billion in the first three years after 2001, and an additional $14 billion has been pledged to cover the period from 2005 to 2011. These figures are less impressive, however, when compared on a per capita basis to other post-conflict situations. For example, in 2003 international aid per capita in Afghanistan was $50 per person. It had risen to $66 by 2005. This fell well short of post-conflict aid packages elsewhere at the same time, such as Mozambique ($111 per capita) or Serbia and Montenegro ($237 per capita).

Worse, a substantial portion of the aid to Afghanistan was swallowed up by the expenses of providing it. In March 2008 the Agency Coordinating Body for Afghan Relief estimated that, of the $15 billion in reconstruction assistance given to Afghanistan since 2001, "a staggering 40 percent has returned to donor countries in corporate profits and consultant salaries."

The Afghan government, meanwhile, has been treated less as a partner than as a nuisance. Because most projects are handled by foreign contractors or international nongovernmental organizations, 75 percent of aid funds have been disbursed and delivered outside of official Afghan government channels. This has reduced the capacity of Afghans to manage such contracts themselves and has increased the costs devoted to security. While the decision to work around the Afghans rather than through them allowed some large construction projects to be completed more easily (albeit at a much higher cost), it reduced the projects' economic benefits to local communities and failed to provide the job opportunities that returning refugees, in particular, need. It also divorced the reconstruction process from the political process, reducing a source of positive patronage that could demonstrate results to local populations.

One way this lack of opportunity showed itself is in the spectacular rise of the opium economy. The export value of the 2007 opium harvest was estimated at $4 billion—more than a third of Afghanistan's gross domestic product. The opium economy funds widespread corruption of government institutions, finances antigovernment militias, and has made the substitution of alternative crops extremely difficult.

The overall mismatch between the large amounts of money spent and the minimal payoff in local employment has exacted a high political price. Rural Afghans, the country's majority, have complained that their needs are being ignored by decision makers in Kabul and abroad. This situation is hardly unique to Afghanistan, of course. But policy failures in Afghanistan, unlike in some other such places, would have international repercussions.

The Worm in the Apple

The Taliban regime was so unpopular with its northern and western neighbors that when the United States sought these neighbors' cooperation to bring down the Taliban in 2001, they proved unusually cooperative. With the exception of Turkmenistan, the Central Asian states allowed the Americans and their allies to deploy troops, open air bases, and route supplies through their countries. Normally hostile Iran also gave its tacit approval to the US invasion and expressed its desire to support a new Afghan government.

The Pakistanis, however, did not follow suit. The Taliban were largely their creation, and they were loath to abandon their clients now that the Taliban seemed on the verge of defeating their Northern Alliance enemies completely. Such a victory would have achieved Pakistan's long-sought goal of dominating Afghanistan as a client state. The Pakistani military in particular saw control of Afghanistan as a way to provide "strategic depth" in its long-running conflict with India.

Of course President Pervez Musharraf decided he could not risk the integrity of his country when presented with an ultimatum to either end support for the Taliban or face destruction along with them. It was a bitter pill—sweetened by an offer of $10 billion in aid. In reality, however, Pakistan never dropped its support for the Taliban and indeed provided refuge for them.

Pakistani calculations assumed that the United States would eventually leave the region, allowing the Taliban to return and retake power. Therefore, although some Al Qaeda members were captured inside Pakistan, Musharraf's government turned a blind eye to Mullah Omar's operations in Baluchistan and claimed to be unable to control the border with Afghanistan in the Northwest Frontier Province. Pakistan also allowed the Taliban to open training camps and to recruit new troops from Pakistan's radical Islamist schools, institutions Musharraf had falsely promised the Americans that he would close.

In spite of press reports and Afghan government complaints about the growing strength of Taliban forces in Pakistan, Washington declared Pakistan a "major non-NATO ally" in 2004, giving it access to higher quality military aid. Pakistan may have taken this as a signal that the United States was not really serious about preserving Afghanistan as an independent state. Whatever the reasons, the failure to get Pakistan to stop its covert support of radical Islamist groups undermined Afghanistan's stability. The significance of this problem would become clearer two years later when the Taliban began a new offensive in Afghanistan, using Pakistan as both their base of operations and as a sanctuary from retaliation.

Mission Unaccomplished

The goodwill and enthusiasm that the Afghan people displayed between the expulsion of the Taliban in 2002 and the presidential elections of 2004 declined sharply after the elections were over. Universal complaints of governmental malfeasance, corruption, and abuses of power steadily reduced confidence in the Karzai administration in the absence of any serious steps to curb the abuses. And this coincided with a growing dissatisfaction over the slow pace of the country's economic development. Afghans, perhaps unrealistically, had expected that the billions of dollars pledged to develop their country would quickly translate into a better standard of living and higher rates of employment. Yet, as the years passed, few improvements reached the rural areas where most Afghans live. Even the more favored residents of Kabul complained that the government appeared incapable of providing such necessities as electricity, drinking water, and transport.

More ominously, security slowly deteriorated, especially on the border with Pakistan, where suicide bombers began for the first time in Afghanistan to operate. According to a UN report, travel safety between 2006 and 2007 declined sharply in large areas of the country, particularly in the south in Kandahar and Helmand, and in the eastern provinces of Paktika, Nangarhar, and Kunar.

Even so, as 2006 began, international newspaper readers could be forgiven for thinking that Afghanistan really represented a "mission accomplished." Despite the problems outlined above, levels of violence still remained relatively low and no big problems appeared to be on the horizon. The Bush administration was so confident of the situation in Afghanistan that it reduced its budgeted aid request from $4.3 billion in fiscal 2005 to $3.1 billion in fiscal 2006. US Secretary of Defense Donald Rumsfeld signed an order in December 2005 to reduce American troop numbers by about 3,000 for the coming year, although a larger NATO force would replace them. The new NATO command would take responsibility over all of Afghanistan except for the east, where the Americans retained direct control.

This rosy scenario wilted as the spring sun melted the winter snows. In May 2006 a riot sparked by a deadly traffic accident involving American troops and local Afghans engulfed Kabul. The rapid spread of the unrest, an ineffective response by the police, and the antigovernment character of the protest demonstrated both the danger of complacency and the declining popularity of Karzai even in normally pro-government Kabul.

Later in the summer, as British and Canadian troops were deployed to Helmand and Kandahar, they confronted a well-armed and full-blown insurgency led by the reinvigorated Taliban. Though the Western forces expected to meet some opposition, their plans and training had focused on providing a peacekeeping shield that would facilitate the introduction of new economic development projects, not on combat. Instead the Western troops experienced the fiercest fighting in Afghanistan since 2001. NATO forces inflicted severe casualties on the Taliban, many of whom retreated back to Pakistan, but troop levels were too low to expel the rebels permanently from the region. Meanwhile, eastern Afghanistan experienced a sharp rise in cross-border attacks from Pakistan's autonomous tribal territories, where Al Qaeda and Taliban forces were becoming dominant.

As 2006 ended, it was clear that levels of violence had spiked: Between 2005 and 2006 suicide bombings increased by more than 400 percent (from 27 to 139), the use of improvised explosive devices more than doubled (from 783 to 1,677), and armed attacks nearly tripled (from 1,558 to 4,542). How could America's "good war" have gotten so badly off track? How could the discredited Taliban have gained the capacity to mount an insurgency among people who had failed to raise a hand to defend them in 2001?

How could America's "good war" have gotten so badly off track?

The explanation lies in defective policies that were never corrected in response to a changing situation. No one policy was so flawed that it alone caused the crisis, but in combination they produced a situation that was difficult to turn around. Turning to the south in 2006, for example, we can see how various policy defects intertwined. The absence of any earlier economic development had left the region dependent on the illicit opium economy. The absence of an international military presence had allowed the Taliban, unimpeded for at least two years, to regroup in an area they knew well. The inability of the Afghan government to provide services and local security or to establish the rule of law reinvigorated local warlords, who exploited public discontent with officials dispatched from Kabul. And while these conditions also existed in other parts of Afghanistan, they only erupted into open warfare in places that had access to Pakistani support and bases. The reaction of the Pakistani government to charges that it was backing an insurgency was worthy of Claude Rains in the film *Casablanca:* shocked, shocked to hear that anyone might think there were armed Taliban using their territory to attack Afghanistan!

The Taliban offensive was premised on the assumption that NATO troops were simply covering for an American departure

from Afghanistan, which they believed Rumsfeld's troop-cut announcement presaged. Believing NATO would be a less committed foe than the Americans, the Taliban were willing to risk fighting conventional battles with the expectation that they could take Kandahar when NATO withdrew. But in fact the Americans increased their troop commitment and, despite disputes among the allies over their willingness to deploy troops into combat zones, NATO did not withdraw from Afghanistan. Troop deployments into the south increased, putting the Taliban on the defensive (but not defeating them).

By 2008 the United States had 33,000 troops in the country, including 13,000 as part of the 47,000-member NATO force. The NATO commander for Afghanistan, General David McKiernan, has requested as many as 15,000 more US troops. Planned levels for the Afghan National Army have increased to 134,000 soldiers from 75,000, and training of the long-neglected national police force (which takes the brunt of casualties in rural areas) has finally began in earnest. These steps have not, however, stopped the spread of insecurity to larger parts of the country. As the generals have been the first to point out, improving the situation in Afghanistan remains as much a political and economic task as a military one, perhaps more so.

The Tipping Point

Afghanistan today is at a tipping point. The legitimacy of the Kabul government, along with its international backers, has been challenged, but its enemies have been unable to incite a national insurrection against it. This has led most ordinary Afghans to stay on the fence politically, waiting to see which side will prevail. Since popular perception of success or failure creates its own reality in Afghanistan, such uncertainty engenders volatility. Small policy changes or unexpected events can have disproportionate impacts, both positive and negative. And 2009 can be counted on to produce both policy changes and unexpected events.

The Obama administration will be revising US military and political strategy for Afghanistan. The planned presidential election in Afghanistan could produce greater stability or disaster, depending on how Afghans view the process. The crisis in Pakistan and its relationship to both the United States and Afghanistan will reach a critical juncture. Looking further ahead, the question will be whether Afghanistan can escape the instability that began with the Soviet invasion in 1979 or be drawn back into it.

The United States is already geared up to address many of the underlying problems created in 2001. Current plans call for US troop strength to increase by 15,000 in 2009 to take primary responsibility for fighting the Taliban under a single command structure. Other NATO forces will then have the option of redeploying to areas where little combat is expected. The delivery of more effective economic aid will also have a higher priority, though it will have a political impact only to the extent that it improves the lives of ordinary Afghans. Infrastructure such as roads, electric grids, natural gas supplies, waterworks, and sewage plants are not exciting to people who already have them, but the vast majority of Afghans live without any such services.

The United States must also come to grips with a failed drug policy that has permitted Afghanistan to become the world's largest producer of opium. New options on the table will include targeting traffickers and corrupt officials rather than farmers, possible legalized production under license (as in Turkey and India), and more realistic plans to create alternative livelihoods for Afghanistan's farmers.

Overhauling a failed Afghan government will prove a greater challenge. The United States and UNAMA never gave serious attention to making the government work and ignored its inefficiencies and its increasing corruption. It is now clear that the state's deficiencies and dependence on foreign support have undermined Afghanistan's fragile stability. But plans to improve the Afghan army and police, which can be implemented with money and more effort, are simple when compared to reforming the civilian administration. Government officials remain poorly trained, poorly paid, and unaccountable to the people they govern. Those in Kabul whose positions depend on maintaining such a dysfunctional system will resist any policies that devolve more political power to communities and regions, the only practical strategy for a country as diverse as Afghanistan.

The presidential election scheduled for 2009 presents Afghanistan with high risks and three possible outcomes. Because the government is unpopular and there is fighting in the Pashtun regions that are Karzai's political base of support, many Afghans believe he will not risk a free election. One tactic would be to cancel the vote in favor of another national *loya jirga* (a grand assembly) that would renew Karzai's mandate without an election. Another tactic might be to remove all credible rivals from the ballot or, failing that, rig the balloting. Any of these outcomes would undermine Karzai's already weakened legitimacy and put Afghanistan's international backers in a difficult position.

A second scenario is a free-for-all election in which so many candidates run that a second-round vote produces a non-Pashtun president, upending Afghan politics in an unpredictable manner. A third, and more hopeful, possibility is that a stronger leader emerges to challenge Karzai by putting together a powerful coalition that serves as a more popular broad-based government when elected. No matter what occurs, most Afghans are convinced that the Americans will call the shots and must therefore bear the responsibility for the result.

Ultimately, if Afghanistan has any hope of regaining stability it must break from the isolation it has endured for more than 120 years. For much of Afghanistan's history, its autocratic rulers saw economic development as a danger rather than an opportunity. This left the country rich in unexploited resources while its people lived in poverty. It also meant that none of its neighbors had any vested economic interests there. Finally, this has begun to change, with projects—encompassing roads, electricity, minerals, and natural gas—that could fundamentally alter Afghanistan's economy and its international relationships.

In September 2008 India completed a 135-mile road connecting Afghanistan's Nimroz province to the Iranian port of Chahbahar, as part of a larger $1.1 billion reconstruction project. Tajikistan and Kyrgyzstan in August agreed to export 1,000 megawatts of electricity through Afghanistan to Pakistan. In May China signed a $3 billion agreement for a 30-year lease to develop Afghanistan's biggest untapped copper deposit, valued at an estimated $88 billion. And plans for a $2 billion Turkmenistan-Afghanistan-Pakistan-India natural gas pipeline were revived in April 2008 when India agreed to join the consortium and share the gas equally with Pakistan.

None of these projects can bring peace to Afghanistan, and without peace they will not succeed. But the roads are already in place, electric lines are being built, and China's determination to develop resources in regions where Western investors are unwilling to risk their capital is well known. None of these projects is being constructed out of charity to the Afghans, but all have the capacity to change everyday lives for a majority of the population. They present the possibility of a payoff for investments in Afghanistan's security. Managing the current crisis should therefore not be treated as an end in itself but must have broader goals. Afghans who have experienced 30 years of war and unrest are all too aware that they would be the first victims of failure.

THOMAS BARFIELD is a professor of anthropology and director of the Institute for the Study of *Muslim Societies and Civilizations* at Boston University.

Pakistan's Perilous Voyage

Turbulence that results from competition among . . . rival centers of power might well propel the nation toward shipwreck. . . .

Farzana Shaikh

The political disarray that has characterized Pakistan since civilian rule was restored this spring brings to mind a bitterly funny passage in *A Case of Exploding Mangoes,* a recently published novel by the Pakistani journalist Mohammad Hanif. In the book, the country's devout military dictator from the 1980s, General Mohammad Zia ul-Haq, known for his contempt for politicians, rises from a prayer mat, wraps his silk dressing gown around his bulging belly, and declares it "the only civilian part of my body and hence out of control."

An out-of-control belly may merit a giggle, but the prospect of an out-of-control Pakistan (which also happens to be a nuclear power) rings alarm bells across Western capitals. And indeed, good reason for alarm may exist. A devastating bomb attack on the Marriott Hotel in Islamabad in September was said to be in retaliation for Pakistan's participation in the US-led war on terror, a war that includes American military incursions against Al Qaeda and Taliban bases inside the country. The attack suggests a dangerous tipping point could be imminent.

The devastating bomb attack on the Marriott Hotel suggests that a dangerous tipping point could be imminent.

Meanwhile, there is no end in sight to the Islamist militancy that engulfs the country's tribal and northwestern regions. A constitutional crisis concerning the reinstatement of judges sacked last November by then-President Pervez Musharraf grows ever more acute. And the economy is in tatters. Inflation is running above 25 percent, its highest level in 30 years, and the rupee is trading at a 10-year low against the dollar. Economic growth, which has averaged 6 percent annually since 2001, is expected to decline to 4.5 percent this year. Food and fuel shortages have reached critical levels, triggering riots in some urban centers. Pakistan's precarious credit rating has both discouraged foreign investment and thwarted the government's efforts to shore up fast-dwindling central bank reserves.

For all these reasons, the nation seems a vessel adrift, in danger of capsizing. Granted, it is not a rudderless ship, nor one without a captain. It is rather a ship under the command of too many captains—all working at cross-purposes and rarely, if ever, accountable to the hapless passengers. In fact, the common image of Pakistan as a state torn between two principal centers of power (the country's military and its civilian rulers) or between two opposing ideologies (the religious and the secular) is no longer very apt.

Instead, what has become clear since general elections in February 2008 is that multiple centers of power, with rival claims to power, now threaten to reconfigure traditional alliances.

The main centers of power today number six, beginning with the recently elected president, Asif Ali Zardari of the Pakistan People's Party (PPP). Zardari controls the government through extraordinary constitutional powers vested in his office, including the right to dismiss ministers and dissolve the parliament. A second center of power is former Prime Minister Nawaz Sharif of the Pakistan Muslim League-Nawaz (PML-N), whose base is Punjab—the country's most powerful province. A third is the so-called "neo-Taliban" or "Pakistani Taliban," spread across the country's tribal regions; they owe broad allegiance to the tribal militant leader Baitullah Mehsud.

A fourth power center is the legal fraternity, which is pursuing a course of civil disobedience intended to force the restoration of senior judges who were summarily dismissed by former President Musharraf. A fifth is the United States, whose proxies (it is said) still haunt the corridors of power. And finally there is the Pakistani army, along with its intelligence services, whose dark, sphinx-like approach to national security is the stuff of legend. The army may yet regain control of the country that it lost this year when General Musharraf's party lost the February elections and Musharraf himself had to resign the presidency in August to avoid impeachment charges.

Lagging far behind in power is an uneasy parliamentary coalition under the nominal control of Prime Minister Yusuf Raza Gilani. His powers have been so comprehensively ceded to Zardari that some say Gilani does not even qualify as the "mayor of Islamabad." (Even Afghan President Hamid Karzai can claim to be the de facto "mayor of Kabul.")

The problem is this: The turbulence that results from competition among these rival centers of power might well propel the nation toward shipwreck, an event that would carry devastating consequences for both Pakistanis and the international community.

A glaring imbalance between elected and un-elected power centers is no surprise to historians of Pakistan. They are well familiar with Pakistan's traditional consolidation of executive authority in the state instead of in popular institutions—as well as with the power of popular protest to force change in a system notoriously resistant to it. Many observers would also acknowledge, however, that this embedded dysfunctionality has resurfaced with unusual speed since the general elections. This perhaps suggests that fundamental political changes are at work today, trends whose long-term consequences could significantly alter the complexion of the state.

The Missing Middle

One such trend is the disappearance of the so-called "moderate middle," which in the past has been relied on to help bridge the divide between the policy preferences of the West, especially the United States, and those of the Pakistani electorate. The steady erosion of this moderate constituency has taken a heavy toll on governance and has all but ruined the chances of forming a coordinated policy to tackle militancy in Pakistan's tribal areas. It has also nearly ruined any chances of easing resentment against the United States, resentment that is only fueled by fears of a US-led invasion to smash Al Qaeda bases inside the country.

The erosion of moderation has been most noticeable in the strains within the coalition government that has been dominated by the PPP and its erstwhile partner, the PML-N. The two parties had agreed in March to enter into a coalition on the basis of an understanding that was said to involve the reinstatement of all judges sacked by Musharraf. But given the two parties' long history of rivalry, sharpened in the context of Pakistan's peculiar tradition of zero-sum-game politics, it is not surprising that before long they were locking horns. In May 2008, the coalition teetered after Sharif decided to withdraw his ministers from the government in protest of the PPP's failure to honor the agreement on reinstating the judges. Sharif, though he kept his party within the coalition, in June further distanced himself from his partners when he joined a week-long demonstration in which lawyers called for the immediate restoration of the sacked judges.

The two main coalition partners came together in early August to force Musharraf's resignation, but their entrenched differences resurfaced within days. Ominously, their divisions had now widened from disagreements over the reinstatement of the judges to recrimination over Zardari's decision to run for president in violation of a document, called the Charter of Democracy, that both parties signed in 2006. This agreement had committed them to fully restore the 1973 constitution, which provided for a "nonpartisan" president stripped of powers to dissolve the parliament and dismiss the government. Zardari's nomination while still in command of his party and his apparent reluctance to curb the extraordinary powers that Musharraf

had vested in the presidency, it was claimed, constituted a major breach of the Charter. The final rupture between the two parties and the collapse of the coalition came in late August.

These partisan differences, though couched in the language of politics and principles, masked rival personal agendas of the sort that have long defined party politics in Pakistan. Zardari and Sharif both regard their organizations as instruments for the promotion of private ends rather than as engines of public policy. In Zardari's case, the private ends amount to his personal campaign to resist a legal challenge mounted by the deposed judges to an amnesty that Zardari received for corruption charges. This grant of amnesty had made possible the return to the country in 2007 of former Prime Minister Benazir Bhutto and Zardari, her husband. (In exchange, they had pledged their party's support for Musharraf as a civilian president.)

> **Zardari and Sharif both regard their organizations as instruments for the promotion of private ends.**

For Sharif, who was ousted by Musharraf in a coup in 1999 and then banished to ignominious exile in Saudi Arabia, the private ends have involved cultivating judges prepared to invalidate a constitutional ban on his seeking the post of prime minister for a third time. Both Zardari and Sharif have avoided laborious consensus building—a process unfamiliar in Pakistan, where politics is typically shaped by conflict rather than compromise.

Also uncommon in Pakistani politics is the voluntary surrender of power—a practice that many unrealistically expected Musharraf to observe after his faction of the Pakistan Muslim League, the PML-Q, was soundly defeated in the February general elections. Although, during the run-up to the elections, Musharraf was briefly seduced by the idea of cultivating a political constituency through the PML-Q, he never lost sight of the fact that political power in Pakistan has historically flowed not from the electorate but from the army.

In a revealing speech in Karachi just weeks before his resignation in August, Musharraf sought to dispel rumors of his imminent political demise by declaring that his "last day" would be the day he lost the support of the army. He added that he did not think "the army [would] ditch me" or "leave me on my own." Coming just days after US Assistant Secretary of State Richard Boucher had in Islamabad publicly scolded Pakistan's politicians for their misplaced priorities in trying to displace Musharraf, the president's statement affirmed the long-established view that as long as regimes, especially military regimes, enjoy the support of the United States, their survival is assured.

Musharraf clearly understood the linkage: At a time of speculation about a breakdown in trust between the United States and the Pakistani army over whether Pakistani forces could wage an effective campaign against tribal militants allied to Al Qaeda and the Taliban, Musharraf tried hard to bank on the claim that, as one who enjoyed the confidence of both Washington and his country's army, he was best placed to salvage this vital relationship.

Musharraf's decision finally to step down, though loudly proclaimed by his political opponents as "a victory for the people," was in fact widely recognized as proof that the exercise of power in Pakistan remains closely tied to support from the army and from the country's foreign benefactor—the United States. The general had lost the support of both.

The exercise of power in Pakistan remains closely tied to support from the army and the United States.

Nation for Hire

Musharraf's resignation was also evidence of a larger truth that has long unsettled the politics of Pakistan—its status as a rentier state. Political scientists generally use the term "rentier state" to describe states that finance more than 40 percent of their expenditures through "revenue accruing directly from abroad." Recently, the term has also come to refer to any state that hires out its services to the highest bidder. Pakistan qualifies neatly on both counts.

Economists have repeatedly drawn attention to the country's heavy dependence on external capital flows, especially from the United States, and have shown that such flows reached their highest levels in the 1960s, the 1980s, and from 2001 onward—times when the United States called on Pakistan's services as a close ally. All three periods coincided with times of military rule, during which high growth was achieved but little investment was made in key social sectors like education and health.

Instead, the three periods saw a significant expansion in Pakistan's defense arsenal—a fact confirmed by recent US congressional reports showing that the bulk of an estimated $12 billion in US aid received by Pakistan since September 2001 has gone to service the needs of the military establishment, especially the army. It is as the beneficiary of this American largesse that the Pakistani military has been expected to deliver certain services as an ally in the US-led war on terror.

Heading the list of the army's obligations has been the elimination of the Taliban and Al Qaeda forces that took refuge in Pakistan's tribal areas after being forced to flee Afghanistan during the US military attack in 2001. However, Washington clearly did not appreciate at that time (distracted as it was by its plans to invade Iraq) that the Pakistani army's role as subcontractor would be compromised by the political ambitions of Musharraf, then the military commander in chief. President Musharraf, running with the hare and hunting with hounds, had already sealed a bargain with the parties of the Islamic religious right, parties that served as mentors and protectors of the Taliban.

This bargain involved resurrecting an "unholy alliance" (first forged in the late 1970s, but with roots that go deeper) between Pakistan's military and the country's clerical establishment. Its terms rested on farming out to religious parties (and their assorted militant subsidiaries) the business of pacifying the tribal areas—in exchange for the religious parties' help in limiting any challenges to the military's right to rule mounted by the so-called "democratic opposition," represented mainly by the PPP.

Initially, there seemed little reason to doubt that the bargain would succeed, since it appeared nicely to meet the needs of all parties. The United States was guaranteed a regular haul of high-value Al Qaeda suspects. The army could count on US largesse as a reward for its endeavors. The religious parties could look forward to entering the political mainstream after years of losing out on the electoral front. And Musharraf, of course, gained time to consolidate his grip on power.

Judge Not

So what disturbed this cozy equilibrium? It was challenged mainly by the expansion of two competing centers of power whose iconic symbols—the mosque and the judge—have in recent months served as reminders of the struggle between the religious and liberal forces that have been embedded in the heart of Pakistan since the establishment of the state. I refer, on one hand, to the consolidation of a powerful and increasingly autonomous militant front which, from its base in the tribal areas of the northwest, seeks to extend Islamic law to the rest of Pakistan; and, on the other, to the emergence of a strident lawyers' movement that is determined to establish the supremacy of constitutional law as shaped by modern democratic institutions. While the two sides may seem to represent two aspects of Pakistan's as-yet-unresolved national identity, the energy now animating both flows directly from decisions Musharraf made in order to shore up his questionable legitimacy.

After reneging on a promise he made in 2004 to stay on as president but give up his role as army chief, Musharraf found his support waning among religious parties. They held him responsible for violating the terms of the informal agreement whereby they, and not the military forces now deployed by the thousands in tribal areas, were to be responsible for pacifying militants concentrated in these areas. Attempts to calm the Islamist opposition during peace talks in 2005 and 2006 proved futile. And Musharraf was forced to make concessions that significantly eroded his regime's authority in the tribal areas and threatened even to challenge its writ in the country's capital, Islamabad.

Islamist militants, most with close links to the tribal and northern regions of North-West Frontier Province, were galvanized into action in July 2007 during a conflict centered around the famous Red Mosque in Islamabad. The mosque had a long-established reputation as a hotbed of Islamic radicalism; its leaders had openly called for President Musharraf's assassination, and had endorsed a series of vigilante actions in the name of Islam against "centers of vice" in the capital. A standoff with security forces ensued, ending in a bloody assault. The incident made the mosque a potent symbol of a movement that remained intent on establishing an Islamic purpose for the state.

A challenge from another direction came in the form of the lawyers' movement. It had begun in March 2007 in a protest against Musharraf's summary dismissal of the country's chief justice on charges of corruption—charges that were overturned by a judicial council four months later. It was after Musharraf decided in December of 2007 to impose emergency rule that this lawyers' revolt was transformed into something resembling a mass civil disobedience movement. Musharraf responded by dismissing 60 more judges, including Chief Justice Iftikhar

Muhammad Chaudhry again (after the judiciary had reinstated him), and packing the courts with judges of his own choosing. His actions fueled further outrage, timed as they were in anticipation of a Supreme Court judgment that was expected to prevent Musharraf from seeking reelection.

At a stroke Musharraf forfeited whatever goodwill he still enjoyed among the liberal middle classes. They had looked to him in 1999 to restore the rule of law (which had been undermined, paradoxically, by Sharif, who as prime minister was engaged in a protracted confrontation with the judiciary). The middle classes also looked to Musharraf to return the country to its original course, which they understood as democracy grounded in constitutional principles. Musharraf underestimated the power that can be exerted by a society in the throes of a minor "civil society revolution"—one led by an increasingly defiant media. It was not long before this grievous miscalculation helped make the chief justice a powerful symbol for those who saw themselves as the rightful heirs of the democratic state envisaged by Pakistan's founder, Muhammad Ali Jinnah.

Washington watched these battles with mounting consternation. Having invested heavily in securing Pakistan's participation in the so-called war on terror, the administration of George W. Bush was not about to get sidetracked by the question of who owned Pakistan. However, the United States could no longer avoid the question of who in Pakistan owned the war on terror. For it was clear that if this war was to succeed, it had to be backed by a popular mandate.

The Murder of Hope

This is where former Prime Minister Bhutto came in. Her return to Pakistan from exile in October of last year (after months of intricate political wrangling overseen by the United States) was meant both to paper over the cracks that were developing in Pakistani politics and to bridge the yawning gap between US and Pakistani perceptions of the conflict with Islamist militants. The carefully orchestrated plan underpinning her return called for the pro-Western Bhutto to serve as prime minister alongside Musharraf as a civilian president—though only after he was reelected while still in command of the army.

Bhutto's liberal political credentials, it was hoped, would also calm the enraged legal fraternity that was clamoring for an independent judiciary. And her cooperation with the pro-Musharraf PML-Q, whose senior leaders enjoyed close relations with segments of the religious right, was expected to lull at least some of the Islamists into believing that they exercised influence. Holding it all together was a power sharing agreement sanctioned by the United States. It obliged Musharraf to issue a presidential ordinance (the now famous National Reconciliation Ordinance) that froze all corruption charges against Bhutto, allowing her to return home without fear of arrest, in exchange for her supporting Musharraf as a civilian president.

With Bhutto and Musharraf thus beholden to the United States and with each in command of resources vital to the United States—respectively, genuine popular support and control of the army—Washington could be forgiven for thinking

that it was finally in a position to steer Pakistan toward its own objectives.

Fate was to decide otherwise. Bhutto's assassination, during a campaign stop in Rawalpindi in December 2007, threw America's carefully laid plans to the wind. Then, as if to compound the disarray, into the confusion stepped the United States' least preferred option as leader of Pakistan: former Prime Minister Sharif. His return to the country from exile ahead of the February general elections was arranged at the insistence of the Saudis, whose importance in Pakistan as a powerful eminence grise is best judged by the fact that even the United States was unwilling to cross them—notwithstanding the threat to US interests posed by Sharif's return.

Sharif intended to claim the mantle previously held by Bhutto, but strictly on his own terms. That he could soon be in position to set those terms became clear immediately after the February 2008 elections, when his party finished in a strong second place behind the PPP. The PML-N also swept the board in Punjab—the country's wealthiest and most populous province—making the party's support vital to the stability of any government.

Sharif, free from any obvious political debt to the United States, moved to define the parameters of his mandate. His priorities centered overwhelmingly on Musharraf, whom Sharif accused of compromising the sovereignty of Pakistan by forcing it into an alliance with the United States and of violating the country's constitution by undermining an independent judiciary.

To Bed, Fellows

Sharif's return to the political scene has brought together forces hitherto opposed to each other. On one side are parties of the religious opposition naturally sympathetic to Sharif's religious conservatism, but moved in particular by his anti-American rhetoric, which seeks to cast the "war on terror" as a war against Islam. On the other side stands the legal fraternity, whose demand for the reinstatement of the deposed judges and for an independent judiciary has also been espoused by Sharif. Indeed, Sharif's open support for these causes has come in sharp contrast to the more muted attitude of the United States, which is now accused of working against the rule of law.

This unusual pattern of alliances could herald a significant shift in the development of Pakistani politics by combining for the first time two very different identities within Pakistan—the religious and the liberal, or as some would have it, the Islamic and the secular. Given the surprising alliance of Islamic parties and legal reformers now supporting Sharif, it perhaps comes as no surprise that, according to a poll published in June by two US think tanks (the New America Foundation and Terror Free Tomorrow), Sharif is the country's most popular leader, with 86 percent of Pakistanis expressing a favorable opinion of him compared to just 13 percent for Zardari.

This state of affairs was not lost on Zardari, who sought to regain lost ground this summer by describing Musharraf as a "relic of the past" and by forging ahead with plans to impeach the president if he insisted on clinging to power. But at the same time, Zardari's resistance to the reinstatement of the judges could inflict lasting damage on his party. For not only has the new president misjudged the popular mood; he also risks losing the moral high ground to Sharif. While the issue of restoring the judges may be an elite concern, it also enjoys wide support insofar as the judges' continuing suspension serves as a reminder of the Musharraf regime, whose unpopularity was conclusively demonstrated in the general elections.

Spinning out of Control?

It might appear that, with Zardari at the helm, time remains, at least for a while, on the side of those still working to allow the original US-backed power sharing agreement to mature, this time under the aegis of Zardari and his PPP. But just how much time does Pakistan have before it again finds itself taking orders from a military chief? The army appears to show little appetite for intervention, at least at this stage; in July, however, it acquired fresh, sweeping powers from the government to tackle the spread of militancy in the tribal region and northern regions of the North-West Frontier Province. It is far from clear whether these powers are restricted to planning military operations or whether they will extend (as some senior officials in the Frontier Province have alleged they will) to a right of veto on the terms of government negotiations with the region's militant groups.

This in turn raises questions about whether the army is still informally playing a lead role in decision making. Indeed, a recent report by the Texas-based think tank Stratfor claimed that since February Musharraf's regime has effectively been replaced by what the report calls "a civil-military hybrid." Stratfor also suggests somewhat ominously that the country's failure to stop the spiral of militant violence has gravely weakened the army, which—like its civilian counterparts in this hybrid arrangement—has simply lost the will or the ability to confront the militant threat. Pakistan, the report concludes, is "spinning out of control."

If so, US patience might wear thin with a government that, by all accounts, remains deeply divided over whether to engage in talks with tribal militants or to intensify military operations in the tribal and northwest regions of the country. The United States strongly opposes negotiations, insisting that militants will use a lull in fighting to regroup, and US opposition has so far preempted any decisive move in favor of negotiations. So too has concern that the new government, having finally secured the tacit approval of a reluctant US administration to oust Musharraf, should not be seen as lacking the muscle to contain the militant threat.

It is worth noting that the launch of the latest military operation in the tribal district of Bajaur in early August—the bloodiest such operation since the new government assumed power—was timed precisely to coincide with the announcement of plans to impeach Musharraf. Soon after his resignation, a ban was imposed with much fanfare on the tribal militant group Tehrik-i-Taliban. The group's leaders have contemptuously dismissed the ban as "meaningless," considering that the organization is not formally registered nor does it possess known financial assets vulnerable to seizure.

These measures have done little in any case to quell speculation that the United States is now determined to continue with unilateral strikes against militant hideouts inside Pakistan and to take direct charge of operations aimed at rooting them out—even at the risk of provoking retaliation from Pakistani forces. Such speculation, fanned by reported skirmishes between US and Pakistani forces in September, ignites considerable anger in Pakistan. It heightens fears that US plans to "go it alone" will intensify the current climate of popular anti-American hostility and encourage further militant attacks on the pattern of the bombing of the Marriott Hotel.

Patience, Patience

Many will probably perceive in this assessment excessive pessimism about the country's future. Nevertheless it is critical, in taking a long view of Pakistan's crisis, to acknowledge the difficulties facing the new government in the current context.

First, the new government, however committed to peace it might be, is gravely hampered by the consequences of a war against Islamist militants that is not of its making. Second, even if peace could be secured with one or more sets of insurgents, the sheer proliferation of militant groups over the past decade means that expectations of immediate gains are unrealistic. Third, if an effort is mounted to formally integrate the tribal areas into the rest of Pakistan so as to introduce economic and social reforms to this most deprived of the country's regions, the results likely would not be apparent for years—and improved conditions would depend on sustaining an extremely fragile peace agreement between warring parties.

Even to begin to overcome these challenges requires a determined move by the now extremely weakened coalition, especially its senior partner, the PPP, to forge a political consensus based on trust. This trust can only be restored in the present circumstances by the immediate reinstatement of the former chief justice and his court. Trust will also require restoring to the parliament its sovereign role as the main forum for political debate, making it once again a place where the country's rulers are held accountable and their performance is measured against public expectations.

Yet, for this to happen, the PPP must fulfill its pledge to curb the constitutional powers of the president to dismiss democratically elected governments; the army and its agencies must be prepared to be held publicly responsible for their actions in the tribal areas and elsewhere, such as Baluchistan; and the United States must understand that its interests in Pakistan would be best secured through what the journalist Graham Usher has aptly described as the exercise of "strategic patience." Like Usher, I remain skeptical about all three prospects. The journey to democracy in Pakistan, it seems, is going to be very long indeed.

FARZANA SHAIKH is an associate fellow at the Royal Institute of International Affairs at Chatham House in London. She is author of the forthcoming *Making Sense of Pakistan* (Columbia University Press, 2009).

From *Current History*, November 2008, pp. 362–368. Copyright © 2008 by Current History, Inc. Reprinted by permission.

The Shiite "Threat" Revisited

"Reverberations from the 2003 invasion of Iraq may last for decades. But an inexorable spread of Sunni-Shiite conflict is only the worst case, and frankly it is not very likely."

Augustus Richard Norton

In the early 1980s, when the shock of the revolution in Iran was still reverberating in North American and European capitals, there was a worry that Iran's revolution would spread like a cancer in the Persian Gulf. The shah of Iran, toppled in January 1979, had been viewed as a surrogate and bulwark of American security in the Gulf. After the shah's fall, concerned US officials would unfold maps showing swaths of green ink marking the countries threatened by Iran. Special note was taken of places where local Shiite communities—presumed allies of Iran—were located. In fact, the fears proved misplaced. While Iran was able to make inroads in Lebanon, especially thanks to the Israeli invasion of 1982, each of the other Gulf governments survived intact.

Now, a quarter century later, the old maps are unfolding once again, and talk of a "Shiite crescent" has resumed. Jordan's King Abdullah, whose kingdom is now host to 700,000 Iraqi refugees, was the first to sound the call in December 2004, but the tune has been picked up by other Arab leaders, the Western press, and some in the Bush administration. Just as before, however, there is much exaggeration in the warnings. None of the Gulf governments is at real risk of being toppled by a Shiite uprising.

US Secretary of State Condoleezza Rice has worked strenuously to construct an alliance of "moderate" Sunni Muslim Arab states, particularly Egypt, Jordan, and Saudi Arabia, to counter the "Shiite threat." These governments are motivated by a combination of justified apprehension about the consequences of the disastrous Iraq War, and by opportunism. Aside from the questionable moderation of the governments in Cairo, Amman, and Riyadh, which neither promote free political life in their own societies nor fully embrace US goals in the region, the wisdom of playing the sectarian card is dubious because it deepens anti-American sentiments among both Shiites and Sunnis.

Sunni Muslims are well aware that the Baghdad government, which enjoys massive support from the Americans, has been implicated in death squad activities and ethnic cleansing operations targeting Sunni Iraqis. Meanwhile, people across the Middle East—in Lebanon, Bahrain, Kuwait, Saudi Arabia, Syria, and certainly in Iraq—see the United States trying to play both sides of the sectarian divide and become only more suspicious of Washington's motives.

"I Thought They Were All Muslims"

The basic problem facing the United States stems from its invasion of Iraq. By crushing the regime led by Saddam Hussein, the Americans gave a huge geopolitical gift to Iran, which is now the most powerful opponent of US hegemony in the Gulf. As American forces struggle to bring order to Iraq, the keenest concern is that the community they have empowered, the Iraqi Shiites, will spurn US influence and ally with Iran. This fear was expressed candidly in late October by US Ambassador Ryan Crocker in Baghdad. He was voicing concern about the strength of Moktada alSadr, whose *Jaysh al-Mahdi* (army of the divinely guided one) is growing in power and support, particularly among the large Shiite underclass. Sadr has been a fierce opponent of the US occupation, and now challenges other Shiite groups in Iraq that are more favorably disposed to cooperating with the Americans.

Ambassador Crocker worried aloud about "Hezbollahization." He was referring to the Shiite Islamists' building of social networks through self-help groups, businesses, service agencies, and community offices, just as Hezbollah ("party of God") had done in Lebanon. Indeed, most of the successful Islamist groups in today's Middle East have built networks of interlinked units that not only help their constituents but also reflect values such as empowerment, self-help, and resistance to oppression. In addition, like Lebanon's Hezbollah, Sadr's Mahdi Army has benefited from Iran's largesse.

It is no exaggeration to say that US leaders were completely surprised by some of the challenges that have emerged from the Iraq War. In a remarkable encounter in January 2003, two months before the Anglo-American invasion, members of the Iraqi opposition were meeting in the Oval Office with President

George W. Bush. Kanan Makiya, an Iraqi-American academic, began speaking about Sunnis and Shiites in Iraq, but Bush interrupted him, puzzled: "I thought they were all Muslims."

Bush would not make the same mistake today. Nonetheless, considerable confusion about the two major sects of Islam persists. Senior US Homeland Security officials, for instance, have been documented identifying Al Qaeda as a Shiite group; it is in fact dogmatically anti-Shiite. In Capitol Hill hearings, congressmen are on record using "Palestinian" as a synonym for Shiite, though there are almost no Palestinian Shiites.

The Heirs of Ali

In all, there are thought to be about 1.3 billion Muslims in the world, and as many as 15 percent of them are members of some branch of Shiism. There are three major Shiite sects, but they all share a special regard for the House of the Prophet Muhammad and the belief that the Prophet's spiritual guidance was transmitted by divine ordination through his descendents, especially through his son-in-law and cousin Ali. (The Sunnis believed caliphs did not need to be descended from the Prophet.) For Shiite Muslims, the holy day Ashura commemorates the martyrdom of one Imam Hussein—the grandson of the Prophet and son of Ali—whose demise in the seventh century, near the city of Karbala in modern-day Iraq, has become a lodestone of modern identity for Shiites, much as the crucifixion of Jesus is central to Christian identity.

The two smaller Shiite sects are the Ismailis, found in small numbers in Syria and Iran, and the Zaydis, who account for a quarter of Yemen's population of 22 million. In the thirteenth century the Ismailis were known as the "Assassins," but today they are respected, prosperous, and deeply involved in education and ecumenical aesthetic pursuits. Their leader is known as the Aga Khan; they number only a couple of million adherents worldwide. (The Druze, an offshoot of the Ismailis, number less than a million and are found in Israel, Syria, and Lebanon. The Alawites, who rule Syria and comprise 11 percent of its population, are often considered to be a Shiite faction as well.) The Zaydis, who ruled Yemen until 1962, embrace a firm moral code in this life but they reject the mystical religious beliefs usually associated with Shiism.

Hezbollah's rivals fear that its ultimate aim is to transform Lebanon into an Islamic state.

Almost all Shiites believe in the eventual return of an imam who will lead the community up to the day of judgment. The largest Shiite sect, the Twelvers, traces the descendents of Muhammad to the Twelfth Imam, who disappeared when he went into occultation more than a millennium ago. In the absence of the Hidden Imam, these believers seek guidance from respected and specially educated clerics, such as Ayatollah Muhammad Hussein Fadlallah of Lebanon, or Ayatollah Ali

Sistani in Najaf, Iraq—by far the world's most influential Shiite cleric. In contrast, religious authority in the majority Sunni sect is much more diffuse.

While Iraq and Iran may come quickly to mind when the topic of Shiism is introduced, Shiites are found in significant numbers in six other Middle Eastern countries, as well as outside the region. By far, the largest concentration of Shiites is in Iran, where they comprise 90 percent of the country's 70 million inhabitants; followed by Iraq, where 60 percent of the population of 27 million are Shiites. There are about 1.3 million in Lebanon. Not counting guest workers, about 2 million Shiite citizens are distributed among Bahrain, Kuwait, Qatar, Saudi Arabia, and the United Arab Emirates.

Except for Bahrain, where they account for 70 percent of the half-million citizens (another 250,000 expatriate workers live on the island), in the other Gulf states the Shiites represent only a small fraction of the total population (ranging from 5 to 8 percent in Saudi Arabia to 25 percent in Kuwait). In fact, some of the largest populations of Shiites are found outside the Gulf and the Middle East. There are locally significant populations in Indonesia, perhaps 6 million in Azerbaijan, approximately 10 million in India, and at least 30 million in Pakistan.

The Fluidity of Identity

Popular authors such as the historian Bernard Lewis promote the view that sectarian identity is a permanent, historically rooted quality that lies at the heart of Middle Eastern politics. Lewis has also popularized the view that a longing for the lost glory of the past lies at the heart of Muslim hostility to the West and to the United States in particular. These can be very self-satisfying perspectives for Western readers because they offer a simple formula for understanding Middle East politics, and they absolve external powers from responsibility for political problems in the region.

A mere century or so ago, sectarian affiliation was neither a particularly important marker of faith nor an important basis for political action. In recent decades, before the present fever of sectarianism infected the region, there were actually several initiatives toward *taqarub* (rapprochement) between Sunnis and Shiites. While these ecumenical impulses were not successful, they hint that assuming an unbridgeable gulf between the sects is a contemporary prejudice.

Although the differentiation of the Shiite and Sunni sects dates to the earliest days of Islam, the political salience of sectarian identity has varied dramatically over the course of history, not to mention in recent decades. For instance, in Iraq and Lebanon well into the 1960s, Shiite Muslims were politically mobilized very successfully by the Communist party. Arab Sunnis and Shiites alike were widely attracted to the ideology of Nasserism in the 1950s and 1960s. In Bahrain, where the sparks of Sunni-Shiite tension have ignited several recent clashes, the Shiites were fervent admirers of Egyptian President Gamal Abdel Nasser just a few decades ago.

By the 1970s in the Arab world, heretofore dominant secular-nationalist ideologies began to be energetically challenged by Sunni Islamist groups, which offered both a critique of the secular state and a call for activism informed by a renewal of piety. In some instances, these groups were overtly hostile to Shiism. Yet it was the self-styled "Islamic Revolution" in predominantly Shiite Iran that offered the most profound critique of the secular state in the Middle East.

If Ayatollah Ruhollah Khomeini and his co-revolutionaries were disappointed by the Sunnis' reluctance to embrace their revolution and its idiosyncratic religio-political structure, the exemplar of a state informed by Islam was still powerful. In Egypt, a few Sunnis were so inspired by the revolution that they converted to Shiism, but their very small numbers underline the limited appeal of Iran's model to Sunnis. The most enthusiastic Sunni embrace of the "Islamic Revolution" came in Lebanon, where Iran founded Hezbollah in the early 1980s, taking advantage of the opportunity created by Israel's 1982 invasion and the long Israeli occupation of southern Lebanon, which ended only in 2000.

People across the Middle East see the United States trying to play both sides of the sectarian divide.

There were a few half-hearted attempts to imitate the Iranian example. In Bahrain, an amateurish coup was thwarted in 1981. In the same period, Kuwait suffered several acts of terrorism emanating from its Shiite community. Bursts of militancy erupted among minority Shiites in Saudi Arabia's Eastern province, but these did not last long. Since then, particularly in the past decade, the Saudi government has taken some steps to lift controls on the public practice of Shiism and has afforded the Shiite community modest levels of representation at the national level. Considering that the dominant Saudi religious group is the puritan Wahhabis, who consider Shiism to be anathema, it was a milestone when Saudi Arabia's King Abdullah received Sadr, the Iraqi Shiite cleric, near the holy city of Mecca.

In Iraq, the Baathist regime turned the screws of repression on Shiites and, in 1980, opportunistically launched what would be an eight-year war to contain the Iranian revolution (with clear support from the United States as well as Sunni-dominated countries, including Saudi Arabia and Kuwait). When that war finally ended in 1988 it was Iran that tasted defeat. Iraq's immense Shiite population, which comprised much of the rank and file in the army, had proved deaf to Iran's clarion.

Nonetheless, hints of the sectarian passions that would later brutally affect Iraqi politics were visible in the spring of 1991. Heeding President George H. W. Bush's call for an uprising to topple Hussein, whose army had just been expelled from Kuwait, many of Iraq's Shiite Muslims joined an intifada against the regime. Iraq's army unleashed a furious and pitiless response.

Iraqi Shiites begged at the Kuwait border for sanctuary, where the US military stood watch. American soldiers might as well have been spectators in Rome's Coliseum. The supplicants were rebuffed and turned back to their wretched fates. No state in the region lifted a finger to help the victims, except

Iran, and Iran did nothing to stanch the bloodshed. An estimated 100,000 Iraqi Shiites were killed. Incredibly, this horrendous moment made so little impression on American war planners in 2003 that the invading US forces did not anticipate the lingering suspicion and contempt that often greeted them among the Iraqi Shiites.

Academic experts in some cases only added to the public's ignorance by pandering to or promoting stereotypes. Johns Hopkins University's Fouad Ajami, who was then testifying before Congress on Islamic radicalism, offered the now famous aphorism: "The Sunnis are homicidal and the Shiites are suicidal." Suicide, he said, "is definitely a Shiite phenomenon because of the ethic of martyrdom and martyrology which is exalted in the Shiite experience and which knows no equivalent in Sunni life." As quotidian examples from Palestine and Israel, Iraq, Afghanistan, Chechnya, and a handful of other locales demonstrate, Ajami's insight does not stand up to the evidence. Sunni Muslims have proved adept at transforming themselves into human bombs at great cost to innocent victims, not least on September 11, 2001.

Religious sect, just as any other form of ascriptive identity, such as race or ethnicity, may be used to rationalize a horrifying variety of outrages against those who are different. Abu Musab al-Zarqawi, the late and savage leader of Al Qaeda in Iraq, certainly understood the divisive potential of sectarian affinity. In 2004 he wrote: "If we succeed in dragging [the Shiites] into the arena of sectarian war, it will become possible to awaken the inattentive Sunnis as they feel imminent danger." Before he died at US hands, Zarqawi ordered numerous suicide attacks against Shiite targets, thereby helping to push Iraq's Sunnis and Shiites into a civil war.

The Case of Lebanon

Lebanon already has fought a civil war along sectarian lines, a war that lasted 15 years, ending only in 1990. Today that country is locked in a tense stalemate that Lebanese fear might end with the eruption of a new civil war. Sectarian passions are inflamed for several reasons: the assassination of former Prime Minister Rafik Hariri in 2005; the 34-day war with Israel in 2006 that brought ruin to Lebanon's economy and destruction to many parts of the country; and the manipulations and encouragement of numerous outside players, including the United States, a variety of European states, Iran, Syria, Israel, Saudi Arabia, and some other Middle Eastern nations. Lebanon has also been cursed with a weak central government and a set of self-interested sectarian leaders who often treat the state as a feeding trough.

The 2006 war started when Hezbollah's paramilitary wing provoked Israel by capturing two Israeli soldiers from Israeli territory, thereby breaking the "rules of the game" that defined the security system in southern Lebanon. The United States encouraged and supported Israel's summer war to disable if not destroy Iran-supported Hezbollah. Israel failed and Hezbollah emerged from the war more or less intact, but surrounded by ruins in southern Lebanon and in the Beirut suburbs where many Shiite supporters of Hezbollah live. The US-backed government in Beirut is now in a fierce test of wills with an opposition that includes not only Shiites, but also many Christians and a number of other Lebanese supporting Hezbollah.

While the wider Arab world celebrated Hezbollah's "victory" in the war, closer to home many questioned the party's motives and the war's consequences, which included an estimated $4 billion to $5 billion in reconstruction costs and a heavy toll in lives and personal property.

Politically, the war divided Lebanon in two. One Lebanon is a coalition of mainly Sunnis, Druze, and Christians who came together after Hariri's assassination. This group, demanding the truth about Hariri's killers and a withdrawal of Syrian forces from Lebanon, mobilized as many as a million protesters in downtown Beirut. After winning the parliamentary elections in May 2005, this coalition was in power during the 2006 war. It accuses Hezbollah of instigating the disastrous war with Israel, and of being an agent of Syria and Iran.

The second Lebanon is also a coalition, consisting mostly of the southern Lebanese Shiite community and large elements of the Christian community—especially the followers of the magnetic Maronite Christian politician and former general Michel Aoun. The "Aounists" and Shiites share a profound sense of victimization in the face of what they see as a corrupt and unresponsive political system.

None of the Gulf governments is at real risk of being toppled by a Shiite uprising.

The slow pace of government payments to those who lost their homes thanks to Israel's relentless bombing is widely viewed as an example of official ineffectiveness, much in contrast to Hezbollah's speedy distribution of $12,000 payments to each family made homeless by the war. The opposition alliance has proved remarkably durable. Most basically, it is trying to expand its share of power at the expense of the traditional Christian elite and the Sunni Muslims. Indeed, it is the threat of a decline in Sunni prerogatives and power in Lebanon that has prompted Saudi Arabia to become a key backer of the government.

In Western circles, Hezbollah and the Aounists are perceived as trying to protect Syria by stifling efforts to authorize an international tribunal to try those accused of responsibility for the killing of Hariri and his associates. (The Syrian regime is widely suspected of having directed the assassination.) There is some truth in the charge, since a weakening of Syria would no doubt weaken its friends in Lebanon.

Back from the Brink

The fall of 2006 was marked by an escalation of tension and demands, including an ultimatum by Hezbollah leader Hasan Nasrallah on October 31 demanding that the government either agree to a national unity government or face widespread demonstrations and other forms of organized pressure such as blockades on the route to the national airport. In conjunction with these demands, all five Shiite members of the government resigned in November. The opposition then noted that, under a 1989 agreement, every major sect must be represented in government. President Emile Lahoud asserted that the government was no longer legitimate (vis-à-vis the question of an international tribune, notably).

To block a vote on the tribunal, Speaker Nabih Berri refused to convene parliament. But in an endrun around the opposition, Prime Minister Fouad Siniora requested action by the United Nations Security Council to mandate an international tribunal. While Siniora's request was of doubtful legality, given Lahoud's refusal to agree to it, the tribunal was approved by the Security Council in May 2007. The tribunal now is a sword of Damocles that swings over the heads of the opposition.

Meanwhile, seven prominent figures have been assassinated since 2005. All of the victims are opponents of Syrian influence in Lebanon; the most recent was killed in a car bombing in September 2007. The result is a climate of fear among pro-government politicians. The political stakes were raised on December 1, 2006, when opposition supporters erected 1,000 tents in Beirut's Riyadh alSulh and Martyr's Square, literally at the feet of the government, and announced that they would not budge until the government succumbed. Massive numbers of people assembled on the first day of the demonstration, immobilizing the commercial heart of Beirut.

As tensions continued to rise, fighting erupted in January 2007 between Sunni gunmen and Shiite protesters. Four people were killed. But Hezbollah at this point stepped back from the brink. Appearing on television, Nasrallah declared that "anyone using a firearm against a Lebanese brother is working for Israel." The situation calmed. It helped that the Lebanese army during this period performed with both neutrality and firmness. Since early 2007 neither side has budged much politically from its position.

While the stalemate has been enormously costly to Lebanon's economy, and while the continuing risk of a new civil war is obvious, the demonstrations are now restrained and usually peaceful. Initially tens of thousands of opposition supporters occupied the tents, but today the tents often stand empty, quiet canvas testaments to the frozen political situation. In all, 10 deaths may be attributed to the demonstrations, which have been under way for a year.

At the same time, however, extremist Sunni groups, some inspired by Al Qaeda, have proliferated in Lebanon. These groups are generally hostile to Shiites. In May 2007, clashes broke out in the Nahr al-Bared Palestinian refugee camp in northern Lebanon. It took the lightly equipped Lebanese army four months to defeat the Sunni group, at the cost of more than 160 dead soldiers and the displacement of more than 34,000 civilians. The urgency of the crisis was further demonstrated in June, when six soldiers from Colombia and Spain serving in the UN mission were killed in the south, following calls by Al Qaeda's number two leader, Ayman al-Zawahiri, for Muslims to confront the "Crusaders," meaning the international soldiers. The attacks led to quiet security contacts between UN officials and Hezbollah, prompting Zawahiri to pointedly criticize Hezbollah.

Hezbollah's rivals fear that its ultimate aim is to transform Lebanon into an Islamic state and that the party is only feigning attachment to Lebanon as a pluralist society. But Nasrallah and his colleagues have claimed frequently that the conditions for establishing a state based on Islamic rule will probably never exist in Lebanon, since such a state could only be established on the basis of broad consent, which is highly unlikely. Whatever dreams Hezbollah might entertain, the conclusion that there will never be widespread support for an Islamic state is a sound one.

A Less Fractious Future?

In his commendably lucid book, *The Shia Revival: How Conflicts within Islam Will Shape the Future,* Vali Nasr emphasizes—in my view overstates—enduring Sunni-Shiite tensions in history. But his argument largely turns on the importance of the mayhem in Iraq as a historical watershed. In the past, social and political conventions kept sectarian distrust and enmity hidden from view. With Iraqi society in chaos and the fate of the state uncertain, the veneers are stripped away, exposing the deep-grained realities. But even if this holds for Iraq, which some respected scholars doubt, it is deceptive to generalize from the Iraqi case. The invasion destroyed the already dry-rotted institutions of a dictatorship, imposed an incompetent occupation on Iraq, empowered a disenfranchised majority, and did so in country where civil society had been obliterated for years. Fortunately, this would be a hard case to replicate.

Even so, the invasion and its aftermath effectively lent validation to Al Qaeda's ideology, and have inspired some anti-Shiite Sunnis to open Al Qaeda "franchises" in places far removed from Iraq. There have been other dubious "accomplishments" as a result of the war. When Hussein was hanged at the end of 2006, he won posthumous fame as a Sunni hero. An Egyptian weekly published a commemorative edition that included a poster depicting the late dictator and captioned: "He lived heroically and died a man."

These developments have had variant impacts in societies where Sunnis and Shiites live side by side. In prosperous Kuwait, the Shiites participate in government, and the Shiite community is defined by several distinct orientations, ranging from secularism and quietism to radicalism. Some Kuwaiti Shiites follow the late and moderate Ayatollah Muhammad Shirazi; others support the Iranian regime; still others adhere to Arab religious authorities, such as Iraq's Sistani. While relations among the sects in Kuwait are generally good, the Salafis (Sunnis who favor a return to an earlier, "purer" form of Islam) are usually hostile to the Shiites. In March 2007, a Kuwaiti Sunni cleric named Uthman al-Khamis announced plans to launch "Tibah" (disclosure), a new satellite channel to warn Muslims of "the Shiite threat."

In Bahrain, where Shiites comprise 70 percent of the population but have suffered considerable discrimination by the government, Lebanon's Hezbollah is extremely popular. Bahrain, though tiny in population, is strategically important to the United States. The Fifth Fleet is headquartered in Bahrain and many US Navy vessels are replenished and repaired there. A growing number of Bahrainis are expressing opposition to the American role in their country, and one can expect this opposition to grow. In fact, Hezbollah's al-Manar satellite station is the most popular source of news in the monarchy. Bahrain is the poorest of the small Arab Gulf states, and many of its disadvantaged Shiites are a rapt audience for Nasrallah. In Manama, the capital, at least three stores sell a variety of Hezbollah literature, DVDs, tee shirts, and decorations. The Bahraini Shiites, moreover, boast a proud and long history of political and economic protests. The minority regime is firmly in place in Bahrain, but much will depend on how wisely it responds to inevitable calls for reform.

Throughout the Middle East, reverberations from the 2003 invasion of Iraq may last for decades. But an inexorable spread of Sunni-Shiite conflict is only the worst case, and frankly it is not very likely. One hopes imaginative political leaders will pursue enlightened and conciliatory policies. A spirit of conciliation is implied, for instance, in a recent observation by King Abdullah of Saudi Arabia: "If sectarianism deepens and spreads, its destructive effect will reflect on everyone. It will foster division, polarization, and isolationism. Our region will drown in a conflict whose outcome cannot be foreseen." Equally important, if leaders in North America, Europe, and Asia are able to escape the conceptual prisons they have built for themselves, a less fractious future is possible.

Augustus Richard Norton, a Current History contributing editor, is a professor in the international relations and anthropology departments at Boston University. He is the author of *Hezbollah: A Short History* (Princeton University Press, 2007).

The Most Dangerous Place in the World

Somalia is a state governed only by anarchy. A graveyard of foreign-policy failures, it has known just six months of peace in the past two decades. Now, as the country's endless chaos threatens to engulf an entire region, the world again simply watches it burn.

JEFFREY GETTLEMAN

When you land at Mogadishu's international airport, the first form you fill out asks for name, address, and caliber of weapon. Believe it or not, this disaster of a city, the capital of Somalia, still gets a few commercial flights. Some haven't fared so well. The wreckage of a Russian cargo plane shot down in 2007 still lies crumpled at the end of the runway.

Beyond the airport is one of the world's most stunning monuments to conflict: block after block, mile after mile, of scorched, gutted-out buildings. Mogadishu's Italianate architecture, once a gem along the Indian Ocean, has been reduced to a pile of machine-gun-chewed bricks. Somalia has been ripped apart by violence since the central government imploded in 1991. Eighteen years and 14 failed attempts at a government later, the killing goes on and on and on—suicide bombs, white phosphorus bombs, beheadings, medieval-style stonings, teenage troops high on the local drug called *khat* blasting away at each other and anything in between. Even U.S. cruise missiles occasionally slam down from the sky. It's the same violent free-for-all on the seas. Somalia's pirates are threatening to choke off one of the most strategic waterways in the world, the Gulf of Aden, which 20,000 ships pass through every year. These heavily armed buccaneers hijacked more than 40 vessels in 2008, netting as much as $100 million in ransom. It's the greatest piracy epidemic of modern times.

In more than a dozen trips to Somalia over the past two and a half years, I've come to rewrite my own definition of chaos. I've felt the incandescent fury of the Iraqi insurgency raging in Fallujah. I've spent freezing-cold, eerily quiet nights in an Afghan cave. But nowhere was I more afraid than in today's Somalia, where you can get kidnapped or shot in the head faster than you can wipe the sweat off your brow. From the thick, ambush-perfect swamps around Kismayo in the south to the lethal labyrinth of Mogadishu to the pirate den of Boosaaso on the Gulf of Aden, Somalia is quite simply the most dangerous place in the world.

> **I've felt the incandescent fury of the Iraqi insurgency. I've spent freezing-cold nights in an Afghan cave. But nowhere was I more afraid than in today's Somalia.**

The whole country has become a breeding ground for warlords, pirates, kidnappers, bomb makers, fanatical Islamist insurgents, freelance gunmen, and idle, angry youth with no education and way too many bullets. There is no Green Zone here, by the way—no fortified place of last resort to run to if, God forbid, you get hurt or in trouble. In Somalia, you're on your own. The local hospitals barely have enough gauze to treat all the wounds.

The mayhem is now spilling across Somalia's borders, stirring up tensions and violence in Kenya, Ethiopia, and Eritrea, not to mention Somalia's pirateinfested seas. The export of trouble may just be beginning. Islamist insurgents with al Qaeda connections are sweeping across the country, turning Somalia into an Afghanistan-like magnet for militant Islam and drawing in hard-core fighters from around the world. These men will eventually go home (if they survive) and spread the killer ethos. Somalia's transitional government, a U.N.-santioned creation that was deathly ill from the moment it was born four years ago, is about to flatline, perhaps spawning yet another doomed international rescue mission. Abdullahi Yusuf Ahmed, the old war horse of a president backed by the United States, finally resigned in December after a long, bitter dispute with the prime minister, Nur Hassan Hussein. Ostensibly, their conflict was about a peace deal with the Islamists and a few cabinet posts. In truth, it may be purely academic. By early this year, the government's zone of control was down to a couple of city blocks. The country is nearly as big as Texas.

Just when things seem as though they can't get any worse in Somalia, they do. Beyond the political crisis, all the elements for a full-blown famine—war, displacement, drought, skyrocketing food prices, and an exodus of aid workers—are lining up again, just as they did in the early 1990s when hundreds of thousands of Somalis starved to death. Last May, I stood in the doorway of a hut in the bone-dry central part of the country watching a sick little boy curl up next to his dying mother. Her clothes were damp. Her breaths were shallow. She hadn't eaten for days. "She will most likely die," an elder told me and walked away.

Just when things seem they can't get any worse in Somalia, they do. Beyond the political crisis, all the elements for a full-blown famine are lining up again.

It's crunch time for Somalia, but the world is like me, standing in the doorway, looking in at two decades of unbridled anarchy, unsure what to do. Past interventions have been so cursed that no one wants to get burned again. The United States has been among the worst of the meddlers: U.S. forces fought predacious warlords at the wrong time, backed some of the same predacious warlords at the wrong time, and consistently failed to appreciate the twin pulls of clan and religion. As a result, Somalia has become a graveyard of foreign-policy blunders that have radicalized the population, deepened insecurity, and pushed millions to the brink of starvation.

Somalia is a political paradox—unified on the surface, poisonously divided beneath. It is one of the world's most homogeneous nation-states, with nearly all of its estimated 9 to 10 million people sharing the same language (Somali), the same religion (Sunni Islam), the same culture, and the same ethnicity. But in Somalia, it's all about clan. Somalis divide themselves into a dizzying number of clans, subclans, sub-subclans, and so on, with shifting allegiances and knotty backstories that have bedeviled outsiders for years.

At the end of the 19th century, the Italians and the British divvied up most of Somalia, but their efforts to impose Western laws never really worked. Disputes tended to be resolved by clan elders. Deterrence was key: "Kill me and you will suffer the wrath of my entire clan." The places where the local ways were disturbed the least, such as British-ruled Somaliland, seem to have done better in the long run than those where the Italian colonial administration supplanted the role of clan elders, as in Mogadishu.

Somalia won independence in 1960, but it quickly became a Cold War pawn, prized for its strategic location in the Horn of Africa, where Africa and Asia nearly touch. First it was the Soviets who pumped in weapons, then the United States.

A poor, mostly illiterate, mainly nomadic country became a towering ammunition dump primed to explode. The central government was hardly able to hold the place together. Even in the 1980s, Maj. Gen. Mohamed Siad Barre, the capricious dictator who ruled from 1969 to 1991, was derisively referred to as "the mayor of Mogadishu" because so much of the country had already spun out of his control.

When clan warlords finally ousted him in 1991, it wasn't much of a surprise what happened next. The warlords unleashed all that military-grade weaponry on each other, and every port, airstrip, fishing pier, telephone pole—anything that could turn a profit—was fought over. People were killed for a few pennies. Women were raped with impunity. The chaos gave rise to a new class of parasitic war profiteers—gunrunners, drug smugglers, importers of expired (and often sickening) baby formula—people with a vested interest in the chaos continuing. Somalia became the modern world's closest approximation of Hobbes's state of nature, where life was indeed nasty, brutish, and short. To call it even a failed state was generous. The Democratic Republic of the Congo is a failed state. So is Zimbabwe. But those places at least have national armies and national bureaucracies, however corrupt. Since 1991, Somalia has not been a state so much as a lawless, ungoverned space on the map between its neighbors and the sea.

In 1992, U.S. President George H.W. Bush tried to help, sending in thousands of Marines to protect shipments of food. It was the beginning of the post-Cold War "new world order," when many believed that the United States, without a rival superpower, could steer world events in a new and morally righteous way. Somalia proved to be a very bad start. President Bush and his advisors misread the clan landscape and didn't understand how fiercely loyal Somalis could be to their clan leaders. Somali society often divides and subdivides when faced with internal disputes, but it quickly bands together when confronted by an external enemy. The United States learned this the hard way when its forces tried to apprehend the warlord of the day, Mohammed Farah Aidid. The result was the infamous "Black Hawk Down" episode in October 1993. Thousands of Somali militiamen poured into the streets, carrying rocket-propelled grenades and wearing flip-flops. They shot down two American Black Hawk helicopters, killing 18 U.S. soldiers and dragging the corpses triumphantly through the streets. This would be Strike One for the United States in Somalia.

Humiliated, the Americans pulled out and Somalia was left to its own dystopian devices. For the next decade, the Western world mostly stayed away. But Arab organizations, many from Saudi Arabia and followers of the strict Wahhabi branch of Sunni Islam, quietly stepped in. They built mosques, Koranic schools, and social service organizations, encouraging an Islamic revival. By the early 2000s, Mogadishu's clan elders set up a loose network of neighborhood-based courts to deliver a modicum of order in a city desperate for it. They rounded up thieves and killers, put them in iron cages, and held trials. Islamic law, or *sharia,* was the one set of principles that different clans could agree on; the Somali elders called their network the Islamic Courts Union.

Mogadishu's business community spotted an opportunity. In Mogadishu, there are warlords and moneylords. While the warlords were ripping the country apart, the moneylords, Somalia's big-business owners, were holding the place together, delivering many of the same services—for a tidy profit, of course—that a government usually provides, such as healthcare, schools, power plants, and even privatized mail. The moneylords went as far as helping to regulate Somalia's monetary policy, and the Somali shilling was more stable in the 1990s—without a functioning central bank—than in the 1980s when there was a government. But with their profits came very high risks, such as chronic insecurity and extortion. The Islamists were a solution. They provided security without taxes, administration without a government. The moneylords began buying them guns.

By 2005, the CIA saw what was happening, and again misread the cues. This ended up being Strike Two.

In a post-September 11 world, Somalia had become a major terrorism worry. The fear was that Somalia could blossom into a jihad factory like Afghanistan, where al Qaeda in the 1990s plotted its global war on the West. It didn't seem to matter that at this point there was scant evidence to justify this fear. Some Western military analysts told policymakers that Somalia was too chaotic for even al Qaeda, because it was impossible for anyone—including terrorists—to know whom to trust. Nonetheless, the administration of George W. Bush devised a strategy to stamp out the Islamists on the cheap. CIA agents deputized the warlords, the same thugs who had been preying upon Somalia's population for years, to fight the Islamists. According to one Somali warlord I spoke with in March 2008, an American agent named James and another one named David showed up in Mogadishu with briefcases stuffed with cash. Use this to buy guns, the agents said. Drop us an e-mail if you have any questions. The warlord showed me the address: no_email_today@yahoo.com.

The plan backfired. Somalis like to talk; the country, ironically, has some of the best and cheapest cellular phone service in Africa. Word quickly spread that the same warlords no one liked anymore were now doing the Americans' bidding, which just made the Islamists even more popular. By June 2006, the Islamists had run the last warlords out of Mogadishu. Then something unbelievable happened: The Islamists seemed to tame the place.

I saw it with my own eyes. I flew into Mogadishu in September 2006 and saw work crews picking up trash and kids swimming at the beach. For the first time in years, no gunshots rang out at night. Under the banner of Islam, the Islamists had united rival clans and disarmed much of the populace, with clan support of course. They even cracked down on piracy by using their clan connections to dissuade coastal towns from supporting the pirates. When that didn't work, the Islamists stormed hijacked ships. According to the International Maritime Bureau in London, there were 10 pirate attacks off Somalia's coast in 2006, which is tied for the lowest number of attacks this decade.

The Islamists' brief reign of peace was to be the only six months of calm Somalia has tasted since 1991. But it was one thing to rally together to overthrow the warlords and another to decide what to do next. A rift quickly opened between the moderate Islamists and the extremists, who were bent on waging jihad. One of the most radical factions has been the Shabab, a multiclan military wing with a strict Wahhabi interpretation of Islam. The Shabab drove around Mogadishu in big, black pickup trucks and beat women whose ankles were showing. Even the other Islamist gunmen were scared of them. By December 2006, some of the population began to chafe against the Shabab for taking away their beloved khat, the mildly stimulating leaf that Somalis chew like bubble gum. Shabab leaders were widely rumored to be working with foreign jihadists, including wanted al Qaeda terrorists, and the U.S. State Department later designated the Shabab a terrorist organization. American officials have said that the Shabab are sheltering men who masterminded the bombings of the U.S. embassies in Kenya and Tanzania in 1998.

Somalia may indeed have sheltered a few unsavory characters, but the country was far from the terrorist hotbed many worry it has now become. In 2006, there was a narrow window of opportunity to peel off the moderate Islamists from the likes of the Shabab, and some U.S. officials, such as Democratic Rep. Donald M. Payne, the chairman of the House subcommittee on Africa, were trying to do exactly that. Payne and others met with the moderate Islamists and encouraged them to negotiate a powersharing deal with the transitional government.

But the Bush administration again reached for the gunpowder. The United States would not do much of the fighting itself, since sending large numbers of ground troops into Somalia with Iraq and Afghanistan raging would have been deemed insane. Instead, the United States anointed a proxy: the Ethiopian Army. This move would be Strike Three.

Ethiopia is one of the United States' best friends in Africa, its government having carefully cultivated an image as a Christian bulwark in a region seething with Islamist extremism. The Ethiopian leadership savvily told the Bush administration what it wanted to hear: The Islamists were terrorists and, unchecked, they would threaten the entire region and maybe even attack American safarigoers in Kenya next door.

Of course, the Ethiopians had their own agenda. Ethiopia is a country with a mostly Christian leadership but a population that is nearly half Muslim. It seems only a matter of time before there is an Islamic awakening in Ethiopia. On top of that, the Ethiopian government is fighting several rebel groups, including a powerful one that is ethnically Somali. The government feared that an Islamist Somalia could become a rebel beachhead next door. The Ethiopians were also scared that Somalia's Islamists would team up with Eritrea, Ethiopia's archenemy, which is exactly what ended up happening.

Not everyone in Washington swallowed the Ethiopian line. The country has a horrendous human rights record, and the Ethiopian military (which receives aid for human rights training from the United States) is widely accused of brutalizing its own people. But in December 2006, the Bush administration shared prized intelligence with the Ethiopians and gave them the green light to invade Somalia. Thousands of Ethiopian troops rolled across the border (many had secretly been in the country for months), and they routed the Islamist troops within a week. There were even some U.S. Special Forces with the Ethiopian units. The United States also launched several airstrikes in an attempt to take out Islamist leaders, and it continued with intermittent cruise missiles targeting suspected terrorists. Most have failed, killing civilians and adding to the boiling anti-American sentiment.

The Islamists went underground, and the transitional government arrived in Mogadishu. There was some cheering, a lot of jeering, and the insurgency revved up within days. The transitional government was widely reviled as a coterie of ex-warlords, which it mostly was. It was the 14th attempt since 1991 to stand up a central government. None of the previous attempts had worked. True, some detractors have simply been war profiteers hell-bent on derailing any government. But a lot of blame falls on what this transitional government has done—or not done. From the start, leaders seemed much more interested in who got what post than living up to the corresponding job descriptions. The government quickly lost the support of key clans in Mogadishu by its harsh (and unsuccessful) tactics in trying to wipe out the insurgents, and by its reliance on Ethiopian troops. Ethiopia and Somalia have fought several wars against each other over the contested Ogaden region that Ethiopia now claims. That region is mostly ethnically Somali, so teaming up with Ethiopia was seen as tantamount to treason.

The Islamists tapped into this sentiment, positioning themselves as the true Somali nationalists, and gaining widespread support again. The results were intense street battles between Islamist insurgents and Ethiopian troops in which thousands of civilians have been killed. Ethiopian forces have indiscriminately shelled entire neighborhoods (which precipitated a European Union investigation into war crimes), and have even used white phosphorous bombs that literally melt people, according to the United Nations. Hundreds of thousands of people have emptied out of Mogadishu and settled in camps that have become breeding grounds for disease and resentment. Death comes more frequently and randomly than ever before. I met one man in Mogadishu who was chatting with his wife on her cellphone when she was cut in half by a stray mortar shell. Another man I spoke to went out for a walk, got shot in the leg during a crossfire, and had to spend seven days eating grass before the fighting ended and he could crawl away.

Death comes more frequently and randomly than ever before. I met one man in Mogadishu who was chatting with his wife on her cellphone when she was cut in half by a stray mortar shell.

It's incredibly dangerous for us journalists, too. Few foreign journalists travel to Somalia anymore. Kidnapping is the threat du jour. Friends of mine who work for the United Nations in Kenya told me I had about a 100 percent chance of being stuffed into the back of a Toyota or shot (or both) if I didn't hire a private militia. Nowadays, as soon as I land, I take 10 gunmen under my employ.

By late January, the only territory the transitional government controlled was a shrinking federal enclave in Mogadishu guarded by a small contingent of African Union peacekeepers. As soon as the Ethiopians pulled out of the capital vicious fighting broke out between the various Islamist factions scrambling to fill the power gap. It took only days for the Islamists to recapture the third-largest town, Baidoa, from the government and install sharia law. The Shabab are not wildly popular, but they are formidable; for the time being they have a motivated, disciplined militia with hundreds of hard-core fighters and probably thousands of gunmen allied with them. The violence has shown no signs of halting, even with the election of a new, moderate Islamist president—one who had, ironically, been a leader of the Islamic Courts Union in 2006.

If the Shabab do seize control of the country, they might not stop there. They could send their battle-hardened fighters in battered four-wheel-drive pickup trucks into Ethiopia, Kenya, and maybe even Djibouti to try to snatch back the Somali-speaking parts of those countries. This scenario has long been part of an ethereal pan-Somali dream. Pursuit of that goal would internationalize the conflict and surely drag in neighboring countries and their allies.

The Shabab could also wage an asymmetric war, unleashing terrorists on Somalia's secular neighbors and their secular backers—most prominently, the United States. This would upend an already combustible dynamic in the Horn of Africa, catalyzing other conflicts. For instance, Ethiopia and Eritrea fought a nasty border war in the late 1990s, which killed as many as 100,000 people, and both countries are still heavily militarized along the border. If the Shabab, which boasts Eritrean support, took over Somalia, we might indeed see round two of Ethiopia versus Eritrea. The worst-case scenario could mean millions of people displaced across the entire region, crippled food production, and violence-induced breaches in the aid pipeline. In short, a famine in one of the most perennially needy parts of the world—again.

The hardest challenge of all might be simply preventing the worst-case scenario. Among the best suggestions I've heard is to play to Somalia's strengths as a fluid, decentralized society with local mechanisms to resolve conflicts. The foundation of order would be clan-based governments in villages, towns, and neighborhoods. These tiny fiefdoms could stack together to form district and regional governments. The last step would be uniting the regional governments in a loose national federation that coordinated, say, currency issues or antipiracy efforts, but did not sideline local leaders.

Western powers should do whatever they can to bring moderate Islamists into the transitional government while the transitional government still exists. Whether people like it or not, many Somalis see Islamic law as the answer. Maybe they're not fond of the harsh form imposed by the Shabab, who have, on at least one occasion, stoned to death a teenage girl who had been raped (an Islamic court found her guilty of adultery). Still, there is an appetite for a certain degree of Islamic governance. That desire should not be confused with support for terrorism.

A more radical idea is to have the United Nations take over the government and administer Somalia with an East Timor-style mandate. Because Somalia has already been an independent country, this option might be too much for Somalis to stomach. To make it work, the United Nations would need to delegate authority to clan leaders who have measurable clout on the ground. Either way, the diplomats should be working with the moneylords more and the warlords less.

But the problem with Somalia is that after 18 years of chaos, with so many people killed, with so many guntoting men rising up and then getting cut down, it is exceedingly difficult to identify who the country's real leaders are, if they exist at all. It's not just Mogadishu's wasteland of blown-up buildings that must be reconstructed; it's the entire national psyche. The whole country is suffering from an acute case of post-traumatic stress disorder. Somalis will have to move beyond the narrow interests of clans, where they have withdrawn for protection, and embrace the idea of a Somali nation.

If that happens, the work will just be beginning. Nearly an entire generation of Somalis has absolutely no idea what a government is or how it functions. I've seen this glassy-eyed generation all across the country, lounging on bullet-pocked street corners and spaced out in the back of pickup trucks, Kalashnikovs in their hands and nowhere to go. To them, law and order are thoroughly abstract concepts. To them, the only law in the land is the business end of a machine gun.

JEFFREY GETTLEMAN is East Africa bureau chief for the *New York Times*.

Reprinted in entirety by McGraw-Hill with permission from *Foreign Policy,* March/April 2009, pp. 61–69. www.foreignpolicy.com. © 2009 Washingtonpost.Newsweek Interactive, LLC.

Will the Kenyan Settlement Hold?

"It is possible that in 10 years' time Kenyans will look back on the current crisis as the turning point at which the country came close to political disintegration, but drew back and established a long-term framework for democratic consolidation."

JOEL D. BARKAN

On the next-to-last day of February, with former UN Secretary General Kofi Annan standing behind them, Kenyan President Mwai Kibaki and opposition leader Raila Odinga signed a historic power sharing agreement, thus ending a nine-week crisis that had threatened to reduce Kenya to another failed or semi-failed African state.

The standoff between the two men and their respective political parties—the Party of National Unity (PNU) and the Orange Democratic Movement (ODM)—followed the flawed presidential election of December 27, 2007. Most domestic and international observers concluded that Odinga had probably won the election with a narrow plurality of the vote, but the Electoral Commission of Kenya (ECK) declared Kibaki the winner two and a half days after the polls closed. The legitimacy of Kibaki's "victory" was further undermined by the fact that the ODM won 99 of 210 seats in the Kenya National Assembly, compared to 43 for the PNU, making the ODM the largest party. Most troubling of all, the elections polarized the country along ethnic lines, as both parties had mobilized ethno-regional constituencies by appealing to voters' sense of identity. Passions ran high on election day as a record 9 million voters—70 percent of the registered electorate—turned out.

Afterwards, a wave of political unrest and inter-ethnic violence not experienced since independence in 1963 was set off by the delay in reporting the outcome, widespread suspicion about the results, and the polarization of the electorate. In the month following, between 1,000 and 1,500 people died as supporters of both sides attacked the other side, burned homes, and so forth. The attacks occurred in urban centers across western Kenya, in areas of the northern Rift Valley with settlements of Kikuyus (the nation's largest ethnic group), and in the slums of Nairobi. About 350,000 Kenyans were displaced from their homes, many permanently. And while some of this violence was spontaneous, most of it was encouraged, albeit indirectly, by political leaders and local elites on both sides of the party divide.

Kenya's economy was deeply affected by the crisis. Tourism, which had been enjoying a boom, evaporated, and the country's horticultural exports to Europe were interrupted. Foreign direct investment ceased overnight and the value of the Kenyan shilling fell by 9 percent. The IMF estimated that the economic losses during the unrest averaged more than $550 million a week, approaching what Kenya receives annually in foreign assistance. The economic effects of the crisis were also felt in Uganda, southern Sudan, Rwanda, and eastern Congo, places whose imports and exports flow through the Kenyan port of Mombasa.

Kenya, moreover, was becoming "zoned." Members of the Kikuyu, who make up 22 percent of the country's population, fled east from towns in western Kenya to the Kikuyu heartland of Central Province. Luos, who make up 13 percent of the population, and Kalenjins, who constitute 14 percent, were chased out of towns such as Naivasha and Nakuru and forced to migrate west to their ancestral homelands.

Progress Interrupted

The national elections in December, which also included voting for the National Assembly and local governments, were the fourth since the reintroduction of multiparty politics in 1992. Each of the previous elections had proceeded better than the one that preceded it, and the hope was that the 2007 poll would also be better than the last.

In 1992, when Kenya held its first multiparty balloting in 24 years, the playing field before the election was not level. Opposition candidates were routinely harassed by the provincial administration and by the police. The electoral commission was neither independent nor neutral. And there was widespread violence in the western Rift Valley, on a scale close to that which occurred this year. The one bright spot in that election was that, for the first time in Kenya's history, roughly 8,000 domestic electoral observers established a toehold in the process, with active diplomatic and financial support from the United States and other like-minded donors.

The 1997 elections were better, but still flawed. They too were marred by ethnic violence in the western Rift Valley and the area south of Mombasa, but the number of domestic observers nearly doubled. Also, the elections were preceded by a series of "mini-constitutional" reforms that, among other things, enlarged the electoral commission to include members nominated by the opposition and eliminated the president's right to unilaterally appoint 12 members of the National Assembly. The 1997 elections resulted in near legislative parity between the government and the opposition. Significantly, from that point on, President Daniel arap Moi, then in his nineteenth year in office, could no longer govern Kenya on his own, and the legislature began to emerge as a meaningful check on executive power.

Kenya's smaller, poorer ethnic groups have been calling for federalism for nearly 50 years.

The 2002 elections were better still. The logistics were improved. Harassment of opposition candidates all but ceased. A cadre of 24,000 domestic monitors covered all polling places. And Kenya experienced, for the first time since independence, a change in government via the ballot box. That election brought Kibaki to power as head of a broad-based pan-ethnic coalition that included not only his own community, the Kikuyu, but also the Luo, Kenya's third-largest ethnic group and the political base of Odinga.

Hopes of a fair and peaceful outcome for the December 2007 elections were therefore high, despite Kenya's polarized political climate. Public opinion polls conducted before the elections indicated that the presidential race was too close to call, and this increased the temptation for both sides to engage in fraud—but most Kenyans, as well as the international community, believed that Kibaki, Odinga, and the ECK would rise to the occasion. After all, democratization arguably had advanced more during Kibaki's presidency than at any time since independence, and the president himself stated that if the voters chose a candidate other than himself, he would "respect the wishes of Kenyans." The election campaign, though marked by isolated incidents of violence, had been largely free and fair. There was widespread confidence in the ECK's preparations for the elections and in the ECK chairman, Samuel Kivuitu. Domestic monitoring efforts, under the umbrella of the Kenya Elections Domestic Observation Forum (KEDOF), were expected to be as robust as they had been in 2002.

The election, it turned out, was arguably the freest and fairest since independence—until its last stages. International observers, including myself, witnessed an election that was reasonably well administered on election day. The polls opened roughly on time; the presiding officers were adequately trained; there were sufficient ballots and other required materials on hand; procedures were largely followed by the presiding officer at each polling station; all or nearly all voters who wished to vote had

done so by the time the polls closed; and though the counting of the paper ballots at the polling stations was slow—in many places continuing until midnight—it was transparent. Agents of the rival candidates signed off on the count and went home thinking that the rest of the process would proceed according to procedures specified by the ECK.

Sadly, they were wrong, as became apparent during the 48 hours following the close of the polls. In upwards of 35 parliamentary constituencies, the tabulation of the vote at constituency headquarters and the reporting of that tally to ECK headquarters in Nairobi were highly flawed. Domestic and international observers found that both sides probably inflated vote totals. They concluded that Kibaki supporters had perpetrated the far greater fraud. The European Union, which mounted the largest international observation effort, involving roughly 130 observers, called for an internationally supervised forensic audit of the tallies—as did the KEDOF.

With the benefit of hindsight, we now see that the international community, including the United States, was too complacent about several aspects of the polling. First, the fact that the register of voters was not fully purged of deceased voters was largely ignored, increasing the likelihood that vote totals could be inflated without (a telltale sign) exceeding the number of voters registered. Second, too much emphasis was placed on the individual leading the ECK, Kivuitu, instead of the ECK as an institution. The international community had lobbied hard for Kivuitu's reappointment as chairman, but paid insufficient attention both to Kibaki's appointment of five new commissioners and to procedures for reporting the vote from the polling stations to the ECK. Third, the international community missed the fact that Kenyan civil society in 2007 had failed to reestablish the robust organization for domestic election observation that it had mounted in 2002. Only 17,000 people observed the elections this time around—7,000 fewer than in 2002—with the result that not all polling stations were covered on election day.

Last but not least, the United States failed to respond quickly to the problems that unfolded during the two days after the election. Indeed, the State Department congratulated the Electoral Commission on its handling of the election on the very day—December 29—when the election came apart at the seams. Washington amended this statement on December 31, the day after Kibaki was hastily sworn in for a second term, but the damage to US credibility had been done.

While it is impossible to argue with certainty that Odinga won the election, it is possible to argue with near certainty that Kibaki did *not* win. Further, an exit poll conducted on election day suggests that the president may have failed to meet the requirement of winning at least 25 percent of the vote in five of Kenya's eight provinces—a test Odinga easily passed.

Fault Lines

The vote, like the opinion surveys that preceded the election, revealed fault lines in Kenyan society—fault lines that threatened to roll back the democratization and economic gains achieved in the five years since Kibaki was elected to succeed President Moi in 2002. Whereas the Moi years were marked by economic stagnation and resistance to democratic reform, Kibaki's administration turned the country around on both fronts. Indeed, the economy in 2007 was growing at nearly 7 percent annually, the highest rate in more than 30 years. A genuine "trickle-down" of benefits, including free universal primary education, and the resurrection of state agencies responsible for the marketing of coffee, tea, meat and milk, had touched the lives of Kenyans in all regions. Investment and tourists were pouring into the country. Civil society, the press, and the parliament had come alive, advancing to unprecedented levels what had been a tortuous quest for democratization. Kenya, it appeared, had been reborn, and President Kibaki should have won reelection handily. Deep schisms, however, existed within the political elite, reflecting the persistent divides in Kenyan society.

Many attribute Kibaki's victory in 2002 to Odinga. Odinga campaigned tirelessly for Kibaki and swung his political allies and followers in Nyanza Province, the heartland of the Luo people, behind Kibaki. A broad multiethnic coalition was formed, the National Rainbow Coalition (NARC), which brought the Kikuyu and Luo together. The formation of NARC was based on a now-controversial memorandum of understanding between Kibaki and Odinga that ostensibly promised Odinga the position of prime minister, which would carry substantial executive power. The coalition, which included other prominent non-Kikuyu leaders from outside Nyanza, was also promised an "equal" number of posts in Kibaki's cabinet should he win the election. After the election, however, Kibaki reneged on the deal—though he did appoint Odinga minister of works and housing. This perceived betrayal planted seeds for the turmoil that erupted five years later.

Kibaki further miscalculated by relying heavily as president on a small group of ministers from his own Kikuyu tribe, as well as from the culturally related Meru and Embu communities. These ministers, dubbed the "Mount Kenya Mafia" because they came from the ethnic groups that inhabit the slopes around Mount Kenya, controlled the key departments of finance, defense, internal security, justice, and information.

Kibaki began his first term in ill health, the result of a debilitating auto accident before the 2002 election and at least one stroke soon after his inauguration. As a consequence, especially during the first half of his presidency, he relied heavily on the "Mafia." This group of mostly older politicians was determined to run Kenya as it had been run during the 1960s and 1970s by the country's first president, Jomo Kenyatta. That is, they meant to pursue sound macroeconomic policies and delegate substantial authority to the civil service and the business community. In marked contrast to Moi, Kibaki and his inner circle did not micromanage either the bureaucracy or the private sector. The result was that individual Kenyans enjoyed more personal freedom, both political and economic, than at any time since independence.

The problem was that many members of other ethnic groups regarded the Mount Kenya Mafia, and thus the Kibaki administration, as favoring the Kikuyu at the expense of their own communities. The Kikuyu, as the largest ethnic group in Kenya, as well as the best educated and most prosperous, have long held a disproportionate number of positions in the civil service and the

professions. Kikuyu are also overrepresented in the business community, which has prospered as the country's economy has regained its dominance in East Africa. As a result, the same perception that had dogged the Kenyatta regime at the end of the 1970s, and that had triggered the ruinous redistribution policies of the Moi era, now confronted Kibaki and his government—that the Kikuyu run the country to serve themselves (even though all regions and ethnic groups have arguably benefited under Kibaki's rule).

Hence, even as Kibaki campaigned for reelection in 2007 on the theme that the country had never had it so good, the opposition, led by Odinga, mobilized the electorate with appeals for change—arguing that a new administration would do a better job of equally distributing the fruits of Kenya's economic and political success across the country's 42 ethnic groups. Odinga and the ODM also called for *majimbo,* the establishment of a federal form of government that would protect the interests of the other ethnic groups. The implicit anti-Kikuyu message was clear.

The Violent Aftermath

This appeal, in addition to a well-organized, well-financed, and colorful campaign by the ODM, enabled Odinga and other prominent non-Kikuyu leaders to rally a majority of Kenyans against Kibaki. Inevitably, the campaign also polarized the country along ethnic lines. While over 90 percent of the Kikuyu and Meru residents around Mount Kenya voted for Kibaki, a similar percentage of Luos in Nyanza voted for Odinga. Odinga also rolled up large majorities of between 55 and 70 percent of the vote in Western Province, the home of the Luhya people; in Rift Valley Province, the homeland of the Kalinjin and a half dozen other small tribes; in Coast Province, which is also inhabited by smaller ethnic groups, as well as most of Kenya's Muslim population; and in North Eastern Province. Odinga obtained a narrow majority in Nairobi, the capital, as well.

As noted previously, Odinga's ODM won many more seats than did Kibaki's PNU. When the seats held by allies of the two parties were added in, the ODM majority became much smaller—roughly 105 to 88, with the balance of the seats not committed to either side. The results, nonetheless, reflected dissatisfaction across Kenya with Kibaki's government. Even within the Kikuyu heartland, more than half the members of Kibaki's cabinet were defeated, as were a substantial number of Kikuyu incumbents, including two members of the old guard—Njenga Karume, the minister of defense, and David Mwiraria, the former minister of finance. The election revealed, in addition to the tensions between the Kikuyu and the other ethnic groups, deep generational divisions within the Kikuyu community. Many younger Kikuyu, especially professionals and members of the business community, believe that Kibaki's "exclusivist" approach to governance has not served their long-term interests nor the interests of the group, because it stokes resentment on the part of the other tribes.

Resentment against the Kikuyu runs particularly deep in the area of the western Rift Valley, in the triangle formed by Nakuru, Eldoret, and Kericho. It is in this area, inhabited by Kenya's white settler community before independence, that most of the killing occurred in the week following the election. In the 1960s and early 1970s, land vacated by the former settlers was purchased by Kikuyu with the assistance of the Kenyan government—then led by Kenyatta, himself a Kikuyu— instead of being returned to the communities from which the land had been taken. This, along with Kikuyu migration into the area as far back as the 1920s, created a domestic Kikuyu diaspora 100 miles west of the Kikuyu's Mount Kenya homeland. It was this group that suffered the most during the post-election violence.

In this context, the election and the violence that followed it made clear that Kibaki and his allies could not govern the country, despite having been sworn in for a second term. Nor could Odinga. Neither Kibaki nor Odinga won more than 46 percent of the vote. Neither was regarded by a majority of Kenyans as their legitimate representative, and it was quickly evident that a negotiated deal between the two principals and their parties was essential for long-term stability and economic wellbeing.

Talks That Nearly Failed

To this end, Kibaki announced on January 7, 2008, that he was prepared to form a government of national unity that presumably would give the ODM a large proportion of seats in the cabinet. Unfortunately, the president and his advisers misunderstood what type of deal would be required to return the country to the peace it had enjoyed before the elections. Moreover, on January 8, Kibaki undermined the prospects for a quick settlement by appointing as vice president Kalonzo Musyoka, the candidate who finished third in the presidential race with roughly 8 percent of the vote. He also appointed 16 people to the cabinet. His spokesperson described the new appointees as only "part" of the cabinet, but the appointments included the most powerful minis tries—finance, internal security, justice, local government, and defense.

The election was arguably the freest and fairest since independence—until its last stages.

These moves may have been meant to signal to Odinga and the ODM that the president was fully in charge. But they were more examples of the self-isolating and ethnically insensitive policies that had already marked the Kibaki presidency. In fact, based on his cabinet appointments, it appeared that Kibaki intended to base his new government on a central-eastern alliance of the Kikuyu, Embu, Meru, and Kamba peoples—versus everybody else.

This was precisely the type of governance that Odinga and his colleagues wanted to end, and they would not settle for mere posts in an expanded cabinet. After making it clear that they did not recognize Kibaki or his hastily appointed government as legitimate, they demanded genuine power sharing between the two sides. This would involve, at a minimum, the creation of a prime minister position—a prime minister who would

exercise real executive power and supervise the day-to-day work of government ministries, and who would be accountable to the National Assembly, *not* to the president. The ODM also demanded at least half the positions in the cabinet and, most important, a new constitution that would guarantee the arrangement, grant greater power to the legislature, and possibly establish a federal form of government.

The leaders of Kenya's smaller, poorer ethnic groups—the "have-nots," compared to the Kikuyu—have been calling for federalism for nearly 50 years. As in India in the 1950s, Nigeria in the 1980s, and Ethiopia in the 1990s, the effort to defuse linguistic and ethnic strife may require restructuring the basic rules of the political game by providing every group a homeland—even though this could result in ethnically homogeneous "zones" in which members of other groups have limited rights. Given the realities of Kenya and other plural societies across Africa, democratization must entail more than the expansion of individual rights, both political and economic. Group rights, to address the ethnic factor, must be afforded too, especially when inequities are perceived.

Kibaki and Odinga thus articulate and represent two different visions of Kenya's political future, and it is not surprising that in the aftermath of the election debacle the two sides quickly fell into stalemate—a condition that persisted for two months, despite carnage and heavy economic costs. During January, each side's strategy was simply to outlast the other. Kibaki, having been sworn in as president and in control of the state apparatus, refused, along with the PNU hard-liners around him, to offer the opposition more than a number of unspecified posts in a "government of national unity." They calculated that Odinga and the ODM, out of financial resources and not in office, would soon cave. The government rebuffed mediation efforts by figures such as Nobel laureate Desmond Tutu; Ghanaian President John Kufuor, then in his capacity as the rotating chair of the African Union (AU); and Mark Malloch Brown, Britain's foreign minister for Africa, Asia, and the UN. From the hard-liners' perspective (especially the minister of justice, Martha Karua), these visitors were meddling in Kenya's internal affairs.

Odinga and the ODM, in contrast, called for international mediation, and announced mass demonstrations to protest Kibaki's rule. They also calculated that they could outlast their adversaries because the economic losses borne by the Kikuyu business class would ultimately force Kibaki to address opposition demands. The result, in the near term, was more violence—including the shooting of several protesters in Kisumu and Nairobi, continued evictions of Kikuyu from the western Rift Valley, and mounting damage to the economy.

Three significant constituencies, one internal and two external, became increasingly alarmed about the possibility that what all regarded as the "anchor state" of East Africa and a symbol of political and economic reform for Africa as a whole was moving closer to the political abyss. The first such constituency was the country's civil society and press (both of which are arguably the most robust on the continent, save perhaps for South Africa's). The second constituency consisted of the heads of AU member states, particularly Kufuor, Abdoulaye Wade of Senegal, Yoweri Museveni of Uganda, Paul Kagame of Rwanda, and Jakaya

Kikwete of Tanzania. All of these leaders stated publicly that a negotiated solution to the crisis had to be found. The third constituency was the international community beyond Africa, led by the United States, Britain, and the EU. They stepped up consultations among themselves and agreed that the best approach was to throw their collective weight behind the AU's position of bringing in Annan to mediate the dispute. This proposal was one Kibaki and the hard-liners around him could not refuse, though it became evident in the negotiations that followed that they did not intend to change their positions.

The obvious questions are if the deal will hold and if the government will function. The answers are unclear.

Following Annan's arrival in late January, the two sides sat down to what became four weeks of talks that yielded little progress. The sides were each represented by three senior leaders, but the principals themselves were not involved. Without them, both sides stuck to their basic positions. For the PNU, this meant expanding the cabinet to accommodate the ODM, and creating a non-executive prime minister position that would be filled by and accountable to the president. Most important from the PNU's standpoint was that any deal would have to be arranged within the framework of the country's existing constitution, which assigns most powers to the president. The ODM leaders said no. They, remembering Kibaki's failure to appoint Odinga prime minister after the 2002 elections, insisted that any deal be cemented by an amendment to the constitution.

Although the talks made little progress, the teams did succeed in defining four issues that had to be addressed for Kenya to achieve a lasting peace. These were ending the violence; providing humanitarian assistance to those who need it; addressing the longstanding political issues underlying the conflict, including the country's constitution; and addressing long-term socioeconomic issues such as land tenure rights, poverty, and inequality. But apart from listing these issues, little was achieved. An uneasy calm spread across Kenya while the talks were under way, but few had any illusions about what would happen if the negotiations failed.

They nearly did fail. As the weeks passed, Annan made his frustrations known and stated the obvious—that both sides must make painful concessions if there was to be a settlement. He gained some assistance on February 18 when US Secretary of State Condoleezza Rice, who was in Africa at the time, flew to Nairobi to put pressure on the principals. Rice's visit, plus her blunt talk to both sides (especially Kibaki and the members of his negotiating team) pushed the talks to completion—though not immediately. Annan spoke in generalities about making hard choices, but Rice said explicitly that resolving the crisis required "genuine power sharing, not *pretend* power sharing." Rice reiterated her view five days later upon returning to the United States. At a tarmac press conference in Washington she again called for genuine power sharing, adding that she was

"disappointed" by the lack of progress since her visit to Nairobi, and that the US-Kenya relationship could not be "business as usual" if the two sides failed to reach an agreement. On the other hand, she said, the international community would stand by Kenya through its crisis should a deal be reached.

On February 25, Annan suspended the talks and announced that he would negotiate directly with Kibaki and Odinga to break the impasse. These new talks took place on February 27, with the participation of AU Chair Kikwete. Kikwete twisted Kibaki's arm by arguing that just as Tanzanian presidents had learned to live with a prime minister and a divided government, Kibaki could too—and that this was essential for peace and prosperity in Kenya and in the region. At that point, Kibaki agreed to a power sharing arrangement very much along the lines proposed by the ODM. Not surprisingly, the deal met with jubilation across western Kenya but with tepid acceptance across Central Province, the Kikuyu heartland.

Now the Hard Part

Although the accord resolves the immediate crisis, the obvious questions are if the deal will hold and if the government will function. The answers are unclear, especially when one notes what the agreement does *not* resolve. Apart from creating a prime minister accountable to the National Assembly, the deal is silent on the constitutional issues facing Kenya—particularly the powers of the president, the specific division of labor between the president and the prime minister, the balance of power between the executive and the legislature, and the parameters of any future federal arrangement. Also unmentioned in the accord are the four sets of issues identified during the negotiations as key to lasting peace. In short, implementing the spirit and the letter of the deal depends entirely on establishing trust between Kibaki and Odinga, and between their respective lieutenants.

The two leaders, in an effort to assure both Kenyans and the international community that they were serious about implementing the accord, moved during the first week of the parliamentary session that convened on March 11 to pass the National Accord and Reconciliation Act and the companion Constitutional Amendment Act. They also released four supplementary agreements. The first creates a commission of inquiry to examine the nature and cause of the violence that engulfed Kenya following the elections. The second establishes a Truth and Reconciliation Commission (TRC) to examine the historical grievances, including land issues, that have divided Kenya since independence in 1963. The TRC, which will function for a maximum of two years, is modeled on a similar body that existed in South Africa following apartheid. The third agreement establishes a committee of experts to review all aspects of the electoral process to ensure that the flaws evident in the 2007 elections are corrected before the next elections. (Significantly, the committee is *not* charged with conducting an audit or recount to determine who actually won the election.) Last is an agreement calling on the National Assembly to establish a statutory basis for a review of the nation's constitution and a referendum on any new or revised constitution.

While the basic power sharing deal is solidified by the passage of the National Accord and Reconciliation Act and the supplementary agreements, the hard work has only begun (as Annan rightly noted at the time the agreement was signed). This is particularly true when it comes to negotiating a new constitution, a subject on which even the supplementary agreement is vague. So what are the prospects for overall success?

One of three scenarios is likely to unfold, depending on how well Kibaki and Odinga are able to work together and keep their respective hard-liners in check. The most optimistic scenario is smooth sailing all the way. This is highly unlikely, especially on the issue of constitutional reform. Kenya has tried three times over the past 15 years to amend its constitution and has failed on two of those occasions. Sorting out a permanent structure for the executive, and deciding whether and in what form power will devolve to subnational units of government, will be particularly difficult. Already there is friction between the PNU and the ODM over which party will control which ministries in the new government.

The second and most likely scenario is muddling through. Under this scenario, negotiations for both the formation of a new government and the resolution of other issues will be protracted—but incremental (if not holistic) solutions will be found that avoid a total breakdown of the power sharing process. Power sharing, however, is in any case not an end in itself and cannot be sustained indefinitely. Rather, it is a mechanism to put Kenya back on track.

The third scenario is, within six to eighteen months, a political divorce, a breakdown, and the resumption of violence. This is also unlikely. While the coalition government will probably not last until the next election, neither will there likely be an acrimonious divorce—if for no other reason than that the leadership on both sides, especially Kibaki and Odinga themselves, have been chastened by the recent crisis.

While one must be cautious in assessing the future, it is possible that in 10 years' time Kenyans will look back on the current crisis as the turning point at which the country came close to political disintegration, but drew back and established a long-term framework for democratic consolidation, peace, and prosperity.

JOEL D. BARKAN is a senior associate at the Center for Strategic and International Studies and a professor emeritus of political science at the University of Iowa.

Mexico's Drug Wars Get Brutal

Given the rising tide of violence and the mounting evidence of drug-related corruption at all levels of government, it is probably fair to say that, so far, the cartels have managed to take the lead in a psychological war against the Mexican state.

FRANCISCO E. GONZÁLEZ

Narco-violence has intensified in Mexico since the early 2000s as a consequence of the Mexican government's crackdown on drug cartels. The spiral of violence has included shootouts on the public squares of big cities in broad daylight. A grenade attack on September 15, 2008, left eight dead and more than one hundred injured on the central square in Morelia (the capital of the state of Michoacán), on a night Mexicans were celebrating the 198th anniversary of their country's independence. The mayhem has included a proliferation of mass executions discovered on isolated ranches in remote areas, as well as in homes in crowded neighborhoods of cities as different and distant as Tijuana, on the border with California, and Mérida, on the Yucatán peninsula.

For most Mexicans, rich and poor, a psychological leap into a state of generalized fear and a perception of acute vulnerability coincided with an increase in gruesome displays of barbarism since the spring of 2006. These acts have included public displays of battered human heads, some thrown into plazas or placed on car rooftops, some thrown outside schools; mutilated torsos hanging from meat hooks; threats and taunts to rival cartels written on walls with the blood of butchered adversaries; and video-postings of torture and beheadings on YouTube.

How did Mexico spiral into this horrific wave of violence? The export of illegal substances to the United States became big business during the Prohibition years (1917–1933), but the seeds for the long-term growth and astounding profitability of the Mexico-US illegal drug trade were sown much earlier. Opiates (morphine and heroin) became a growing business in the United States in the wake of the American Civil War (1861–1865) and the two world wars (1914–1918 and 1939–1945). Since the nineteenth century, farmers in northwest Mexico had grown the opium poppies that satisfied part of this demand.

Mexico also became one of the ports of entry for cocaine. It was sold commercially and developed a mass market in the United States in the 1880s as a cure-all for everything from discolored teeth to flatulence. Smugglers from the Andean

countries and their US networks used Mexico and the Caribbean as gateways to supply the illegal market that served Hollywood's and New York's glamorous sets in the 1950s and 1960s. Cocaine remained a luxury item that only the well-to-do could afford until the early 1980s, when crack cocaine invaded the streets of America's large cities, wreaking havoc particularly in poor African-American and Hispanic neighborhoods.

Mexican seasonal migrant workers in the 1920s introduced to Americans the smoking of cannabis leaves. A mass market for cannabis consumption did not develop, however, until the rise of the counterculture of the 1960s and 1970s. Lastly, a mass market for synthetic drugs such as methamphetamines developed in the 1990s in the United States, and Mexican drug cartels became dominant suppliers of these too.

For decades Mexico and the United States have pursued very different antidrug strategies. The United States launched the original "war on drugs" under President Richard Nixon in the early 1970s. This policy contained both domestic and very prominent international components, explicitly targeting Mexico as a key site for the eradication of opium crops and marijuana, as well as the Andean countries for the eradication of coca. Successive Mexican governments, on the other hand, pursued what analysts have dubbed a "live and let live" approach. This system, characterized by a working relationship between some Mexican authorities and drug lords, prevailed between the 1940s and the 1990s.

This does not mean that Mexican presidents or most high-ranking bureaucrats, governors, and military high commanders were involved in the illegal drug trade. It does mean, however, that given Mexico's complex and fragmented territorial politics, the country's governors, mayors, military officers, and police chiefs retained some autonomy to advance their interests and those of their allies, including drug traffickers.

The kingpins bought access to the Mexico-US border, and this access allowed them to expand their production and smuggling activities. The authorities in turn stuffed their pockets with cash— but also, crucially, kept relative public peace and a semblance of law and order through the containment (rather than the destruction) of drug syndicates. Direct confrontation meant risking public disorder and violence, and indeed whenever authorities went after traffickers, bloody shootouts ensued. But such confrontations were the exceptions rather than the rule. For those involved on both sides of the game, mutually understood rules and practices prevailed. Authorities did not tolerate open turf wars among competing cartels, and they prohibited them from harming innocent civilians through extortion, kidnappings, or assassinations.

Rising Violence

Mexican authorities came under increased pressure from the United States to clamp down on drug cartels after the 1985 murder of an American Drug Enforcement Administration (DEA) officer. Enrique Camarena, a DEA agent working under-cover in Mexico, had exposed big ranches in the state of Chihuahua where traffickers cultivated cannabis with the full knowledge of some federal authorities, military officers, and state and local officials. The traffickers captured and killed Camarena, and the discovery of his tortured, decomposing body created a furor in US public opinion. Footdragging by the authorities investigating the case convinced Americans that highly placed individuals in the government of President Miguel de la Madrid were involved with the traffickers.

By the time a new president, Carlos Salinas, expressed eagerness to join the United States in a free trade agreement in 1989, the Mexican government had to show that it was doing all it could to clean house. Salinas allowed DEA agents to return to work in Mexico and his government spent resources strengthening military and police operations against traffickers. In parallel, changes enacted under the administration of George H.W. Bush altered the long-standing equilibrium of the Mexico-US illegal drug trade. In 1989–90, Washington committed large-scale material resources, military training, and intelligence to try to bust the Andean cocaine trade. After years of engagement, the United States contributed to the demise of Colombia's main syndicates, the Medellín and Cali cartels, and to largely shutting down the Caribbean–Gulf of Mexico cocaine route. By the late 1990s, the battle lines had been redrawn and Mexico had ended up in the eye of the storm.

The demise of the Colombian cartels allowed the Mexican syndicates, which formerly had worked for the Colombians, to take over. The virtual closure of the Caribbean route strengthened the Central America–Mexico route by land and the Pacific Ocean route toward Mexico's western coast. Despite official efforts by Salinas's successor, President Ernesto Zedillo, drug traffic increased in the late 1990s and some Mexican authorities continued to be on the drug lords' payroll. The most embarrassing instance was revealed in 1997, when Zedillo's drug czar, General Jesús Gutiérrez Rebollo, was exposed as a beneficiary of the top leader of the Juárez cartel. The confluence of higher spending by Mexican governments to combat drug trafficking and higher illegal drug flows through the country's territory set the stage for a serious increase in narco-violence in the late 1990s.

This increase in drug-related violence coincided in 2000 with the loss of the presidency by the Institutional Revolutionary Party (PRI) for the first time in Mexico's history. Vicente Fox, of the center-right National Action Party (PAN), assumed the presidency promising many changes, among them the defeat of the drug cartels. Some analysts think that even before Fox became president, PAN governments at the state and local levels in the early 1990s had pursued a more principled approach to combating drug trafficking, which had resulted in higher levels of drug-related violence in border states such as Baja California and Chihuahua. Fox purged and reorganized the federal police forces and tried to extradite captured drug lords to the United States.

This policy, though effective at raising the number of individuals arrested and drug shipments confiscated, fell far short of the government's objective of defeating the cartels. Moreover, the capture of some cartel leaders was tantamount to kicking hornets' nests without having the means to spray the rattled insects. The capture of Benjamín Arellano Félix, head of the Tijuana cartel, in 2002, and of Osiél Cárdenas Guillén, head of the Gulf cartel, in 2003, led to a vicious war within and among the criminal organizations, as upcoming drug leaders battled to assert or reassert control over territory, resources, and manpower. The change in the balance of power among the cartels led to new alliances. The Gulf, Tijuana, and Juárez cartels struck deals to take on another bloc made up of the Sinaloa, Milenio, Jalisco, and Colima cartels.

Likewise, the reorganized police forces soon succumbed to the bribes and threats of the criminal syndicates. Government infiltration continued to such an extent that a spy for a drug cartel was discovered working in the president's office in 2005. Violence had gotten so out of control by 2004–05 that Fox implemented an operation involving 1,500 army and federal police officers in Mexico-US border cities. In this context, the conflict intensified and started mutating into the bloody spectacle that Mexicans witness today.

Calderón's War

Felipe Calderón, also from the PAN, took over the presidency from Fox on December 1, 2006. Calderón won a fiercely contested and extremely close election against the candidate of the center-left Party of the Democratic Revolution (PRD), Andrés Manuel López Obrador. Throughout the campaign, public opinion surveys had shown that Mexican citizens' top concerns were lack of economic opportunities, and crime and general insecurity. Shortly after assuming office, Calderón declared a war on drugs by deploying the Mexican military in a series of large-scale operations that by the end of 2008 had involved close to 40,000 troops and 5,000 federal police.

The decision to bring the armed forces into the fray was controversial, and observers disagreed about the reasons the president raised the stakes in this way, investing his political capital in the war on drugs. During the presidential campaign Calderón had not hinted that this policy would come to define his government.

Some analysts highlighted a political explanation, according to which weak incoming presidents in contemporary Mexico have to carry out spectacular acts early on to establish their authority, boost their standing with the public, and help gain some autonomy over groups within the Mexican political class that try to limit their scope of action. From this perspective, Calderón may have ordered the military surge against the drug cartels to "turn the page" on the then- raging postelectoral conflict with the PRD candidate. Given the contentious electoral results, López Obrador had declared himself the "legitimate" president. Calderón's decisive action showed in effect who was the real commander-in-chief.

Other analysts have argued that the political explanation sounds like a conspiracy theory. The main reason behind the military surge, they suggest, was the incoming adminstration's realization that the cartels were dominating more territory and public spaces and that if this process were left unchecked, it could lead to a situation of state failure similar to the one that Colombia had to endure. Also, according to this view, a war on drugs had existed in all but name during Fox's term. Given the ineffectiveness of police forces in combating the syndicates, Calderón was left without any option but to involve the military.

In fact these two explanations are not mutually exclusive. Calderón might have decided to pursue a war on drugs given, first, genuine concern regarding the uncontrolled violence in parts of the country, including his home state of Michoacán; and, second, his wish to make the armed forces key allies in the context of the postelectoral conflict with López Obrador and the PRD. Regardless of the mix of motivations for launching the surge against traffickers, in the short term Calderón has reaped higher political than operational benefits. Opinion polls show that a majority of the Mexican public supports the president's stance against the cartels. By mid-2007, the postelectoral conflict and López Obrador's continuing maneuvers to discredit Calderón had disappeared from the headlines. But dominating the news instead has been a brutal intensification of drug-related violence.

The Corruption Conundrum

Operationally, Calderón's war against drugs has already resulted in the arrests of more than a dozen top drug lords and record seizures of arms, cash, and drugs. Yet the campaign started as, and it remains, a steep uphill battle. The main conundrum is still the ineffectiveness of law enforcement in Mexico. Aside from questions of jurisdiction (Mexico's federal structure means that approximately 3,800 law enforcement institutions exist throughout the country), the root cause of the problem is the drug cartels' extensive penetration of government agencies and co-optation of government officials. This is a hurdle that is almost impossible to overcome without somehow depriving the drug lords of the astounding profits they currently make.

Indeed, the paradox of tougher enforcement is that, as the cost of doing business in the illegal drug trade rises, the street price of drugs goes up too, thereby raising profit margins. The result is that some drug traffickers and would-be traffickers may decide that pursuing this line of business is becoming prohibitively risky, but as long as profits from the trade remain so out

of line compared with any other economic activity, there will always be individuals ready to risk their lives.

Studies of drug gang members in cities like Chicago have shown that only the "top dogs" make stratospheric profits, while most of the rank and file make so little that they have second and third jobs, while still living with their mothers! Yet, no matter how low the probability of making it to the top, individuals will take a chance on the dangers of the drug trade if their social conditions are precarious enough and their opportunities for advancement are negligible. And it goes without saying that conditions of hopelessness and extreme life choices abound in developing countries such as Mexico. As long as these conditions persist, and as long as the system put in place to counter the narcotics trade leads to the generation of exceptional profits, there will continue to be individuals willing to play this lottery.

The generation of exceptional profits, moreover, also provides the plentiful cash that drug lords use to buy into the system. Only now are we realizing the extent to which top Mexican authorities are in the pay of the drug lords. Since at least the Camarena affair, and probably for much longer, Mexicans had assumed that the cartels had bought off some among the political elite. But never before have so many top ranking law enforcers been exposed as under Calderón. They have been exposed at the local, state, and federal levels, and have ranged from the lowliest privates among the ranks to the head of Mexico's Interpol office and the federal government's drug czar.

Only now are we realizing the extent to which top Mexican authorities are in the pay of the drug lords.

Even though many officials might refuse to collaborate with the drug cartels irrespective of the pecuniary gains on offer, the criminal syndicates also compel cooperation by issuing threats and sometimes carrying them out. The assassination in May 2008 of Edgar Millán Gómez, the acting chief of Mexico's federal police, allegedly in retribution for the arrest in January of one of the top leaders of the Sinaloa cartel, increased the sense of vulnerability even for those who go about their daily lives surrounded by bodyguards.

Fate did not help the government's cause when a small jet carrying Mexico's top law enforcement officials—including the interior secretary and Calderón's closest political ally, Juan Camilo Mouriño, as well as the country's antidrug prosecutor, José Luis Santiago Vasconcelos—crashed in downtown Mexico City on November 4, 2008, killing all on board. Even though official evidence has suggested that turbulence caused the accident, conspiracy theories have spread around Mexico, fueling the sense that the government has suffered another blow, this time at its core.

In the two years since the start of Calderón's war on drugs, the government has raised the stakes for the cartels by hitting them with full military force. The cartels have responded with an intensification of both their turf wars and their war against the

Mexican state. As a result, drug-related violence has spread from states where it has been endemic for years into states that had not seen drug-related violence before. The number of dead almost doubled in just one year—from 2,700 in 2007 to more than 5,300 in 2008. Given the rising tide of violence and the mounting evidence of drug-related corruption at all levels of government, it is probably fair to say that, so far, the cartels have managed to take the lead in a psychological war against the Mexican state.

I noted earlier that Calderón's drug war has yielded higher short-term political than operational benefits. However, some political implications of the war could have a big impact on the operational capacity for waging it. The most important of these political implications has been Calderón's ability to get the US government to accept that the war on drugs is a matter of co-responsibility. In effect, Calderón has managed to bring the United States into the eye of the storm.

> **Calderón has managed to bring the United States into the eye of the storm.**

Washington Lends a hand

Colombia receives the lion's share of US anti-narcotics aid in Latin America—this has been the case for several decades. But Calderón's declaration of a war on drugs in Mexico got the attention of President George W. Bush and the US Congress in 2007. As a result, a $1.4 billion, three-year program, the Mérida Initiative, started operating in December 2008. The aim is to assist the Mexican government wage the war against drugs by helping it with technology and training.

There is no doubt that, in the case of Colombia, the agreement between Presidents Andrés Pastrana and Bill Clinton, which led to the creation of Plan Colombia in 2000, has proved a game changer. In the late 1990s, analysts and policy makers talked about Colombia as a potential failed state. Although the US Government Accountability Office has shown that Plan Colombia has not been a great success in terms of curbing the production of coca and the transportation of cocaine, it has undoubtedly strengthened the Colombian state and its capacity to strike against non-state actors, notably guerrillas and paramilitary groups. Colombia, which until recently possessed an underdeveloped military, has come a long way in eight years, and the central government's presence around the country's territory is stronger than ever.

These benefits have been very costly in some regards. Aerial fumigation to eradicate coca plants has damaged legal crops and produced adverse health effects in those exposed to the herbicides. The number of dead and displaced as a result of the intensification of the conflict since the early 2000s has grown enormously. News of extensive human rights violations has made headlines around the world. And yet, the plan's contribution to strengthening the state—and thereby to reestablishing a still precarious but nonetheless basic sense of security for many Colombians, particularly in big cities—has meant that a substantial majority of that country's public favors the continuation of President Alvaro Uribe's policies, and of Colombia's cooperation with the United States.

What then for Mexico? There is danger in carrying the Colombia-Mexico analogy too far. After all, the United States does not share a border with Colombia, let alone a 2,000-mile one as it does with Mexico. For Mexico, the danger of an escalating war on drugs, with the United States helping to strengthen Mexican authorities' firepower, is that some of the extreme conditions created in Colombia since 2000 could be repeated. For the United States, the danger from such an escalation is potentially far greater than in its engagement with Colombia. An escalation of the war on drugs in Mexico could spill over into US territory. Indeed, an April 2008 report by the US National Drug Intelligence Center, part of the Department of Justice, found evidence of Mexican smuggling operations in all but two states (Vermont and West Virginia) of the union. Drug-related violence connected with the Mexican cartels has been increasingly reported in cities of the American southwest, from San Diego to Phoenix, Las Vegas, and Dallas.

Some analysts have gone so far as to start calling this a borderless war. This is no doubt an exaggeration. But there is also no doubt that unless US authorities can control the massive trafficking of weapons, cash, and chemical precursors of drugs that originate in the United States and are shipped into Mexico, America risks exposing its "soft underbelly," a term now often used to describe its southern border. As it is, some 90 percent of armaments confiscated from the cartels comes from the more than 7,000 gun outlets situated on US soil within 50 miles of the Mexican border.

The stakes for the United States in Mexico, thus, are much higher than they could ever be in Colombia. Supplying the Mexican government with technology and training to help prop up its fighting capabilities is an important first step, but it is not enough. Without seriously denting the demand for illegal drugs and preventing the southbound flow of weapons, cash, and drug-making chemicals, the United States will keep feeding the flames that threaten to consume the basis for civilized life in Mexico.

FRANCISCO E. GONZÁLEZ is an associate professor of politics and Latin American studies at Johns Hopkins University's School of Advanced International Studies. He is the author of *Dual Transitions from Authoritarian Rule: Institutionalized Regimes in Chile and Mexico, 1970–2000* (Johns Hopkins University Press, 2008).

Dangerous Liaisons

As Farc guerrillas drag Latin America to the brink of war, ratings for Colombia's ultra-right Álvaro Uribe soar. Now the left is determined to divorce itself from the group.

ALICE O'KEEFFE

Orlando Ordoñez no longer looks like a *guerrillero*. He is clean-shaven, with suit, shiny boots and long hair slicked into a neat ponytail. Calloused hands and a worn expression on his broad face are the only clues to his past: Ordoñez spent ten years rising through the ranks of the Revolutionary Armed Forces of Colombia (Farc), Latin America's oldest and most powerful guerrilla army. By the time he left in 2005, he was, as describes himself, a high-ranking *comandante*, managing millions of dollars of the group's profits from extortion and drug trafficking.

Ordoñez experienced the moral decline of the Farc from the inside. He joined as an idealistic 28-year-old, attracted by the organisation's revolutionary agenda. "When I joined, being a *guerrillero* was a source of pride," he says. "We had the respect of the Colombian people." Initially, he looked after a small territory where peasants grew crops including coca, and the Farc charged the drug traffickers a tax for the service. It was only in the late 1990s that he realised the organisation was increasingly producing and trafficking drugs itself. "The ideology was changing."

His disillusionment grew over time. He discovered that other *comandantes* had been abusing, threatening and displacing peasants in the areas they controlled. "Our reputation in those communities suffered very badly." Then he was given a promotion, and moved into a position where he was expected to buy influence with politicians, businessmen and police. "I was unhappy with my life, and with the Farc," he says. He took the potentially life-threatening decision to desert and handed himself in to the army.

Ordoñez is now training at a community television station, and hopes to persuade others to demobilise. "I want all the *guerrilleros* to know that if they want to really make a difference, they should rejoin Colombian society. If they want to work for the left-wing cause, this is a democracy and they are free to do that."

At present, the Colombian left is in a sorry state. Unlike much of the rest of Latin America, where centre-left and left-wing

administrations have become increasingly common, Colombia is governed by a right-wing, militaristic, pro-business president, Álvaro Uribe. After winning two elections by large majorities on the promise that he would smash the guerrillas with a "strong hand", he saw his popularity recently hit 84 per cent. The opposition is floundering. This is even though the country has one of the most unequal societies in the world: its cities are filled with shiny 4x4s, designer beauty queens and chichi shopping malls, but in its slums and rural areas 50 per cent of the population lives in poverty.

No Support

Those on the left in Colombia have one explanation for their lack of popularity: the Farc effect. "It is our greatest problem," says José Sanín Vásquez, director of the trade union research institute Escuela Nacional Sindical. "If being on the left means wanting change, then the Farc has become ultra-right-wing. It is a great obstacle to change in this country." It is a mark of how far the Farc has fallen that, despite great injustices in Colombia, it commands almost no support from any section of society. In a recent Gallup poll, all but 3 per cent of Colombians said they had an unfavourable opinion of the Farc.

Trade unionists, human rights campaigners, community leaders and left-wing politicians all have the same complaint: their credibility is continually damaged by insinuations in politics and the media that they are "guerrilla sympathisers" (Uribe has made a habit of smearing his critics, including Amnesty International and other NGOs, in this way). "It suits the government to describe the Farc as left-wing, as that way it stigmatises the opposition," says Sanín. "It suits the Farc because it gives it a certain legitimacy. Meanwhile, the real left in Colombia is completely squashed between the two."

The Farc was founded in 1964, and headed by a peasant leader and member of the Communist Party known as Manuel Marulanda, or "Tirofijo." Its members came from existing peasant militias, but during the 1960s and 1970s it adopted a Marxist ideology. As other guerrilla groups in Colombia and across Latin America have been defeated or drawn into mainstream politics, the Farc has continued to wage an implacable war against the Colombian state, fuelled increasingly by profits from the drugs trade. It also specialises in kidnapping and extortion, with some of its hostages—most notoriously the former presidential candidate Ingrid Betancourt—kept in jungle hideouts for years.

The impact of the guerrilla movement in Colombia has been particularly devastating because it has given rise to an array of right-wing paramilitary groups, which sprang up around the country during the 1990s. Their aim was to protect the interests of large landowners and they were brutally dismissive of the rights of the civilian population, taking revenge on anyone they considered to be a guerrilla supporter. The armed groups from left and right have contributed to a bloody and seemingly intractable civil war, in which the value of human life has been disregarded by both sides. Tens of thousands of Colombians—usually from the poorest communities—have been killed, and three million more displaced; the country has the world's second-largest internally displaced population, outstripped only by Sudan's.

Harsh Discipline

The highest estimated figure for Farc membership stands at 30,000, though the Colombian government claims that numbers have fallen to around 8,000. Its soldiers are drawn largely from the most deprived social groups, attracted by the offer of a basic wage. "I always liked guns, and what's more I come from a very poor family. The Farc told me they would help me if I joined," says Francisco, a softly spoken 22-year-old from a peasant family in the Antioquian region, who joined the group when he was 17. Like many Farc foot soldiers, he is illiterate. "They taught me all about the ideology and to sing the revolutionary anthems. They taught us that the Farc would bring the Cuban Revolution to Colombia. Once I was trained, they gave me a gun and set me missions, like collecting a certain amount of base [coca paste] from a particular area, and bringing it back to the camp."

The conditions for recruits are harsh: the group operates from bases deep inside Colombia's vast, dense jungles, where disease is rife and resources are scarce. Discipline is brutal; those who break the rules are subjected to trials, or "war councils." "When somebody broke the rules, they would tie them up and present them in front of the group to decide their punishment," says Francisco. "If they had a good record, they might be given a chance. If they had stolen food from the store tent or something, and had done it a number of times, they would be given the maximum penalty. Often they would just tie people up and punish them for nothing."

In Colombia, it has long been widely accepted across the political spectrum that although the Farc continues to use Marxist rhetoric, it has abandoned any claim to political legitimacy. "The foot soldiers are still taught the ideology, and believe it," says Jaime Echevarría, another former member who did not want his real name published. Jaime has a university education, but had lost his job and was destitute when he was recruited to the Farc's urban division. "But to judge by my contact with the higher

ranks and the secretariat [the Farc's seven-man governing body], I would say they have left that behind. They are businessmen."

The increasingly public alliance between the Farc and the Venezuelan president, Hugo Chávez, which reared its head last month, has served to bolster Uribe's position and further demoralise the Colombian left. The extent of the collaboration between the two is a matter of debate—the Colombian government claims to have evidence that Chávez has provided the Farc with funds, although he denies this. He has, however, made no secret of his political support (as reported in the NS of 11 February). The two countries were brought to the brink of war in March following an illegal raid by Colombian troops into Ecuadorian territory, during which one of the Farc secretariat, Raú Reyes, was killed. Ecuador was understandably furious, but Chávez went further, ordering troops to the border and announcing a minute's silence in Reyes's honour.

> **Thankfully, we were spared annihilation because we did not ally ourselves closely with Chávez.**

"Venezuela does not support the Farc, but Chávez has made a strategic alliance with them," says Fernando Gerbasi, formerly Venezuela's ambassador in Colombia and now a professor of international relations at the Universidad Metropolitana in Caracas.

Having turned its back on the political arena at home, the Farc has focused on building up international support, effectively playing on tensions between right-wing Colombia and its "21st-century socialist" neighbour. With a huge amount of military aid pouring into Colombia from the United States—around $5bn since 2000—its neighbours, with comparatively scant military resources, understandably fear that the country has become a foothold from which the US can extend its influence in the region.

"The danger is that the US would like Colombia to be its proxy for an anti-Chávez campaign," says Rodrigo Pardo, editor of the Colombian political magazine Cambio. "That would be disastrous for regional relations."

Strengthening Uribe

Gustavo Petro, a senator for Colombia's left-wing opposition Polo Democrático Alternativo party, describes himself as a personal friend of Chávez. He believes that the Venezuelan president allowed himself to be persuaded that the Farc offered the only way of challenging the Uribe administration, and protecting himself against American aggression.

"This was a grave error, and if he had consulted us it never would have happened," Petro says. "The relationship between the Farc and the Latin American left represents a mortal danger for the left." He despairs that the crisis has once again boosted the popularity of the already unchallengeable Uribe. "It has affected the left in Colombia profoundly. We have been damaged—thankfully, we were spared annihilation because we did not ally ourselves closely with Chávez."

Meanwhile, the Uribe administration continues to implement controversial policies, virtually unchecked by a serious opposition. Colombia is opened up to business while trade unionists fear for their lives; millions of dollars are poured into the military while the displaced population is abandoned to live in squalid poverty. The government offers cash incentives for the murder of suspected *guerrilleros*—last month, it gave a $2.6m reward to a Farc soldier who killed another member of the secretariat and delivered his hand to the authorities in a plastic bag.

"There is a lot of work for the left to do in this country," says Petro with a weary smile."

Call in the Blue Helmets

Peacekeeping: Can the UN cope with increasing demands for its soldiers?

Call it peacekeeping, peace-enforcement, stabilisation or anything else, but one thing is clear: the world's soldiers are busier than ever operating in the wide grey zone between war and peace.

The United Nations has seen a sixfold increase since 1998 in the number of soldiers and military observers it deploys around the world. About 74,000 military personnel (nearly 100,000 people including police and civilians, and increasing fast) are currently involved in 18 different operations—more than any country apart from the United States. And it is not just the UN that is in high demand. NATO, the European Union and the African Union (AU), as well as other coalitions of the willing, have some 74,000 soldiers trying to restore peace and stability in troubled countries. Added to their number come the more than 160,000 American, British and other troops in Iraq.

The "war on terror" is one cause of this military hyperactivity. But Jean-Marie Guéhenno, the UN's under-secretary for peacekeeping, also sees more hopeful reasons. The growing demand for blue helmets, he says, is a good sign that a number of conflicts are ending.

This is only partly true. In Congo, southern Sudan and Liberia—the UN's three biggest operations—the blue helmets are shoring up peace agreements. But in countries such as Lebanon or Côte d'Ivoire, they are at best holding the line between parties still in conflict.

One reason for the surge in UN peacekeeping is that Africa, the region most in need of peacekeepers, is least able to provide for itself. The AU is trying to improve its peacekeeping capacity, but is desperately short of resources. It has handed over its operation in Burundi to the UN. Now it wants the blue helmets to help relieve its 7,000 hard-pressed AU peacekeepers in Sudan's troubled region of Darfur.

The Sudanese government has long resisted such a deployment, accusing the UN of being an agent of the West. But under sustained international pressure to halt what Washington regards as genocide, it has grudgingly agreed to allow in a "hybrid" UN and AU force. An advance party of 24 police advisers and 43 military officers, wearing blue berets and AU armbands, has started to arrive in Darfur to test Sudan's co-operation. According to a three-phase plan, the force will be built up into a contingent of 17,000 soldiers and 3,000 police officers.

Can the UN take on another onerous peacekeeping operation? Mr Guéhenno says the world already faces two kinds of "overstretch": the military sort, in which many armed forces of many leading countries are badly strained by foreign operations; and "political overstretch", in which the world's political energies are focused on just a few acute problems while the UN is left to deal as best it can with many chronic or less visible conflicts.

Mr Guéhenno is cautious about what he can achieve in Darfur. He says he may get the soldiers, given the right political conditions, but is worried about getting enough "enablers"—the crucial specialised units and equipment that enhance the ability of a force to move and operate. These include army engineers and logisticians, field hospitals and nurses, heavy-lift aircraft and transport helicopters, as well as proper command-and-control and intelligence-gathering: in other words, the wherewithal of modern Western expeditionary forces. These capabilities are in short supply and are expensive; the few countries that have them are using them, and the others can't afford them.

In a region as vast as Darfur, an effective UN force would need to be highly mobile, and make use both of unmanned surveillance drones and special forces. It would need to sustain itself in a harsh environment, some 1,400km (870 miles) from the nearest harbour and with few airfields. Engineers could drill for water, but would be under pressure to share it with local populations and with refugees. And then there is the problem of time. On current plans it would take six to nine months to build up to full strength in Darfur. Having to merge with the AU adds further complications to the command structure.

Finding a Fire Engine

Apart from military capability, or lack of it, there is the question of political will. Who will risk their soldiers' lives, and their valuable military assets, in a faraway conflict? NATO, the world's foremost military alliance, has struggled for months to find a few thousand additional soldiers—and a few extra helicopters—to back up its troops fighting in southern Afghanistan.

By contrast, European countries moved with unusual speed when the UN appealed for its hapless mission in Lebanon to be reinforced last summer in order to end the war between Israel and Hizbullah. Within weeks of a ceasefire being called in August, French and Italian peacekeepers were coming ashore. It was the first time that sizeable Western forces had donned blue helmets since the unhappy days of the war in Bosnia.

But there were particular reasons for this. Lebanon, of course, is more easily accessible than Afghanistan or Darfur. But it is also less dangerous than southern Afghanistan, and European governments regard the Israeli-Arab conflict as much closer to their interests than the effort to pacify rebellious Pashtun tribesmen.

Kofi Annan, the former UN secretary-general, liked to say that the UN is the only fire brigade that must go out and buy a fire engine before it can respond to an emergency. The Security Council must first authorise an operation and pass a budget, and then the

Current UN Peacekeeping Missions

Location	Mission Name	Year of Deployment	Number of Personnel*
Congo	MONUC	1999	22,167
Liberia	UNMIL	2003	18,382
Southern Sudan	UNMIS	2005	13,021
Lebanon	UNIFIL	1978	11,431
Côte d'Ivoire	UNOCI	2004	11,150
Haiti	MINUSTAH	2004	3,142
Kosovo	UNMIK	1999	4,631
Burundi	ONUB	2004	3,142
Ethiopia and Eritrea	UNMEE	2000	2,687
Timor-Leste	UNMIT	2006	1,340
Golan Heights (Israel/Syria)	UNDOF	1974	1,247
Cyprus	UNFICYP	1964	1,069
Afghanistan[a]	UNAMA	2002	850
Western Sahara	MINURSO	1991	459
Georgia	UNOMIG	1993	419
Middle East[b]	UNTSO	1948	374
Sierra Leone[a]	UNIOSIL	2006	298
India and Pakistan	UNMOGIP	1949	113

*Includes military, police and civilians

[a]Political or peace-building missions

[b]Egypt, Jordan, Israel, Lebanon and Syria

Source: United Nations

secretariat beseeches governments to contribute forces and arranges the means to transport them. This system has created a two-tier structure: powerful countries decide the missions (and pay for them) while poor countries such as India, Pakistan, Bangladesh, Nepal and Jordan supply the soldiers. They receive a payment for doing so; this becomes for some a subsidy for their own armed forces, while the deployment also provides their troops with training.

Idealists such as Sir Brian Urquhart, a former UN under secretary-general, believe it is high time the UN had its own "fire engine": a permanent force that could deploy quickly to stop conflicts before they spin out of control. The UN's founding fathers envisioned some kind of international army, but all proposals for a standing UN force have foundered—partly because of political objections to giving the UN too much power, partly because of the practical difficulties of recruiting, training and paying for such a force.

After the failure of the UN in the mid-1990s to stop blood-letting in Somalia, Rwanda and the Balkans, many argued it would be better for those who are properly equipped to deal with putting out the fires of conflict. In 1999, it was NATO that stopped the killing of ethnic Albanians in Kosovo, while a force led by Australia halted the conflict in East Timor. A year later, in Sierra Leone, the quick deployment of about 1,000 British soldiers helped save what was then the UN's largest peace-keeping mission from collapsing under attack by rebels of the Revolutionary United Front.

All this seemed to confirm that the UN could take on only soft peacekeeping and "observer" missions with co-operation from the warring sides. But in 2000 a panel headed by Lakhdar Brahimi recommended a complete rethink of UN peacekeeping. The United Nations, it acknowledged, "does not wage war"; but its operations nevertheless had to "project credible force" and be ready to distinguish between victim and aggressor.

Mr Brahimi's central recommendation was the creation of multinational brigades around the world ready to deploy at short notice. This idea of pre-assembling bits of the fire engine has made only fitful progress. But other proposals have been acted on. They include the creation of a more powerful headquarters to oversee the UN effort; stockpiling of equipment; compilation of lists of military officers, police and other experts who will be on *call* to join UN missions; and the meshing of peacekeeping with ordinary policing, government reform and economic development.

New missions are now much more likely to be given robust mandates authorising them to use "all necessary means" under Chapter VII of the UN Charter: in other words, aggressive military force. In places such as Congo and Haiti, the UN has even been accused of using too much force.

Since the world is likely to need large numbers of peacekeepers for the foreseeable future, a further option is being explored: "leasing" the fire engine by hiring private security companies to do more of the work. Don't expect anything to happen quickly, though. The world, and especially the Americans, has moved a long way towards the privatisation of war. But for many, the privatisation of peacekeeping is still a step too far.

UNIT 4

Political Change in the Developing World

Unit Selections

Key Points to Consider

• What are the current trends in democracy in different parts of the world?

• What accounts for Asia's democracy backlash?

• What challenges does India face in expanding it influence?

• What challenges does new South African president Jacob Zuma face?

• How do new findings challenge the conventional wisdom regarding Muslim views of democracy?

• What do prospects for democracy in the Arab world depend on?

• How does the 1979 Iranian Revolution continue to affect the country's politics and economics?

• What problems does Brazil face in finding a balance between its regional and global roles?

• Why is the success of Venezuela's revolution uncertain?

Student Website

www.mhcls.com

Internet References

Latin American Network Information Center—LANIC
   http://www.lanic.utexas.edu
ReliefWeb
   http://www.reliefweb.int/w/rwb.nsf
World Trade Organization (WTO)
   http://www.wto.org

A history of authoritarian rule and the lack of a democratic political culture have hampered efforts to extend democracy to many parts of the developing world. Authoritarian colonial rule and the failure to prepare colonies adequately for democracy at independence help to account for the present situation. Even when there was an attempt to foster parliamentary government, the experiment failed frequently, largely due to the lack of a democratic tradition and a reliance on political expediency. Independence-era leaders frequently resorted to centralization of power and authoritarianism, either to pursue ambitious development programs or more often simply to retain power. In some cases, leaders experimented with socialist development schemes that emphasized ideology and the role of party elites. The promise of rapid, equitable development proved elusive, and the collapse of the Soviet Union further discredited this strategy. Other countries had the misfortune to come under the rule of tyrannical leaders who were concerned only with enriching themselves and who brutally repressed anyone with the temerity to challenge their rule. Although there are a few notable exceptions, the developing world's experiences with democracy since independence have been limited.

Democracy's "third wave" brought redemocratization to Latin America during the 1980s after a period of authoritarian rule. The trend toward democracy also spread to some Asian countries, such as the Philippines and South Korea, and by 1990 it reached sub-Saharan Africa, too. The results of this democratization trend have been mixed so far. While democracy has increased across the world, the pace of democratic change has slowed recently; and in some instances democratic reform has regressed. There has been a backlash against democracy in some parts of Asia, particularly illustrated by the armed forces' intervention into the politics of some countries. Although Latin America has been the developing world's most successful region in establishing democracy, widespread dissatisfaction due to corruption, inequitable distribution of wealth, and the threats to civil rights have produced a left wing, populist trend in the region's politics recently. The trend has been most evident in Venezuela, although it exists in several countries of the region at varying degrees. Venezuelan president Hugo Chavez's efforts to change the constitution to eliminate term limits has led some to view this populist trend as drifting toward authoritarian rule.

Africa's experience with democracy has also been varied since the third wave of democratization swept over the continent beginning in 1990. Although early efforts resulted in the ouster of many leaders, some of whom had held power for decades, and international pressure forced several countries to hold multiparty elections, the political landscape in Africa includes consolidating democracies and states still mired in conflict. Among the success stories is Ghana, which held elections in late 2008 that resulted in the opposition leader defeating the ruling party's candidate. South Africa, the continent's biggest success story, held its fourth round of democratic elections in April 2009. The elections took place amid allegations of corruption against the

© Thomas Hartwell/2003

new president, Jacob Zuma, and featured a nasty split in the ruling African National Congress. Although South Africa continues to face major challenges, its democracy remains vibrant. Ghana and South Africa stand in sharp contrast to the circumstances in some other parts of Africa. Congo's 2006 elections brought a state of tenuous peace to most of the country although sporadic fighting continued in the eastern part of the country until the arrest of rebel leader Laurent Nkunda in early 2009. Nigeria's 2007 elections were flawed, and the country continues to face widespread corruption and political unrest in the Niger Delta region.

Political change has begun in the Middle East, but it will be a long-term challenge. Iraq continues to face the task of reconciling its Sunni, Shiite, and Kurdish communities, and the threat of violence remains. The role of Islam in the region and its compatibility with democracy continues to be a major issue. The results of a new study indicate that, contrary to conventional wisdom, Muslims favor free speech, rule of law, and self-determination while rejecting terrorism. Iran's June 2009 elections will provide more insight into the continuing impact of factors that helped shape the country's 1979 revolution. Prospects for broader democratic reform in the region will depend on the success of efforts to reframe the political debate.

While there has been significant progress toward democratic reform around the world, there is no guarantee that these efforts will be sustained. Although there has been an increase in the percentage of the world's population living under democracy, nondemocratic regimes still exist. Furthermore, some semi-democracies hold elections but citizens lack full civil and political rights. International efforts to promote democracy often tend to focus on elections rather than on the long-term requirements of democratic consolidation. More effective ways of promoting and sustaining democracy must be found in order to expand freedom further in the developing world.

Asia's Democracy Backlash

Leaders of nations like Cambodia, Laos, and Vietnam have begun to debate how they can apply a Chinese model to their own nations.

JOSHUA KURLANTZICK

So intense is the chaos in the Bangladeshi capital of Dhaka that to an outsider it often seems miraculous that the city actually functions. At intersections, mobs of rickshaws, motorcycles, and luxury cars vie for space with vendors and homeless people wandering in all directions. Sidewalks are crowded with so many people—the megacity is one of the largest in the world—that you must push through the pack just to move.

Normally, the city's politics mirrors its daily life. For years, university students allied with either of the two major parties have led boisterous rallies and street protests at election time, demonstrations often so fevered that they descend into violence. Vendors sell huge numbers of vernacular and English-language newspapers, which offer tens of thousands of words of political coverage.

But over the past two years, Dhaka—or at least its politics—has quieted considerably. In January 2007, a caretaker government preparing for a new Bangladeshi election stepped down, probably because of pressure from the military, and the army soon asserted itself even more. Working only barely behind the scenes, it organized a new government, declared a state of emergency, and soon detained thousands of political activists, putatively as part of a campaign to eliminate graft from politics. After promises to hold a new election, the military and its caretaker regime scheduled voting for the late date of December 2008.

Across the region, armed forces once believed confined to their barracks have begun to reassert their power.

Bangladesh is hardly unique in experiencing undemocratic developments. Asia once was regarded as the vanguard of a global wave of democratization that, over the past three decades, has swept through southern Europe, Latin America, and Africa as well. In recent years, however, Asia has witnessed a democracy backlash. Across the region, armed forces once believed

confined to their barracks have begun to reassert their power. Quasi-authoritarian rulers in Sri Lanka, Cambodia, the Philippines, and other nations have drastically strengthened the power of the state, unleashing security forces on political opponents, using emergency decrees to consolidate power, and cracking down on civil society. And in the region's most repressive states, such as Myanmar (formerly Burma), progress toward greater freedom appears to have stalled entirely.

Quasi-authoritarian rulers in Sri Lanka, Cambodia, the Philippines, and other nations have drastically strengthened the power of the state.

The Freedom Façade

South and Southeast Asia in the late 1990s and early in this decade rode the crest of a wave of democratization that encompassed much of the developing world. During the Asian financial crisis in the late 1990s, protesters in Indonesia toppled the long-ruling dictator Suharto and established a new, multiparty political system. In Malaysia at roughly the same time, protesters lashed out at the authoritarian rule of Mahathir Mohamad. Liberalization spread to East Timor, then a part of Indonesia, and after a bloody conflict Timor won its independence and established a nascent democracy. Cambodia emerged from years of civil war to hold a series of elections in the 1990s.

Even long-suffering Myanmar, ruled since 1962 by the military, seemed ready to change, as the junta released pro-democracy opposition leader Daw Aung San Suu Kyi from house arrest in 2002 and allowed her to tour the country. She drew massive crowds hopeful for political change and proclaimed "a new dawn for the country."

As economies grew rapidly and publics became more politically active, nations such as Thailand and Bangladesh drew up liberal constitutions supposedly designed to strengthen civil society, protect minority rights, and check the power of entrenched actors like the military and powerful business interests. In vibrant Asian cities like Bangkok and Kuala Lumpur, where rapid growth had produced towering skylines, sleek new roads, and flashy shopping districts, the idea of military coups now seemed obsolete.

But recent years have revealed that some of this democratization was a façade. (To be sure, Asia's longest-established democracies, Japan and India, suffer few of these weaknesses; and South Korea and Taiwan, though unruly, do not seem at risk of backsliding.) In some cases, the apparent vibrancy reflected merely economic liberalization, and democracy had not sunk deep roots.

Quasi-authoritarian states like Singapore and Malaysia did understand the need for financial transparency, since that was critical to attracting the foreign investment that has powered their economic miracles. Yet Singapore and Malaysia—like China and, to some extent, Vietnam—have managed to build walls around their political processes, promoting financial and economic transparency while using subtle means to undermine political liberalization. They have held highly controlled elections while allowing few other facets of democracy, such as union organizing, independent media, or trade associations. Foreign investors, who care mostly about financial probity, offer little protest about these dual policies, and have said nothing when countries like Malaysia jail activists.

Economic transparency in Southeast Asia has not necessarily signified political liberalization.

Even countries in South and Southeast Asia that seem more democratic than Malaysia still have papered over major flaws. Few have established effective methods of probing state corruption or electoral fraud. Despite holding elections and writing constitutions, many Asian nations have never assimilated a central premise of democracy—the idea that once a party loses it must respect the system by serving as a loyal opposition, working within the established political framework and honoring constitutional rules.

Instead, from the Philippines to Bangladesh to Thailand—where large popular movements in the past have overthrown dictators—individuals and organized groups dissatisfied with the results of free elections have continually taken their cases to the streets. Because these nations constantly rely on "people power" to change governments, they have invested little in building democratic institutions or in promoting equitable development.

In Manila, street protests nicknamed People Power 2 toppled President Joseph Estrada in 2001 and brought to power his vice president, Gloria Macapagal Arroyo. Although Estrada had been far from flawless in office—he packed his administration with unqualified cronies and became enmeshed in vast corruption scandals—he had been popularly elected. Three years later, similar demonstrations almost brought Arroyo down.

In Bangladesh, political parties run by two women who reportedly detest each other, Sheikh Hasina Wazed and Begum Khaleda Zia, have taken this unwillingness to capitulate to rules to a perverse extreme. When one party wins an election, the opposition often responds with waves of paralyzing strikes and protests, attempting to make the country ungovernable. These strikes only foster political violence. Numerous assaults on party gatherings have occurred, including a 2004 grenade attack against Sheikh Hasina's entourage in which 21 people were killed.

Asians, meanwhile, have not entirely banished the men in green. Although militaries rarely intervened in domestic politics in the late 1990s and early in this decade, few Asian countries have established complete civilian control over their armed forces. (In several nations, like Pakistan and Myanmar, the military never truly left politics.) In many South Pacific nations such as Fiji, military officers have constantly threatened coups, sometimes successfully toppling governments. In the Philippines and Bangladesh (as in Kazakhstan and Uzbekistan, among other countries), security forces have continued to operate unencumbered by laws, killing suspected opponents of whichever government is in power, running off-the-books businesses, and trafficking in weapons and drugs.

The Fading Beacon

At the same time, over the past decade the balance of power among external actors in Southeast and South Asia has shifted dramatically. For decades, the United States was the major external power in Asia, and in the late 1990s and early in this decade Washington rhetorically committed itself to pushing for democratization and better governance in the region.

In the past five years, however, this commitment has weakened. The war on terror has consumed the White House's attention and undermined America's moral standing. Demanding counterterrorism cooperation in Asia, the United States often has ignored efforts by countries such as Cambodia and Malaysia to use the war on terror to crack down on critics—for example, through Malaysia's Internal Security Act, a colonial-era relic that allows for detention without trial.

Focused on Iraq, the United States also has had little time to confront problems like the ongoing human rights crisis in Myanmar, where the army's scorched-earth tactics—which include widespread rape—have displaced nearly 1 million people in the eastern part of the country, and where the junta this year held, just days after a catastrophic cyclone hit, a sham national "referendum" designed to strengthen its control.

Washington did help to push Myanmar onto the agenda of the United Nations Security Council after the junta's crackdown on the so-called Saffron Revolution in 2007. But when the Security Council refused to take tough action, the administration of George W. Bush declined to invest more time and resources in the issue. Some US officials suggested that China should lead the effort to bring reform to Myanmar, a task for which Beijing has shown little appetite; it was China, in fact, that blocked UN action against Myanmar. The United States, meanwhile, does not even have an ambassador in the country.

More generally, scandals at Abu Ghraib in Iraq, Guantanamo Bay in Cuba, and other prisons have damaged the United States' image as a guarantor of freedom. Authoritarian nations like China and Russia, both of which are flexing their muscles in Asia, now have a ready response to American criticism of their human rights records—the United States, they argue, is no better. (For years, China has responded to the State Department's annual report on human rights in China with its own paper on human rights in America; Beijing now has considerable evidence it can marshal in its report.)

In the late 1990s, many reformers and activists in Asia wanted to be associated with the United States and its blossoming democracy promotion outfits, like the National Endowment for Democracy, the National Democratic Institute, and the International Republican Institute. By the mid-2000s, America's image in Asia had plummeted so far that many activists took pains not to be linked to US funding. And President Bush's linking of democracy promotion to the war in Iraq led citizens of many nations to associate democratization with images of turmoil televised from Baghdad.

Model Competitors

As America's standing has weakened, China and Russia have made impressive gains in the region. Indeed, they are advertising their undemocratic systems—according to which they have moderately liberalized their economies while avoiding concurrent political reform—as development models that Asian countries should emulate. China and Russia also emphasize a doctrine of noninterference, arguing that countries should not intervene in other nations' internal affairs—interference that could include sanctioning human rights violators or supporting pro-democracy movements.

Beijing in particular, employing more effective diplomacy than the United States—and with a growing aid program that now outstrips American assistance in countries like the Philippines, Myanmar, and Cambodia—has transformed its image in Asia from that of an economic and political threat to a more benign neighbor, and even a model. China promotes its style of development through a rising number of training programs for top leaders and mid-level technocrats in countries like Vietnam, Laos, and Pakistan. It also provides sufficient aid and investment to authoritarian nations to render meaningless Western efforts to influence the regime in Myanmar, for example, or to pressure the Cambodian government into improving its human rights climate.

Russia, for its part, has begun to wield greater influence in Central Asia, where many top leaders still have Soviet backgrounds. With the growing cash hoard it is accumulating because of the high price of oil, Russia has funded the creation of new NGO-like organizations that *fight* democracy promotion efforts in Central Asia, while providing assistance to Central Asian autocrats and training to some of their security forces.

Some Asian countries appear to be listening to Beijing and Moscow. Leaders of nations such as Cambodia, Laos, and Vietnam have begun to debate how they can apply a Chinese model to their own nations. At the same time that Beijing promotes a non-democratic model, China's growing power also ties the United States' hands in Asia. When faced with antidemocratic behavior across the region, Washington must be increasingly careful how it responds, for fear of pushing these countries more firmly into Beijing's orbit.

Revenge of the Autocrats

Over the past five years, all these trends have coalesced, creating Asia's democracy backlash. The dangerous mix of years of venal and corrupt rule in countries like Bangladesh and the Philippines, combined with the failure to build institutions for funneling protest into peaceful channels, has finally exploded. In East Timor, disgruntled young men descended last year on the streets of Dili, the low-rise capital, to fight it out with knives and slingshots. Until foreign troops intervened, rioters burned block after city block, leaving Dili a morass of charred and gutted buildings. In Bangladesh in 2007, thousands of protesters charged through Dhaka's alleys and tin-roofed slum dwellings. They attacked stores and clashed with riot police and thousands of soldiers, battling with stones and sticks until demonstrators fled the scene, their faces bleeding and clothes ripped apart.

Militaries have asserted themselves in Asian nations beyond Bangladesh. In Thailand, another supposedly consolidated democracy, the army seized power in a September 2006 coup. The coup followed months of street demonstrations against the government of then–Prime Minister Thaksin Shinawatra, a popularly elected leader who had used his power to neuter the courts, civil society, and the Thai bureaucracy, and to launch a war against drugs that killed thousands of innocent citizens. The Thai military soon shredded the country's reformist constitution, written in 1997.

In Fiji, the military seized power in December 2006 and amassed emergency powers, announcing that it did so to battle corruption and that it would hold elections in far-off 2010. The Fijian armed forces then censored the press and arrested at least two dozen prominent activists.

At first, many liberals embraced these military interventions. In Bangladesh, crowds initially cheered the takeover as a balm against the corruption and political violence that had created chaos in the run-up to the January 2007 election, in which at least 45 people were killed. In a poll taken in October 2006 by the Bangladeshi newspaper *Daily Star,* most respondents had expressed anger at "inter-party bickering, unbridled corruption [and] total lack of governance."

Likewise, many middle class Bangkok residents hailed the coup-makers. Thai girls celebrated the takeover by placing flowers in army tanks in the capital. Reform-minded Thai liberals (and some Western commentators), from newspaper editors to academics, praised the military for stepping in.

The generals, however, proved incapable of ruling. Asian military rulers who take power today must deal with far more complex and globalized economies than was the case in the 1960s and 1970s. They also must deal with publics that have become accustomed to democracy, and are less willing to abide by martial law and bans on political activity.

In Fiji, the government reserve bank admitted that the coup had depressed economic development. In Thailand, the army vacillated between reassuring investors and implementing measures such as currency interventions and new protectionist laws that terrified many foreign businesses. The military also demonstrated it did not understand how to interact with the modern media: The army cracked down on the press in 2007 and even banned CNN when it aired an interview with Thaksin, even as activists in Bangkok became more openly critical of the military regime.

Reforms under Siege

At the same time that these outright coups against democracies have been occurring, many of the region's other governments have used subtler means of undermining political freedoms. In quasi-authoritarian Cambodia, Prime Minister Hun Sen has consolidated near-total power over the past five years, using the legal system, which he dominates, to arrest opponents and silence prominent critics for defaming the government. He also has co-opted nearly the entire political opposition, so that his party is left with virtually no one arrayed against it in the legislature. A possible new gusher of oil to be exploited off Cambodia's shores will only add to Hun Sen's power, since it will further decrease the influence of foreign donors over his regime. In Vietnam, the government has arrested pro-democracy lawyers and other activists trying to build a political opposition.

Sri Lanka also has become a major offender. In December 2006, after a peace process with separatist Tamil Tigers collapsed, the government issued new emergency laws giving it greater power to control the media and civil society. Since then, the conservative Sri Lankan government, which is allied with Sinhalese hard-line nationalist parties, has become more and more repressive, using the civil war against the Tamil Tigers to crack down more broadly on legitimate dissent.

Over the past two years, according to Amnesty International, at least 10 journalists in Sri Lanka have been killed, while several others have disappeared or have been jailed under the emergency laws and tortured. The disappearances have extended beyond writers: Last year, the UN's working group on disappearances documented more such vanishings in Sri Lanka than in any other country in the world. Meanwhile, the Sri Lankan government has been expelling Tamils from the capital, Colombo, for no reason other than their ethnic background. The situation is unlikely to improve soon, as the government has recently stepped up its war against the Tamil Tigers, attacking them across the north of the country with heavy troop deployments.

The Philippines, a longstanding bastion of democracy, also has backslid badly. This year Freedom House downgraded its rating for the Philippines from "free" to "partly free." Indeed, it warned, "Asia's oldest democracy has become increasingly dysfunctional." Citing vast corruption and potential rigging of voting machinery, Freedom House also alleges that the Philippine military has had a hand in the killings of hundreds of activists, particularly left-leaning activists, in recent years. Journalists have been targets, with a rising number of reporters murdered as well. Two years ago, too, President Arroyo invoked emergency rule and then used that legislation to arrest many anti-government activists.

In Myanmar, of course, the regime responded to the 2007 Saffron Revolution with a brutal and bloody crackdown, after which thousands of monks and other activists were killed or tossed in prison. Then the junta exploited the devastating May 2008 cyclone to consolidate its hold on power, resisting all international efforts to use the disaster to push for political reform.

The Jakarta Model

Still, the trend is not all negative. In Thailand in 2007, a year after the coup, voters did elect a new government. The period spent under military rule left the country in such turmoil, however, that it now faces a near future of unstable governments and, possibly, frequent elections. In recent months, street protests have continued to dominate Bang-kok, leading to clashes with security forces and even a protester takeover of the prime minister's offices. The elected prime minister, Samak Sundarvej, was forced out of office in September 2008, though his party still controlled the government.

In Malaysia, elections early this year, in which opposition parties won a far larger share of the vote than normal, suggested a possible opening of the political system. The kingdom of Bhutan held its first democratic elections in March 2008. And in Nepal, autocratic rule by the monarchy has given way to a democratic process, although recent elections brought into the government former Maoist insurgents, already known for their harsh repression of dissent.

But one young Asian democracy stands out. A decade ago, Indonesian protesters carrying fire-bombs and machetes rampaged through downtown Jakarta, furious over years of political repression and the country's impending economic collapse. Many took out their anger on Indonesia's Chinese minority, which controlled a high percentage of the nation's wealth. Mobs focused on ethnic Chinese–owned businesses such as shopping malls and gold stores, and men on motorcycles led some of the rioters to selected Chinese-owned shops, where they locked the proprietors inside and burned the buildings to the ground. Perhaps as many as 70,000 Chinese Indonesians fled the country, and many more escaped Jakarta for quieter parts of the archipelago, like Bali.

Other types of inter-ethnic and inter-religious violence raged through remote regions such as Aceh and the Maluku Islands, where warring bands of men chopped off their enemies' heads and posted them on spikes alongside roads.

Only a decade later, Indonesia has made astonishing strides, and can claim to have become the most stable democracy in Southeast Asia. Leaders have been pushing to enshrine minority rights, opening the political field to ethnic Chinese politicians: At least 30 Indonesian Chinese ran for parliament in 2004 elections.

And the acceptance of minority rights, in a nation where 10 years ago mobs burned ethnic Chinese alive, is but one sign of Indonesia's transformation. The government of President Susilio Bambang Yudhyono has tried to inculcate a stronger democratic culture. Yudhyono, himself a former general, was elected in 2004 in the first direct presidential poll in Indonesian history, and since then he has led a truly progressive government.

Rather than focusing on the elite, capital-centered politics of the kind found in Manila or Bangkok, the administration has built democratic culture from the grassroots, aggressively decentralizing power and bringing more control over local politics to local politicians, while also offering greater autonomy to regions of the country like Aceh, which suffered a 30-year-long separatist war. Thus far, though the region's erst-while rebels have engaged in sporadic firefights, the peace process in Aceh has mostly held, with rebels laying down arms, the Indonesian military withdrawing troops from the region, and Aceh holding local elections.

The decentralization has strengthened and stabilized rural democracy. A report by *Asia Times* found that in recent years voters have removed nearly 40 percent of local-level incumbents, fostering a healthy climate of accountability. Local-level democracy, *Asia Times* noted, is also healing religious differences and reducing the threat of political Islam, since Muslims and Christians are teaming up to form local tickets. And, combined with economic decentralization, the political decentralization has provided provincial and local governments with more resources, which they can use to improve social welfare.

Under Yudhyono, the state has strengthened Indonesian institutions designed to hold powerful politicians accountable. The president, for example, has backed court decisions that overturned Internal Security Act–like laws that protected Indonesian leaders from criticism and had been used in the past to jail political opponents. Increased accountability in turn has strengthened average Indonesians' belief in the democratic system.

Democratic Inroads

Almost alone among Southeast Asian leaders, Yudhyono also has realized that Asian nations must push for democracy among their neighbors if political liberalization is to entrench itself in the region. He has recognized that the most antidemocratic

countries, like Myanmar, breed the type of instability that spreads transnational problems like drugs and illegal migration to the rest of Asia.

While most Southeast Asian leaders avoid even talking about Myanmar, Yudhyono has openly warned Myanmar officials that their country must move faster on its constitution-drafting process and work toward implementing democracy. In Thailand and even India, by contrast, leaders said little after the Saffron Revolution crackdown. India's petroleum minister even visited Myanmar to sign new contracts while the Saffron protests were still going on.

The recent changes within Indonesia have proved popular with the public. Opinion polls not only give Yudhyono high marks; they also strongly and repeatedly endorse democracy. In one comprehensive poll conducted by the Indonesia Survey Institute, 82 percent of respondents said that they supported democracy—even as Thais in Bangkok welcomed military rule. Indonesian opposition parties also have proved willing to resolve electoral losses within the political system, rather than demanding the overthrow of the government.

Clearly Indonesia still faces high hurdles, including military officers reluctant to give up powers they gained during the 30-year Suharto era, and judges too often unwilling to punish military abuses. Before Yudhyono stands, as expected, for reelection in 2009, he will have to build a more consolidated and organized party around his progressive values to ensure that his ideas live on.

Yet Indonesia's transformation offers examples to other Asian states of how to consolidate a vibrant democracy. Indeed, before the region's democracy backlash gains more strength, progressive leaders from Cambodia to Bangladesh would be wise to pay attention to Jakarta. The United States, too, must pay more attention to a region that is economically dynamic and once seemed on the edge of total democratization. If Washington backs antidemocrats, it abandons its image as a guarantor of freedoms, and opens the door wider for other actors, like China, to make greater gains in the region.

JOSHUA KURLANTZICK, a Current History contributing editor, is a visiting scholar at the Carnegie Endowment for International Peace. He is the author of *Charm Offensive: How China's Soft Power Is Transforming the World* (Yale University Press, 2007).

From *Current History,* November 2008, pp. 375–380. Copyright © 2008 by Current History, Inc. Reprinted by permission.

India Held Back

The country still faces a series of domestic and external challenges that remain significant hurdles on the path to great power status.

SUMIT GANGULY

How is India faring in its rise as a significant economic and diplomatic player in Asia and beyond? Certainly, reasons for optimism exist. In the late 1980s the country's economy began to exceed its traditionally anemic "Hindu rate of growth" (a joke introduced by the late Indian economist, Raj Krishna, based on the economic concept of a "secular rate of growth"). Also, at the end of the cold war, India dispensed with its hoary commitment to nonalignment and its reflexive anti-Americanism. Finally, India disproved the polemical claim that, despite the country's democracy and federalism, it would prove unable to contain ethnic separatism of the sort that was unleashed by the collapse of the poly-ethnic Soviet Union and Yugoslavia.

India may yet emerge as a major power in Asia, with its influence extending well beyond its immediate vicinity. However, as a quick survey of events in the past year demonstrates, the country still faces a series of domestic and external challenges that remain significant hurdles on the path to great power status. These challenges include an economic conundrum, fractious internal politics, growing governance problems, and difficulties both in tackling indigenous Islamic extremism and in improving relations with India's ever-nettlesome neighbor, Pakistan.

While India has so far defied all doomsday scenarios constructed for it, its ability to deal with and indeed overcome its structural shortcomings ultimately will determine whether it can transcend its role in South Asia and emerge as a global power of some consequence.

Persistent Poverty

In late August 2008, the World Bank released a major study that provided some rather disturbing evidence about the persistence of absolute poverty in India. According to the report, the segment of the population living on less than $1.25 a day in all of South Asia had fallen from 60 percent to 40 percent between 1981 and 2005. More specifically, within India, it had declined from 60 percent to 42 percent during the same period. Yet, despite this progress, the study concluded that well over 400 million Indians were still eking out a living on less than $1.25 a day in 2005.

Beyond this startling revelation, the Indian economy has been reeling this year from two important exogenous shocks—the high prices of both petroleum and food on the global market. Petroleum products' dramatic rise in cost has dealt a particularly hard blow to India's economy. India's gross domestic product, after achieving 9 percent growth in 2007, will grow by about 7 percent at best this year, according to even the most optimistic forecasts. The greatest concern to most Indian policy makers, however, is not slowing growth but a sharp spike in inflation—which now hovers close to 13 percent.

These statistics should give the Indian government pause, especially because they represent such a contrast to the bulk of the past decade, when the country has managed to grow by over 8 percent annually. Given that India has steadily registered high growth rates since it embarked on economic liberalization following an unprecedented fiscal crisis in 1991, the country's failure to make a greater dent in endemic poverty is somewhat puzzling.

The country's failure to make a greater dent in endemic poverty is somewhat puzzling.

Of course aggregate statistics, however compelling, do not adequately capture India's economic realities. Other evidence helps provide a different view of India's economic future. For example, one of India's largest industrial conglomerates, Tata, is on the verge of producing the world's cheapest car, the Nano, which is expected to be priced at $2,500 and will meet the latest European emission standards. Parts of India are emerging as manufacturing hubs for major automotive firms, especially Hyundai.

Moreover, India's economic success is hardly confined to the industrial sector. The country's information technology sector continues to boom despite the current global economic downturn. According to the National Association of Software and Services Companies (the apex organization of Indian information technology businesses), growth in India's information technology sector has been staggering over recent years. In 1998 the sector accounted for 1.2 percent of India's GDP. By

2007, this figure had reached 5.2 percent. The same organization predicts that the information technology sector, and related areas in business-process outsourcing, will contribute as much as $64 billion to India's economy in 2008.

The success of India's information technology sector and its business-process outsourcing is not an entirely unknown phenomenon to many Americans. Indeed, this very success became fodder for populist outrage during the 2004 presidential election when, for the first time, white collar industries were seeing jobs transferred to India and elsewhere from the United States. But not as well known is India's continuing success in the pharmaceutical industry. In this sector, which initially focused on the production of cheap generic drugs, some of the most successful players are now investing in developing new drugs and are attracting the attention of foreign drug makers. In June of this year, for instance, India's largest pharmaceutical company, Ranbaxy, sold a 70 percent stake in its equity to a Japanese firm, Daiichi Sankyo, for $4.6 billion.

India's economic situation, in short, is complex and varied. The economy features sustained general growth and innumerable success stories. Even so, there is no denying that compelling economic challenges still plague the nation. The evidence from India and elsewhere shows that posting high rates of economic growth and boasting highly successful economic sectors will not alone result in the reduction of endemic poverty. To make significant strides in poverty reduction, India will need to go beyond market-oriented growth strategies and devise imaginative public policies.

There are no panaceas for poverty. As argued by, among others, Amartya Sen, the Indian Nobel laureate, the country must invest more in primary education and health care. Yet increased spending alone will not improve the lot of India's poor. Currently, India spends 3 percent of GDP on education. However, for complex reasons, a disproportionate segment of this expenditure is directed toward higher education. Hence the quality of primary schooling in India remains quite uneven. Some of India's states—especially Kerala, Tamil Nadu, and Himachal Pradesh—have made primary education a priority, with impressive results. But a large number of other states have grossly neglected their public schools, with disastrous consequences.

India spends close to 6 percent of its GDP on health care, but its public hospitals for the most part are in shambles. There is little or no oversight of public hospitals and maladministration is rampant. The country's wealthy, of course, have opted out of the public health care system and enjoy standards of health care comparable to those in the advanced industrial states.

India, however, cannot emerge as a great power with mere enclaves of excellence amid vast swaths of grinding poverty, economic disparity, and social inequality. These internal cleavages invariably will contribute to political instability and thereby hobble India's ambitions for major power status.

Disharmony Rules

To a considerable degree, the economic hurdles that confront India result directly from the country's fractious and increasingly coarse politics. The political spectrum in India ranges from two Communist parties—the Communist Party of India and the Communist Party of India (Marxist)— which steadfastly refuse to countenance market-oriented reforms at the national level, to parties that remain committed to such reforms, such as the middle-of-the road Congress and the right-of-center Bharatiya Janata Party (BJP).

The width of the political spectrum and the virtual absence of one-party dominance in India's parliament for over two decades have meant that the forging of a political consensus on many issues of national significance can easily be held hostage to either parochial political or rigidly ideological concerns. Such a situation confronted the Indian polity in July this year when the Communists and their allies in the parliament withdrew support for the Congress-led regime of Prime Minister Manmohan Singh over the government's pursuit of a major civilian nuclear agreement with the United States.

This agreement, which will allow India to participate in normal global nuclear commerce, won the approval of the 45-nation Nuclear Suppliers Group in September. The US Congress granted its imprimatur to the deal on October 1. India until now has been excluded from nuclear energy commerce because of its unwillingness to sign the Nuclear Nonproliferation Treaty and because of its pursuit of nuclear weapons outside the ambit of the global nonproliferation regime. Under the terms of the pact, India has agreed to separate its nuclear establishment into two segments. Fourteen of its existing power reactors will be brought under International Atomic Energy Agency safeguards while another eight, presumably connected to India's nuclear weapons program, will remain off limits. Over time, the agreement should make a meaningful contribution to meeting India's burgeoning energy needs while reducing the country's acute dependence on imported petroleum products and fossil fuels.

The Communists and their allies opposed the agreement strictly on ideological grounds. Indeed, one prominent Communist leader, Prakash Karat, made no secret of the fact that his hostility toward the deal was based on his belief that it would contribute to greater Indo-US diplomatic amity. The BJP, for its part, displayed political opportunism in its crassest form. When in power in the early part of this decade, the party was instrumental in dramatically improving relations with the United States and had even initiated preliminary negotiations on the civilian nuclear agreement. However, when Prime Minister Singh decided to send the carefully negotiated agreement to the Nuclear Suppliers Group for its approval, the Communists, a group of small parties allied with them, and the BJP chose to attack the deal with vigor in the hope of bringing the government down and hastening new national elections.

In the end, though the government was hit with unproven, scurrilous allegations of bribing key parliamentary supporters during negotiations over the pact (though some overt political horse-trading certainly occurred), the Singh administration prevailed. It did not lose its parliamentary majority, and it managed to send the agreement off to the Nuclear Suppliers Group.

Nevertheless, the episode again underscored the ideological rigidity and political crassness that have come to characterize Indian politics. The outrageous behavior of parties at the two extremes of the political spectrum showed that even those well-schooled in the craft of parliamentary democracy were willing to violate one of its most fundamental and cherished tenets, the principle of loyal opposition. And this is not the first occasion when the BJP has resorted to such crude parliamentary tactics. Shortly after its electoral defeat in the national elections of 2004, the leadership of the BJP often resorted to obstreperous behavior to impede routine parliamentary proceedings.

Ideological rigidity and political crassness have come to characterize Indian politics.

These sorts of political tactics, aggravating India's ideological, regional, and personal divides, represent a serious impediment to the forging of a consensus on policies that would promote and sustain economic growth while also aiming at poverty reduction.

Stubborn Insurgencies

Tragically, as the Singh government focused its energies on fending off the BJP's attacks and the Communists' attempts to unseat it over the nuclear deal, long-simmering discontent within the majority Muslim population in the disputed state of Jammu and Kashmir flared up once again in July. The Indian-controlled portion of this state has been the site of an ethno-religious insurgency since 1989. The insurgency had its origins in the exigencies of domestic Indian politics. However, once the insurgency erupted, significant Pakistani support for and involvement in it expanded its scope and increased its duration. In recent years, an Indian counterinsurgency strategy combining fierce repression with political concessions had managed to restore a large degree of normalcy. Nevertheless, a reservoir of disaffection from the Indian state remained in the region.

The immediate precipitant of this summer's crisis was a decision by the coalition government in the state to hand over some 100 acres of publicly owned land to the Shri Amarnath Shrine Board, a quasi-public body that oversees annual Hindu pilgrimages to a prominent Himalayan shrine. Once the government had announced its decision to build shelters for the Hindu pilgrims on the land, Syed Ali Shah Geelani, a local Islamist leader with pronounced pro-Pakistani sentiments, mobilized his followers, claiming that the decision to hand over the land was part of an unfolding and sinister plot to settle Hindus in the region.

The Islamist's claims were entirely mendacious. However, his inflammatory rhetoric fired the popular imagination of young Kashmiris who harbor considerable resentment against the Indian state for the dislocations they have experienced during the insurgency of the past two decades. Soon public demonstrations started to rock the Kashmir valley. Faced with this apparent groundswell of discontent, one of the partners in the coalition regime, the Peoples' Democratic Party, abruptly withdrew its support for the land transfer. But the Congress Party refused to go along to take the same step.

In late July the regional government collapsed. India's central government took over the affairs of the state, also replacing the governor. The new governor, a highly respected former bureaucrat, Narendra Nath Vohra, in an attempt to assuage the feelings of the aggrieved Muslim population, rescinded the land transfer. His decision, however, led Hindu chauvinists in Jammu, the southern part of the state, to start a violent agitation. As matters threatened to spin completely out of control, the central government intervened again and sought to address the grievances of both constituencies. Negotiations proved successful in containing the agitation in Jammu, but violent demonstrations persisted in the Kashmir valley.

Unfortunately, the renewed agitation and very possibly a recrudescence of the insurgency in Kashmir are not the only challenges to authority that face the Indian state today. At least two other sources of violent discontent stalk the land. The first is a resurgence of the Naxalite movement. This movement had its origins among a group of neophyte Maoist guerrillas in the state of West Bengal in the late 1960s. They had started their violent agitation in the village of Naxalbari, from which the movement derives its name. By the early 1970s, largely through a strategy of harsh repression, the Indian state had managed to effectively suppress the movement.

To the dismay and shock of India's policy makers, the Naxalite menace has seen a dramatic resurgence. In 2006 as many as 165 districts in 14 states were facing periodic attacks from Naxalite guerrillas. The central government, while it has recognized the problem, has yet to devise a coordinated strategy to deal with this renewed threat to public order and wellbeing. To a large extent, India's federal structure hobbles the development of a uniform, nationwide strategy to tackle this problem. Unless law and order break down almost completely, the central government cannot intervene in the day-to-day law-and-order problems of particular states. Nor can the central government send in paramilitary forces without the express invitation and consent of state governments.

Moreover, the attempts by some states to confront the problem have actually worsened matters. In the state of Chhattisgarh, for example, authorities have created a village-based vigilante organization, the Salwa Judum (literally "peace mission"). This entity—composed of villagers armed with crude weaponry and lacking in training, organization, and control—has engaged in mayhem while attempting to counter the Naxalites. In the process, far from containing the Naxalite threat, the Salwa Judum may have contributed to the swelling of the rebels' ranks.

What explains the seemingly abrupt resurgence of this movement? There are no clear-cut answers. Popular accounts tend to emphasize the growing impact of India's fitful embrace of a more market-oriented economic development strategy and the concomitant inequalities that it has helped generate. This argument, though seemingly persuasive, is not entirely satisfactory because substantial economic inequity has been a constant of the Indian socioeconomic landscape since independence. Even so, economic disparities—combined with growing awareness of them and mobilization based on those grievances—certainly help to explain the return of the Naxalites. The sources of this malady in any case need to be carefully identified as India's central government and constituent states seek to devise strategies to contain and suppress it.

Homegrown Terrorists

The other critical security threat confronting the Indian state is the rise of homegrown Islamic extremism. The sources of this threat are complex but more readily explicable than the Naxalite menace. During this past year, India has faced a spate of bombings in major cities including Jaipur in May and Ahmedabad in July. A little-known organization, the Indian Mujahideen—widely believed to be linked with the banned Students Islamic Movement of India—has claimed responsibility for some of these bomb attacks. A series of five coordinated bombings in New Delhi on September 13, 2008, represented perhaps the most daring and brazen of these attacks, even though the loss of life was not as great as in previous bombings.

Muslims, who constitute India's largest minority, do not amount to a cultural or social monolith. Social class, sect, language, and regional affiliations divide them. However, the rise of a form of Hindu jingoism has contributed to a sense of siege among the Muslim community at large. Worse still, a pogrom against various Muslim communities in the western state of Gujarat in 2002, and a failure to prosecute its perpetrators, helped to radicalize a segment of young Muslim men.

Indian intelligence organizations now claim that many of these disaffected men have been trained in Bangladesh and Pakistan to carry out acts of mayhem, sabotage, and terror in India. It is impossible to confirm the veracity of these claims. However, circumstantial evidence does suggest that such external involvement in and support for terrorism is not beyond the realm of possibility. Bangladesh and especially Pakistan both have a record of supporting various dissident and insurgent movements in India.

As a consequence of the rise of a virulent Hindu nationalist movement since the 1980s, Muslim communities across India have been the objects of both increased opprobrium and violence. Worse still, a government-commissioned analysis of the status of Muslims in India, the Justice Rajinder Sachar Commission Report of 2006, provides a disturbing portrait of the Muslim community's poor representation in the realm of government employment. For example, even though Muslims comprise about 13 percent of India's population, a mere 3 percent can be found in the elite Indian administrative service, 1.8 percent in the exclusive Indian foreign service, and 4 percent in the powerful Indian police service.

Significantly lower educational attainments among Muslims as a whole explain, in considerable part, their failure to enter these critical governmental bodies. But how the Indian state seeks to redress these significant disparities in the years ahead will in large measure shape the evolution of the Muslim community's ties and loyalties to the Indian state. In turn, influential and successful members of the Muslim community must also suggest possible strategies for addressing the community's needs, for promoting social and cultural reform, and for eschewing violence. An absence of such leadership will inevitably provide political fodder to Hindu zealots who whip up populist hatred against Muslims.

A Fraught Relationship

In addition to the domestic troubles stemming from economic inequity, political squabbling, and ethno-religious tensions, India faces a very serious challenge in its relations with an increasingly unstable neighbor, Pakistan. Despite Pakistan's tenuous transition to democracy in February of this year, the problems accumulated from years of authoritarian misrule and chicanery still plague the country. Most importantly, despite the resignation of General Pervez Musharraf from the presidency in August, the military in Pakistan remains primus inter pares. It is far from clear that President Asif Ali Zardari and the minority regime of the Pakistan People's Party in parliament will be able to curb drastically the substantial powers of the military establishment any time soon.

And as long as the Pakistani military remains an important force in the country's political order, it will be exceedingly difficult for any civilian regime to improve relations with India. This was amply demonstrated in July when members of the reconstituted Taliban carried out a suicide bomb attack on the Indian embassy in Kabul, Afghanistan. Despite official denials from Pakistan, both India and the United States have publicly implicated Pakistan's powerful Inter-Services Intelligence Directorate in planning and masterminding this attack. Not surprisingly, the fitful bilateral peace process between India and Pakistan, the so-called "composite dialogue" that began in 2004, is now in considerable jeopardy.

Given Pakistan's present internal political disarray, the recent upheaval in Indian-controlled Kashmir, and the upcoming elections in India next year, it is most unlikely that any tangible progress will be made soon in Indo-Pakistani relations. Even if another meeting within the framework of the composite dialogue is held this year, the ensuing discussions will be little more than perfunctory.

Over the Horizon

The Singh regime's inability to forestall the dramatic bomb blasts in Jaipur, Ahmedabad, and New Delhi; its slow and clumsy response to the widespread disturbances in Jammu and Kashmir; its failure swiftly to contain spiraling inflation: All this in combination with the anti-incumbency propensities of the Indian voter bodes ill for the present government in the national elections due in 2009. Unless in the next several months the administration can start addressing critical questions of both internal security and economic stability, its future in the next elections is virtually foreordained. Some Indian political analysts are already predicting the demise of the Singh regime based on its failure to prevent the multiple bombings in the nation's capital.

Some Indian political analysts are already predicting the demise of the Singh regime.

In any case, it is easy to anticipate how the principal opposition party, the BJP, will campaign. It will unfailingly exploit the present administration's very real shortcomings and insist that it will tackle India's challenges with more alacrity and efficacy. And the BJP is not the only bête noire that the Congress Party faces in the next elections. In the large, poor, populous state of Uttar Pradesh, the current lower-caste chief minister, Kumari Mayawati, has already made clear her national ambitions. Whether she will be able to mobilize significant support beyond her political base in her home state and northern India remains an open question.

More to the point, even if she and her Bahujan Samaj Party were to win a substantial number of parliamentary seats, they would still have to forge a coalition with other political parties to form a government. Such a regime would inevitably prove unstable, as regional, ideological, and personal differences would soon come to the fore and threaten any coalition. While India has had some experience with coalition governments, none has been known for its longevity or stability.

As the year nears its end, the Indian polity, though not facing any threat to its viability, nevertheless confronts a range of domestic and external challenges that will severely tax the resources of the next regime in office. So long as India remains weighed down by its various burdens—and lacks a national consensus on critical policies pertaining to economic growth, poverty alleviation, secularism, and relations with contentious neighbors—it inevitably will fail to realize its potential for great power status.

SUMIT GANGULY, a *Current History* contributing editor, is a professor of political science and director of research at the Center on American and Global Security at Indiana University.

From *Current History,* November 2008, pp. 369–374. Copyright © 2008 by Current History, Inc. Reprinted by permission.

Bring Me My Machine Gun

SCOTT JOHNSON AND KAREN MACGREGOR

South Africa has never had a president like Jacob Zuma. For one thing, the 67-year-old self-educated "farm boy" (his own words) has five wives and at least 20 children. On special occasions like weddings and funerals he decks himself out in traditional Zulu finery: leopard skin, headdress and spear. "A leader is a person who doesn't sit back," he tells NEWSWEEK. "Who will do things and make mistakes and be corrected. Who is not reserved." In contrast to the statesmanly lawyer Nelson Mandela and Thabo Mbeki, Mandela's Latin-quoting successor, Zuma revels in his tribal roots. "In a sense, he is our first real African president," says his close friend Jeremy Gordin, author of "Zuma: A Biography." "Mandela . . . came from Xhosa royalty. Mbeki was [educated] in England. But Zuma is a real African, and this real Africanness and lack of sophistication, combined with a real shrewdness, is very compelling."

But also troubling. The continent is littered with the wreckage of countries that were driven into the ground by similarly charismatic postcolonial leaders in the name of revolutionary justice. Africans call them Big Men—demagogues who rose to power promising a better share of the wealth for their followers and railing against anyone who stood in the way. Zuma practically invites the comparison, even down to his choice of a theme song: the Zulu antiapartheid anthem "Lethu Mshini Wami"—"Bring Me My Machine Gun." As head of the ruling African National Congress, however, he's facing only token opposition in this week's South African presidential election. Zuma is extraordinarily intelligent, despite his lack of formal schooling. But he's inheriting some vast challenges: crime-ravaged cities, a reeling economy and the country's ongoing AIDS crisis, among other things. Unemployment among black youth is hovering around 50 percent. Even so, Zuma seems confident he's up to his new job.

For good or ill, the next president is a lot different from his predecessors.

His critics ask just what he's up to. Three years ago he was acquitted of rape charges brought against him by a family friend. The judge ruled that the sex had been consensual, but Zuma's cavalier remarks offended many observers—he even argued that the woman had invited his attention by wearing a short dress. And on April 6, barely two weeks before Election Day, the attorney general's office dropped the last 14 outstanding charges of fraud,

racketeering and corruption against the candidate, eliminating the last obstacle to his rise. "The majority of the people in this country are very happy," Zuma told NEWSWEEK after the decision, vehemently denying any wrongdoing. "They think justice has been done." Still, roughly half the likely voters in one recent poll said they believed he was guilty—and many said they would vote for him anyway. Opposition politicians have begun legal proceedings to keep the case alive. "I have never been corrupt, and I'm fighting corruption within my organization," says Zuma. "So that is not going to be a problem."

Questions of integrity aside, Zuma has shared something else with many of Africa's Big Men: a hardscrabble childhood. He was 4 when his father died. His mother found work as a domestic in the city of Durban, but she couldn't afford to send the boy to school. Instead he herded cattle in the countryside. He was still in his teens when a relative recruited him for the ANC in 1959. Four years later he was arrested and sentenced to 10 years in prison for conspiring against the apartheid regime. He was jailed with Mandela on Robben Island.

The experience only reinforced Zuma's commitment to the revolution after his release. He eventually rose to be the ANC's intelligence chief, based in Zambia at the party's headquarters in exile. When one of his best operatives was compromised on a mission inside South Africa in 1985, Zuma instructed a member of an ANC cell in Durban to take the heat instead, so the operative could escape. The cell member, a young man named Mo Shaik, was arrested along with two of his brothers. Their father was detained and suffered a stroke; his mother died of a heart attack. Mo and his brother Yunis were tortured and spent a year in solitary confinement. "Zuma later apologized to my father for all that had happened, and he ensured that everything would be OK with my family," says Mo. "Zuma knows the difference between those who made sacrifices and those who seek to take advantage now."

Zuma and the Shaiks grew even closer after he returned home in 1990, when the ANC was unbanned. Zuma allegedly received nearly $600,000 in financial help from another of the brothers, Schabir Shaik, a successful businessman. Both men insist it was only a loan, and according to Zuma it has been repaid. But Schabir was subsequently convicted of corruption and fraud. He was released this March for undisclosed health reasons after serving two years and four months of a 15-year sentence.

But Zuma kept fighting until the charges against him were dropped—not because the case was weak, the prosecutor announced, but merely because the filing of charges had come to appear politically motivated. "I've got no ill feelings," Zuma says now. "I'm not going for revenge." But some of his allies have vowed to go after the "witches," "snakes" and "mischievous forces of darkness" responsible for the charges against him. And the candidate himself has filed a libel suit against one South African cartoonist who depicted him as a thug about to rape a woman labeled "Justice."

But in some ways Zuma offers new hope for a unified South Africa. He demurs at being called the country's first Zulu president. "The Zuluness is not the big issue," he says. "I've always looked at myself first as a South African—a black South African who always fought for the interests of the oppressed."

His allies have vowed to go after the 'witches' and 'snakes' responsible for the charges.

In fact, he has a strong record as a man who transcends ethnic and even racial barriers. He had a vital role 10 years ago in ending the virtual civil war between the ANC and armed followers of Zulu political leader Mangosuthu Buthelezi, a conflict that left thousands dead. In the past couple of years Zuma has reached out to the country's white-minority Afrikaners, calling them "the white tribe of Africa." One problem: many English-speaking South Africans now feel left out. Recently the president-to-be met for three hours with a delegation from the country's second-largest labor union, Solidarity, with 130,000 mostly Afrikaner members. (He speaks at least a little Afrikaans himself.) "He doesn't always take up your concerns and be a Mr. Fix-It, but he does listen," says Dirk Hermann, the union's head. "And that's hugely important for us. He's like a Zulu king, sitting under his tree, listening to his tribe." Zuma's challenge now is to make sure his tribe includes everyone in South Africa.

Who Will Speak for Islam?

JOHN L. ESPOSITO AND DALIA MOGAHED

At the heart of the moving puzzle the world faces over the next quarter century are the diverse Muslim populations, collectively known as the "Global Muslim Community." Spanning the globe and speaking nearly every language, they are united by one faith—Islam. Collectively, they make up one-fifth of the world's population and sit on 75 percent of its oil wealth. Understanding the emerging trends of these societies is perhaps the world's leading strategic imperative.

But who will speak for Islam in the future—on democracy, the role of women, or violence? Over six years ending in 2007, the Gallup organization undertook more than 50,000 interviews (representative of the 1.3 billion Muslims who reside in more than 35 nations with majority or significant Muslim populations) in an effort to explore current trends and examine the future. The results, reflective of more than 90 percent of the world's Muslim community, are the end product of the most comprehensive survey of its kind ever conducted; they defy conventional wisdom and the inevitability of a global conflict—even as the wars in Iraq and Afghanistan continue.

Dealing a blow to the foundations of the "clash of civilizations" theory, our data shows a strong Muslim affinity for democratic values. Far from hating Americans for their freedom, Muslims around the world describe and admire the Western tradition of democratic governance, while seeing their faith as a source of progress and balance. Allowed the political space, leaders drawing both on democracy and Islam's rich tradition will overshadow secular liberals and conservative theocrats as the leaders of tomorrow. These Muslim democrats will appeal to Islam's self-image of justice to argue for minority rights, gender justice, and the rule of law. The focus will be heavily on economic development and job creation through free trade and entrepreneurship.

This evolving future will find women at the forefront. Women comprise the majority of university students in several countries, and the percentage of women in Iran, Malaysia, the United Arab Emirates (UAE), and Egypt that attends university is on a par with that of Western Europe and South Korea. These women tell us that they expect their full rights and see their religion as essential to progress. Instead of a misogynistic corpus of ossified medieval edicts, Muslim women see their sacred law as a vibrant work in progress. They associate *shariah* compliance with "justice for women," "scientific advancement," and "protecting human rights." Therefore, we should not expect a move toward secular Western norms as more women take center stage. Muslim women will make progress within their own cultural and religious context. They neither wish to be preached at, nor to be patronized by, their Western sisters—but will welcome partnerships of equals, especially those involving capacity-building and technology transfer. These empowered women will surely focus on the socio-economic bottom quartile of their societies where the education gender gap is greatest. To address this, they will lead the charge for strong laws and educational programs for both men and women promoting Islam's injunction to "read." If democratic values and women's rights are expected to play a prominent role into the future, what will this mean for the level of public support for violence?

Public support for terrorism is already in decline, even as public anger toward the United States inches upward. What are we to make of these trends and what does it mean for the future? It would be dangerous to conclude that, since these two trends are moving in opposite directions, that public sympathy for anti-U.S, terrorism is unrelated to public sentiment toward America and its policies. Instead, there appears to be a multivariable model that takes anti-U.S. sentiment, subtracts moral objections to attacks on civilians, and arrives at the level of public support for anti-U.S, terrorism. Using this model, we've identified three groups: pro-U.S, mainstream Muslims: those who have favorable opinions of the United States and refuse to support anti-U.S. terrorism (35 percent of those polled); skeptical mainstream Muslims: those who have negative opinions of the United States but still refuse to support anti-U.S, terrorism (55 percent); and politically radicalized Muslims: those who have negative opinions of the United States and support anti-U.S. terrorism (7 percent).

The middle—the skeptical mainstream—is growing. As the wars in Iraq and Afghanistan rage on, anti-American sentiment continues to build, but so does the majority's disgust with and moral objection to terrorism. Not only are Muslims the primary victims of terrorism and war, but a major religious campaign is growing against the terrorist tactics used in the conflicts in Iraq and Afghanistan. At the same time, mullahs are taking on militants via a number of channels: from religious programming warning against the sins of freelance violence to de-radicalization of terrorists through moderate religious education in Yemen and Saudi Arabia, to collective clerical declarations against "unqualified" *fatwas* (religious edicts).

However, while clerics may tell young people that Islam teaches that 70 years of tyranny is better than one day of chaos and bloodshed, they thus far have failed to offer an alternative means for addressing grievances. Those who call for change through democratic means have, in many cases, been arrested and shut out of the political process. For this reason, in the absence of real change, appeals to Islamic morality will not reach everyone. The politically radicalized will likely decrease but remain over the next quarter century. Their rage surpasses—and thus rationalizes away—their moral objection to terrorism.

It is here where the battle of the future will be fought: not for the "soul of Islam," but for the "road to reform." Will those calling for peaceful change be effective and thus draw energy away from those who insist violence is justified? The battle will not be about theology or readings of the Koran. Instead, the ideological battle of the future will focus on convincing the hardened residual supporters of terrorism that progress can be achieved without brutality. To fully understand the future, we must first accurately read the present.

Who Speaks for Islam Today?

What do Muslims believe, what do they want, and what do they really think? While Muslim rulers and clergy have often cast themselves as spokespersons of the religion, both a modern, educated—but Islamically oriented—elite and heads of Islamic movements, mainstream and militant, attempt to speak for Islam. However, in recent years, vocal extremists and terrorists have monopolized the conversation. They claim to speak for more than a billion Muslims, to champion their causes and address their grievances in the name of Islam, citing religious texts and issuing *fatwas.*

This situation is further compounded in the West by media-savvy, self-proclaimed "Muslim reformers," who wage a battle of experts and pseudo-experts. Contending voices offer competing interpretations of what Islam is, who Muslims are, and what they believe and want. In responding effectively to global terrorism, U.S. foreign policymakers require insight into the "hearts and minds" of Muslims globally and a better understanding of how Muslim majorities see the world, and, in particular, how they regard the United States. Policymakers have had to rely on wildly differing "experts" who, however well-credentialed, often lacked the global data to back up their "reading" of the Muslim world. Direct access to Muslim public opinion avoids the grand theories, individual political agendas, and ideologies that can blur important insights. Rather than relying on those speaking *for* or *about* Muslims, leaders must cut through these competing voices and hear directly from the vast majority of ordinary people.

The conventional wisdom, based upon deeply held stereotypes and presuppositions has often fallen back on an intuitive sense that the Muslim world is riven by hatred of the West, and in particular America, envy at our success, religious fanaticism, poverty, and unemployment—and that this noxious stew breeds extremism and terrorism.

While the atrocities and acts of terrorism committed by violent extremists are often enshrouded in religious rhetoric, Islamic tradition and law place limits on the use of violence and reject terrorism, hijackings, and hostage-taking. As with other faiths, today, a radical fringe ignores, distorts, and misinterprets mainstream and normative doctrines and laws.

Anger at the United States, a sense of being disrespected, and widespread religiosity would seem like an explosive combination. However, Gallup data verifies that a majority of Muslims—like a majority of Americans—are gravely concerned about religious extremism and terrorism. And no wonder: since *they* have been the primary victims of Muslim terrorism. Asked their greatest fears, respondents in majority Muslim countries cite "being a victim of a terrorist attack" even more frequently than do Americans. Residents of majority Muslim societies are in fact at least as likely as the American public to reject attacks on civilians. While 6 percent of Americans think attacks that target civilians are "completely justified," in Saudi Arabia, it's 4 percent, and in both Lebanon and Iran, this figure is 2 percent.

A majority of Muslims are gravely concerned about religious extremism and terrorism. No wonder: since they have been the primary victims.

Even in London, since the bombings of July 7, 2007, data shows that terrorists remain a fringe group. Asked to rate the moral acceptability of using violence in the name of a "noble cause" on a 5-point scale, the proportion of Muslims in London who chose a low rating of 1 or 2 was 81 percent, compared with 72 percent of the British public overall. In France, the corresponding numbers were 77 percent of Parisian Muslims vs. 79 percent of the French public; in Germany, 94 percent of Muslims in Berlin vs. 75 percent of the German public.

Despite widespread disapproval of the George W. Bush administration, only a minority sympathizes with the attacks of 9/11. To understand what drives public support for terrorism, we chose to look at the most extreme fringe—the 7 percent of the population who see the 9/11 attacks as completely justifiable and have an unfavorable view of the United States (the "politically radicalized") and compared them to the rest (the mainstream). Where is terrorism finding a sympathetic ear and heart?

Perhaps our most significant finding is, paradoxically, the lack of a finding: there is no statistical correlation between level of religiosity and extremism among respondents. While 94 percent of the high conflict group says religion is an important part of their daily lives, a statistically identical 90 percent of the mainstream says the same thing. And no significant difference exists between high conflict and mainstream respondents in mosque attendance.

Gallup probed respondents further and actually asked both those who condoned and condemned extremist acts why they said what they did. The responses fly in the face of conventional wisdom. For example, in Indonesia, the largest Muslim majority country in the world, many of those who condemned terrorism cites humanitarian or religious justifications to support their response. One woman said, "Killing one life is as sinful as killing the whole world," paraphrasing a passage in the Koran.

On the other hand, not a single respondent who condoned the attacks of 9/11 cited the Koran for justification. Instead, this group's responses are markedly secular and worldly—speaking in terms of revenge and revolution, not religion. For example, one respondent said, "The U.S. government is too controlling toward other countries, seems like colonizing." A primary catalyst or driver of extremism, often seen as inseparable from the threat to Muslim religious and cultural identity, is the threat of political domination and occupation. The politically radicalized convey a strong sense of being "dominated" or even "occupied" by the West. Responding to an open-ended question, they cite "occupation/U.S. domination" as their greatest fear. In contrast, while concerned about American influence, the mainstream respondents' top concern centers on economic problems.

The interplay of the political and the religious is likewise strongly reflected in radical and mainstream responses to open-ended Gallup questions such as, "What can the West do to improve relations with the Muslim World?" and, "What is the most important thing the United States could do to improve the quality of life of people like you in this country?" Reflecting the importance of respect for Islam, the most frequent responses given by both groups are: more respect, consideration and understanding of Islam as a religion; not underestimating the status of Arab/Muslim countries; and being fair and less prejudiced. In addition, the politically radicalized respondents reflects the priorities of self-determination and democracy, and gave equal importance to the need for political independence. When asked, they respond that the West should stop interfering and meddling in their internal affairs; they cite a U.S colonizing presence and desire to control natural resources.

The politically radicalized are far more intense in their belief that Western political, military, and cultural domination is a major threat. When asked to define their greatest fears about the future of their country, the politically radicalized most frequently cite interference in their internal affairs by other countries, national security, colonization, occupation, and fear of U.S. dominance. In contrast, mainstream respondents rank economic problems as their top concern. Fully half of the politically radicalized polled by Gallup say that to "sacrifice one's life for a cause one believes in" is "completely justifiable." This contrasts strikingly with only 18 percent of the mainstream. Thus, although both groups are concerned about Western bias and political interference in their affairs, the greater intensity and fear expressed by the politically radicalized predisposes them to have a more sympathetic ear to terrorists—if their grievances are not addressed.

Democracy and Islam

For years, pundits have debated whether Islam and democracy are compatible. Only one in four nations where Muslims constitute a majority of the population have democratically elected governments, though many more make this claim even as their "elections" result in fairytale outcomes. Tunisia's president, Zine al-Abidine Ben Ali, won 99.4 percent of the vote in the 1999 presidential elections, and 94.5 percent in 2004. In Egypt, Hosni Mubarak in 1999 won with 94 percent and in 2005 with 88.6 percent of the vote. Indeed, a majority of Muslim governments control or severely limit opposition political parties and non-governmental organizations.

Despite these realities, Gallup data reveals that majorities of Muslims want free speech and a free press, and believe in self-determination, democracy, and the rule of law. (However, the same majority also believes that Western powers—especially the United States—will not allow democracy to truly flourish in the Islamic world.) Yet, when asked what they admire most about the West, Muslims frequently mention political freedom, liberty, fair judicial systems, and freedom of speech.

However, while Muslims say they admire freedom and an open political system, Gallup surveys suggest that they do not believe they must choose between Islam and democracy, but rather, that the two can co-exist. Their ideas of self-determination do not require a separation of religious concepts and the politics. Muslims surveyed indicate widespread support for *shariah*—Islamic principles that govern all aspects of life from the mundane to the most complex. While majorities of Muslims report they want *shariah* as a source—but not the sole source—of legislation, they differ as to what that might mean: formal constitutional lip service, a system where no law is contrary to *shariah* values, or where a country's laws are a blend of those derived from Western legal codes and selected Islamic laws. Surprisingly, though *shariah* is often thought of as inherently unfair to women, there are no large differences between men and women regarding support for the incorporation of *shariah* into governance.

For Muslims, the presence of *shariah* as a source of legislation does not conflict with drafting a constitution that would allow freedom of speech. Substantial majorities in all nations surveyed—the highest being 99 percent in Lebanon, 94 percent in Egypt, 92 percent in Iran, and 91 percent in Morocco—say that if they were drafting a constitution for a new country, they would guarantee freedom of speech (defined as "allowing all citizens to express their opinions on political, social, and economic issues of the day"). Support is also strong in most Muslim majority nations for freedom of religion and freedom of assembly. Thus, support for *shariah* does not mean that Muslims want a theocracy to be established in their countries. Only minorities in each country say they want religious leaders to be directly in charge of drafting their country's constitution, writing national legislation, drafting new laws, determining foreign policy and international affairs, and deciding how women dress in public or what is televised or published in newspapers.

Women will play a key role in this future transformation of the Muslim world. In sharp contrast to the popular image of silent submissiveness, Gallup findings on women in countries that are predominantly Muslim or have sizable Muslim populations hardly show that they have been conditioned to accept second-class status. Majorities of women—as well as men—in virtually every country surveyed say that women deserve the same legal rights as men, to vote without influence from family members, to work at any job where they are qualified, and even to serve in the highest levels of government.

In Saudi Arabia, for example, where as of this writing, women were not allowed to vote or drive, majorities of women say that women should be able to drive a car by themselves (61 percent), vote without influence (69 percent), and work at any job for which they are qualified (76 percent). Egyptian women, who have faced far fewer restrictions than their Saudi counterparts, speak even more strongly in favor of women's rights, with 88 percent of Egyptian women saying that they should be allowed to work at any job for which they are qualified. In Egypt, as in other parts of the Muslim world, this attitude is not just a theory, as a full third of professional and technical workers in Egypt are women, on a par with Turkey and South Korea. In the United Arab Emirates and Iran, women make up the majority of university students.

Radical Fringe vs. the Mainstream

So now we return to our central question: who will speak for Islam in the future? Will a radical fringe continue to monopolize our understanding of this global community or will representative voices break through? Will we see the emergence of a reality closer to the vision of the Muslim majority, or one which reflects the twisted ideology of a few? How we approach the next phase of the "war on terror" very will influence answers to these questions. In other words, who the world allows to speak for Islam today will drive who will speak for Islam in the future.

As the world witnesses the seventh anniversary of the September 11 terrorist attacks and the U.S.-led "war on terror" begins its eighth year, hard questions must be asked about the core assumptions that are guiding policy in this battle. Are they leading to actions that help eliminate or inadvertently increase extremism? Who is speaking for Islam in this assessment?

A common question in Washington and the West since 9/11, reinforced by widespread anti-Americanism in the Arab and Muslim world has been: why do they hate us? The mantra-like response, however, "they hate for who we are: our democracy, freedoms, gender equality, and way of life," is plain wrong—worse, it further obscures the facts necessary to bridge the divide. Many have spoken of a clash of civilizations. These fears have been compounded by the tendency to equate widespread anti-Americanism across the Muslim world with terrorists' blind hatred of America and the West; to conflate the mainstream majority of Muslims with a small militant minority, and thus normative Islam with violence and terrorism.

Taking a vocal fringe to represent Islam and Muslims in general inevitably leads to characterizing the war on terror as a "clash of civilizations." Some analysts and policy makers have even drawn an analogy between the Cold War and the current global war on terror calling it the "decisive ideological struggle of our time" and have recommended analogous strategies. After all, it is argued, both conflicts were fought on the battlefield and over people's hearts and minds. Instead of a battle between Western values and communism, however, we now have a struggle between Western values and "radical Islam."

Using a 'Cold War II' paradigm to think of the current gulf between the West and Muslims, confuses two very different conflicts.

However, when mainstream Muslims are allowed to speak for Islam, a very different picture emerges. Our analysis points to serious flaws in the "Cold War II" paradigm and the real danger in confusing these two very different conflicts. Instead, Gallup data suggests that it is more constructive to think of the current conflict not as a battle with Islam, or even within Islam, but rather a competition for the "road to reform." Will widely held grievances be addressed through violence or votes? Two widely differing scenarios represent our choice of futures.

Which Voice Will Dominate?

Scenario One: *the mainstream Muslim majority is marginalized by a vocal and violent minority.* The war on terror is defined in the West as Cold War II or World War III. Islam and/or Arab culture rather than political and economic grievances are identified as the cause of radicalization, violence, and terrorism. This diagnoses drives decisions to carry out large-scale social engineering projects aimed at imposing Western culture as an alternative to Islam. This is coupled with aggressive military buildup in the region as a part of a Cold War-like containment and deterrence policy. To carry out these policies, American leaders are forced to foster even closer and more unconditionally supportive ties to local dictators. Public sentiment flares up at these rulers' foreign and domestic policies and is then squashed by even more draconian repression tactics. The relationship between the United States and majority Muslim publics follows a downward spiral as the fears of many are realized: Western (particularly American) intervention or dominance persists or grows in Muslim countries such as Iran, Pakistan, or Afghanistan; the Palestinian-Israeli conflict flares up again; Muslim regimes become more repressive, continue to use global terrorism as an excuse to further tighten their grip on power, silencing mainstream as well as extremist opposition; despite their rhetoric, Western powers' continue their support for repressive regimes at the expense of homegrown democratization movements.

As a result, political and economic grievances further alienate the politically radicalized, feeding the growth of political and religious extremism and global terrorism. Militant opposition groups re-emerge or grow in Egypt, North Africa, the Persian Gulf, and South Asia. In a worst case scenario, violence and revolution lead to the destabilization of regimes and the emergence of leaders whom neither mainstream Muslim populations nor the West favor, bringing greater insecurity and instability that threatens U.S. and Western interests.

Scenario Two: *the mainstream Muslim majority is engaged and able to address widely held concerns peacefully.* Political grievances (authoritarian, non-representative and repressive governments, corruption and economic stagnation) rather than simply Islam or Muslim culture are seen as the targets for reform. The U.S. and Europe use their political, economic, and military leverage to pressure their Muslim allies to broaden political participation, develop independent government institutions and strong civil societies that limit corruption and increase respect for human rights. Western governments will provide substantial aid for economic and educational development and, at the same time, cut back on arms sales and such high-profile symbols as oversized embassies, military bases, ships, and troops—all of which emphasize American and European armed presence, and the tangible threat of dependency, intervention, and domination.

Muslim societies will change through evolution—not revolution. Rulers will become more accountable to their people and governments more independent and pragmatic in their relations with the West. They begin to reflect better the interests, desires, and values of their people. However, greater democratization does not mean secularization (institutional separation of religion and the state) in most Muslim societies, but a synthesis of greater freedoms and the recognition of religious values as *a*—not *the*—source of law. In most instances, *shariah* will not be the only source of law, but theocracies have been avoided as Muslim majorities have indicated their opposition to such measures. Greater interaction with the West occurs because of common political and economic interests as well as admiration for science, technology, and many of the principles and values of the West, particularly the United States.

A New Direction

Defining the current conflict as a battle between Western values and Islam (or even "radical" Islam) misses the root cause of terrorism while energizing the very perception that fuels sympathy for it—that Islam itself is under attack. In no uncertain terms, the Gallup poll begins to expose the danger of acting on the Cold War II analogies. Indeed, the very premise of Washington's Cold War policy was convincing people that communism was bad and that American democracy was good. But the current and future struggle to come to grips with the interaction of the Western and Muslim worlds is about not appearing to denigrate Islam or impose a secular democracy that excludes faith, because it is this perception that fuels extremist sentiment and alienates those mainstream Muslims who want a democracy compatible with religious values.

The Cold War involved bringing down repressive communist governments in places such as Eastern Europe, where the ruling elites were largely unpopular with the people. But the "war on terror" involves, at times, propping up unpopular repressive governments as a safeguard against terrorism and Islamic fanaticism. Ironically, this support fuels more animosity against the United States and thus empowers violent extremists. Indeed, many have claimed that "blue jeans and *Playboy*" brought down the Soviet Union as much as did strong military deterrence. In

sharp contrast, today it is precisely America's military presence in Muslim lands and a perceived threat to Muslim identity and culture that extremists exploit to gain support. Should this continue, it will likely only intensify the attractiveness of their argument in the future.

From many Muslims' point of view, the conflict with the West is about policy, not principles or values. Through their eyes, it looks like a global civil rights struggle much more than a clash between superpowers. Viewed through this lens, seemingly inexplicable crises such as the Muslim reaction to the incendiary Danish cartoons depicting the Prophet Mohammed published in *Jyllands-Posten* in September 2005, come into sharper focus—as does a more effective strategy forward.

Muslim rioters were not angry because they did not understand the value of free speech in principle—many cite this liberty as among the most admired aspects of the West. Instead, the Danish cartoons were simply the "trigger" igniting the combustible fuel of widespread perceptions of Western domination, denigration of Islam and Muslims, and injustice. Lessons learned from America's civil rights struggle help clarify how to begin to create the conditions by which the silenced majority may start speaking for Islam rather than the vocal and violent fringe. It will require a shift in public diplomacy and policy.

Empowering the Silenced Majority

The Bush administration quite correctly adopted a three-pronged strategy to fight global terrorism: military, economic, and public diplomacy. But, while the military can kill, capture, and contain terrorists, it is not equipped to fight against global terrorism—which is fundamentally a war of ideas, ideology, and policy. Economic measures have been useful: they have identified and cut off financial support for terrorists. But these two methods target only terrorists who, regardless of their power to intimidate us, represent only a small percentage of the Muslim population. Neither the military nor economic option is equipped to address the conditions—now or in the future—that radicalize mainstream Muslims and increase the growth of terrorist recruits. Public diplomacy, however, targets the broader Muslim world, the mainstream majority.

A successful public diplomacy strategy will require public affairs efforts, such as exchange programs and education, to foster mutual understanding in conjunction with foreign policies that reflect shared goals. Past tendencies to reduce public diplomacy to a public relations campaign are based on the flawed premise that the main problem is, "they don't know or understand us." Likewise, simplistic attribution to religious or cultural causes or differences (*i.e.,* "Islam is a violent religion; Muslims don't want democracy") gets us nowhere.

Many Muslims know America quite well and have studied, visited, or lived here. Many admire America's principles and values but fault us for not living up to them. The cause of anti-Americanism is not who we are but what we do. Western governments will need to look beyond militant ideologues or autocratic Muslim rulers, even those who are now our allies, but who use global terrorism as a smokescreen for greater political control and repression. Over the next quarter century, policymakers will require a better understanding of how global Muslim majorities see the world and, in particular, how they regard the United States.

How to Improve Relations?

In the battle for the road to reform, whose outcome determines who will speak for Islam in the future, our diplomatic goals must be to marginalize the violent extremists while building bridges with the mainstream majority. Through an accurate assessment of the current conflict, appropriate language will naturally flow whereby terrorists are positioned as deviant, not devotees of Islam.

The term at the center of this war of words is "jihad." Today, *jihad* continues to have multiple meanings: the personal struggle to lead a good or virtuous life, to fulfill family responsibilities, to clean up a neighborhood, to fight drugs, or to work for social justice. *Jihad* is also used to refer to both wars of liberation and resistance as well as global acts of terror. But many mainstream Muslim theologians have asserted that radicals who encourage a "*jihad* against the infidels" employ a faulty reading of the Koran.

The multiple meanings of *jihad* were captured in a 2001 Gallup Poll in which 10,004 adults in nine predominantly Muslim countries were asked an open-ended question: "Please tell me in one word (or a very few words) what *jihad* means to you." In the four Arab nations polled (Lebanon, Kuwait, Jordan, and Morocco), the most frequent descriptions of *jihad* were, "duty toward God," a "divine duty," or a "worship of God"—with no reference to warfare. However, in three non-Arab Muslim countries (Pakistan, Iran, and Turkey), significant minorities mentioned "sacrificing one's life for the sake of Islam/God/a just cause," or "fighting against the opponents of Islam." An outright majority mentioned this in Indonesia.

The two broad meanings of *jihad,* nonviolent and violent, are contrasted in a well-known prophetic tradition that reports the Prophet Muhammad returning from battle to tell his followers, "We return from the lesser *jihad* [warfare] to the greater *jihad.*"

The greater *jihad* is the more difficult and more important struggle against ego, selfishness, greed, and evil. But it is important to note that for Muslims, whether *jihad* means a struggle of the soul or the sword, it is in both cases a just and ethical struggle. The word *jihad* has only positive connotations. This means that calling acts of terrorism *jihad* risks not only offending many Muslims, but also inadvertently handing radicals the moral advantage they so desperately desire. The recent State Department recommendation to avoid using the word "jihadist" to describe terrorists is therefore a welcome blow to Al Qaeda's rhetorical frame.

In the battle for the road to reform—the outcome of which will determine who will speak for Islam in the future—our diplomatic goals must focus on marginalizing the violent extremists while building bridges to, and with, the mainstream majority.

The good news, for the next quarter century, at least, is that nine of ten Muslims are mainstream—and they want better relations with the West.

The good news, for the next quarter century at least, is that nine out of ten Muslims are in the mainstream. Moreover, both the mainstream and politically radicalized want better relations with the West, coexistence not conflict. However, the politically radicalized do believe that the West uses a double standard in its promotion of democracy and human rights, and fear Western intervention, invasion, and domination. If 7 percent (91 million) of the 1.3 billion Muslims worldwide remain politically radicalized and continue to feel politically dominated, occupied, and disrespected, the West's opportunity to address these drivers of extremism will be as great as the challenge of succeeding. In light of our broad-based data, we now know how to create public diplomacy programs that are informed by what people *actually* think and want: respect for Islam and Muslims, technological and economic development, more sensitivity to the implications of strong, visible support for authoritarian regimes, and diplomacy—above all—rather than the threat of military intervention.

JOHN L. ESPOSITO, University Professor and professor of Religion and International Affairs, Georgetown University, and **DALIA MOGAHED,** senior analyst and executive director of the Gallup Center for Muslim Studies, are co-authors of *Who Speaks for Islam? What a Billion Muslims Really Think* (Gallup Press. 2007).

Free at Last?

BERNARD LEWIS

The Arab World in the Twenty-First Century

As the twentieth century drew to an end, it became clear that a major change was taking place in the countries of the Arab world. For almost 200 years, those lands had been ruled and dominated by European powers and before that by non-Arab Muslim regimes—chiefly the Ottoman Empire. After the departure of the last imperial rulers, the Arab world became a political battleground between the United States and the Soviet Union during the Cold War. That, too, ended with the collapse of the Soviet Union in 1991. Arab governments and Arab dynasties (royal or presidential) began taking over. Arab governments and, to a limited but growing extent, the Arab peoples were at last able to confront their own problems and compelled to accept responsibility for dealing with them.

Europe, long the primary source of interference and domination, no longer plays any significant role in the affairs of the Arab world. Given the enormous oil wealth enjoyed by some Arab rulers and the large and growing Arab and Muslim population in Europe, the key question today is, what role will Arabs play in European affairs? With the breakup of the Soviet Union, Russia ceased to be a major factor in the Arab world. But because of its proximity, its resources, and its large Muslim population, Russia cannot afford to disregard the Middle East. Nor can the Middle East afford to disregard Russia.

The United States, unlike Europe, has continued to play a central role in the Arab world. During the Cold War, the United States' interest in the region lay chiefly in countering the growing Soviet influence, such as in Egypt and Syria. Since the end of the Cold War, U.S. troops have appeared occasionally in the region, either as part of joint peace missions (as in Lebanon in 1982-83) or to rescue or protect Arab governments from their neighboring enemies (as in Kuwait and Saudi Arabia in 1990–91). But many in the Arab world—and in the broader Islamic world—have seen these activities as blatant U.S. imperialism. According to this perception, the United States is simply the successor to the now-defunct French, British, and Soviet empires and their various Christian predecessors, carrying out yet another infidel effort to dominate the Islamic world.

Increasing U.S. involvement in the Middle East led to a series of attacks on U.S. government installations during the 1980s and 1990s. At first, Washington's response to the attacks was to withdraw. After the attacks on the U.S. marine barracks in Beirut in 1983 and on the U.S. component of a United Nations mission in Mogadishu in 1993, Washington pulled out its troops, made angry but vague declarations, and then launched missiles into remote and uninhabited places. Even the 1993 attack on the World Trade Center, in New York City, brought no serious rejoinder. These responses were seen by many as an expression of fear and weakness rather than moderation, and they encouraged hope among Islamist militants that they would eventually triumph. It was not until 9/11 that Washington felt compelled to respond with force, first in Afghanistan and then in Iraq, which were perceived as the sources of these attacks.

Other powers, both external and within the region, are playing increasingly active roles. Two neighboring non-Arab but predominantly Muslim countries, Iran and Turkey, have a long history of involvement in Arab affairs. Although the Turks, no doubt because of their past experience, have remained cautious and defensive, mainly concerned with a possible threat from Kurdish northern Iraq, the Iranians have become more active, especially since Iran's Islamic Revolution entered a new militant and expansionist phase. The broader Islamic world, free from outside control for the first time in centuries, is also naturally interested in events in the heartland of Islam. China and India, which will share or compete for primacy in Asia and elsewhere in the twenty-first century are also taking an interest in the region.

The Challenge of Peace

The political landscape within the Arab world has also changed dramatically since the end of the Cold War. Pan-Arabism, which once played a central role in the region, has effectively come to an end. Of the many attempts to unite different Arab countries, all but one, the unification of North and South Yemen after they were briefly separated by an imperial intrusion, have failed. Since the death of Egyptian President Gamal Abdel Nasser, in 1970, no Arab leader has enjoyed much support outside his own country. Nor has any Arab head of state dared to submit his attainment or retention of power to the genuinely free choice of his own people.

At the same time, issues of national identity are becoming more significant. Non-Arab ethnic minorities—such as the Kurds in Iran, Iraq, and Turkey and the Berbers in North

Africa—historically posed no major threat to central governments, and relations were generally good between Arabs and their non-Arab Muslim compatriots. But a new situation arose after the defeat of Saddam Hussein in the Persian Gulf War. The U.S. invasion of Iraq in 1991 had a strictly limited purpose: to liberate Kuwait. When this was accomplished, U.S. forces withdrew, leaving Saddam in control of his armed forces and free to massacre those of his subjects, notably Kurds and Shiites, who had responded to the United States' appeal for rebellion. Saddam was left in power, but his control did not extend to a significant part of northern Iraq, where a local Kurdish regime in effect became an autonomous government. This region was largely, although not entirely, Kurdish and included most of the Kurdish regions of Iraq. For the first time in modern history, there was a Kurdish country with a Kurdish government—at least in practice, if not in theory. This posed problems not only for the government of Iraq but also for those of some neighboring countries with significant Kurdish populations, notably Turkey. (Because of the strong opposition of these neighbors, the creation of an independent Kurdish state in the future seems unlikely. But a Kurdish component of a federal Iraq is a serious possibility.)

Another major problem for the region is the Palestinian issue. The current situation is the direct result of the policy, endorsed by the League of Nations and later by the United Nations, to create a Jewish national home in Palestine. With rare exceptions, the Arabs of Palestine and the leading Arab regimes resisted this policy from the start. A succession of offers for a Palestinian state in Palestine were made—by the British mandate government in 1937, by the United Nations in 1947—but each time Palestinian leaders and Arab regimes refused the offer because it would have meant recognizing the existence of a Jewish state next door. The struggle between the new state of Israel and the Palestinians has continued for over six decades, sometimes in the form of battles between armies (as in 1948, 1956, 1967, and 1973) and more recently between Israeli citizens and groups that are variously described as freedom fighters or terrorists.

The modern peace process began when President Anwar al-Sadat, of Egypt, fearing that the growing Soviet presence in the region was a greater threat to Arab independence than Israel could ever constitute, made peace with Israel in 1979. He was followed in 1994 by King Hussein of Jordan and, less formally, by other Arab states that developed some commercial and quasi-diplomatic contacts with Israel. Dialogue between Israel and the Palestine Liberation Organization led to some measure of formal mutual recognition and, more significant, to a withdrawal of Israeli forces from parts of the West Bank and the Gaza Strip and the establishment of more or less autonomous Palestinian authorities in these places.

But the conflict continues. Important sections of the Palestinian movement have refused to recognize the negotiations or any agreements and are continuing the armed struggle. Even some of those who have signed agreements—notably Yasir Arafat—have later shown a curious ambivalence toward their implementation. From the international discourse in English and other European languages, it would seem that most of the Arab states and some members of the Palestinian leadership have resigned themselves to accepting Israel as a state. But the discourse in Arabic—in broadcasts, sermons, speeches, and school textbooks—is far less conciliatory, portraying Israel as an illegitimate invader that must be destroyed. If the conflict is about the size of Israel, then long and difficult negotiations can eventually resolve the problem. But if the conflict is about the existence of Israel, then serious negotiation is impossible. There is no compromise position between existence and nonexistence.

Running on Empty

The state of the region's economy, and the resulting social and political situation, is a source of increasing concern in the Arab world. For the time being, oil continues to provide enormous wealth, directly to some countries in the region and indirectly to others. But these vast sums of money are creating problems as well as benefits. For one thing, oil wealth has strengthened autocratic governments and inhibited democratic development. Oil-rich rulers have no need to levy taxes and therefore no need to satisfy elected representatives. (In the Arab world, the converse of a familiar dictum is true: No representation without taxation.)

In addition to strengthening autocracy, oil wealth has also inhibited economic development. Sooner or later, oil will be either exhausted or replaced as an energy source, and the wealth and power that it provides will come to an end. Some more far-sighted Arab governments, aware of this eventuality, have begun to encourage and foster other kinds of economic development. Some of the Persian Gulf states are showing impressive expansion, especially in tourism and international finance. But the returns accruing from these sectors are still limited compared to the enormous wealth derived from oil.

Oil wealth has also led to the neglect or abandonment of other forms of gainful economic activity. From 2002 to 2006, a committee of Arab intellectuals, working under the auspices of the United Nations, produced a series of reports on human development in the Arab world. With devastating frankness, they reviewed the economic, social, and cultural conditions in the Arab world and compared them with those of other regions. Some of these comparisons—reinforced by data from other international sources—revealed an appalling pattern of neglect and underdevelopment.

Over the last quarter of a century, real gdp per capita has fallen throughout the Arab world. In 1999, the gdp of all the Arab countries combined stood at $531.2 billion, less than that of Spain. Today, the total non-oil exports of the entire Arab world (which has a population of approximately 300 million people) amount to less than those of Finland (a country of only five million inhabitants). Throughout the 1990s, exports from the region, 70 percent of which are oil or oil-related products, grew at a rate of 1.5 percent, far below the average global rate of six percent. The number of books translated every year into Arabic in the entire Arab world is one-fifth the number translated into Greek in Greece. And the number of books, both those in their original language and those translated, published per million people in the Arab world is very low compared with the figures for other regions. (Sub-Saharan Africa has a lower figure, but just barely.)

The situation regarding science and technology is as bad or worse. A striking example is the number of patents registered in the United States between 1980 and 2000: from Saudi Arabia, there were 171; from Egypt, 77; from Kuwait, 52; from the United Arab Emirates, 32; from Syria, 20; and from Jordan, 15—corhpared with 16,328 from South Korea and 7,652 from Israel. Out of six world regions, that comprising the Middle East and North Africa received the lowest freedom rating from Freedom House. The Arab countries also have the highest illiteracy rates and one of the lowest numbers of active research scientists with frequently cited articles. Only sub-Saharan Africa has a lower average standard of living.

Another shock came with the 2003 publication in China of a list of the 500 best universities in the world. The list did not include a single one of the more than 200 universities in the Arab countries. Since then, new rankings have appeared every year. The Arab universities remain absent, even from the relatively short list for the Asia-Pacific region. In an era of total and untrammeled independence for the Arab world, these failings can no longer be attributed to imperial oppressors or other foreign malefactors.

One of the most important social problems in the Arab world, as elsewhere in the Islamic world, is the condition of women. Women constitute slightly more than half the population, but in most Arab countries they have no political power. Some Muslim observers have seen in the depressed and downtrodden status of the female Arab population one of the main reasons for the underdevelopment of their society as compared with the advanced West and the rapidly developing East. Modern communications and travel are making these contrasts ever more visible. Some countries, such as Iraq and Tunisia, have made significant progress toward the emancipation of women by increasing opportunities for them. In Iraq, women have gained access to higher education and, consequently, to an ever-widening range of professions. In Tunisia, equal rights for women were guaranteed in the 1959 constitution. The results have been almost universal education for women and a significant number of women among the ranks of doctors, journalists, lawyers, magistrates, and teachers, as well as in the worlds of business and politics. This is perhaps the most hopeful single factor for the future of freedom and progress in these countries.

Another social problem is immigrant communities in the Arab world, which have received far less attention than Arab immigrant communities in Europe. These immigrants are attracted by oil wealth and the opportunities that it provides, and they undertake tasks that local people are either unwilling or unable to perform. 1 rus is giving rise to new and growing alien communities in several Arab countries, such as South Asians in the United Arab. The assimilation of immigrants from one Arab country into another has often proved difficult, and the acceptance of non-Arab and non-Muslim immigrants from remoter lands poses a more serious problem.

All these problems are aggravated by the communications revolution, which is having an enormous impact on the Arab population across all social classes. Even in premodern times, government control of news and ideas in the Islamic countries was limited—the mosque, the pulpit, and, above all, the pilgrimage—provided opportunities for the circulation of both information and ideas without parallel in the Western world. To some extent, modern Middle Eastern governments had learned how to manipulate information, but that control is rapidly diminishing as modern communications technology, such as satellite television and the Internet, has made people in the Arab countries, as elsewhere, keenly aware of the contrasts between different groups in their own countries and, more important, of the striking differences between the situations in their countries and those in other parts of the world. This has led to a great deal of anger and resentment, often directed against the West, as well as a countercurrent striving for democratic reform.

The Rise of the Radicals

Most westerners saw the defeat and collapse of the Soviet Union as a victory in the Cold War. For many Muslims, it was nothing of the sort. In some parts of the Islamic world, the collapse of the Soviet Union represented the devastating loss of a patron that was difficult or impossible to replace. In others, it symbolized the defeat of an enemy and a victory for the Muslim warriors who forced the Soviets to withdraw from Afghanistan. As this latter group saw it, the millennial struggle between the true believers and the unbelievers had gone through many phases, during which the Muslims were led by various lines of caliphs and the unbelievers by various infidel empires. During the Cold War, the leadership of the unbelievers was contested between two rival superpowers, the United States and the Soviet Union. Since they—the Muslim holy warriors in Afghanistan—had disposed of the larger, fiercer, and more dangerous of the two in the 1980s, dealing with the other, they believed, would be comparatively easy.

That task was given a new urgency by the two U.S. interventions in Iraq: that during the brief Persian Gulf War of 1990–91 and the 2003 invasion that resulted in the overthrow of Saddam and the attempt to create a new and more democratic political and social order. Opinions differ on the measure of the United States' achievements so far, but even its limited success has been sufficient to cause serious alarm, both to regimes with a vested interest in the survival of the existing order and, more important, to groups with their own radical plans for overthrowing it.

In the eyes of Islamist radicals, both of these wars have constituted humiliating defeats for Islam at the hands of the surviving infidel superpower. This point has been made with particular emphasis by Osama bin Laden, a Saudi who played a significant role in the war against the Soviets in Afghanistan and subsequently emerged as a very articulate leader in the Islamic world and as the head of al Qaeda, a new Islamist radical group. He has repeatedly made his case against the United States, most notably in his declaration of jihad of February 1998, in which he elaborated three grievances against the infidel enemies of Islam. The first was the presence of U.S. troops in Saudi Arabia, the holy land of Islam. The second was the use of Saudi bases for an attack on Iraq, the seat of the longest and most glorious period of classical Islamic history. The third was U.S. support for the seizure of Jerusalem by what he contemptuously called "the statelet" of the Jews.

Another claimant for the mantle of Islamic leadership is the Islamic Republic of Iran. The 1979 Iranian Revolution constituted a major shift in power, with a major ideological basis, and had a profound impact across the Muslim world. Its influence was by no means limited to Shiite communities. It was also very extensive and powerful in countries where there is little or no Shiite presence and where Sunni-Shiite differences therefore have little political or emotional significance. The impact of the Iranian Revolution in the Arab countries was somewhat delayed because of the long and bitter Iran-Iraq War (1980–88), but from the end of the war onward, Iran's influence began to grow, particularly among Shiites in neighboring Arab countries. These populations, even in those places where they are numerous, had for centuries lived under what might be described as a Sunni ascendancy. The Iranian Revolution, followed by the regime change in Iraq in 2003, gave them new hope; the Shiite struggle has once again, for the first time in centuries, become a major theme of Arab politics. This struggle is very important where Shiites constitute a majority of the population (as in Iraq) or a significant proportion of the population (as in Lebanon, Syria, and parts of the eastern and southern Arabian Peninsula). For some time now, the eastern Arab world has seen the odd spectacle of Sunni and Shiite extremists occasionally cooperating in the struggle against the infidels while continuing their internal struggle against one another. (One example of this is Iran's support for both the strongly Sunni Hamas in Gaza and the strongly Shiite Hezbollah in Lebanon.)

The increasing involvement of Iran in the affairs of the Arab world has brought about major changes. First, Iran has developed into a major regional power, its influence extending to Lebanon and the Palestinian territories. Second, although the rift between the Sunnis and the Shiites is significant, Iran's involvement has rendered it less important than the divide between both of them and their non-Arab, non-Muslim enemies. Third, just as the perceived Soviet threat induced Sadat to make peace with Israel in 1979, today some Arab leaders see the threat from Iran as more dangerous than that posed by Israel and therefore are quietly seeking accommodation with the Jewish state. During the 2006 war between Israeli forces and Hezbollah, the usual pan-Arab support for the Arab side was replaced by a cautious, even expectant, neutrality. This realignment may raise some hope for Arab-Israeli peace.

The Struggle for the Future

For much of the twentieth century, two imported Western ideologies dominated in the Arab world: socialism and nationalism. By the beginning of the twenty-first century, these worldviews had become discredited. Both had, in effect, accomplished the reverse of their declared aims. Socialist plans and projects were put in place, but they did not bring prosperity. National independence was achieved, but it did not bring freedom; rather, it allowed foreign overlords to be replaced with domestic tyrants, who were less inhibited and more intimate in their tyranny. Another imported European model, the one-party ideological dictatorship, brought neither prosperity nor dignity—only tyranny sustained by indoctrination and repression.

Today, most Arab regimes belong to one of two categories: those that depend on the people's loyalty and those that depend on their obedience. Loyalty may be ethnic, tribal, regional, or some combination of these; the most obvious examples of systems that rely on loyalty are the older monarchies, such as those of Morocco and the Arabian Peninsula. The regimes that depend on obedience are European-style dictatorships that use techniques of control and enforcement derived from the fascist and communist models. These regimes have little or no claim to the loyalty of their people and depend for survival on diversion and repression: directing the anger of their people toward some external enemy—such as Israel, whose misdeeds are a universally sanctioned public grievance—and suppressing discontent with ruthless police methods. In those Arab countries where the government depends on force rather than loyalty, there is clear evidence of deep and widespread discontent, directed primarily against the regime and then inevitably against those who are seen to support it. This leads to a paradox—namely, that countries with pro-Western regimes usually have anti-Western populations, whereas the populations of countries with anti-Western regimes tend to look to the West for liberation.

Both of these models are becoming less effective; there are groups, increasing in number and importance, that seek a new form of government based not primarily on loyalty, and still less on repression, but on consent and participation. These groups are still small and, of necessity, quiet, but the fact that they have appeared at all is a remarkable development. Some Arab states have even begun to experiment, cautiously, with elected assemblies formed after authentically contested elections, notably Iraq after its 2005 election.

In some countries, democratic opposition forces are growing, but they are often vehemently anti-Western. The recent successes of Hamas and Hezbollah demonstrate that opposition parties can fare very well when their critiques are cast in religious, rather than political, terms. The religious opposition parties have several obvious advantages. They express both their critiques and their aspirations in terms that are culturally familiar and easily accepted, unlike those of Western-style democrats. In the mosques, they have access to a communications network—and therefore tools to disseminate propaganda—unparalleled in any other sector of the community. They are relatively free from corruption and have a record of helping the suffering urban masses. A further advantage, compared with secular democratic opposition groups, is that whereas the latter are required by their own ideologies to tolerate the propaganda of their opponents, the religious parties have no such obligation. Rather, it is their sacred duty to suppress and crush what they see as antireligious, anti-Islamic movements. Defenders of the existing regimes argue, not implausibly, that loosening the reins of authority would lead to a takeover by radical Islamist forces.

Lebanon is the one country in the entire region with a significant experience of democratic political life. It has suffered not for its faults but for its merits—the freedom and openness that others have exploited with devastating effect. More recently, there have been some hopeful signs that the outside exploitation and manipulation of Lebanon might at last be diminishing.

The Palestinian leadership has been gone for decades; Syria was finally induced to withdraw its forces in 2005, leaving the Lebanese, for the first time in decades, relatively free to conduct their own affairs. Indeed, the Cedar Revolution of 2005 was seen as the beginning of a new era for Lebanon. But Lebanese democracy is far from secure. Syria retains a strong interest in the country, and Hezbollah—trained, armed, and financed by Iran—has become increasingly powerful. There have been some signs of a restoration of Lebanese stability and democracy, but the battle is not yet over, nor will it be, until the struggle for democracy spreads beyond the borders of Lebanon.

Today, there are two competing diagnoses of the ills of the region, each with its own appropriate prescription. According to one, the trouble is all due to infidels and their local dupes and imitators. The remedy is to resume the millennial struggle against the infidels in the West and return to God-given laws and traditions. According to the other diagnosis, it is the old ways, now degenerate and corrupt, that are crippling the Arab world. The cure is openness and freedom in the economy, society, and the state—in a word, genuine democracy. But the road to democracy—and to freedom—is long and difficult, with many obstacles along the way. It is there, however, and there are some visionary leaders who are trying to follow it. At the moment, both Islamic theocracy and liberal democracy are represented in the region. The future place of the Arab world in history will depend, in no small measure, on the outcome of the struggle between them.

Iran in Search of Itself

The intertwined sources of Iranians' identity—Iranian nationalism, Islam, and Westernization—remain an uncomfortable mix.

MAHMOOD SARIOLGHALAM

February 2009 will mark the thirtieth anniversary of the Iranian Revolution. After three decades, the conceptions that shaped the Islamic Revolution of 1979 are still alive and floating about.

The course that a revolutionary polity follows is heavily influenced by the way its leaders perceive their own roles, their society, and the world at large. In the case of the Iranian revolution, the fundamental perception that underpinned events was that a need existed for "an end to foreign intervention." This view of history is still ubiquitous, and Iranian leaders consistently express their distrust of foreigners and especially Westerners. Indeed, resentful references to Iran's past experiences with the West remain a significant part of most politicians' rhetoric. And the constitution of the Islamic Republic of Iran is rife with institutional and conceptual attempts to focus the nation's attention inward.

This preoccupation among the elites and some other segments of society with "foreign intervention" leads one to believe that such a perception is not just analytical in nature but rather an in-grained feature of the Iranian political psyche. And as is the case in all revolutions, deviation from the original path threatens the raison d'etre of a consolidated revolutionary order. For three decades now, the Islamic Revolution in Iran has remained loyal to its original roots.

With good intentions and a cosmopolitan orientation, President Akbar Hashemi Rafsanjani strived to concentrate on economic reconstruction during his two consecutive presidential terms, from 1989 to 1997. This new focus seemed logical after a long and devastating eight-year war with Iraq (1980–1988). Rafsanjani's successor, Mohammad Khatami, undertook an even more ambitious project, the launching of civil society and democracy in Iran. His imaginative pivot seemed to fit in with the post-Soviet trend toward democratization in the developing world.

Ultimately, however, neither president succeeded in his aims. They both discounted the underlying reality that the principles of the Iranian constitution and its supporting institutions are designed to hamper "foreign influence and intervention" in the country. Mixing with the alien world—and, even worse, emulating outsiders' political and economic constructions—sinfully threatened the revolution's raison d'etre. More dangerously, a global outlook had the potential to activate and organize groups out of sync with the cultural inheritance of the Islamic Revolution, such as digital professionals and individualist non-populists.

In Iran, isolationism was never the unintended consequence of a novel political movement; instead, it constituted a historically driven way of perceiving the world. It was an intended preference. So not only did the two presidents' endeavors for 16 years (1989–2005) reflect a departure from the fixations of a revolutionary order, but Iranian society itself was unprepared to shoulder the two presidents' colossal national objectives of democracy and economic privatization. Iran's presidential election of June 2005 brought the derailed revolutionary order back on its original track.

The China Difference

Revolutions resist reform. They are not flexible enough to make transitions. The Chinese Revolution stands out as an exception, thanks to a leadership that was inspired more by Chinese nationalism than by Marxist dogmatism. To be sure, the Iranian and Chinese experiences feature striking correlations: Both countries were humiliated in the nineteenth and twentieth centuries; both underwent revolutions; and both revolutions led to endogenous politics and overstressed political sovereignty and freedom from foreign influence. The Chinese, however, realized fairly quickly that economic wealth is the bedrock of any power, even ideological power. The Chinese also realized that developing countries, if they are to accumulate wealth, are obliged to connect to the core, to the Western world.

In particular, the Chinese realized this ground rule: that the more a country is structurally linked to the American economy, the more it will have access to technology, markets, and investment opportunities. (In 2007, almost 30,000 patents were registered in California, while Brazil could claim only 93.) The correctness of China's judgment is unmistakably demonstrated by statistics such as these: From 1998 through 2008, China attracted some $500 billion in foreign investment; and China's foreign exchange reserves increased from a meager $20 billion in 1987 to $1.9 trillion by the end of September 2008.

When comparing China and Iran, cultural factors are crucial. In China, an overwhelming consensus exists between the state and substantial sectors of society, a consensus that the country's future depends on its integration into the global economy. Importantly, the Chinese and the Iranians diverge in the way they handle their fears of the international system. China is a nation-state in which, increasingly since the early 1980s, pragmatic considerations of the national interest have taken precedence over political or ideological concerns. Iran is still striving to achieve this kind of nationalism because of the isolationist impulses introduced by inward looking policies and also because the country's shift from tribal to national politics, which is a part of the post-revolutionary national electoral process, is still incomplete. China's nationalism is indisputable. Iranian nationalism has yet to be transformed from its current sentimentalism into a rational, binding, constructive, and pervasive nationalism.

More importantly, consensus-building processes in China are hierarchical, collective, and lasting. In contrast, consensus building among Iranians is unconventional, thanks in part to centuries-old *center-of-the-universe* rule by monarchical despots. Chinese authoritarianism in imperial days featured hierarchy in the ruling courts and even in society; Iranians, meanwhile, were ruthlessly dismissed as subjects while despots and kings hogged the spotlight and took all decision making on themselves. Iranians, with little experience of or training in collective decision making, incessantly quarrel among themselves. They delight in avoiding definitions. Consensus building is impaired by deficiencies in listening and coordinating. Ambiguity is regarded as a virtue—even children learn to hone this technique for survival and entertainment. And transparency and clarity are viewed as signs of naiveté and as invitations for distrust.

Political Paradoxes

At the center of this unpromising situation are paradoxical issues of identity and the way identity relates to the modern world. The intertwined sources of Iranians' identity—Iranian nationalism, Islam, and Westernization—remain an uncomfortable mix. Over time, Islam and Iranian nationalism have peacefully converged, providing space for each other. However, when Westernization as a way of life becomes involved, contradictions immediately surface. Islam and liberalism are at odds with one another, and stand at opposite ends of the philosophical spectrum. Islam as a worldview cannot be secularized. As a culture and as a reference point for morality, it can nurture itself alongside a liberal economic or even political order—but not easily.

Understood objectively, the idea of "Islamic democracy" is a conceptual fabrication. True, Islam promotes its own logic of collectivism and consultation. But this is philosophically and institutionally distinct from the underpinnings of liberal democracy. Since Islam is not a secular ideology, it cannot be integrated with a liberalism permeated by secularism, individualism, and pluralistic consensus. No nation can claim to sustain a cohesive social construct on the basis of two contradictory philosophical pillars, namely Islam and liberalism.

Yet Islam is an integrated part of Iranian society and politics, and will remain so. Thus, in the Iranian context, the question of whether Islam and variations of liberalism can coexist, and to what degree, and how, presents a major philosophical and political challenge to those who would like to see Iran's paradoxes resolved and the country move toward stability and advancement. And the most consequential theoretical challenge is whether it is possible to preserve an Islamist order at home while the world is managed by liberal means.

A problem that complicates matters further is the fact that politics in Iran is a zero-sum game. Adherents of one identity cannot, either philosophically or practically, combine with or even build coalitions with advocates of other groups, since their basic definitions are at odds with one another. Iran's body politic, in contrast to Turkey's, is not broad enough to contain all political orientations. Many of Iran's policy dilemmas can be understood in light of the incompatibility of the country's three sources of identity. This conflict acts as a drag on this slowly maturing nation-state.

Islamists Versus Globalists

Iran's identity paradox has repercussions in many layers of the country's society, its economic institutions, and its differentiated culture.

Turkey and Malaysia, through industrialization and their market economies, have advanced further than Iran toward accommodating the Islamic identity paradox. They have seemingly (albeit arduously) achieved an emerging consensus, both on the street and in the corridors of power, that they must join the processes of economic and political globalization. In Iran, the settlement of the identity paradox will be the result of a political reconciliation between the Islamists and the globalists. The cornerstone of such a settlement, it seems to me, could be learned from the Chinese communists: national economic prosperity and accumulation of wealth.

This is why the concept of "regime change," as an American policy prescription regarding Iran, is a superficial and ill-conceived approach to a complex society and body politic. In the end, Iranians themselves need to rise above theoretical quarrels and focus on what is constructive for their country's advancement. If economic progress is any guiding principle, fellow Muslim countries like Malaysia or nearby Turkey and the United Arab Emirates can certainly serve as examples.

But the economy plays a complicated role in Iranian politics. In all rentier states, where the government relies on income from other nations and so does not need the support of its citizens to justify its policies, state-society relations will necessarily be a one-way street. Today, some 85 percent of the economic activity in Iran is conducted by the state. The government's command over national resources and particularly petroleum income leaves insufficient room for private economic activity. Under such a model of political economy, the pursuit of democratic ideals is illusory in the short to medium term.

Democratization requires an active and empowered private sector. As Milton Friedman pointed out in his classic *Capitalism and Freedom,* "If economic power is joined to political power, concentration seems inevitable. On the other hand, if economic power is kept in separate hands from political power, it can serve as a check and a counter to political power." The political future of Iran lies in how its economy evolves, the degree to which citizens become less dependent on state employment, and the emergence of tendencies that would expedite the rise of a vibrant and organized private economic sector. Without these developments, no state with independent revenues—such as Iran's oil income—will feel compelled to delegate authority or to hold itself accountable for its domestic or foreign policies.

Enter the Engineers

When analyzing Iran's politics, Western media and other observers tend to concentrate on clerics as the most critical group. This is an oversimplified depiction of Iran's convoluted political world. In fact, clerics do not run the machinery of the Iranian government. Furthermore, Iran's diplomatic corps and the majority of the members of the parliament are not clerics.

Interestingly, a sizable group of Iranian professionals and technocrats, many of them Western-educated and most of them engineers, believe that democracy is an "alien concept" and part of a Western conspiracy to regain control of Iran. Indeed, the political influence of officials with engineering degrees in post-revolutionary Iran should not be underestimated. Their ritual religious orthodoxy is often quite deep, and they tend not to question or challenge basic assumptions, though a good majority of them are not well versed in Islamic law or thinking. The engineers' conceptual poverty in social, economic, and political theory is one reason that Iranian statecraft has experienced an endless process of trial and error. Every time the engineers in various state institutions engage in another round of self-teaching, the country's progress is disrupted by another round of experimentation with novel modalities.

As noted by many European and Middle Eastern scholars who have written on engineers' and physicians' unschooled entry into fundamentalist waters in the Arab world, in most cases when these two professional groups set foot in politics, diversity is unrecognized, parochialism is applauded, and there is only one answer to every question and one solution to every problem. An engineering-based mental construct leaves little space for nuance, subtlety, sophistication, gray-area options in problem solving, or a long-term orientation toward society and politics. This binary-oriented and project-based approach to Iran's domestic politics as well as its foreign policy has created a short-term perspective on complex human processes. It is no surprise that even the reformists under former President Khatami—mostly engineers and physicians—dubbed their mission a "project for democracy," as if it were another dam or highway construction project.

In much of the developing world, politicians with engineering or medical degrees tend to conform easily to the proclivities of the core leadership. Yet Iran is not exactly another

Soviet-style state. Over the past two decades, some sectors of Iranian society have audaciously adopted the underlying ideas associated with globalization. Despite the fact that Iran's society is highly stratified, levels of tolerance among citizens have expanded. Members of the Iranian parliament engage in lively and unhindered debate on economic issues. The movie industry criticizes political practices in amorphous and subtle ways. In Tehran alone, one can identify startling cultural variations, from genuine Islamic orthodoxy to Beverly Hills styles of living.

In Iranian politics, there are elections almost every year. There is even some rotation of power. Some 3,000 officials are replaced following presidential elections. There are also policy debates, though all this takes place within a predominantly singular school of thought. A minority of Iranian society has abandoned politics altogether and is busy living a plush life. The nouveau riche barely watch Iranian television. They spend their vacations abroad, and in cozy north Tehran cafés mingle with Iranian-American visitors from West Los Angeles and Bethesda, talking about the latest concerts in Dubai and fashion shows in Milan.

To be sure, the economic umbilical cord keeps a substantial portion of the population dependent on the state and its subsidies. In an assured fashion, a healthy majority religiously and gleefully supports the ideological minarets of the state. Yet contrary to conventional wisdom, a majority of Shiite clerics are open to discussion, diverse views, and conceptual challenges in their seminary settings. If one investigates the traditions of Shiite clerics from a historical perspective, one finds that radicalism, either as a way of thinking or as a political method, is typically deemed a form of irrational exuberance. Indeed, Iranian radicalism can be traced to the practices of the Iranian left more than to the Islamists. Generally speaking, the various intellectual groups in Iran are more or less atomized, urban-based, and trapped in ivory-tower deductive analysis.

Most of the exotic colors in this rainbow portrait of Iran's society are not institutionalized; they are forces of history, state building, and survival, and must be reckoned with. But two lasting institutions persist among a majority of Persians of all stripes: love of life and a passion for proximity to power.

The Struggle for Iran's Soul

During the Iran-Iraq War in the 1980s, there naturally existed a sweeping consensus for defending Iran's territorial integrity, and for the revolutionary apparatus. After the war, however, two orientations toward national issues began to surface: the revolutionary and the internationalist schools of thought. (Similar parallels can be drawn from the Chinese and Soviet experience in the 1970s.) The Rafsanjani presidency provided momentum and organization to the internationalist school. Hassan Rouhani, Iran's chief nuclear negotiator under Khatami, is a demure and sophisticated member of this elitist group (the international-ists). Khatami himself, a media-savvy political idealist, uncomfortably but inevitably falls into this category as well. Even Ali Larijani, speaker of the Iranian parliament, according to Iran's typically opaque politics and using an elastic definition of globalization, counts as an inter-nationalist. Mohammad Bagher Qalibaf, Tehran's mayor, has gradually been elbowed into this family as well.

These politicians have one characteristic in common: medium to extensive exposure to the complexities of the international milieu. In the public domain, a majority of economists, diplomats educated in international affairs, technocrats, and intellectuals belong to this group. Members of this school of thought attach importance to Iran's global standing and national wealth, and to the economic well-being of the average citizen. For them, economic development, access to information technology, education, efficiency, and globalization should be the concerns of the state, even an Islamic state.

In contrast, the revolutionary school champion unerring Islamic sovereignty, the plight of the Muslim world, and a genuine struggle against imperialism. Advocates for the revolutionary school of thought consider Islam an all-encompassing ideology. From their perspective, there is no need to extend a hand to foreigners; Islamic dignity dictates distance. They argue that the international landscape is founded on oppression, conspiracy, and anti-Islam sentiment. It is all controlled and directed by capitalists. The outside world is merely the extension of a vast economic and political conglomerate.

The revolutionary group believes that most national efforts should aim to preserve the ideological order, and it defines the West as Iran's adversary. The internationalist group, however, does not dissociate the domestic structure from global dynamics, the national economy from foreign policy, and national security from economic development. While the former group believes that Iran should focus on its internal agenda and maintain a calculated distance from the alien world, the latter promotes economic development and believes Iran should join the World Trade Organization and become a normal member of the international community.

The revolutionary school asserts that Iran's security is guaranteed when it dissociates itself from the economic and political impositions of the international capitalist system led by the United States. The internationalist school presumes that Iran's national security stems from its economic interdependence with the international community, and argues that Iran should focus on producing national wealth, engage in economic diplomacy, and busy itself with soft politics. Whereas the threat perceptions of the revolutionaries are fundamentally in the area of existential and security issues, the internationalists perceive economic and social problems, aggravated by isolation, as the underlying security threats to the country.

Self-Esteem Issues

From a sociopolitical perspective, the two schools of thought reflect a divergence of opinion within Iranian society. Their interpretations of life, politics, and the world are part of the realities of the complex layers of Iran. The revolutionary group's members feel at odds with and are insecure while dealing with foreigners. They are philosopher-politicians, welded to history. The internationalists have a more robust self-esteem and are willing to compete, to influence, and to be influenced. They are worldly politicians, and are convinced that efficiency results from professionalism and internationalism.

The two groups and their affiliates have learned to coexist. They both have media, institutions, and gatherings to express and promote themselves. Their philosophical differences underscore the challenge of delineating an overwhelming national consensus for the country's future direction, of the sort achieved by Turkish and Malaysian elites and societies. Time is of essence for revolutionary states if they wish to precipitate coherence and consensus, in terms of both definition and conduct. Historical evidence substantiates the idea that, whenever philosophical discussions among elites give way to policy debates, a nation-state is born. Iran is no exception. From this vantage point, the Iranian Revolution has been constructive and encouraging in that it has generated indispensable discourse among Iranians, helping them to draw delicate lines defining identity, politics, state, society, and the globe. Vibrant debate between internationalists and revolutionaries is decidedly flourishing in Iran's evolving and maturing society.

The Necessary Trial

Iran is a land of philosophy, mystics, and ideology cloaked in pride and an imperial mentality. Its identity is not a twentieth century extension of colonial constructs. For old nations, history is both a blessing and a limitation. In retrospect, the Islamic Revolution was a necessary trial. In the long run it will inadvertently address Iran's identity paradox, and hopefully will help resolve the country's polar contradictions. In this respect, a rational, respectful, and two-way communication channel with the West will prove crucial. A sustained, consensus-based, and practical mélange of Islam and Iranian pride will have to be established in order for a broad consensus to be reached among society's various layers.

Populism may be a subject that political scientists dismiss, but populist social debate and upheaval are historically indispensable in fashioning an organized society. Political scientists need to remain mindful of the arduous social processes that produced mature nation-states in nineteenth century Europe and Japan and twentieth century Latin America. Ultimately, a self-assured identity is required if Iran is to relinquish its visceral disdain for the West's vices, past imperfections, and appreciation for economic privatization and, far more importantly, if it is to develop a sense of responsibility about the future. Confidence is the crowning virtue of the strong.

Ultimately, a self-assured identity is required if Iran is to relinquish its visceral disdain for the West.

The Foreign Policy Labyrinth

Iran's constitutional framework and revolutionary inertia have led to a number of paradoxes in the country's foreign policy behavior. Article 153 of the constitution specifies that "it is forbidden for any hegemonic power to dominate Iran's natural resources, economy, army, and other pillars of the state." Three intertwined paradoxes stand out in Iranian global conduct. First, Iran desires to be a normal state carrying out ordinary functions at the international level while simultaneously striving to be a revolutionary state with defiant rhetoric. Second, Iran questions the unjust nature of the international system administered by major industrial countries while it also seeks to influence the very same international system. Third, Iran attempts to develop its economy while it fails to accept the role of multinational corporations or Western governments in facilitating its entry into international markets for technology, capital, and commodities. To express it in a simple dichotomy, Iran alternates between revolutionary idealism and political realism.

Iran desires to be a normal state carrying out ordinary functions at the international level while simultaneously striving to be a revolutionary state with defiant rhetoric.

These oscillations breed discontinuity, they protract vulnerability, and they limit diplomacy to tactical and short-term interactions. For other countries, the short-term behavior of Iran's state institutions creates uncertainties and ambiguities in pursuing common objectives. Nonetheless, these complications in Iranian foreign policy are a vivid manifestation of Iran's aforementioned identity paradoxes. Therefore, both Iranians and the world need to practice patience while Iran's social contract develops, either through intensification of internal debate or through the effects of globalization.

Iranian policies that have consistently received the most attention are Tehran's support for militant Palestinian groups, its opposition to Arab-Israeli peace negotiations, and its nuclear program. These policies stem from Iran's revolutionary legacy. However, Iran's offensive posturing of the 1980s has given way to a defensive one in the 1990s and the current decade. In fact, Iran today is a status quo power. Tehran's links to groups in Iraq, Afghanistan, Lebanon, and elsewhere are components of an Iranian containment policy.

As with most states' foreign policies, Iran's is an extension of its domestic structures. In this context, Tehran's foreign policy behavior is an enterprise devoted to maintaining and defending the post-revolutionary apparatus. Thus America needs to pay more attention to the social complexities within Iran than to the political pronouncements of its politicians. US policy toward Iran should cease to orient itself around Tehran's rhetoric, which after all consists of the clichés and rhetorical twists typical of revolutionary states.

And certainly American military intervention in Iran would be rejected by Iranians from all walks of political life. The last time Washington intervened in Iran, overthrowing Prime Minister Mohammad Mossadegh in 1953, Islamic fundamentalism was born as a political ideology, and spread from Iran through the entire Middle East. Military threats against Iran will only intensify nationalist feelings among all Iranians, postpone the country's economic development, and reactivate political radicalism in the region.

American military intervention in Iran would be rejected by Iranians from all walks of political life.

Security issues are at the center of the nuclear confrontation between Iran and the United States. The nuclear issue cannot reach resolution unless the larger security concerns of both sides are addressed. Americans cannot hope that Tehran will be dissuaded from crossing the nuclear threshold while Washington continues, at least theoretically, to promote regime change, however implicit and rhetorical the possibility might be. Likewise, for the purposes of easing security tensions, Iran cannot hope for a consequential dialogue with the United States without artfully and astutely modifying its approach toward the Palestinian-Israeli conflict. This is pivotal for any potential rapprochement with the West in general and the United States in particular.

Security paranoia in Tehran leads to a confrontational policy toward the United States. Iran's security doctrine is shaped by a central threat perception among decision makers in Tehran: the seeming bipartisan strategic consensus in Washington to unseat the Islamic Republic of Iran. In fact, the application of regime change toward Iran is neither theoretically sound nor politically possible. And there is actually precedent for an American approach founded on dealing with Iran's policies rather than its polity. In the Shanghai Communiqué of February 28, 1972, former US President Richard Nixon and Chinese Prime Minister Zhou Enlai concluded that:

> There are essential differences between China and the United States in their social systems and foreign policies. However, the two sides agreed that countries, regardless of their social systems, should conduct their relations on the principles of respect for the sovereignty and territorial integrity of all states, nonaggression against other states, noninterference in the internal affairs of other states, equality and mutual benefit, and peaceful coexistence.

Like the People's Republic of China, the Islamic Republic of Iran will have to travel through its evolution according to its own internal logic. Based on geopolitical and geo-economic reality, Iran is the most powerful country in the Middle East. Both Iran and the United States have containment policies regarding each other. These policies necessarily serve domestic constituencies. But it is time now for accurate analysis and pragmatic deliberations grounded in geopolitical realism.

A Work in Progress

Members of today's Iranian elites had one fundamental objective in mind when they were in their 20s and 30s: Iran's independence and national sovereignty. This has been achieved. At this point, however, well into the twenty-first century, complete political sovereignty is not an objective that most nations pursue. Even powerful countries such as Japan and the United States do not enjoy total sovereignty, let alone China, South Korea, or Turkey. More than 50 percent of wealth in Malaysia is owned by non-Malaysians. Interdependence, outsourcing, and regional integration are very real.

The roots of the Islamic Republic of Iran can be traced through the country's long history of struggle to acquire political sovereignty. But a majority of Iranians today are more interested in gradual reform. By 2020, Iran's population is expected to exceed 100 million. Almost two-thirds of this population will be below the age of 30. Opportunities for all, economic efficiency, accountability, and improvement of Iran's global image are the primary concerns of average citizens. And the hope in Iran is for a generational shift in the coming decade. Iranians are rummaging through fiction and nonfiction to explore their new strengths and appetites. The revolution served as an event allowing them to mull over, reevaluate, and reinvent their identity and future.

Iran's development, in short, is a work in progress. Regrettably, the country's economic development is overshadowed now by its overwhelming security concerns. But if Iranians can focus on producing wealth, if the nation as a whole recognizes that it is compelled to join in the processes of globalization, then Iran can enjoy higher moral status and greater political sovereignty.

Mahmood Sariolghalam is a professor of international relations at Shahid Beheshti University (formerly the National University of Iran) in Tehran.

From *Current History*, December 2008, pp. 425–431. Copyright © 2008 by Current History, Inc. Reprinted by permission.

Lula's Brazil

A Rising Power, but Going Where?

"One of the most interesting features of the Lula years has been a pessimistic view of the international system combined with a belief that there is scope for an activist and assertive foreign policy."

ANDREW HURRELL

As the world enters a period of increasing challenges to US hegemony, attention shifts naturally to rising powers, emerging nations, threshold states, and regional powers. Such states obviously will be central to the dynamics of the balance of power in the twenty-first century, as well as to the possible emergence of new concert-style groupings of major powers. But these states will also be crucial to the development of international institutions and global governance. Indeed, the current detachment from—or outright opposition to—existing international organizations on the part of many of these nations represents one of the most important weaknesses in the global institutional order.

Think of the major emerging economies' distancing themselves from the World Bank and International Monetary Fund, or the opposition (led by Brazil and India) to developed countries' preferences in the World Trade Organization (WTO), or the effective breakdown of the global aid regime in the face of the emergence of new aid donors such as China and India. These countries are substantively critical to the management of major global challenges such as climate change and nuclear proliferation. And they are procedurally critical if international institutions are to reestablish legitimacy and a degree of representativeness.

Ranking just after China and India, Brazil figures prominently in almost all lists of emerging states and regional powers. As US Secretary of State Condoleezza Rice put it: "In the twenty-first century, emerging nations like India, China, Brazil, Egypt, Indonesia, and South Africa are increasingly shaping the course of history. . . ." But there are other reasons to focus on Brazilian foreign policy. For many on the left (especially in Europe), for many inside Brazil, and for many in the developing world, the assertive foreign policy of the government of President Luiz Inácio Lula da Silva (Lula) is seen as a progressive force in global affairs.

Lula and the Workers Party government may well have been tainted at home by corruption and an association with old-style Brazilian machine politics. They may have followed an orthodox domestic macroeconomic policy and made little progress on structural reforms in areas such as taxation, land redistribution, or tackling violent crime. Nonetheless, Brazil's foreign policy (along with

its conditional cash-transfer program to reduce poverty) is widely regarded as a great success story, as well as a potential bellwether for the global strategies of other emerging powers.

A Nationalist Worldview

The Lula government that came to power in January 2002 sought to differentiate its own more assertively nationalist foreign policy from that of its predecessor, which it portrayed as insufficiently resolute in the defense of Brazilian interests and too closely tied to the acceptance of the liberalizing and globalizing agenda of the 1990s. The incoming administration brought with it a view of foreign policy that stressed both the instability of the international environment and the growing concentration of political and military power, wealth, and ideological sway on the part of the United States and its developed-country allies.

Reflecting a deep-rooted strand of nationalist thought in Brazil (on both right and left), this approach to foreign affairs regards the global economy as containing more constraints and snares than opportunities. It views globalization as a force working to reinforce the power of the developed world while creating new sources of instability (especially in relation to recurrent financial crises) and promoting politically dangerous and morally unacceptable inequality (both within and across countries).

Political power, according to this view, was used throughout the post–cold war period to incorporate developing economies into the globalized system. Developed nations and the international institutions that they control have exploited developing countries' external financial vulnerability, created new forms of coercion and conditionalities, and imposed new economic norms that have generally reflected and reinforced their own political power and the interests of the core economies.

Even before the presidency of George W. Bush, many in Brazil and in particular many who later were associated with the Lula government suspected that the liberal norms of the 1990s concerning human rights, democracy, and free markets had been used in selective ways to reflect narrow national interests. Since the terrorist attacks of September 11, 2001, many have suspected Washington of exploiting new security threats to mobilize support at home and abroad for the projection and expansion of US power.

Within this harsh and conflict-oriented view of the international system, Brazil is seen as vulnerable—on one hand because of its internal inequalities, social cleavages, and incomplete development and, on the other, because of its continued external weaknesses and its absence from international decision-making structures. Yet the country is not without options. Indeed, one of the most interesting features of the Lula years has been a pessimistic view of the international system combined with a belief that there is scope for an activist and assertive foreign policy. Foreign policy discussions repeatedly invoke the idea that Brazil is not small or insignificant and that it has room to maneuver in a world where, despite all the challenges, unipolarity is more apparent than real.

Facing "hegemonic structures of power," Brazil needs to reassert its national autonomy, according to the currently prevalent line of thinking. It needs to form coalitions with other developing states in order to reduce its external vulnerability and increase its bargaining power, and to work, however modestly, toward a more balanced world order. Brazil should seek "to increase, if only by a margin, the degree of multipolarity in the world," as the foreign minister, Celso Amorim, put it.

Building up technological capacity also matters, as can be seen in Brazil's determination to continue protecting its industrial base. Because the proposed Free Trade Area of the Americas is seen as a threat in this regard, the Lula administration has downplayed and significantly diluted the negotiations. Likewise, the government has placed renewed emphasis on the long-term goal of developing the country's nuclear technological capacity (seeking to preserve industrial secrets while maintaining good relations with the global inspection regime).

The Multilateral Route

The cornerstones of Brazilian foreign policy have followed from this general outlook. The Lula years have witnessed efforts to increase Brazil's presence in international institutions—including a (so far unsuccessful) campaign for permanent membership in the UN Security Council, and a (successful) drive to join the core group of states negotiating in the World Trade Organization's Doha Round of talks. Brazil has sought to expand relations with other major developing countries—especially India, China, and South Africa—while launching a more activist policy toward Africa and, to a lesser extent, the Middle East.

The Lula administration has also intensified relations within South America. It has attempted to deepen and broaden Mercosur, the common market that, in addition to Brazil, includes Argentina, Paraguay, Uruguay, and now Venezuela. Lula's apparent aim is to shift Mercosur's focus from purely economic relations toward the development of a political bloc. And Brazil has launched the Union of South American nations, a fledgling intergovernmental organization that will unite Mercosur with the region's other major free-trade bloc, the Andean Community, as part of a continuing process of South American integration.

Brazilian officials have sought to portray foreign policy as the external face of the Lula govern-ment's domestic social commitment. As Lula put it: "Alongside the theme of security, the international agenda should also privilege those issues which aim at the eradication of asymmetries and injustices, such as the struggle against social and cultural exclusion, the genuine opening of the markets of the rich countries, the construction of a new financial architecture, and the imperative of combating hunger, disease, and poverty."

In keeping with both its perceived identity and its power-related interests, Brazil continues to for-swear a hard-power strategy in favor of a heavy emphasis on multilateralism. The Lula administration is attempting to exploit what one observer has called Brazil's diplomatic GNP: its capacity for effective coalition-building and insider activism within international institutions, as well as its ability to frame its own interests in terms of arguments for greater justice. Thus, mobilizing claims for greater representational fairness (as with membership in the Security Council) and distributional justice (as with the promotion of a global hunger fund) has been a central tool of Brazil's recent foreign policy.

> Brazil has been viewed in Washington as a potentially moderating force in the region, especially in relation to Chávez in Venezuela and Morales in Bolivia.

Notwithstanding this concentration on soft power, however, it is worth noting that the past five years have seen the first glimmering of a more focused discussion of links between foreign policy and military strategy. This has few concrete implications for current policy, but it represents a new development that could have a significant impact in the future, especially if security relations in the region deteriorate.

A Return to History?

Where does Lula's foreign policy fit within the broader historical picture? How much does it represent a sharp discontinuity with the past? In fact, assertions that Brazil is destined to play a more influential role in world affairs have a long history inside the country. The intensity of these predictions has varied across time. At times ideas about national greatness have been little more than vague aspirations—hardly tied to practical political action or concrete foreign policies and commonly engendering a good deal of cynicism. At other times they have assumed a much more direct role in the shaping of foreign policy, as in the 1970s when high growth rates seemed to establish Brazil as an upwardly mobile middle power, if not one moving ineluctably toward eventual great power status. In this respect, the claim that Brazil should be seen as a major player speaks to a long tradition of thought, and some critics have interpreted the Lula foreign policy in terms of "nostalgia" for the idea of *Brasil-potência* (Brazil as a power).

The third-worldism (*terceiro-mundismo*) of the Lula years also feeds into another debate with deep historical roots that reflects the complex origins of Brazil's international identity. On one hand, Brazil was formed as part of the process of European colonial settlement, a process that involved subjugation of indigenous peoples. Brazil's elites have seen themselves as part of the West in cultural and religious terms and the country harbors a strong tradition of liberalism, including Western ideas about international law and society. On the other hand, Brazilian society has been shaped by the legacies of colonialism and poverty, the imperatives of economic development, and longstanding connections to Africa, the Middle

East, and Asia—connections created most powerfully by the slave trade but also by other waves of immigration.

This duality has remained an important element of Brazilian discussions about where the country "fits in." The cold war years witnessed a persistent and often highly politically charged debate as to whether Brazil was part of the West in its battle against communism and the Soviet Union or a member of the third world in its struggle for development and a greater role in international affairs.

Embracing the Third World

In general terms, the developmentalist line won out. Brazil came to place great emphasis on the pursuit of national autonomy, the politicization of international economic relations, and complaints against the freezing of the international power structure by the powers that be. By the end of the 1960s the close alignment with the United States that followed a coup in 1964 had given way to a broader and more pragmatic approach. Relations with Washington varied between cool and distant, and Brazil sought to diversify its foreign and economic relations, expanding ties with Western Europe, Japan, the socialist countries, and, increasingly, the third world.

Thus, Brazil played a prominent role in such third world forums as the Group of 77 (a United Nations coalition of developing countries) and was heavily engaged in debates during the 1970s regarding a "New International Economic Order." Brazil's embrace of the third world was not as thoroughgoing as India's—and it certainly did not include calls for global revolution, as China's did before 1978—but it did figure prominently in the country's sense of itself and its place in the world.

The developmentalist-nationalist stance was closely tied to economic policy. Brazil's economic policies for much of the post-1945 period relied on a strategy of import substitution, subsidies to strategic sectors, large-scale direct investment in state-owned enterprises, technological nationalism, and a deeply rooted belief in the imperative of continued growth even at the cost of high inflation. The project of national economic development came to be institutionally embedded within and around the Brazilian state and was backed by a wide array of powerful interest groups and a relatively high degree of elite consensus.

It also gave rise to a set of unspoken assumptions whose influence continues to be apparent in Brazilian foreign policy: the importance of defending economic and political sovereignty; the imperative of developing a more prominent international role for the nation; and the suspicion that the United States is more likely to be a hindrance than a help in securing the country's upward progress.

This pattern of foreign policy was not significantly affected by the return to civilian rule in 1985. It began to change, however, by the early 1990s, as the established economic model came under increasing strain, as Brazil along with other countries in the region moved toward economic liberalization, and as the end of the cold war seemed to force acceptance of the reality of both a unipolar world and economic globalization.

The Cardoso Legacy

How far Brazil actually abandoned its foreign policy traditions and embraced "neoliberal globalization"—especially under the government of Fernando Henrique Cardoso from 1994 to 2002—is a subject bitterly contested inside the country. (One important trend in recent years has been a politicization of foreign policy, both within the foreign ministry and in Brazilian politics more generally.)

It is certainly true that the central preoccupation of the Cardoso administration was with economic stabilization and economic reform rather than foreign policy. It is also the case that the Cardoso government tended to stress the need for Brazil to accommodate itself to US power and to liberal globalization. Brazil showed a greater willingness to accept many of the dominant norms of the post–cold war period. For example, the country moved during the 1990s toward increased acceptance of international norms controlling missile technology, arms exports, and nuclear proliferation.

Similarly, in relation to the environment, Brazil moved sharply away from its defensiveness of the 1980s toward an acknowledgement of the legitimacy of international concerns about environmental matters. Brazil came to accept the activities of nongovernmental organizations, which before had often been denounced as subversive, and it engaged more positively in international negotiations, especially in the process leading to the 1992 Earth Summit in Rio. A parallel move could be seen in relation to international human rights.

It is true, as well, that Brazilian foreign policy during the 1990s frequently demonstrated national reticence, as captured by Cardoso's view that "to provoke friction with the United States is to lose," or by a comment in his memoirs that Brazil's capacity to influence the region politically remained limited. Thus, while action to help maintain democracy in Paraguay was viable, thoughts of involvement in Colombia were resisted as something Brazil was not "yet" able to contemplate.

Nevertheless, Cardoso's own view of the international system and of Brazilian development was never that of a straightforward neoliberal. And over the course of the decade his foreign policy shifted in a more critical and nationalist direction. Even if his approach had achieved its important initial purpose of reestablishing Brazil's international political and economic credibility, by the late 1990s the Cardoso foreign policy of "autonomy via participation" had come to face increasingly serious challenges. The relative optimism with which policy makers had viewed the post–cold war international environment was giving way to a greater emphasis on Brazil's international economic vulnerability and the difficulty of translating into concrete results the country's adaptation to global liberal norms.

There are important differences between Cardoso and Lula, but they cannot be simplified in terms of a contrast between "pro-Western liberalizer" and "progressive third-worldist." Cardoso believed the changing structures of global capitalism meant that there was little alternative but to adapt to globalization and that the potential political opportunities for successful foreign policy activism were limited. But he combined this pragmatic view of the world with a significant degree of optimism that structural reform at home was both possible and necessary and that democracy had become an overriding value.

The Lula government, by contrast, has been rather modest in its domestic policy ambitions, stressing economic orthodoxy and large-scale targeted social programs. But it has combined this domestic accommodation with a high degree of optimism as to what can be achieved abroad.

Regional Destiny?

How is Lula's foreign policy working out? Let us look first at South America. The Latin-Americanization of Brazil's foreign policy in fact goes back to the late 1970s. By the end of the 1990s it was already common to talk of Mercosur as part of Brazil's "destiny" (as opposed to the Free Trade Area of the Americas, which was seen as an option). Nevertheless, it is clear that the Lula government has worked hard to develop a more prominent role in Latin America. Especially during the first Lula administration, the body language (if you will) of assertive regional leadership was highly visible, however much it was couched in the rhetoric of "non-hegemonic leadership."

Brazil has sought to expand relations with other major developing countries—especially India, China, and South Africa.

The Lula government has committed considerable rhetorical energy and high-level political effort in particular to relaunching Mercosur; to restoring with neighboring states economic ties that had frayed during the Argentinian economic crisis at the start of the millennium; to seeking new areas for cooperation, such as with anti-poverty initiatives; and to indicating in a variety of ways a greater willingness to bear costs and make some concessions in order to help sustain the regionalist project.

Brasilia has also been prepared to assume a more assertive political role in the region—in the sense of an expansion of party-to-party relations and greater involvement in politically contested areas, such as Brazil's leadership of the UN peace mission to Haiti (where it has 1,200 troops on the ground) and its recent expressions of willingness to mediate in Colombia.

Yet it is in relation to the region that the limits of Brazil's foreign policy appear in sharpest light. Mercosur itself is now far more divided than at any time in its history. Its already weak institutional structures have not been strengthened, and it is difficult to believe that Venezuela's 2005 accession will do anything other than weaken them still further. The early activism of the Lula years was too personalist and too voluntarist to have much of an institutional impact, and there has been a yawning gap between the rhetoric of leadership and the concrete political, military, and economic resources made available to sustain substantive achievements.

Lula's foreign policy overestimates the willingness of the region to fall into line behind Brazilian pretensions to a global role as the region's leader. In fact, there have been across Latin America numerous instances of resistance to Brazil's role—in opposition, for example, to its campaign for UN Security Council membership and to Brazilian candidates in international organizations. Brazil's foreign policy has also underestimated the readiness of many in the region to find an accommodation with Washington (a readiness likely to become more noticeable in a post-Bush world). And perhaps most difficult, Brazil's pretensions to regional leadership have encountered Venezuela's Hugo Chávez—both as a leader with his own ideas about hemispheric integration and as a symptom of deep-rooted discontent within Latin America.

If the measure of success for Brazil's regional strategy is the creation of a regional bloc with a significant degree of internal cohesion and a capacity to increase the region's power in the world, then there can be little doubt that the strategy has failed. It is crucial, however, to note the structural factors both shaping Brazil's regional policy and constraining its actions.

Compared to 20 years ago, Brazil is now much more firmly enmeshed in the region, and it has to live with the spillovers and externalities that go with ever greater social, economic, and energy interdependence. In this respect Brazil is living with the consequences of a sustained period of successful regional integration. Not only have economic, infrastructural, and energy ties increased, but the protracted violence and the narco-economy of the Andean region have had profound effects on patterns of violence in Brazil's cities.

Equally important, the political complexion of the region has changed dramatically in ways that make it very difficult for Brazil to steer regional developments or to project its own model. The *chavismo* emanating from Venezuela may not establish itself as a stable counter-narrative to political and economic liberalism, but it is more than a purely local or transitory phenomenon, and it reflects the widely perceived failures of economic liberalism, the narrowness of many accounts of electoral democracy, and a powerful resurgence of economic nationalism.

Brazil has thus become ever more entangled in an unstable and crisis-prone area without its being clear that the country has the economic or military resources to play a leadership role. The regional story of the past five years is in some ways better understood in terms of damage limitation under difficult conditions than in terms of the projection of regional leadership.

Relations with Washington

There is a common but mistaken view that relations between Brazil and the United States have historically been harmonious. It is true that there have been periods of close relations, such as the years following Brazil's entry into the Second World War and following the coup in 1964. Still, for much of the cold war era the relationship was not especially close; on the contrary, it was characterized by real clashes of interest (especially over economic and trade issues), by deep divergences in the two countries' views of the international system, and by a recurrent sense of mutual frustration. More recent policy making in Brazil has aimed at prudent coexistence with the United States, possible collaboration, and minimal collision, but it has shied away from any kind of special relationship. Many Brazilians share the traditional nationalist perception that Washington is a potential obstacle to Brazil's progress.

Lula's foreign policy overestimates the willingness of the region to fall into line behind Brazilian pretensions to a global role as the region's leader.

There is also strong and widespread opposition to US policy in Colombia, which is seen as dangerously militarizing conflicts in the Andean region. US policy has also revived in some quarters the old fear that the United States poses a threat to the sovereignty of the Amazon. (The other element of this fear is that viewing tropical forests as part of the common heritage of humanity will lead to calls for the international administration of the region.) And, of course, the unilateralism and interventionism of the Bush years have fueled anti-Americanism even in a country in which such sentiments have traditionally been weak (compared to, say, Mexico or Argentina).

On the other hand, recent relations with Washington have actually been rather cordial. There has, after all, not been much to quarrel about. US foreign policy has obviously been focused elsewhere. And the integrating impulses of the 1990s had already faded by the end of that decade, as is evident in the absence within the United States of either the foreign policy will or the domestic political support to negotiate a Free Trade Area of the Americas.

Much is made of the unique position of the United States, the degree to which (unlike all other modern great powers) it faces no geopolitical challenge from within its region, and how it has been able to prevent, or more accurately to contain, the influence of extra-regional powers. But the other important regional aspect of US power is that country's ability to avoid deep entanglements and mostly to escape from lower-level conflicts within its backyard that could ensnare and divert it. Washington has been able to take the region for granted and, for long periods, to avoid having a regional policy at all—as has arguably been the case since 2001.

And there has been space for some shared interests with Brazil. New issues such as biofuels have provided a basis for cooperation. After the brief and absurd portrayal of Lula in some neoconservative quarters as part of a South American axis of evil, Brazil has been viewed in Washington as a potentially moderating force in the region, especially in relation to Chávez in Venezuela and Evo Morales in Bolivia. While Brazil's economy has not been growing as fast as China's or India's, foreign investment has been rising fast and economic stability has been maintained. Brazilian diplomats, though formally rejecting any role as "bridge-builders," have sometimes stressed the country's moderating influence and fire-fighting role.

Still, limits to an active or close relationship with Washington remain. Brazil has to maintain a very delicate balancing act that would be upset, both within the region and inside Brazil, by any attempt to act as a provider of regional order on behalf of the United States. Serious differences persist over the two countries' preferred models of regional economic integration: Brazil rejects the US notion of integration along the lines of the North American Free Trade Agreement.

There has been considerable frustration in Washington, as well, over Brazil's determination in trade talks to press for deeper agricultural liberalization in the United States and the European Union while resisting further trade and investment openings in Brazil. And on the issue of climate change, Brazil has firmly maintained its position that the internationally accepted formula of "common but differentiated responsibilities" means that the United States and the developed world have a duty to take the lead in reducing greenhouse gas emissions (including accepting binding targets) and to provide funds and technology to help developing countries reduce their emissions.

Above all, the US-Brazilian relationship features none of the sorts of concrete political, security, or economic interests that have underpinned the strategic realignment that has taken place in the case of US-Indian relations. Brazil is not closely linked to major American geopolitical interests, as India is with China, Pakistan, and the issue of nuclear proliferation. The economic relationship with Brazil is nothing like America's with India. Nor is there a large Brazilian diaspora in the United States pushing for improved ties.

Southern Strategy

If Brazil's aspirations for regional leadership and its relations with the United States have so far produced limited gains, the same might be said of the Lula administration's vaunted South-South diplomacy.

Critics of Brazil's attempted solidarity with emerging economies say the policy has generated more rhetoric than concrete achievement.

In 2003, Brazil, along with India and South Africa, formed within the World Trade Organization a coalition of developing countries—the Group of 20—that decided to block the Doha round of trade talks until their demands were met. For many orthodox economists, the G-20 coalition shackles Brazil's true interests as a major agricultural exporter with powerful stakes in trade liberalization. Although South-South trade has increased, the core of Brazil's external economic relations remains with the developed world.

The critics of South-South diplomacy, both in Brazil and elsewhere, argue that economic engagement with the developed world should be given far higher priority—especially since China appears to be emerging more as a competitor to Brazil than an ally. According to this view, China's failure to support Brazil's bid for a seat on the UN Security Council demonstrates that Brazilian talk of "strategic partnerships" with India and China is radically out of line with Brazil's actual status in the foreign policies of those countries. Some observers have also noted that Brazil's efforts to gather support for its Security Council membership and its broader attempts at southern solidarity have at times led the country to compromise on its commitment to human rights.

And yet, although there has indeed been a gap between some of the rhetoric and the concrete achievements in South-South diplomacy, the critics' arguments underestimate the way in which Brazilian foreign policy has contributed to perceptions that global power is more diffuse than had appeared to be the case even five years ago. Brazil's weight as a player in international trade, for example, is limited, but its activism and assertiveness have worked to convince many that Brazil has to be part of any stable global trade regime for reasons of political legitimacy as much as narrow economic logic. In relation to climate change, Brazil has helped to shift the focus of negotiations back toward recognition of global warming as a shared and common problem, and has advanced the notion that the responsibilities and burdens of the developed and developing world need to be differentiated.

In general, Lula's Southern strategy forms a clear contrast to the nearly total disappearance of third world self-identification on the part of China, as well as, in Indian foreign policy, the displacement of nonalignment and the relative downgrading of multilateralism. In part, Brazil's approach reflects its relative power position. Brazil is a threshold state that seeks entry into the ranks of the powerful, but for whom coalitions with other developing countries continue to make political sense.

But Brazil's foreign policy under Lula has also reflected a powerful set of ideas about nationalism, development, and globalization that resonate both in the country and across Latin America. As Brazil seeks to carve out a regional and global position for itself as an emerging power, its foreign policy is likely to continue to be marked by tensions among the different facets of the nation's strategy and identity—as a leader of the South, as a potential bridge between North and South, and as a rising power that uses the rhetoric of South-South solidarity and claims for global justice for its own instrumental purposes.

ANDREW HURRELL is director of the Center for International Studies at Oxford University and a faculty fellow of Nuffield College, Oxford. He is the author of *On Global Order: Power, Values, and the Constitution of International Society* (Oxford University Press, 2007).

An Empty Revolution
The Unfulfilled Promises of Hugo Chávez

Francisco Rodríguez

On December 2, when Venezuelans delivered President Hugo Chávez his first electoral defeat in nine years, most analysts were taken by surprise. According to official results, 50.7 percent of voters rejected Chávez's proposed constitutional reform, which would have expanded executive power, gotten rid of presidential term limits, and paved the way for the construction of a "socialist" economy. It was a major reversal for a president who just a year earlier had won a second six-year term with 62.8 percent of the vote, and commentators scrambled to piece together an explanation. They pointed to idiosyncratic factors, such as the birth of a new student movement and the defection of powerful groups from Chávez's coalition. But few went so far as to challenge the conventional wisdom about how Chávez has managed to stay in power for so long.

Although opinions differ on whether Chávez's rule should be characterized as authoritarian or democratic, just about everyone appears to agree that, in contrast to his predecessors, Chávez has made the welfare of the Venezuelan poor his top priority. His government, the thinking goes, has provided subsidized food to low-income families, redistributed land and wealth, and poured money from Venezuela's booming oil industry into health and education programs. It should not be surprising, then, that in a country where politics was long dominated by rich elites, he has earned the lasting support of the Venezuelan poor.

That story line may be compelling to many who are rightly outraged by Latin America's deep social and economic inequalities. Unfortunately, it is wrong. Neither official statistics nor independent estimates show any evidence that Chávez has reoriented state priorities to benefit the poor. Most health and human development indicators have shown no significant improvement beyond that which is normal in the midst of an oil boom. Indeed, some have deteriorated worryingly, and official estimates indicate that income inequality has increased. The "Chávez is good for the poor" hypothesis is inconsistent with the facts.

My skepticism of this notion began during my tenure as chief economist of the Venezuelan National Assembly. In September 2000, I left American academia to take over a research team with functions broadly similar to those of the U.S. Congressional Budget Office. I had high expectations for Chávez's government and was excited at the possibility of working in an administration that promised to focus on fighting poverty and inequality. But I quickly discovered how large the gap was between the government's rhetoric and the reality of its political priorities.

Soon after joining the National Assembly, I clashed with the administration over underfunding of the Consolidated Social Fund (known by its Spanish acronym FUS), which had been created by Chávez to coordinate the distribution of resources to antipoverty programs. The law establishing the fund included a special provision to ensure that it would benefit from rising oil revenues. But when oil revenues started to go up, the Finance Ministry ignored the provision, allocating to the fund in the 2001 budget only $295 million—15 percent less than the previous year and less than a third of the legally mandated $1.1 billion. When my office pointed out this inconsistency, the Finance Ministry came up with the creative accounting gimmick of rearranging the law so that programs not coordinated by the FUS would nevertheless appear to be receiving resources from it. The effect was to direct resources away from the poor even as oil profits were surging. (Hard-liners in the government, incensed by my office's criticisms, immediately called for my ouster. When the last moderates, who understood the need for an independent research team to evaluate policies, left the Chávez camp in 2004, the government finally disbanded our office.)

Chávez's political success does not stem from the achievements of his social programs or from his effectiveness at redistributing wealth. Rather, through a combination of luck and manipulation of the political system, Chávez has faced elections at times of strong economic growth, currently driven by an oil boom bigger than any since the 1970s. Like voters everywhere, Venezuelans tend to vote their pocketbooks, and until recently, this has meant voting for Chávez. But now, his mismanagement of the economy and failure to live up to his pro-poor rhetoric have finally started to catch up with him. With inflation accelerating, basic foodstuffs increasingly scarce, and pervasive chronic failures in the provision of basic public services, Venezuelans are starting to glimpse the consequences of Chávez's economic policies—and they do not like what they see.

Fake Left

From the moment he reached office in 1999, Chávez presented his economic and social policies as a left-wing alternative to the so-called Washington consensus and a major departure from the free-market reforms of previous administrations. Although the differences were in fact fairly moderate at first, the pace of change accelerated significantly after the political and economic crisis of 2002–3, which saw a failed coup attempt and a two-month-long national strike. Since then, the Venezuelan economy has undergone a transformation.

The change can be broadly characterized as having four basic dimensions. First, the size of the state has increased dramatically. Government expenditures, which represented only 18.8 percent of GDP in

1999, now account for 29.4 percent of GDP, and the government has nationalized key sectors, such as electricity and telecommunications. Second, the setting of prices and wages has become highly regulated through a web of restrictions in place since 2002 ranging from rigid price and exchange controls to a ban on laying off workers. Third, there has been a significant deterioration in the security of property rights, as the government has moved to expropriate landholdings and private firms on an ad hoc basis, appealing to both political and economic motives. Fourth, the government has carried out a complete overhaul of social policy, replacing existing programs with a set of high-profile initiatives—known as the misiones, or missions—aimed at specific problems, such as illiteracy or poor health provision, in poor neighborhoods.

Views differ on how desirable the consequences of many of these reforms are, but a broad consensus appears to have emerged around the idea that they have at least brought about a significant redistribution of the country's wealth to its poor majority. The claim that Chávez has brought tangible benefits to the Venezuelan poor has indeed by now become commonplace, even among his critics. In a letter addressed to President George W. Bush on the eve of the 2006 Venezuelan presidential elections, Jesse Jackson, Cornel West, Dolores Huerta, and Tom Hayden wrote, "Since 1999, the citizens of Venezuela have repeatedly voted for a government that—unlike others in the past—would share their country's oil wealth with millions of poor Venezuelans. "The Nobel laureate economist Joseph Stiglitz has noted, "Venezuelan President Hugo Chávez seems to have succeeded in bringing education and health services to the barrios of Caracas, which previously had seen little of the benefits of that country's rich endowment of oil." Even The Economist has written that "Chávez's brand of revolution has delivered some social gains."

One would expect such a consensus to be backed up by an impressive array of evidence. But in fact, there is remarkably little data supporting the claim that the Chávez administration has acted any differently from previous Venezuelan governments—or, for that matter, from those of other developing and Latin American nations—in redistributing the gains from economic growth to the poor. One oft-cited statistic is the decline in poverty from a peak of 54 percent at the height of the national strike in 2003 to 27.5 percent in the first half of 2007. Although this decline may appear impressive, it is also known that poverty reduction is strongly associated with economic growth and that Venezuela's per capita GDP grew by nearly 50 percent during the same time period—thanks in great part to a tripling of oil prices. The real question is thus not whether poverty has fallen but whether the Chávez government has been particularly effective at converting this period of economic growth into poverty reduction. One way to evaluate this is by calculating the reduction in poverty for every percentage point increase in per capita income—in economists' lingo, the income elasticity of poverty reduction. This calculation shows an average reduction of one percentage point in poverty for every percentage point in per capita GDP growth during this recovery, a ratio that compares unfavorably with those of many other developing countries, for which studies tend to put the figure at around two percentage points. Similarly, one would expect pro-poor growth to be accompanied by a marked decrease in income inequality. But according to the Venezuelan Central Bank, inequality has actually increased during the Chávez administration, with the Gini coefficient (a measure of economic inequality, with zero indicating perfect equality and one indicating perfect inequality) increasing from 0.44 to 0.48 between 2000 and 2005.

Poverty and inequality statistics, of course, tell only part of the story. There are many aspects of the well-being of the poor not captured by measures of money income, and this is where Chávez's supporters claim that the government has made the most progress—through its misiones, which have concentrated on the direct provision of health, education, and other basic public services to poor communities. But again, official statistics show no signs of a substantial improvement in the well-being of ordinary Venezuelans, and in many cases there have been worrying deteriorations. The percentage of underweight babies, for example, increased from 8.4 percent to 9.1 percent between 1999 and 2006. During the same period, the percentage of households without access to running water rose from 7.2 percent to 9.4 percent, and the percentage of families living in dwellings with earthen floors multiplied almost threefold, from 2.5 percent to 6.8 percent. In Venezuela, one can see the misiones everywhere: in government posters lining the streets of Caracas, in the ubiquitous red shirts issued to program participants and worn by government supporters at Chávez rallies, in the bloated government budget allocations. The only place where one will be hard-pressed to find them is in the human development statistics.

Remarkably, given Chávez's rhetoric and reputation, official figures show no significant change in the priority given to social spending during his administration. The average share of the budget devoted to health, education, and housing under Chávez in his first eight years in office was 25.12 percent, essentially identical to the average share (25.08 percent) in the previous eight years. And it is lower today than it was in 1992, the last year in office of the "neoliberal" administration of Carlos Andrés Pérez—the leader whom Chávez, then a lieutenant colonel in the Venezuelan army, tried to overthrow in a coup, purportedly on behalf of Venezuela's neglected poor majority.

In a number of recent studies, I have worked with colleagues to look more systematically at the results of Chávez's health and education misiones. Our findings confirm that Chávez has in fact done little for the poor. For example, his government often claims that the influx of Cuban doctors under the Barrio Adentro health program is responsible for a decline in infant mortality in Venezuela. In fact, a careful analysis of trends in infant and neonatal mortality shows that the rate of decline is not significantly different from that of the pre-Chávez period, nor from the rate of decline in other Latin American countries. Since 1999, the infant mortality rate in Venezuela has declined at an annual rate of 3.4 percent, essentially identical to the 3.3 percent rate at which it had declined during the previous nine-year period and lower than the rates of decline for the same period in Argentina (5.5 percent), Chile (5.3 percent), and Mexico (5.2 percent).

Even more disappointing are the results of the government's Robinson literacy program. On October 28, 2005, Chávez declared Venezuela "illiteracy-free territory." His national literacy campaign, he announced, had taught 1.5 million people how to read and write, and the education minister stated that residual illiteracy stood at less than 0.1 percent of the population. The achievement received considerable international recognition and was taken at face value by many specialists as well as by casual observers. A recent article in the San Francisco Chronicle, for example, reported that "illiteracy, formerly at 10 percent of the population, has been completely eliminated." Spanish President Jose Luis Rodríguez Zapatero and UNESCO's general director, Koïchiro Matsuura, sent the Venezuelan government public letters of congratulation for the achievement. (After Matsuura's statement, the Chávez's administration claimed that its eradication of illiteracy had been "UNESCO-verified.")

But along with Daniel Ortega of Venezuela's IESA business school, I looked at trends in illiteracy rates based on responses to the Venezuelan National Institute of Statistics' household surveys. (A full presentation of our study will appear in the October 2008 issue of the journal Economic

Development and Cultural Change.) In contrast to the government's claim, we found that there were more than one million illiterate Venezuelans by the end of 2005, barely down from the 1.1 million illiterate persons recorded in the first half of 2003, before the start of the Robinson program. Even this small reduction, moreover, is accounted for by demographic trends rather than the program itself. In a battery of statistical tests, we found little evidence that the program had had any statistically distinguishable effect on Venezuelan illiteracy. We also found numerous inconsistencies in the government's story. For example, it claims to have employed 210,410 trainers in the anti-illiteracy effort (approximately two percent of the Venezuelan labor force), but there is no evidence in the public employment data that these people were ever hired or evidence in the government budget statistics that they were ever paid.

The Economic Consequences of Mr. Chávez

In fact, even as the conventional wisdom has taken hold outside of Venezuela, most Venezuelans, according to opinion surveys, have long been aware that Chávez's social policies are inadequate and ineffective. To be sure, Venezuelans would like the government's programs—particularly the sale of subsidized food—to remain in place, but that is a far cry from believing that they have reasonably addressed the nation's poverty problem. A survey taken by the Venezuelan polling firm Alfredo Kellery Asociados in September 2007 showed that only 22 percent of Venezuelans think poverty has improved under Chávez, while 50 percent think it has worsened and 27 percent think it has stayed the same.

At the same time, however, Venezuelan voters have given Chávez credit for the nation's strong economic growth. In polls, an overwhelming majority have expressed support for Chávez's stewardship of the economy and reported that their personal situation was improving. This is, of course, not surprising: with its economy buoyed by surging oil profits, Venezuela had enjoyed three consecutive years of double-digit growth by 2006.

But by late 2007, Chávez's economic model had begun to unravel. For the first time since early 2004, a majority of voters claimed that both their personal situation and the country's situation had worsened during the preceding year. Scarcities in basic foodstuffs, such as milk, black beans, and sardines, were chronic, and the difference between the official and the black-market exchange rate reached 215 percent. When the Central Bank board received its November price report indicating that monthly inflation had risen to 4.4 percent (equivalent to an annual rate of 67.7 percent), it decided to delay publication of the report until after the vote on the constitutional reform was held.

This growing economic crisis is the predictable result of the gross mismanagement of the economy by Chávez's economic team. During the past five years, the Venezuelan government has pursued strongly expansionary fiscal and economic policies, increasing real spending by 137 percent and real liquidity by 218 percent. This splurge has outstripped even the expansion in oil revenues: the Chávez administration has managed the admirable feat of running a budget deficit in the midst of an oil boom.

Such expansionary policies were appropriate during the deep recession that Venezuela faced in the aftermath of the political and economic crisis of 2002–3. But by continuing the expansion after the recession ended, the government generated an inflationary crisis. The problem has been compounded by efforts to address the resulting imbalances with an increasingly complex web of price and exchange controls coupled with routine threats of expropriation directed at producers and shopkeepers as

a warning not to raise prices. Not surprisingly, the response has been a steep drop in food production and widening food scarcity.

A sensible solution to Venezuela's overexpansion would require reining in spending and the growth of the money supply. But such a solution is anathema to Chávez, who has repeatedly equated any call for spending reductions with neoliberal dogma. Instead, the government has tried to deal with inflation by expanding the supply of foreign currency to domestic firms and consumers and increasing government subsidies. The result is a highly distorted economy in which the government effectively subsidizes two-thirds of the cost of imports and foreign travel for the wealthy while the poor cannot find basic food items on store shelves. The astounding growth of imports, which have nearly tripled since 2002 (imports of such luxury items as Hummers and 15-year-old Scotch have grown even more dramatically), is now threatening to erase the nation's current account surplus.

What is most distressing is how predictable all of this was. Indeed, Cháveznomics is far from unprecedented: the gross contours of this story follow the disastrous experiences of many Latin American countries during the 1970s and 1980s. The economists Rudiger Dornbusch and Sebastian Edwards have characterized such policies as "the macroeconomics of populism." Drawing on the economic experiences of administrations as politically diverse as Juan Perón's in Argentina, Salvador Allende's in Chile, and Alan García's in Peru, they found stark similarities in economic policies and in the resulting economic evolution. Populist macroeconomics is invariably characterized by the use of expansionary fiscal and economic policies and an overvalued currency with the intention of accelerating growth and redistribution. These policies are commonly implemented in the context of a disregard for fiscal and foreign exchange constraints and are accompanied by attempts to control inflationary pressures through price and exchange controls. The result is by now well known to Latin American economists: the emergence of production bottlenecks, the accumulation of severe fiscal and balance-of-payments problems, galloping inflation, and plummeting real wages.

Chávez's behavior is typical of such populist economic experiments. The initial successes tend to embolden policymakers, who increasingly believe that they were right in dismissing the recommendations of most economists. Rational policy formulation becomes increasingly difficult, as leaders become convinced that conventional economic constraints do not apply to them. Corrective measures only start to be taken when the economy has veered out of control. But by then it is far too late.

My experience dealing with the Chávez government confirmed this pattern. In February 2002, for example, I had the opportunity of speaking with Chávez at length about the state of the Venezuelan economy. At that point, the economy had entered into a recession as a result of an unsustainable fiscal expansion carried out during Chávez's first three years in office. Moderates within the government had arranged the meeting with the hope that it would spur changes in the management of the public finances. As a colleague and I explained to Chávez, there was no way to avoid a deepening of the country's macroeconomic crisis without a credible effort to raise revenue and rationalize expenditures. The president listened with interest, taking notes and asking questions over three hours of conversation, and ended our meeting with a request that we speak with his cabinet ministers and schedule future meetings. But as we proceeded to meet with officials, the economic crisis was spilling over into the political arena, with the opposition calling for street demonstrations in response to Chávez's declining poll numbers. Soon, workers at the state oil company, PDVSA, joined the protests.

In the ensuing debate within the government over how to handle the political crisis, the old-guard leftists persuaded Chávez to take a hard line. He dismissed 17,000 workers at PDVSA and sidelined moderates within his government. When I received a call informing me that our future meetings with Chávez had been canceled, I knew that the hard-liners had gained the upper hand. Chávez's handling of the economy and the political crisis had significant costs. Chávez deftly used the mistakes of the opposition (calling for a national strike and attempting a coup) to deflect blame for the recession. But in fact, real GDP contracted by 4.4 percent and the currency had lost more than 40 percent of its value in the first quarter of 2002, before the start of the first PDVSA strike on April 9. As early as January of that year, the Central Bank had already lost more than $7 billion in a futile attempt to defend the currency. In other words, the economic crisis had started well before the political crisis—a fact that would be forgotten in the aftermath of the political tumult that followed.

The government's response to the crisis has had further consequences for the Venezuelan economy. The takeover of PDVSA by Chávez loyalists and the subordination of the firm's decisions to the government's political imperatives have resulted in a dramatic decline in Venezuela's oil-production capacity. Production has been steadily declining since the government consolidated its control of the industry in late 2004. According to OPEC statistics, Venezuela currently produces only three-quarters of its quota of 3.3 million barrels a day. Chávez's government has thus not only squandered Venezuela's largest oil boom since the 1970s; it has also killed the goose that lays the golden egg. Despite rising oil prices, PDVSA is increasingly strained by the combination of rising production costs, caused by the loss of technical capacity and the demands of a growing web of political patronage, and the need to finance numerous projects for the rest of the region, ranging from the rebuilding of Cuban refineries to the provision of cheap fuel to Sandinista-controlled mayoralties in Nicaragua. As a result, the capacity of oil revenues to ease the government's fiscal constraints is becoming more and more limited.

Plowing the Sea

Simón Bolívar, Venezuela's independence leader and Chávez's hero, once said that in order to evaluate revolutions and revolutionaries, one needs to observe them close up but judge them at a distance. Having had the opportunity to do both with Chávez, I have seen to what extent he has failed to live up to his own promises and Venezuelans' expectations. Now, voters are making the same realization—a realization that will ultimately lead to Chávez's demise. The problems of ensuring a peaceful political transition will be compounded by the fact that over the past nine years Venezuela has become an increasingly violent society. This violence is not only reflected in skyrocketing crime rates; it also affects the way Venezuelans resolve their political conflicts. Whether Chávez is responsible for this or not is beside the point. What is vital is for Venezuelans to find a way to prevent the coming economic crisis from igniting violent political conflict. As Chávez's popularity begins to wane, the opposition will feel increasingly emboldened to take up initiatives to weaken Chávez's movement. The government may become increasingly authoritarian as it starts to understand the very high costs it will pay if it loses power. Unless a framework is forged through which the government and the opposition can reach a settlement, there is a significant risk that one or both sides will resort to force.

Looking back, one persistent question (in itself worthy of a potentially fascinating study in international political economy) will be how the Venezuelan government has been able to convince so many people of the success of its antipoverty efforts despite the complete absence of real evidence of their effectiveness. When such a study is written, it is likely that the Chávez administration's strategy of actively lobbying foreign governments and launching a high-profile public relations campaign—spearheaded by the Washington-based Venezuela Information Office—will be found to have played a vital role. The generous disbursement of loans to cash-strapped Latin American and Caribbean nations, the sale of cheap oil and heating gas to support political allies in the developed and developing worlds, and the covert use of political contributions to buy the loyalty of politicians in neighboring countries must surely form part of the explanation as well.

But perhaps an even more important reason for this success is the willingness of intellectuals and politicians in developed countries to buy into a story according to which the dilemmas of Latin American development are explained by the exploitation of the poor masses by wealthy privileged elites. The story of Chávez as a social revolutionary finally redressing the injustices created by centuries of oppression fits nicely into traditional stereotypes of the region, reinforcing the view that Latin American underdevelopment is due to the vices of its predatory governing classes. Once one adopts this view, it is easy to forget about fashioning policy initiatives that could actually help Latin America grow, such as ending the agricultural subsidies that depress the prices of the regions exports or significantly increasing the economic aid given to countries undertaking serious efforts to combat poverty.

The American journalist Sydney Harris once wrote that "we believe what we want to believe, what we like to believe, what suits our prejudices and fuels our passions." The idea that Latin American governments are controlled by economic elites may have been true in the nineteenth century, but is wildly at odds with reality in a world in which every Latin American country except Cuba has regular elections with large levels of popular participation. Much like governments everywhere, Latin American governments try to balance the desire for wealth redistribution with the need to generate incentives for economic growth, the realities of limited effective state power, and the uncertainties regarding the effectiveness of specific policy initiatives. Ignoring these truths is not only anachronistic and misguided; it also thwarts the design of sensible foreign policies aimed at helping the region's leaders formulate and implement strategies for achieving sustainable and equitable development.

It would be foolhardy to claim that what Latin America must do to lift its population out of poverty is obvious. If there is a lesson to be learned from other countries' experiences, it is that successful development strategies are diverse and that what works in one place may not work elsewhere. Nonetheless, recent experiences in countries such as Brazil and Mexico, where programs skillfully designed to target the weakest groups in society have had a significant effect on their well-being, show that effective solutions are within the reach of pragmatic policymakers willing to implement them. It is the tenacity of these realists—rather than the audacity of the idealists—that holds the greatest promise for alleviating the plight of Latin America's poor.

FRANCISCO RODRÍGUEZ, Assistant Professor of Economics and Latin American Studies at Wesleyan University, was Chief Economist of the Venezuelan National Assembly from 2000 to 2004.

UNIT 5

Population, Resources, Environment, and Health

Unit Selections

Key Points to Consider

- What accounts for the demographic changes around the world?

- What are the implications of these trends in demography?

- What is the impact of increased demand for water?

- What is the controversy over water resources?

- What are the obstacles to reducing pollution from cooking fires?

- How might climate refugees be better protected?

- What are the ways to improve health care in the developing world?

- What is the link between a sustainable environment and health?

- How does illness contribute to poverty?

Student Website
www.mhcls.com

Internet References

Earth Pledge Foundation
http://www.earthpledge.org
EnviroLink
http://envirolink.org
Greenpeace
http://www.greenpeace.org
Linkages on Environmental Issues and Development
http://www.iisd.ca/linkages/
Population Action International
http://www.populationaction.org
The Worldwatch Institute
http://www.worldwatch.org

The developing world's population continues to increase at an annual rate that exceeds the world average. The average fertility rate (the number of children a woman will have during her life) for all developing countries is 2.9, while for the least developed countries the figure is 4.9. Although growth has slowed considerably since the 1960s, world population is still growing at the rate of over 70 million per year, with most of this increase taking place in the developing world. Increasing population complicates development efforts, puts added stress on the ecosystem, and threatens food security. World population surpassed 6 billion toward the end of 1999 and, if current trends continue, could reach 9 billion or more by 2050. Even if, by some miracle, population growth was immediately reduced to the level found in industrialized countries, the developing world's population would continue to grow for decades.

Almost one-third of the population in the developing world is under the age of 15, with that proportion jumping to 40 percent in the least developed countries. The population momentum created by this age distribution means that it will be some time before the developing world's population growth slows substantially. Some developing countries have achieved progress in reducing fertility rates through family planning programs, but much remains to be done. At the same time, reduced life expectancy, especially related to the HIV/AIDS epidemic, is having a significant demographic impact especially in sub-Saharan Africa.

Over a billion people live in absolute poverty, as measured by a combination of economic and social indicators. As population increases, it becomes more difficult to meet the basic human needs of the citizens of the developing world's citizens. Indeed, food scarcity looms as a major problem as the world struggles with a global food crisis, triggered by higher demand, skyrocketing oil prices, and the diversion of agricultural production to biofuels. Larger populations of poor people also places greater strains on scarce resources and fragile ecosystems. Growing demand for water is rapidly depleting available supplies. Competition for scarce water resources not only affects agricultural production, but it also threatens to spark conflict. Deforestation for agriculture and fuel, as well as to meet demand for timber, has reduced forested areas and contributed to erosion, desertification, and global warming. In an effort to reduce illegal logging, some developing countries have initiated certification programs to ensure that timber is harvested sustainably. Intensified agricultural production, particularly of cash crops, has depleted soil. This necessitates increased fertilization, which is costly and also produces runoff that contributes to water pollution. Greenhouse gas emissions are accelerating climate change, the adverse effects of which will be felt first by the developing world. Up until now, little has been done to prepare for the inevitable climate refugees that are certain to result from climate change.

Economic development has not only failed to eliminate poverty but has actually exacerbated it in some ways. Ill-conceived economic development plans have diverted resources from more productive uses and contributed to environmental degradation.

© The McGraw-Hill Companies/Barry Barker, photographer

Large-scale industrialization, sometimes unsuitable to local conditions, also increases pollution. If developing countries try to follow Western consumption patterns, sustainable development will be impossible. Furthermore, economic growth without effective environmental policies can lead to the need for more expensive clean-up efforts later in the future.

Divisions between the North and the South on environmental issues became evident at the 1992 Rio Conference on Environment and Development. The conference highlighted the fundamental differences between the industrialized world and developing countries over the causes of and the solutions to global environmental problems. Developing countries pointed to consumption levels in the North as the main cause of environmental problems and called on the industrialized countries to pay most of the costs of environmental programs. Industrialized countries sought to convince developing countries to conserve their resources in their efforts to modernize and develop.

These divisions have deepened on the issues of climate and greenhouse gas emissions. The Johannesburg Summit on Sustainable Development, a follow-up to the Rio conference, grappled with many of these issues, achieving some modest success in addressing water and sanitation needs.

Rural-to-urban migration has caused an enormous influx of people to the cities, lured by the illusion of opportunity in cities and the attraction of urban life. As a result, urban areas in the developing world increasingly lack infrastructure to support this increased population and also have rising rates of pollution, crime, and disease. The fact that environmental factors account for about one-fifth of all diseases in developing countries illustrates the link between health and environmental issues. Disease also depletes family resources, contributing to poverty and debt. Environmental decline also makes citizens more vulnerable to natural disasters. Sustainable development is essential to reduce poverty and curtail the spread of diseases. Improving access to affordable health care in the poor countries would also contribute to reducing poverty. The HIV/AIDS epidemic in particular has forced attention on public health issues, especially in Africa. Africans account for 70 percent of the over 40 million AIDS cases worldwide. Besides the human tragedy that this epidemic creates, its implications for development are enormous. The loss of skilled and educated workers, the increase in the number of orphans, and the economic disruption that the disease causes will have a profound impact in the future. Population, environment, and basic health care clearly represent huge challenges for the developing countries.

Booms, Busts, and Echoes

How the biggest demographic upheaval in history is affecting global development.

DAVID E. BLOOM AND DAVID CANNING

For much (and perhaps most) of human history, demographic patterns were fairly stable: the human population grew slowly, and age structures, birth rates, and death rates changed very little. The slow long-run growth in population was interrupted periodically by epidemics and pandemics that could sharply reduce population numbers, but these events had little bearing on long-term trends.

Over the past 140 years, however, this picture has given way to the biggest demographic upheaval in history, an upheaval that is still running its course. Since 1870 death rates and birth rates have been declining in developed countries. This long-term trend toward lower fertility was interrupted by a sharp, post–World War II rise in fertility, which was followed by an equally sharp fall (a "bust"), defining the "baby boom." The aging of this generation and continued declines in fertility are shifting the population balance in developed countries from young to old. In the developing world, reductions in mortality resulting from improved nutrition, public health infrastructure, and medical care were followed by reductions in birth rates. Once they began, these declines proceeded much more rapidly than they did in the developed countries. The fact that death rates decline before birth rates has led to a population explosion in developing countries over the past 50 years.

Even if the underlying causes of rapid population growth were to suddenly disappear, humanity would continue to experience demographic change for some time to come. Rapid increases in the global population over the past few decades have resulted in large numbers of people of childbearing age (whose children form an "echo" generation). This creates "population momentum," where the populations of most countries, even those with falling birth rates, will grow for many years, particularly in developing countries.

These changes have huge implications for the pace of economic development. Economic analysis has tended to focus on the issue of population numbers and growth rates as factors that can put pressure on scarce resources, dilute the capital-labor ratio, or lead to economies of scale. However, demographic change has important additional dimensions. Increasing average life expectancy can change life-cycle behavior affecting education, retirement, and savings decisions—potentially boosting the financial capital on which investors draw and the human capital that strengthens economies. Demographic change also affects population age structure, altering the ratio of workers to dependents. This issue of *F&D* looks at many facets of the impact of demographic change on the global economy and examines the policy adjustments needed in both the developed and the developing world.

Sharp Rise in Global Population

The global population, which stood at just over 2.5 billion in 1950, has risen to 6.5 billion today, with 76 million new inhabitants added each year (representing the difference, in 2005, for example, between 134 million births and 58 million deaths). Although this growth is slowing, middle-ground projections suggest the world will have 9.1 billion inhabitants by 2050.

These past and projected additions to world population have been, and will increasingly be, distributed unevenly across the world. Today, 95 percent of population growth occurs in developing countries. The populations of the world's 50 least developed countries are expected to more than double by the middle of this century, with several poor countries tripling their populations over the period. By contrast, the population of the developed world is expected to remain steady at about 1.2 billion, with declines in some wealthy countries.

The disparity in population growth between developed and developing countries reflects the considerable heterogeneity in birth, death, and migration processes, both over time and across national populations, races, and ethnic groups. The disparity has also coincided with changes in the age composition of populations. An overview of these factors illuminates the mechanisms of population growth and change around the world.

Total fertility rate. The total world fertility rate, that is, the number of children born per woman, fell from about 5 in 1950 to a little over 2.5 in 2006 (see Figure 1). This number is projected to fall to about 2 by 2050. This decrease is attributable largely to changes in fertility in the developing world and can be ascribed to a number of factors, including declines in infant

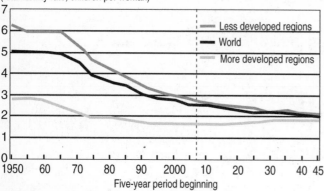

(total fertility rate; children per woman)

Figure 1 Smaller Families. Fertility rates are tending to converge at lower levels after earlier sharp declines.

Source: United Nations, *World Population Prospects*, 2004.

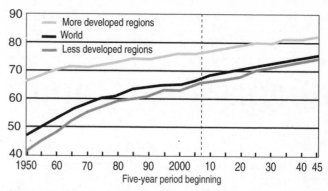

(life expectancy in years)

Figure 2 Living Longer. Life expectancy is continuing to rise, but there are big differences between rates in well-off and poorer countries.

Source: United Nations, *World Population Prospects*, 2004.

mortality rates, greater levels of female education and increased labor market opportunities, and the provision of family-planning services.

Infant and child mortality decline. The developing world has seen significant reductions in infant and child mortality over the past 50 years. These gains are primarily the result of improved nutrition, public health interventions related to water and sanitation, and medical advances, such as the use of vaccines and antibiotics. Infant mortality (death prior to age 1) in developing countries has dropped from 180 to about 57 deaths per 1,000 live births. It is projected to decline to fewer than 30 by 2050. By contrast, developed countries have seen infant mortality decline from 59 deaths per 1,000 live births to 7 since 1950, and this is projected to decline further still, to 4 by 2050. Child mortality (death prior to age 5) has also fallen in both developed and developing countries.

Life expectancy and longevity. For the world as a whole, life expectancy increased from 47 years in 1950–55 to 65 years in 2000–05. It is projected to rise to 75 years by the middle of this century, with considerable disparities between the wealthy industrial countries, at 82 years, and the less developed countries, at 74 years (see Figure 2). (Two major exceptions to the upward trend are sub-Saharan Africa, where the AIDS epidemic has drastically lowered life expectancy, and some of the countries of the former Soviet Union, where economic dislocations have led to significant health problems.) As a result of the global decline in fertility, and because people are living longer, the proportion of the elderly in the total population is rising sharply. The number of people over the age of 60, currently about half the number of those aged 15 to 24, is expected to reach 1 billion (overtaking the 15–24 age group) by 2020 and almost 2 billion by 2050. The proportion of individuals aged 80 or over is projected to rise from 1 percent to 4 percent of the global population by 2050.

Age distribution: working-age population. Baby booms have altered the demographic landscape in many countries. As the experiences of several regions during the past century show, an initial fall in mortality rates creates a boom generation in which high survival rates lead to more people at young ages than in earlier generations. Fertility rates fall over time, as parents realize they do not need to give birth to as many children to reach their desired family size, or as desired family size contracts for other reasons. When fertility falls and the baby boom stops, the age structure of the population then shows a "bulge" or baby-boom age cohort created by the nonsynchronous falls in mortality and fertility. As this generation moves through the population age structure, it constitutes a share of the population larger than the cohorts that precede or follow. This creates particular challenges and opportunities for countries, such as a large youth cohort to be educated, followed by an unusually large working-age (approximately ages 15–64) population, with the prospect of a "demographic dividend," and characterized eventually by a large elderly population, which may burden the health and pension systems (see Figure 3).

Migration. Migration also alters population patterns. Globally, 191 million people live in countries other than the one in which they were born. On average during the next 45 years, the United Nations projects that over 2.2 million individuals will migrate annually from developing to developed countries. It also projects that the United States will receive by far the largest number of immigrants (1.1 million a year), and China, Mexico, India, the Philippines, and Indonesia will be the main sources of emigrants.

Urbanization. In both developed and developing countries, there has been huge movement from rural to urban areas since 1950. Less developed regions, in aggregate, have seen their population shift from 18 percent to 44 percent urban, while the corresponding figures for developed countries are 52 percent to 75 percent. A new UN report says that in 2007 the worldwide balance will tip and more than half of all people will be living in urban areas. This shift—and the concomitant urbanization of areas that were formerly peri-urban or rural—is consistent with the shift in most countries away from agriculturally based economies.

A new UN report says that in 2007 the worldwide balance will tip and more than half of all people will be living in urban areas.

(ratio of working-age to non-working-age population)

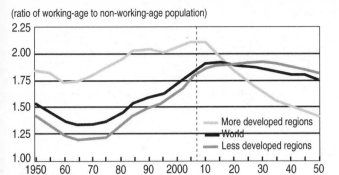

Figure 3 Tracking the Bulge. Developing countries are nearing the peak of their opportunity to benefit from a high ratio of workers to dependents.

Source: United Nations, *World Population Prospects*, 2004.

(world population, aged 80+; millions)

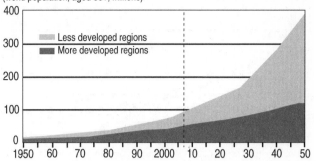

Figure 4 Retiree Boom. The number of people living past 80 is projected to rise sharply, but labor shortages could drive up living costs for retirees.

Source: United Nations, *World Population Prospects*, 2004.

The existence and growth of megacities (that is, those with 10 million or more residents) is a late-20th-century phenomenon that has brought with it special problems. There were 20 such cities in 2003, 15 in developing countries. Tokyo is by far the largest, with 35 million people, followed by (in descending order) Mexico City, New York, São Paulo, and Mumbai (all with 17 to 19 million). Cities in general allow for economies of scale—and, most often, for a salutary mix of activities, resources, and people—that make them centers of economic growth and activity and account, in some measure, for their attractiveness. As continued movement to urban areas leads to megacities, however, these economies of scale and of agglomeration seem to be countered, to some extent, by problems that arise in transportation, housing, air pollution, and waste management. In some instances, socioeconomic disparities are particularly exacerbated in megacities.

What Is the Impact on Economies?

The economic consequences of population growth have long been the subject of debate. Early views on the topic, pioneered by Thomas Malthus, held that population growth would lead to the exhaustion of resources. In the 1960s, it was proposed that population growth aided economic development by spurring technological and institutional innovation and increasing the supply of human ingenuity. Toward the end of the 1960s, a neo-Malthusian view, focusing again on the dangers of population growth, became popular. Population control policies in China and India, while differing greatly from each other, can be seen in this light. Population neutralism, a middle-ground view, based on empirical analysis of the link between population growth and economic performance, has held sway for the past two decades. According to this view, the net impact of population growth on economic growth is negligible.

Population neutralism is only recently giving way to a more fine-grained view of the effects of population dynamics in which demographic change does contribute to or detract from economic development. To make their case, economists and demographers point to both the "arithmetic accounting" effects of age structure change and the effects of behavioral change caused by longer life spans (see box).

Arithmetic accounting effects. These effects assume constant behavior within age and sex groups, but allow for changes in the relative size of those groups to influence overall outcomes. For example, holding age- and sex-specific labor force participation rates constant, a change in age structure affects total labor supply.

As a country's baby-boom generation gets older, for a time it constitutes a large cohort of working-age individuals and, later, a large cohort of elderly people. The span of years represented by the boom generation (which determines how quickly this cohort moves through the age structure) and the size of the population bulge vary greatly from one country to another. In all circumstances, there are reasons to think that this very dynamic age structure will have economic consequences. A historically high proportion of working-age individuals in a population means that, potentially, there are more workers per dependent than previously. Production can therefore increase relative to consumption, and GDP per capita can receive a boost.

Life cycle patterns in savings also come into play as a population's age structure changes. People save more during their working-age years, and if the working-age cohort is much larger than other age groups, savings per capita will increase.

Behavioral effects. Declining rates of adult mortality and the movement of large cohorts through the global population pyramid will lead to a massive expansion in the proportion of elderly in the world population (see the projections for 2050 in Figure 4). Some simple economic projections show catastrophic effects of this aging. But such projections tend to be based on an "accounting" approach, which assumes that age-specific behavior remains unchanged and ignores the potentially significant effects of behavior change.

The aging of the baby-boom generation potentially promotes labor shortages, creating upward pressure on wages and downward pressure on the real incomes of retirees. In response, people may adjust their behavior, resulting in increased labor force participation, the immigration of workers from developing countries, and longer working lives. Child mortality declines can also have behavioral effects, particularly for women, who tend to be the primary caregivers for children. When the reduced fertility effect of a decrease in child mortality is in place, more women participate in the workforce, further boosting the labor supply.

How Much Can the Human Life Span Be Stretched?

In most of the world, children born today can expect to live for many decades longer than their ancestors born in the 19th or early 20th centuries. In Japan, life expectancy at birth is now 82 years, and other regions have also made great progress as medical and public health advances, improved nutrition, and behavioral changes encouraged by improved education have combined to reduce the risk of death at all ages. But how far can these increases in longevity go?

Continuing increases in life expectancy in low-mortality populations have led some demographers to forecast further gains. Kenneth Manton, Eric Stallard, and H. Dennis Tolley, for example, estimate that populations with extremely healthy lifestyles—that is, with an absence or near-absence of risk factors such as infectious disease, smoking, alcohol abuse, and obesity, and the presence of health-promoting behaviors such as a healthy diet and exercise—could achieve a life expectancy of between 95 and 100 years.

But others have reached different conclusions. Nan Li and Ronald Lee estimate that life expectancy in the United States will rise from a 1996 figure of 76.3 to 84.9 by 2050, with that in Japan rising from 80.5 to 88.1. S. Jay Olshansky, Bruce Carnes, and Aline Desesquelles predicted in 1990 that life expectancy at birth would not surpass 85 years, even in low-mortality settings. Death rates, they argued, would not fall sufficiently for life expectancy to rise rapidly, and earlier increases were driven largely by dramatic reductions in infant and child mortality, which could not recur (Samuel Preston, on the other hand, observes that 60 percent of the life expectancy increase in the United States since 1950 is due to mortality declines in people over the age of 50). Perhaps more important, they saw no reason why the future should necessarily mirror the past—new threats to health such as influenza pandemics, antibiotic resistance, and obesity could reverse gains made in recent decades; technological improvements could stall and the drugs needed to counter the diseases of aging might not be found; and environmental disasters, economic collapse, or war could derail health systems at the same time that they weaken individuals' ability to protect their own health.

The Missing Link

Demographic effects are a key missing link in many macroeconomic analyses that aim to explain cross-country differences in economic growth and poverty reduction. Several empirical studies show the importance of demographics in explaining economic development.

East Asia's baby boom. East Asia's remarkable economic growth in the past half century coincided closely with demographic change in the region. As infant mortality fell from 181 to 34 per 1,000 births between 1950 and 2000, fertility fell from six to two children per woman. The lag between falls in mortality and fertility created a baby-boom generation: between 1965 and 1990, the region's working-age population grew nearly four times faster than the dependent population. Several studies have estimated that this demographic shift was responsible for one-third of East Asia's economic growth during the period (a welcome demographic dividend).

Labor supply and the Celtic Tiger. From 1960 to 1990, the growth rate of income per capita in Ireland was approximately 3.5 percent a year. In the 1990s, it jumped to 5.8 percent, well in excess of any other European economy. Demographic change contributed to the country's economic surge. In the decade following the legalization of contraceptives in 1979, Ireland saw a sharp fall in the crude birth rate. This led to decreasing youth dependency and a rise in the working-age share of the total population. By the mid-1990s, the dependency burden in Ireland had dropped to a level below that in the United Kingdom.

Two additional demography-based factors also helped fuel economic growth by increasing labor supply per capita. First, while male labor force participation rates remained fairly static, the period 1980–2000 saw a substantial increase in female labor force participation rates, particularly among those aged between 25 and 40. Second, Ireland historically had high emigration levels among young adults (about 1 percent of the population a year) because its economy was unable to absorb the large number of young workers created by its high fertility rate. The loss of these young workers exacerbated the problem of the high youth dependency rate. The decline in youth cohort sizes and rapid economic growth of the 1990s led to a reversal of this flow, resulting in net in-migration of workers, made up partly of return migrants and also, for the first time, substantial numbers of foreign immigrants.

Continued high fertility in sub-Saharan Africa. Demographic change of a very different type can account for slow economic development. Much of sub-Saharan Africa remains stalled at the first stage of a demographic transition. Fertility rates actually increased a bit from the 1950s through the 1970s and only recently have begun a slow fall. As swollen youth cohorts have entered the labor force, an inadequate policy and economic environment in most countries has prevented many young people from being able to engage in productive employment. The existence of large dependent populations (in this case, of children) has kept the proportion of working-age people low, making it more difficult for these economies to rise out of poverty.

Looking to the Future

Based on the indicators that are available, we can make a few important points:

- *All signs point to continued but slowing population growth.* This growth will result in the addition of roughly 2.5 billion people to the world population, before it stabilizes around 2050 at about 9 billion. Managing this increase will be an enormous challenge, and the economic consequences of failing to do so could be severe.
- *The world's population is aging rapidly.* The United Nations predicts that 31 percent of China's population in 2050—432 million people—will be age 60 or older. The corresponding figures for India are 21 percent and 330 million. No longer can aging be thought of as just a developed-world phenomenon.
- *International migration will continue, but the extent is unclear.* The pressures that encourage people to migrate—above all, the lure of greater economic well-being in the

developed countries—will undoubtedly persist, but the strength of countervailing policy restrictions that could substantially stanch the flow of migrants is impossible to predict.

- *Urbanization will continue, but the pace is also hard to predict.* Greater economic opportunities in the cities will surely continue to attract migrants from rural areas, but environmental and social problems may stymie growth.

Getting the Focus Right

Rapid and significant demographic change places new demands on national and international policymaking. Transitions from high mortality and fertility to low mortality and fertility can be beneficial to economies as large baby-boom cohorts enter the workforce and save for retirement. Rising longevity also tends to increase the incentives to save for old age.

The ability of countries to realize the potential benefits of the demographic transition and to mitigate the negative effects of aging depends crucially on the policy and institutional environment. Focusing on the following areas is likely to be key:

Health and nutrition. Although it has long been known that increased income leads to improved health, recent evidence indicates that good health may also be an important factor in economic development. Good nutrition in children is essential for brain development and for allowing them to become productive members of society. Health improvements—especially among infants and children—often lead to declines in fertility, above and beyond the heightened quality of life they imply. Focusing on the diseases of childhood can therefore increase the likelihood of creating a boom generation and certain positive economic effects. Countries wishing to accelerate fertility declines may benefit from focusing on access to family-planning services and education about fertility decisions.

> **The ability of countries to realize the potential benefits of the demographic transition and to mitigate the negative effects of aging depends crucially on the policy and institutional environment.**

Education. Children are better able to contribute to economic growth as they enter the workforce if they have received an effective education. East Asia capitalized on its baby boom by giving its children a high-quality education, including both general schooling and technical skills, that equipped them to meet the demands of an ever-changing labor market. Ireland also profited from its baby boomers by introducing free secondary schooling and expanding tertiary education.

Labor market institutions. Restrictive labor laws can limit a country's ability to benefit from demographic change, particularly when they make it unduly difficult to hire and fire workers or to work part-time. International outsourcing, another controversial subject, may become an increasingly important means of meeting the demand for labor.

Trade. One way that East Asian countries provided their baby-boom cohorts with productive opportunities was by carefully opening up to international trade. By providing a new avenue for selling the region's output, this opening helped countries avoid the unemployment that could have arisen. We have found that open economies benefit much more from demographic change than the average, and that closed economies do not derive any statistically significant benefit from age structure changes.

Retirement. Population aging will require increased savings to finance longer retirements. This will likely affect financial markets, rates of return, and investment. In addition, as more people move into old age, health care costs will tend to increase, with the expansion of health care systems and growth in long-term care for the elderly. As nontradable, labor-intensive sectors with a low rate of technical progress, health care and elder care may slow economic growth. The ability of individuals to contribute to the financing of their retirement may be hampered by existing social security systems, many of which effectively penalize individuals who work beyond a fixed retirement age.

Although demographic changes are generally easier to predict than economic changes, the big picture outlook is nonetheless unclear. Indeed, many forces that affect the world's demographic profile are highly unpredictable. Will an outbreak of avian flu or another disease become pandemic, killing many millions and decimating economies? What happens if these diseases are, or become, drug-resistant? Conversely, scientific advances in areas such as genomics, contraceptive methods, or vaccines for diseases such as AIDS or malaria could save and improve millions of lives. Global warming and other environmental change could completely alter the context of demographic and economic predictions. Or—to take things to extremes—wars could result in massive premature mortality, thereby rendering irrelevant most predictions about demographic and related economic changes.

References

Bloom, David E., and David Canning, 2004, "Global Demographic Change: Dimensions and Economic Significance," in *Global Demographic Change: Economic Impacts and Policy Challenges,* proceedings of a symposium, sponsored by the Federal Reserve Bank of Kansas City, Jackson Hole, Wyoming, August 26–28, pp. 9–56.

Lee, Ronald, 2003, "The Demographic Transition: Three Centuries of Fundamental Change," *Journal of Economic Perspectives,* Vol. 17 (Fall), pp. 167–90.

National Research Council, 1986, *Population Growth and Economic Development: Policy Questions* (Washington: National Academies Press).

DAVID E. BLOOM is Professor of Economics and Demography and **DAVID CANNING** is Professor of Economics and International Health at the Harvard School of Public Health.

Emerging Water Shortages

LESTER BROWN

Africa's Lake Chad, once a landmark for astronauts circling Earth, is now difficult for them to locate. Surrounded by Cameroon, Chad, Niger, and Nigeria—all countries with fast-growing populations—the lake has shrunk 96 percent in forty years. The region's soaring demand for irrigation water coupled with declining rainfall is draining dry the rivers and streams that feed the lake. As a result, Lake Chad may soon disappear entirely, its whereabouts a mystery to future generations.

The shrinkage of Lake Chad isn't unique. The world is incurring a vast water deficit—one that is largely invisible, historically recent, and growing fast. Because the deficit comes largely from aquifer overpumping, it is often discovered only when wells go dry.

This global water deficit is the result of demand tripling over the last half-century. The drilling of millions of irrigation wells has pushed water withdrawals beyond recharge rates, in effect leading to groundwater mining. The failure of governments to limit pumping to the sustainable yield of aquifers means that water tables are now falling in countries that contain more than half the world's population, including the big three grain producers—China, India, and the United States.

Beyond these traditional sources of water insecurity, climate change is now affecting water supplies. Rising temperatures are boosting evaporation rates, altering rainfall patterns, and melting the glaciers that feed rivers during the dry season. As the glaciers melt, they are threatening to convert perennial rivers such as the Ganges in India and the Yellow in China into seasonal rivers, increasing both water and food insecurity. With the earth's climate system and its hydrological cycle so intertwined, any changes in climate will alter the hydrological cycle.

The link between water and food is strong. We each drink on average nearly 4 liters of water per day in one form or another, while the water required to produce our daily food totals at least 2,000 liters—500 times as much. This helps explain why 70 percent of all water use is for irrigation. Another 20 percent is used by industry, and 10 percent goes for residential purposes. With the demand for water growing in all three categories, competition among sectors is intensifying, with agriculture almost always losing. Though most people recognize that the world is facing a future of water shortages, not everyone has connected the dots to see that this also means a future of food shortages.

Water Tables Falling

Scores of countries are overpumping aquifers as they struggle to satisfy their growing water needs. Most aquifers are replenishable, but not all are. When most of the aquifers in India and the shallow aquifer under the North China Plain are depleted, the maximum rate of pumping will be automatically reduced to the rate of recharge.

Fossil aquifers, however, aren't replenishable. For these—the vast U.S. Ogallala aquifer, the deep aquifer under the North China Plain, or the Saudi aquifer, for example—depletion brings pumping to an end. Farmers who lose their irrigation water have the option of returning to lower-yield dryland farming if rainfall permits. But in more arid regions, such as in the southwestern United States or the Middle East, the loss of irrigation water means the end of agriculture.

Falling water tables are already adversely affecting harvests in some countries, including China, which rivals the United States as the world's largest grain producer. A groundwater survey released in Beijing in August 2001 revealed that the water table under the North China Plain, an area that produces over half of the country's wheat and a third of its corn, is falling fast. Overpumping has largely depleted the shallow aquifer, forcing well drillers to turn to the region's deep aquifer, which isn't replenishable.

Falling water tables, the conversion of cropland to non-farm uses, and the loss of farm labor in provinces that are rapidly industrializing are combining to shrink Chinas grain harvest. The wheat crop, grown mostly in semiarid northern China, is particularly vulnerable to water shortages. After peaking at 123 million (metric) tons in 1997, the harvest has fallen, coming in at 105 million tons in 2007, a drop of 15 percent.

A World Bank study indicates that China is mining underground water in three adjacent river basins in the north—those of the Hai, which flows through Beijing and Tianjin; the Yellow, and the Huai, the next river south of the Yellow. Since it takes 1,000 tons of water to produce one ton of grain, the shortfall in the Hai basin of nearly 40 billion tons of water per year (one ton equals one cubic meter) means that when the aquifer is depleted, the grain harvest will drop by 40 million tons—enough to feed 120 million Chinese.

As serious as water shortages are in China, they are even more serious in India, where the margin between food consumption and survival is precarious. To date, India's 100 million farmers have drilled 21 million wells, investing some $12 billion in wells and pumps. In a survey of India's water situation, Fred Pearce reported in the *New Scientist* that "half of India's traditional hand-dug wells and millions of shallower tube wells have already dried up, bringing a spate of suicides among those who rely on them. Electricity blackouts are reaching epidemic proportions in states where half of the electricity is used to pump water from depths of up to a kilometer."

As water tables fall, well drillers are using modified oil-drilling technology to reach water, going as deep as 1,000 meters in some locations. In communities where underground water sources have dried up entirely, all agriculture is rain-fed and drinking water must be trucked in. Tushaar Shah, who heads the International Water Management Institutes groundwater station in Gujarat, says of India's water situation, "When the balloon bursts, untold anarchy will be the lot of rural India."

India's grain harvest, squeezed both by water scarcity and the loss of cropland to nonfarm uses, has plateaued since 2000. This helps explain why India reemerged as a leading wheat importer in 2006. A 2005 World Bank study reports that 15 percent of India's food supply is produced by mining groundwater. Stated otherwise, 175 million Indians are fed with grain produced with water from irrigation wells that will soon go dry.

As water tables fall, the energy required for pumping rises. In both India and China, the rising electricity demand from irrigation is satisfied largely by building coal-fired power plants.

Pakistan, a country with 164 million people that is growing by 3 million per year, is also mining its underground water. In the Pakistani part of the fertile Punjab plain, the drop in water tables appears to be similar to that in India. Observation wells near the twin cities of Islamabad and Rawalpindi show a fall in the water table between 1982 and 2000 that ranges from one to nearly two meters a year.

Iran, a country of 71 million people, is overpumping its aquifers by an average of 5 billion tons of water per year, the water equivalent of one third of its annual grain harvest. Under the small but agriculturally rich Chenaran Plain in northeastern Iran, the water table was falling by 2.8 meters a year in the late 1990s. New wells being drilled both for irrigation and to supply the nearby city of Mashad are responsible. Villages in eastern Iran are being abandoned as wells go dry, generating a flow of "water refugees."

Saudi Arabia, a country of 25 million people, is as water-poor as it is oil-rich. Relying heavily on subsidies, it developed an extensive irrigated agriculture based largely on its deep fossil aquifer. After several years of supporting wheat prices at five times the world market level, the government was forced to face fiscal reality and cut the subsidies. Its wheat harvest dropped from a high of 4.1 million tons in 1992 to 2.7 million tons in 2007, a drop of 34 percent.

In neighboring Yemen, a nation of 22 million, the water table under most of the country is falling by roughly 2 meters a year as water use outstrips the sustainable yield of aquifers. In western Yemen's Sana'a Basin, the estimated annual water extraction of 224 million tons exceeds the annual recharge of 42 million tons by a factor of five, dropping the water table 6 meters per year. World Bank projections indicate the Sana'a Basin—site of the national capital, Sana'a, and home to 2 million people—may be pumped dry by 2010.

In the search for water, the Yemeni government has drilled test wells in the basin that are more than a mile deep—depths normally associated with the oil industry—but they have failed to find water. Yemen must soon decide whether to bring water to Sana'a, possibly by pipeline from coastal desalting plants, if it can afford it, or to relocate the capital. Either alternative will be costly and potentially traumatic.

In Mexico—home to a population of 107 million that is projected to reach 132 million by 2050—the demand for water is outstripping supply. Mexico City's water problems are well known. Rural areas are also suffering. In the agricultural state of Guanajuato, the water table is falling by two meters or more a year. In the northwestern state of Sonora, farmers once pumped water from the Hermosillo aquifer at a depth of 10 meters. Today they pump from more than 122 meters. At the national level, 51 percent of all the water extracted from underground is from aquifers that are being overpumped.

Since the overpumping of aquifers is occurring in many countries more or less simultaneously, the depletion of aquifers and the resulting harvest cutbacks could come at roughly the same time. And the accelerating depletion of aquifers means this day may come soon, creating potentially unmanageable food scarcity.

Scarcity Crossing National Borders

Historically, water scarcity was a local issue. It was up to national governments to balance water supply and demand. Now this is changing as scarcity crosses national boundaries via the international grain trade. Since it takes 1,000 tons of water to produce one ton of grain, as noted earlier, importing grain is the most efficient way to import water. Countries are, in effect, using grain to balance their water books. Similarly, trading in grain futures is in a sense trading in water futures.

After China and India, there is a second tier of smaller countries with large water deficits—Pakistan, Algeria, Egypt, and Mexico. The latter three already import much of their grain. With its population outgrowing its water supply, Pakistan too may soon turn to world markets for grain.

The Middle East and North Africa—from Morocco in the west through Iran in the east—has become the world's fastest-growing grain import market. The demand for grain is driven both by rapid population growth and by rising affluence, much of the latter from the export of oil. With virtually every country in the region pressing against its water limits, the growing urban demand for water can be satisfied only by taking irrigation water from agriculture.

Overall, the water required to produce the grain and other farm products imported into the Middle East and North Africa last year approached the annual flow of the Nile River at Aswan. In effect, the region's water deficit can be thought of as another Nile flowing into the region in the form of imported food.

It is often said that future wars in the Middle East will more likely be fought over water than oil, but in reality the competition for water is taking place in world grain markets. The countries that are financially the strongest—not necessarily those that are militarily the strongest—will fare best in this competition.

Knowing where grain deficits will be concentrated tomorrow requires looking at where water deficits are developing today. Thus far, the countries importing much of their grain have been smaller ones. Now we are looking at fast-growing water deficits in both China and India, each with more than a billion people.

As noted earlier, overpumping is a way of satisfying growing food demand that virtually guarantees a future drop in food production when aquifers are depleted. Many countries are in essence creating a "food bubble economy"—one in which food production is artificially inflated by the unsustainable mining of groundwater. At what point does water scarcity translate into food scarcity?

David Seckler and his colleagues at the International Water Management Institute, the world's premier water research group, summarized this issue well: "Many of the most populous countries of the world—China, India, Pakistan, Mexico, and nearly all the countries of the Middle East and North Africa—have literally been having a free ride over the past two or three decades by depleting their groundwater resources. The penalty for mismanagement of this valuable resource is now coming due and it is no exaggeration to say that the results could be catastrophic for these countries and, given their importance, for the world as a whole."

Water Scarcity Yields Political Stresses

We typically measure wellbeing in economic terms, in income per person, but water wellbeing is measured in cubic meters or tons of water per person. A country with an annual supply of 1,700 cubic meters of water per person is well supplied with water, able to comfortably meet agricultural, industrial, and residential needs. Below this level,

stresses begin to appear. When water supply drops below 1,000 cubic meters per person, people face scarcity. Below 500 cubic meters, they face acute scarcity. At this level people are suffering from hydrological poverty—living without enough water to produce food or, in some cases, even for basic hygiene.

The world's most severe water stresses are found in North Africa and the Middle East. While Morocco and Egypt have fewer than 1,000 cubic meters per person per year, Algeria, Tunisia, and Libya have fewer than 500. Some countries, including Saudi Arabia, Yemen, Kuwait, and Israel, have less than 300 cubic meters per person per year. A number of sub-Saharan countries are also facing water stress, including Kenya and Rwanda.

While national averages indicate an adequate water supply in each of the world's three most populous countries—China, India, and the United States—regions within these countries also suffer from acute water shortages. Water is scarce throughout the northern half of China. In India, the northwestern region suffers extreme water scarcity. For the United States, the southwestern states from Texas to California are experiencing acute water shortages.

Although the risk of international conflict over water is real, so far there have been remarkably few water wars. Water tensions tend to build more within societies, particularly where water is already scarce and population growth is rapid. Recent years have witnessed conflicts over water in scores of countries. Perhaps the most common of these is the competition between cities and farmers, particularly in countries like China, India, and Yemen. In other countries the conflicts are between tribes, as in Kenya, or between villages, as in India and China, or upstream and downstream water users, as in Pakistan or China. In some countries local water conflicts have led to violence and death, as in Kenya, Pakistan, and China.

One water flash point involves the way water is divided between Israelis and Palestinians. A United Nations report notes that "nowhere are the problems of water governance as starkly demonstrated as in the Occupied Palestinian Territories" Palestinians experience one of the highest levels of water scarcity in the world. But the flash point is as much over inequity in the distribution of water as it is over scarcity. The Israeli population is roughly double that of the Palestinians, but it gets seven times as much water. As others have noted, peace in the region depends on a more equitable distribution of the region's water. Without this, the peace process itself may dry up.

At the global level, most of the projected population growth of nearly 3 billion by 2050 will come in countries where water tables are already falling. The states most stressed by the scarcity of water tend to be those in arid and semiarid regions, with fast-growing populations and a resistance to family planning. Many of the countries high on the list of failing states are those where populations are outrunning their water supplies, among them Sudan, Iraq, Somalia, Chad, Afghanistan, Pakistan, and Yemen.

Although spreading water shortages are intimidating, we have the technologies needed to raise water use efficiency, thus buying time to stabilize population size. Prominent among these technologies are those for more water-efficient irrigation, industrial water recycling, and urban water recycling. Unless population can be stabilized in these countries, the continually shrinking supply of water per person will put still more stress on already overstressed governments.

LESTER BROWN is the founder and president of the Earth Policy Institute and the 1991 Humanist of the Year. This article is an excerpt from Brown's newly released book, *Plan B 3.0: Mobilizing to Save Civilization*, which can be downloaded for free from www.earthpolicy.org.

Water Warriors

**Declaring water a right, not a commodity, a global
water justice movement is growing.**

MAUDE BARLOW

*Thousands have lived without love, not one without
water.*

—W.H. Auden, *First Things First*

A fierce resistance to the corporate takeover of water has grown in every corner of the globe, giving rise to a coordinated and, given the powers it is up against, surprisingly successful water justice movement. "Water for all" is the rallying cry of local groups fighting for access to clean water and the life, health and dignity that it brings. Many of these groups have lived through years of abuse, poverty and hunger. Many have been left without public education and health programs when their governments were forced to abandon them under World Bank structural adjustment policies. But somehow, the assault on water has been the great standpoint for millions. Without water there is no life, and for thousands of communities around the world, the struggle over the right to their own local water sources has been politically galvanizing.

A mighty contest has grown between those (usually powerful) forces and institutions that see water as a commodity, to be put on the open market and sold to the highest bidder, and those who see water as a public trust, a common heritage of people and nature, and a fundamental human right. The origins of this movement, generally referred to as the global water justice movement, lie in the hundreds of communities around the world where people are fighting to protect their local water supplies from pollution, destruction by dams and theft—be it from other countries, their own governments or private corporations such as bottled water companies and private utilities backed by the World Bank. Until the late 1990s, however, most were operating in isolation, unaware of other struggles or the global nature of the water crisis.

Latin America was the site of the first experiments with water privatization in the developing world. The failure of these projects has been a major factor in the rejection of the neoliberal market model by so many Latin American countries that have said no to the extension of the North American Free Trade Agreement to the Southern Hemisphere and that have

forced the big water companies to retreat. A number of Latin American countries are also opting out of some of the most egregious global institutions. This past May Bolivia, Venezuela and Nicaragua announced their decision to withdraw from the World Bank's arbitration court, the International Centre for the Settlement of Investment Disputes (ICSID), in no small measure because of the way the big water corporations have used the center to sue for compensation when the countries terminated private delivery contracts.

Latin America, with its water abundance, should have one of the highest per capita allocations of water in the world. Instead, it has one of the lowest. There are three reasons, all connected: polluted surface waters, deep class inequities and water privatization. In many parts of Latin America, only the rich can buy clean water. So it is not surprising that some of the most intense fights against corporate control of water have come out of this region of the world.

The first "water war" gained international attention when the indigenous peoples of Cochabamba, Bolivia, led by a five-foot, slightly built, unassuming shoemaker named Oscar Olivera, rose up against the privatization of their water services. In 1999, under World Bank supervision, the Bolivian government had passed a law privatizing Cochabamba's water system and gave the contract to US engineering giant Bechtel, which immediately tripled the price of water. In a country where the minimum wage is less than $60 a month, many users received water bills of $20 a month, which they simply could not afford. As a result, La Coordinadora de Defensa del Agua y de la Vida (Coalition in Defense of Water and Life), one of the first coalitions against water privatization in the world, was formed and organized a successful referendum demanding the government cancel its contract with Bechtel. When the government refused to listen, many thousands took to the streets in nonviolent protest and were met with army violence that wounded dozens and killed a 17-year-old boy. On April 10, 2000, the Bolivian government relented and told Bechtel to leave the country.

The Bolivian government had also bowed to pressure from the World Bank to privatize the water of La Paz and in 1997 gave Suez, a French-based multinational, a thirty-year contract to supply water services to it and El Alto, the hilly region surrounding the capital, where thousands of indigenous peoples live. From the beginning, there were problems. Aguas del Illimani, a Suez subsidiary, broke three key promises: it did not deliver to all the residents, poor as well as rich, leaving about 200,000 without water; it charged exorbitant rates for water hookups, about $450, equivalent to the food budget of a poor family for two years; and it did not invest in infrastructure repair or wastewater treatment, choosing instead to build a series of ditches and canals through poor areas of La Paz, which it used to send garbage, raw sewage and even the effluent from the city's abattoirs into Lake Titicaca, considered by UNESCO a World Heritage site. To add insult to injury, the company located its fortresslike plant under the beautiful Mount Illimani, where it captured the snowmelt off the mountain and, after rudimentary treatment, piped it into the homes of families and businesses in La Paz that could pay. The nearest community, Solidaridad, a slum of about 100 families with no electricity, heat or running water, had its only water supply cut off. Its school and health clinic, built with foreign-aid money, could not operate because of a lack of water. It was the same all through El Alto.

An intense resistance to Suez formed. FEJUVE, a network of local community councils and activists, led a series of strikes in January 2005, which crippled the cities and brought business to a halt. This resistance was a prime factor in the ousting of presidents Gonzalo Sánchez de Lozada and Carlos Mesa. Their replacement, Evo Morales, the first indigenous president in the country's history, negotiated Suez's departure. On January 3, 2007, he held a ceremony at the presidential palace celebrating the return of the water of La Paz and El Alto after a long and bitter confrontation. "Water cannot be turned over to private business," said Morales. "It must remain a basic service, with participation of the state, so that water service can be provided almost for free."

Although they have received less international attention, similar battles over privatized water have raged in Argentina. Río de la Plata (Silver River) separates Buenos Aires, the Argentine capital, from Montevideo, the capital of Uruguay. For 500 years, it has also been called Mar Dulce (Sweet Sea) because its size made people think it was a freshwater sea. Today, however, the river is famous for something else: it is one of the few rivers in the world whose pollution can be seen from space. On March 21, 2006, the Argentine government rescinded the thirty-year contract of Aguas Argentinas, the Suez subsidiary that had run the Buenos Aires water system since 1993, in no small part because the company broke its promise to treat wastewater, continuing to dump nearly 90 percent of the city's sewage into the river. In another broken promise, the company repeatedly raised tariffs, for a total increase of 88 percent in the first ten years of operation. Water quality was another issue; water in seven districts had nitrate levels so high it was unfit for human consumption. An April 2007 report by the city's ombudsman stated that most of the population of 150,000 in the southern district of the city lived with open-air sewers and contaminated drinking water.

Yet as Food and Water Watch reports, the Inter-American Development Bank continued to fund Suez as late as 1999,

despite the mounting evidence that the company was pulling in 20 percent profit margins while refusing to invest in services or infrastructure. Outrageously, with the backing of the French government, Suez is trying to recoup $1.7 billion in "investments" and up to $33 million in unpaid water bills at the ICSID. Suez had just (in December 2005) been forced out of the province of Santa Fe, where it had a thirty-year contract to run the water systems of thirteen cities. The company is also suing the provincial government at the ICSID for $180 million. Close on the heels of the Buenos Aires announcement, Suez was forced to abandon its last stronghold in Argentina, the city of Córdoba, when water rates were raised 500 percent on one bill.

In all cases, strong civil society resistance was key to these re treats. A coalition of water users and residents of Santa Fe, led by Alberto Múñoz and others, actually organized a huge and successful plebiscite, in which 256,000 people, about a twelfth of the population of the province, voted to rescind Suez's contract. They convened a Provincial Assembly on the Right to Water with 7,000 activists and citizens in November 2002, which set the stage for the political opposition to the company. The People's Commission for the Recovery of Water in Córdoba is a highly organized network of trade unions, neighborhood centers, social organizations and politicians with a clear goal of public water for all, and was instrumental in getting the government to break its contract with Suez. "What we want is a public company managed by workers, consumers and the provincial government, and monitored by university experts to guarantee water quality and prevent corruption," says Luis Bazán, the group's leader and a water worker who refused employment with Suez.

Mexico is a beachhead for privatization across the region, with its elites having access to all the water they need and also controlling governments at most levels of the country. Only 9 percent of the country's surface water is fit for drinking, and its aquifers are being drawn down mercilessly. According to the National Commission on Water, 12 million Mexicans have no access to potable water whatsoever and another 25 million live in villages and cities where the taps run as little as a few hours a week. Eighty-two percent of wastewater goes untreated. Mexico City has dried up, and its 22 million inhabitants live on the verge of crisis. Services are so poor in the slums and outskirts of the city that cockroaches run out when the tap is turned on. In many "colonias" in Mexico City and around the country, the only available water is sold from trucks that bring it in once a week, often by political parties that sell the water for votes.

In 1983 the federal government handed over responsibility for the water supply to the municipalities. Then in 1992 it passed a new national water bill that encouraged the municipalities to privatize water in order to receive funding. Privatization was supported by former President Vicente Fox, himself a former senior executive with Coca-Cola, and is also favored by the current president, Felipe Calderón. The World Bank and the Inter-American Development Bank are actively promoting water privatization in Mexico. In 2002 the World Bank provided $250 million for infrastructure repair with conditions that municipalities negotiate public-private partnerships. Suez is deeply entrenched in Mexico, running the water services for part of Mexico City, Cancún and about a dozen other cities. Its wastewater division, Degremont, has a large contract for San Luis Potosí and several other cities as well. The privatization of water has become a top priority for the Mexican water commission, Conagua. As in other countries, privatization in Mexico has brought exorbitant water rates, broken promises and cutoffs to those who cannot pay. The Water Users Association in Saltillo, where a consortium of Suez and the Spanish company Aguas de Barcelona run the city's water systems, reports that a 2004 audit by the state comptroller found evidence of contractual and state law violations.

A vibrant civil society movement has recently come together to fight for the right to clean water and resist the trend to corporate control in Mexico. In April 2005 the Mexican Center for Social Analysis, Information and Training (CASIFOP) brought together more than 400 activists, indigenous peoples, small farmers and students to launch a coordinated grassroots resistance to water privatization. The Coalition of Mexican Organizations for the Right to Water (COMDA) is a large collection of environmental, human rights, indigenous and cultural groups devoted not only to activism but also to community-based education on water, its place in Mexico's history and the need for legislation to protect the public's right to access. Their hopes for a government supportive of their perspective were dashed when conservative candidate Calderón won (many say stole) the 2006 presidential election over progressive candidate Andrés Manuel López Obrador. Calderón is working openly with the private water companies to cement private control of the country's water supplies.

O ther Latin American cities or countries rejecting water privatization include Bogotá, Colombia (although other Colombian cities, including Cartagena, have adopted private water systems); Paraguay, whose lower house rejected a Senate proposal to privatize water in July 2005; Nicaragua, where a fierce struggle has been waged by civil society groups and where in January 2007 a court ruled against the privatization of the country's wastewater infrastructure; and Brazil, where strong public opinion has held back the forces of water privatization in most cities. Unfortunately, resistance in Peru, where increased rates, corruption and debt plague the system, has not yet reversed water privatization. Likewise, in Chile, resistance to water privatization is very difficult because of the entrenched commitment to market ideology of the ruling elites, although there is hope that the center-left government of Michelle Bachelet will be more open to arguments for public governance of Chile's water supplies.

From thousands of local struggles for the basic right to water—not just throughout Latin America but in Asia-Pacific countries, Africa and the United States and Canada—a highly organized international water justice movement has been forged and is shaping the future of the world's water. This movement has already had a profound effect on global water politics, forcing global institutions such as the World Bank and the United Nations to admit the failure of their model, and it has helped formulate water policy inside dozens of countries. The movement has forced open a debate over the control of water and challenged the "Lords of Water" who had set themselves up as the arbiters of this dwindling resource. The growth of a democratic global water justice movement is a critical and positive development that will bring needed accountability, transparency and public oversight to the water crisis as conflicts over water loom on the horizon.

MAUDE BARLOW is the author of *Blue Covenant: The Global Water Crisis and the Coming Battle for the Right to Water* (New Press), from which this article was adapted.

Soot from Third-World Stoves Is New Target in Climate Fight

Elisabeth Rosenthal

"It's hard to believe that this is what's melting the glaciers," said Dr. Veerabhadran Ramanathan, one of the world's leading climate scientists, as he weaved through a warren of mud brick huts, each containing a mud cookstove pouring soot into the atmosphere.

As women in ragged saris of a thousand hues bake bread and stew lentils in the early evening over fires fueled by twigs and dung, children cough from the dense smoke that fills their homes. Black grime coats the undersides of thatched roofs. At dawn, a brown cloud stretches over the landscape like a diaphanous dirty blanket.

In Kohlua, in central India, with no cars and little electricity, emissions of carbon dioxide, the main heat-trapping gas linked to global warming, are near zero. But soot—also known as black carbon—from tens of thousands of villages like this one in developing countries is emerging as a major and previously unappreciated source of global climate change.

While carbon dioxide may be the No. 1 contributor to rising global temperatures, scientists say, black carbon has emerged as an important No. 2, with recent studies estimating that it is responsible for 18 percent of the planet's warming, compared with 40 percent for carbon dioxide. Decreasing black carbon emissions would be a relatively cheap way to significantly rein in global warming—especially in the short term, climate experts say. Replacing primitive cooking stoves with modern versions that emit far less soot could provide a much-needed stopgap, while nations struggle with the more difficult task of enacting programs and developing technologies to curb carbon dioxide emissions from fossil fuels.

In fact, reducing black carbon is one of a number of relatively quick and simple climate fixes using existing technologies—often called "low hanging fruit"—that scientists say should be plucked immediately to avert the worst projected consequences of global warming. "It is clear to any person who cares about climate change that this will have a huge impact on the global environment," said Dr. Ramanathan, a professor of climate science at the Scripps Institute of Oceanography, who is working with the Energy and Resources Institute in New Delhi on a project to help poor families acquire new stoves.

"In terms of climate change we're driving fast toward a cliff, and this could buy us time," said Dr. Ramanathan, who left India 40 years ago but returned to his native land for the project.

Better still, decreasing soot could have a rapid effect. Unlike carbon dioxide, which lingers in the atmosphere for years, soot stays there for a few weeks. Converting to low-soot cookstoves would remove the warming effects of black carbon quickly, while shutting a coal plant takes years to substantially reduce global CO_2 concentrations.

But the awareness of black carbon's role in climate change has come so recently that it was not even mentioned as a warming agent in the 2007 summary report by the Intergovernmental Panel on Climate Change that pronounced the evidence for global warming to be "unequivocal." Mark Z. Jacobson, professor of environmental engineering at Stanford, said that the fact that black carbon was not included in international climate efforts was "bizarre," but "partly reflects how new the idea is." The United Nations is trying to figure out how to include black carbon in climate change programs, as is the federal government.

In Asia and Africa, cookstoves produce the bulk of black carbon, although it also emanates from diesel engines and coal plants there. In the United States and Europe, black carbon emissions have already been reduced significantly by filters and scrubbers.

Like tiny heat-absorbing black sweaters, soot particles warm the air and melt the ice by absorbing the sun's heat when they settle on glaciers. One recent study estimated that black carbon might account for as much as half of Arctic warming. While the particles tend to settle over time and do not have the global reach of greenhouse gases, they do travel, scientists now realize. Soot from India has been found in the Maldive Islands and on the Tibetan Plateau; from the United States, it travels to the Arctic. The environmental and geopolitical implications of soot emissions are enormous. Himalayan glaciers are expected to lose 75 percent of their ice by 2020, according to Prof. Syed Iqbal Hasnain, a glacier specialist from the Indian state of Sikkim.

These glaciers are the source of most of the major rivers in Asia. The short-term result of glacial melt is severe flooding in mountain communities. The number of floods from glacial lakes is already rising sharply, Professor Hasnain said. Once the glaciers shrink, Asia's big rivers will run low or dry for part of the year, and desperate battles over water are certain to ensue in a region already rife with conflict.

Doctors have long railed against black carbon for its devastating health effects in poor countries. The combination of health and environmental benefits means that reducing soot provides a "very big bang for your buck," said Erika Rosenthal, a senior lawyer at Earth Justice, a Washington organization. "Now it's in everybody's self-interest to deal with things like cookstoves—not just because hundreds of thousands of women and children far away are dying prematurely."

> **"Now it's in everybody's self-interest to deal with things like cookstoves—not just because hundreds of thousands of women and children far away are dying prematurely."**
>
> —Erika Rosenthal

In the United States, black carbon emissions are indirectly monitored and minimized through federal and state programs that limit small particulate emissions, a category of particles damaging to human health that includes black carbon. But in March, a bill was introduced in Congress that would require the Environmental Protection Agency to specifically regulate black carbon and direct aid to black carbon reduction projects abroad, including introducing cookstoves in 20 million homes. The new stoves cost about $20 and use solar power or are more efficient. Soot is reduced by more than 90 percent. The solar stoves do not use wood or dung. Other new stoves simply burn fuel more cleanly, generally by pulverizing the fuel first and adding a small fan that improves combustion.

That remote rural villages like Kohlua could play an integral role in tackling the warming crisis is hard to imagine. There are no cars—the village chief's ancient white Jeep sits highly polished but unused in front of his house, a museum piece. There is no running water and only intermittent electricity, which powers a few light bulbs.

The 1,500 residents here grow wheat, mustard and potatoes and work as day laborers in Agra, home of the Taj Majal, about two hours away by bus.

They earn about $2 a day and, for the most part, have not heard about climate change. But they have noticed frequent droughts in recent years that scientists say may be linked to global warming. Crops ripen earlier and rot more frequently than they did 10 years ago. The villagers are aware, too, that black carbon can corrode. In Agra, cookstoves and diesel engines are forbidden in the area around the Taj Majal, because soot damages the precious facade.

Still, replacing hundreds of millions of cookstoves—the source of heat, food and sterile water—is not a simple matter. "I'm sure they'd look nice, but I'd have to see them, to try them," said Chetram Jatrav, as she squatted by her cookstove making tea and a flatbread called roti. Her three children were coughing.

She would like a stove that "made less smoke and used less fuel" but cannot afford one, she said, pushing a dungcake bought for one rupee into the fire. She had just bought her first rolling pin so her flatbread could come out "nice and round," as her children had seen in elementary school. Equally important, the open fires of cookstoves give some of the traditional foods their taste. Urging these villagers to make roti in a solar cooker meets the same mix of rational and irrational resistance as telling an Italian that risotto tastes just fine if cooked in the microwave.

In March, the cookstove project, called Surya, began "market testing" six alternative cookers in villages, in part to quantify their benefits. Already, the researchers fret that the new stoves look like scientific instruments and are fragile; one broke when a villager pushed twigs in too hard.

But if black carbon is ever to be addressed on a large scale, acceptance of the new stoves is crucial. "I'm not going to go to the villagers and say CO_2 is rising, and in 50 years you might have floods," said Dr. Ibrahim Rehman, Dr. Ramanathan's collaborator at the Energy and Resources Institute. "I'll tell her about the lungs and her kids and I know it will help with climate change as well."

Population, Human Resources, Health, and the Environment

Getting the Balance Right

Anthony J. McMichael

The UN's World Commission on Environment and Development (WCED)—the "Brundtland Commission," chaired by Gro Harlem Brundtland—released its seminal report *Our Common Future* in 1987.[1] Much has changed on the global environment front since then, only some of which was (or could have been) anticipated by that report. As human population continues to grow and as human societies, cultures, and economies become more interconnected against the background crescendo of "globalization" in recent decades, the collective human impact on the biosphere has increasingly assumed a global and systemic dimension. While issues like climate change, freshwater deficits, and degradation of food-producing systems and ocean fisheries were appearing on the horizon in 1987, they have now moved to the foreground. Today, it is evident that these momentous changes pose threats not only to economic systems, environmental assets, infrastructural integrity, tourism, and iconic nature, but also to the stability, health, and survival of human communities. This realization—along with the fact that human-induced global environmental changes impinge unequally on human groups—heightens the rationale for seeking sustainable development.

While the WCED report explored the rationale and the path toward sustainable development, the extent of subsequent large-scale environmental problems arising from the scale and the energy and materials intensity of prevailing modes of development could not have been fully anticipated in 1987. Indeed, paradoxically, concern over world population growth had temporarily receded in the mid-1980s, reflecting the prevailing mix of politics and optimism. The optimism derived from the apparent alleviation of hunger that had been achieved by the Green Revolution of the 1970s and 1980s in much of the developing world, and from the downturn in fertility rates in at least some developing regions. Today, however, the population issue is reemerging in public discussion, reflecting renewed recognition that population growth, along with rising consumption levels, is exacerbating climate change and other global environmental changes.[2]

If the commission's assessment were re-run this decade, its updated terms of reference would necessarily focus more attention on the social and health dimensions of the "development" process, both as inputs and, importantly, as outcomes. The charge to the commission, which focused on the often-conflicted relationship between economic activity and environmental sustainability, was framed at a time when the orthodox Rostovian view (that economic development occurs in five basic stages from "traditional society" to "age of high mass consumption") still remained influential.[3] Today, human capital and social capital—both of which were first properly understood and factored into the development calculus in the 1990s, along with the need for sound governance—are better recognized as prerequisites for environmentally sustainable development. At the same time, realization is growing that the attainment of positive human experience is the core objective of human societies.[4] In contrast, the commission's primary mandated focus was on how to reconcile environmental sustainability with social-economic development. That orientation afforded little stimulus to considering why, in human experiential terms, achieving such a balance is not an end in itself, but is a prerequisite for attaining human security, well-being, health, and survival. Why else do we seek sustainability?

People, Resources, Environment, and Development

The UN General Assembly Resolution A/38/161 of 1983 establishing the WCED specified that the commission would "take account of the interrelationships between people, resources, environment and development."[5] The full text of the resolution emphasized—as did the commission's name—the dual need for long-sighted environmental management strategies and greater cooperation among countries in seeking a sustainable development path to the common future. Two words in the quoted phrase are of particular interest: "people" and "resources."

Reference to "people," rather than to "populations," seems to emphasize the *human* dimension. However, it also distracts from issues of fertility and population size—a distraction that probably reflected two prevailing circumstances. In the 1980s—when world population growth was at its historic high—the United States's conservative Reagan Administration withheld international aid from family planning because of its perceived links with abortion counseling. This ill-informed and culturally high-handed approach, coming from a powerful country with great financial influence over UN policies, was complemented by the fact that many low-income countries considered that issues of fertility and population size were their own business. Nevertheless, and to its credit, the WCED report directly addressed the question of population size and its environmental consequences, urging lower fertility rates as a prerequisite for both poverty alleviation and environmental sustainability.

The word "resources" is ambiguous; it could be taken to refer to natural environmental resources or to human resources (human capital, including education and health status). To what extent did the WCED consider human well-being and health in relation to changing environmental conditions, population size, and resources? "Many such changes are accompanied by life-threatening hazards," stated the WCED in its overview of the report,[6] suggesting that the report would indeed explore how the state of the natural environment, our basic habitat, sets limits on human well-being, health, and survival, both now—and of particular relevance to sustainability—in future. Indeed, in launching the report in Oslo, on 20 March 1987, Chair Brundtland said:

> Our message is directed towards people, whose wellbeing is the ultimate goal of all environment and development policies. . . . If we do not succeed in putting our message of urgency through to today's parents and decision makers, we risk undermining our children's fundamental right to a healthy, life-enhancing environment.[7]

Despite these promising statements, the report itself gave only limited attention to considering how environmental degradation and ecological disruption affect the foundations of human population health. The report focused primarily on the prospects for achieving an "ecologically sustainable" form of social and economic development that conserves the natural environmental resource base for future human needs. It paid little attention to the fact that the conditions of the world's natural environment signify much more than assets for production, consumption, and economic development in general; the biosphere and its component ecosystems and biophysical processes provide the functions and flows that maintain life processes and therefore good health. Indeed, all extant forms of life have evolved via an exquisite dependency on environmental conditions.

This somewhat restricted vision on the part of the WCED is not surprising. Indeed, such a perspective has been reflected often in subsequent forays of UN agencies into the rationale and objectives of sustainable development—forays that have consistently overlooked or sometimes trivialized the role of sustainable development as a precondition to attaining well-being, health, and survival (see the box on for the example of the UN's Millennium Development Goals).[8] In defense of the report, however, it does state:

It is misleading and an injustice to the human condition to see people merely as consumers. Their well-being and security—old age security, declining child mortality, health care, and so on—are the goal of development.[9]

In the 1980s and early 1990s, there was little evidence and understanding of the relationship between environmental conditions, ecological systems, and human health. For example, the First Assessment Report of the Intergovernmental Panel on Climate Change (IPCC), released in 1991, contained only passing reference to how global climate change would affect human health.[10] The IPCC report reviewed in detail the risks to farms, forests, fisheries, feathered and furry animals, to settlements, coastal zones, and energy generation systems. In contrast, it glossed cursorily over the risks to human health (and gave undue emphasis to solar ultraviolet exposure and skin cancer, which is very marginal to the climate change and health topic).

There was, then, only a rudimentary awareness that the profile and scale of environmental hazards to human health were undergoing a profound transformation. For instance, the human health risks due to stratospheric ozone depletion, first recognized during the late 1970s and early 1980s, had been easily understood. They belonged to the familiar category of direct-acting hazardous environmental exposures. An increase in ambient levels of ultraviolet radiation at Earth's surface would increase the risks of skin damage and skin cancer and would affect eye health (for example, cataract formation). Recognition of this straightforward risk to human biology facilitated the ready international adoption of the Montreal Protocol in 1987, requiring national governments to eliminate release of ozone-destroying gases (mostly chlorofluorocarbons, nitrous oxide, and methyl bromide).

In contrast, the great diversity of (mostly) less direct-acting but potentially more profound risks to human health from changes to Earth's climate system, agroecosystems, ocean fisheries, freshwater flows, and general ecosystem functioning (such as pollination, nutrient cycling, and soil formation) were only dimly perceived in the 1980s. Those health risks received relatively little attention in the WCED report, which focused instead on health hazards related to inadequate water supply and sanitation, malnutrition, drug addiction, and exposure to carcinogens and other toxins in homes and the workplace.

An Incomplete Model of Health Determinants

In discussing population health, the WCED report took a largely utilitarian view, discussing good health as an input to economic development and, specifically, as stimulus to the reduction of fertility and poverty. In this respect it was in good company: both the pioneering sanitary revolution of nineteenth-century England and World Health Organization's International Commission on Macroeconomics and Health, established in 2000, espoused the same rationale: good health fosters national wealth. To the extent that the WCED report addressed the determinants of population health, it focused mainly on the contributions of

Millennium Development Goals: How Much Progress Has Been Made?

By coincidence, the 20-year anniversary of the Brundtland report nearly coincides with the halfway mark of another UN project, the Millennium Development Goals (MDGs), 2000–2015.[1] The MDGs were launched in 2000 against a backdrop of increasing attention on what was termed "ecologically sustainable development" in large part stimulated by the WCED report. They encompass eight goals (each with associated targets): to eradicate extreme poverty and hunger; achieve universal primary education; promote gender equality and empower women; reduce child mortality; improve maternal health; combat HIV/AIDS, malaria, and other diseases; ensure environmental sustainability; and develop a global partnership for development.

Achievement of the MDGs is becoming increasingly improbable as time passes. Some headway has been made in relation to poverty reduction and child school enrollment. But there has been little alleviation of hunger and malnutrition, maternal mortality, and infant-child death rates (which have declined by around one sixth in poorer countries, well short of the two-thirds reduction target).

Inevitably, progress toward the goals has varied between regions and countries. China, for example, has made social and health advances on many fronts, albeit at the cost of increasingly serious environmental degradation. In contrast, in sub-Saharan Africa, no country is coming close to halving poverty, providing universal primary education, or stemming the devastating HIV/AIDS epidemic. More than 40 percent of persons in sub-Saharan Africa live in extreme poverty.

One quarter of the world's children aged less than 5 are underfed and underweight. This, as a proportion, is an improvement on the figure of one third in 1990. However, in sub-Saharan Africa and South Asia, nearly half the children remain underweight, and gains are minimal.

The total number of people living with AIDS has increased by nearly 7-million since 2001, to a total now of 40 million. Neither malaria nor tuberculosis is being effectively curtailed, with the attempt to reduce tuberculosis being threatened further by the recent emergence of strains with more extreme forms of antimicrobial resistance.

Perhaps this lack of progress is in part reflected in the UN's failure to explore and emphasize the primary interconnected role of Goal 7 for the achievement of the MDGs overall. Goal 7 seeks "environmental sustainability"—and achieving this particular goal is the bedrock for attaining most of the targets of the other seven goals. Without an intact and productive natural environment and its life-supporting global and regional systems and processes (such as climatic conditions, ocean vitality, ecosystem functioning, and freshwater circulation), the prospects are diminished for food production, safe drinking water adequate household and community energy sources, stability of infectious disease agents, and protection from natural environmental disasters.

The subsequent treatment by the UN of Goal 7 in relation to its health implications has been rather superficial, and mostly in relation to familiar, localized, environmental health hazards. For example, the UN's 2007 report on the MDGs focuses particularly on how Goal 7 relates to child diarrhoeal diseases. It states:

The health, economic and social repercussions of open defecation, poor hygiene and lack of safe drinking water are well documented. Together they contribute to about 88 per cent of the deaths due to diarrhoeal diseases—more than 1.5 million—in children under age five. Infestation of intestinal worms caused by open defecation affects hundreds of millions of predominantly school-aged children, resulting in reduced physical growth, weakened physical fitness and impaired cognitive functions. Poor nutrition contributes to these effects.[2]

More encouraging is the recent, wider-visioned approach taken by the UN Millennium Project, undertaken for the Commission on Sustainable Development.[3] This project's definition of "environmental sustainability" refers explicitly to the health impacts of environmental changes, and states as follows:

Achieving environmental sustainability requires carefully balancing human development activities while maintaining a stable environment that predictably and regularly provides resources such as freshwater, food, clean air, wood, fisheries and productive soils and that protects people from floods, droughts, pest infestations and disease.[4]

Notes

1. UN Secretary General, Millennium Development Goals (New York. United Nations, 2000), http://www.un.org/millenniumgoals/goals.html (accessed 23 August 2007).

2. United Nations, *The Millennium Development Goals Report 2007* (New York: United Nations, 2007).

3. J. Sachs and J. McArthur, "The Millennium Project: A Plan for Meeting the Millennium Development Goals," *Lancer* 365, no. 9456 (2005): 347–53.

4. Y. K. Nayarro, J. McNeely, D. Melnick, R. R. Sears, and G. Schmidt-Traub, *Environment and Human Wellbeing: A Practical Strategy* (New York: UN Millennium Project Task Force on Environmental Sustainability, 2005).

economic development, health care systems, and public health programs—and not on the fundamental health-supporting role of the natural environment and its ecosystem services.

The report noted the success of some relatively poor nations and provinces, such as China, Sri Lanka, and Kerala State in India, in lowering infant mortality and improving population health by investing in education (especially for girls), establishing primary health clinics, and enacting other health-care programs. The report extended this analysis, citing the history of the well-documented mortality decline in the industrial world—which preceded the advent of modern drugs and medical care, deriving instead from betterment of nutrition, housing, and hygiene. Progressive policies, strong social institutions, and innovative health care and public health protection (especially against infectious diseases), without generalized gains in national wealth, the report's authors said, can be sufficient to raise population health markedly.

This important insight, though, makes no explicit reference to the role of wider environmental conditions. While the control of mosquito populations with window-screens and insecticides certainly confers some health protection, for example, land-use practices, surface water management, biodiversity (frogs and birds eat mosquitoes), and climatic conditions can affect mosquito ecology and mosquito-borne disease transmission more profoundly. The issue must be tackled at both levels.

In fairness, understanding the patterns and determinants of human population health within a wider ecological frame has been impeded by strong cultural and intellectual undercurrents. The rise of modern western science and medicine, in concert with the contemporary ascendancy of neo-liberalism and individualism, has recast our views of health and disease in primarily personal terms. The Christian biblical notion from two thousand years ago of the Four Horsemen of the Apocalypse as the major scourges of population health and survival—war, conquest, famine, and pestilence—has been replaced by today's prevailing model of health and disease as predominantly a function of individual-level consumer behaviors, genetic susceptibility, and access to modern health care technologies.

In addition to this cultural misshaping of our understanding, our increasing technological sophistication has created the illusion that we no longer depend on nature's "goods and services" for life's basic necessities. In this first decade of the twenty-first century, however, we are being forcibly reminded of that fundamental dependence. Hence, a repeat WCED report, written now, would give much higher priority to the relationship between biosphere, environmental processes, human biological health, and survival.

Footprints, Environmental Conditions, and Human Well-being

It is interesting that the WCED report was being drafted at about the time when, according to recent assessments, the demands and pressures of the global human population were first over-reaching the planet's carrying capacity.[11]

In the time since the publication of the report, the "ecological footprint" has become a familiar concept. For any grouping of persons, it measures the amount of Earth's surface required to provide their materials and food and to absorb their wastes. Collectively, humankind reached a point in the mid-1980s when it began to exceed the limit of what Earth could supply and absorb on a sustainable basis. Since then, the human population has moved from having a precariously balanced environmental budget that left nothing in reserve to a situation today in which we are attempting to survive on a substantial, growing,

overdraft: our global standard-of-living is estimated to be at the level that requires approximately 1.3 Earths (see Table).[12] We are therefore consuming and depleting natural environmental capital. This explains the accruing evidence of climate change, loss of fertile soil, freshwater shortages, declining fisheries, biodiversity losses and extinctions. This is not a sustainable trajectory, and it is what, generically, the WCED report exhorted the world to avoid.

In the 1980s, there was more ambivalence about the population component of the "footprint" concept. The absolute annual increments in human numbers were at a historical high, and many demographers and some enlightened policymakers were concerned that population growth needed constraining. That view faced an emergent western political ethos that eschewed family planning, abortion counseling, and governmental intervention. In the upshot, population growth has begun to slow in a majority of countries. Meanwhile, this is being offset by the rapid rise in wealth and consumption in many larger developing countries, including China, India, Brazil, and Mexico.

This planet simply cannot support a human population of 8 to 10 billion living at the level of today's high-income country citizens. Each of those citizens, depending on their particular country, needs 4 to 9 hectares of Earth's surface to provide materials for their lifestyle and to absorb their wastes. Meanwhile, India's population of 1.2 billion has to get by with less than 1 hectare per person. With an anticipated world population of 8 to 10 billion living within Earth's limits, there would be no more than about 1.5 hectares of ecological footprint per average-person—and this arithmetic would limit the resources available for other species. To comply equitably with this limit will necessitate radical changes in value systems and social institutions everywhere.

Global Environment: Emerging Evidence

The Brundtland Commission foresaw at least some of the impending serious erosion of large-scale environmental resources and systems. Indeed, the WCED report judged that by early in the twenty-first century, climate change might have increased average global temperatures sufficiently to displace agricultural production areas, raise sea levels (and perhaps flood coastal cities), and disrupt national economies. This apparently has not yet happened, although very recent scientific reports point strongly to an acceleration in the climate change process,[13] as the global emissions of carbon dioxide from fossil-fuel combustion and of other greenhouse gases from industrial and agricultural activities alter the global climate faster than previously expected.

Several other adverse environmental trends have emerged since 1987. Accessible oil stocks may now be declining—thereby stimulating an (ill-judged) scramble to divert food-grain production into biofuel production as an alternative source of liquid energy.[14] It has also become apparent that human actions are transforming the global cycles of various elements other than carbon, particularly nitrogen, phosphorus, and sulfur.[15] Human agricultural and industrial activity now generates as much biologically activated nitrogen (nitrogenous

Table 1 Changes in Key Global Indicators of Environment and Population Health (1987–2007)

	1987 (1985–1989)	2007 (2005–2009)	Comments
World population size	4.9 billion	6.7 billion	Slight reduction in absolute annual increment
Annual population growth rate	1.7%	1.2%	
Fertility rate (births/woman)	3.4	2.4	
Percent over age 65 years	6%	8%	Low-income countries have increased from 4% to 5.5%
Life expectancy, years	65	68	
Maternal mortality (per 100,000 births)	430	400	
Under 5 mortality, per 1,000 births	115	70	
Infant mortality, per 1,000 births	68	48	
Primary schooling	~60%	82%	See also Figure 1
Malnutrition prevalence	870 million	850 million	Recent increase, relative to the turn of century (~ 820 million)
Child stunting, less than age 5, prevalence	~ 30%	25%	Down from 35% circa 1950, but a persistent and serious problem in sub-Saharan Africa (highest prevalence) and South Asia
HIV/AIDS, prevalent cases	10 million	40 million	
AIDS deaths per year	~ 0.2 million	3.2 million	
Lack safe drinking water	1.3 billion (27%)	1.1 billion (15%)	Percent of world population shown in brackets
Lack sanitation	2.7 billion (54%)	2.6 billion (40%)	Percent of world population shown in brackets
CO_2 atmospheric concentration	325 parts per million	385 parts per million	Approx 0.5% rise per year, currently accelerating. (Pre-industrial concentration 275 parts per million)
Increase in average global temperature relative to 1961–1990 baseline	0.1 degrees Celsius	0.5 degrees Celsius	Warming faster at high latitude, especially in northern hemisphere
Global ecological footprint	1.0 planet Earths	1.3 planet Earths	Estimate of number of planet Earths needed to supply, sustainably, the world population's energy, materials and waste disposal needs

Source: Compiled from various international agency reports, databases, and scientific papers.

compounds such as ammonia) as do lightning, volcanic activity, and nitrogen-fixation on the roots of wild plants. Meanwhile, worldwide land degradation, freshwater shortages, and biodiversity losses are increasing. Those environmental problems were all becoming evident in the mid-1980s and were duly referred to in the WCED report, albeit without particular connection to considerations of human health.

Some other large-scale environmental stresses, however, were not evident in the 1980s. The scientific community had not anticipated the acidification of the world's oceans caused by absorption of increasingly abundant atmospheric carbon dioxide. This acidification—global average ocean pH has declined by a little over 0.1 points during the past several decades—endangers

the calcification processes in the tiny creatures at the base of the marine food web. Nor was much attention paid to the prospect of loss of key species in ecosystems, such as pollinating insects (especially bees). Both those processes are now demonstrably happening, further jeopardizing human capital development, poverty alleviation, and good health.

During 2001–2006, the Millennium Eco-system Assessment (MA) was conducted as a comprehensive international scientific assessment with processes similar to those of IPCC. The MA documented the extent to which recent human pressures have accelerated the decline of stocks of many environmental assets, including changes to ecosystems.[15] The MA also projected likely future trends. This assessment documented how several other globally significant environmental graphs peaked in the mid-1980s. On land, the annual per capita production of cereal grains peaked and has subsequently drifted sideways and, recently, downwards. The harvest from the world's ocean fisheries also peaked at that time and has subsequently declined slowly—albeit with compensatory gains from aquaculture. These emergent negative trends in food-producing capacity jeopardize attempts to reduce hunger, malnutrition, and child stunting—a key target area of the Millennium Development Goals (see the box on next page).

The WCED report, if rewritten today, would presumably take a more integrative and systems-oriented approach to the topic of environmental sustainability and would incorporate greater awareness of the risks posed to human well-being and health.

Trends in Human Capital and Population Health

As discussed, the original UN resolution calling for the WCED report referred ambiguously to "resources." Within the overarching environmental context of the commission, the intended reference of that word may well have been to environmental resources (such as oil, strategic and precious metals, water supplies, etc.). Interestingly, the WCED treated the word as referring primarily to *human* resources in chapter 4, titled "Population and Human Resources."

The global population was 4.9 billion at the time the WCED report was published, and now exceeds 6.7 billion. It continues to increase by more than 70 million persons annually. Because overall fertility rates have declined a little faster than was previously expected, the current "medium" UN projection for population growth by 2050 is for a total of approximately 9.1 billion.[16] Most of that increase will occur in the low-income countries, predominantly in rapidly expanding cities.

Population growth necessarily increases demands on the local environment. But as the WCED report correctly argued, "the population issue is not solely about numbers."[17] Population size, density, and movement are part of a larger set of pressures on the environment. In some regions, resource degradation occurs because of the combination of poverty and the farming of thinly populated drylands and forests. Elsewhere, per-person levels of consumption and waste generation are the critical drivers of environmental stress. Extrapolation of current global economic trends foreshadows a potential five- to tenfold increase in economic activity by 2050. But this looks increasingly unachievable without radical changes in world technological choices and economic practices. The current experience of China is salutary in this regard: that country's rapid economic growth is engendering huge problems of freshwater supply, air quality, environmental toxins in food, desertification of western provinces—and, now, the world's largest national contribution to greenhouse gas emissions.

Is there an upside to population? "People," stated the WCED report, "are the ultimate resource. Improvements in education, health, and nutrition allow them to better use the resources they command, to stretch them further."[18] How have we progressed since 1987 in providing these improvements?

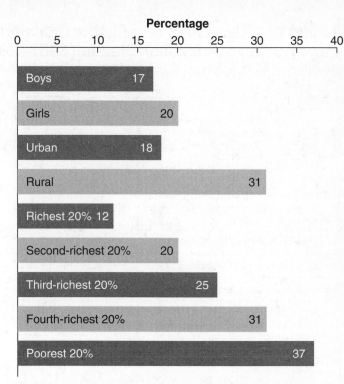

Figure 1 Children of primary school age not in school, by sex, place of residence, and household wealth, 2005

Source: United Nations, *Millennium Development Goals Report 2007* (New York: United Nations, 2007), http://www.un.org/millenniumgoals/goals.html (accessed 23 August, 2007).

Access to primary schooling has increased since 1987 (see Table 1). In particular, the proportion of young girls completing primary school has increased (starting from a lower base than for boys). Figure 1 on this page shows current proportions of the world's children not in primary schooling by key categories. Impediments persist in the form of poverty, parental illiteracy, civil war, and Islamic extremism (banning female education).

Beyond environmental stresses and deficits, the task of improving population health faces other, systemic difficulties. As my colleague C. D. Butler and I wrote last year:

> The gap between rich and poor, both domestically and internationally, has increased substantially in recent decades. Inequality between countries has weakened the United Nations and other global organisations and institutions. Foreign aid has declined, replaced by claims that market forces and the removal of trade-distorting subsidies will reduce poverty and provide public goods, including health care and environmental stability.[19]

Hunger and malnutrition persist at high levels (see box). Famines in Africa remain frequent, and 300 million people in India are undernourished. Further, the almost 50 percent prevalence of underweight children in sub-Saharan Africa and South Asia causes widespread stunting of growth, intellectual development, and energy levels. Yet elsewhere, hundreds of millions of people in all continents are overfed and, via obesity, at increased risk of diabetes and heart disease.

Over the past two decades, demographic and epidemiological transitions have become less orderly than was anticipated

Recent Trends in Population Health

Human health experienced unprecedented gains last century. Globally, average life expectancy approximately doubled from around 35 years to almost 70 years.[1] Rises in life expectancy have slowed a little in recent years in high-income countries. Meanwhile, rises are continuing (from a lower base) in much of the rest of the world. However, the regional picture is very uneven, and some divergence has occurred. The rise in life expectancy has stalled in much of sub-Saharan Africa, various ex-Soviet countries, North Korea, and Iraq (see the figure on the next page). Meanwhile, health inequalities persist both between and within countries and reflect, variously, differences in economic circumstance, literacy, social institutions, and political regimen.

Improved food supply is the likely cause of much of the health gain in modern western populations. The second agricultural revolution, which began in eighteenth-century Europe, brought mechanization, new cultivars, and, eventually, fossil fuel power. Consequently, the millennia-old pattern of subsistence crises diminished and then disappeared. The greater security and abundance of food apparently explains why adult males in northern European countries have grown around 10 centimeters taller and 20–30 kilograms heavier than their eighteenth-century predecessors.[2] Others have argued that improved food quality and safety raised the resistance of better-nourished persons to infectious diseases.[3]

Despite these gains, an estimated 850 million persons remain malnourished. In absolute terms, that figure has grown since the time of the WCED report, including over the past decade.[4] Meanwhile, it has become increasingly evident in both high-income and lower-income countries that an abundance of food energy, especially in the form of refined and selectively produced energy-dense (high fat, high sugar) foods, poses various serious risks to health.

In the 1980s, the general assumption was that these non-communicable diseases appear in the later stages of economic development and would increase with further gains in wealth and modernity. However it has become clear in the past two decades that these diseases, particularly heart disease, hypertensive stroke, and type 2 diabetes, are increasing markedly in lower-income populations as they undergo urbanization, and dietary change. The burden of cardiovascular disease—which accounts for around 30 percent of all deaths in today's world—will continue this shift to low- and middle-income countries. This, plus the persistent infectious disease burden, particularly in poorer subpopulations, will further increase global health inequalities.[5]

Notes

1. A. J. McMichael, M. McKee, V. Shkolnikov, and T. Vaikonen, "Mortality Trends and Setbacks: Global Convergence or Divergence?" *Lancet* 363, no. 9415, (2004): 1155–59.

2. R. W. Fogel, *The Escape from Hunger and Premature Death, 1700–2100: Europe, American and the Third World* (Cambridge: Cambridge University Press, 2004).

3. T. McKeown, R. G. Brown, and R. Record, "An Interpretation of the Modern Rise of Population in Europe," *Population Studies* 26 no. 3 (1972): 345–82.

4. Food and Agriculture Organization of the United Nations (FAO), *The State of Food Insecurity in the World 2004* (Rome: FAO, 2005).

5. M. Ezzati et al., "Rethinking the 'Diseases of Affluence' Paradigm: Global Patterns of Nutritional Risks in Relation to Economic Development." *PLoS Medicine* 2, no.5 (2005), e133.doi.10.1371/journal.pmed.0020133.

by conventional demographic models. There has been considerable divergence between countries in trends in death rates (life expectancy) and fertility rates. National health trends (see box), particularly in poor and vulnerable populations, are falling increasingly under the shadow of climate change and other adverse environmental trends.

In many, but not all low-income countries, fertility rates have declined faster than might have been predicted. However, in some countries (such as East Timor, Nigeria, and Pakistan) fertility remains high (4–7 children per woman). In some regions, the fertility decline has led to an economically and socially unbalanced age structure, especially in China, where in the wake of their "one-child policy," the impending dependency ratio is remarkably high—many fewer young adults will have to provide economic support for an older, longer-living generation.

In some other countries, population growth has declined substantially because of rapid falls in life expectancy.[20] Russia and parts of sub-Saharan Africa have very different demographic characteristics, and yet common elements may underlie their downward trends in life expectancy. Both regions lack public goods for health.[21] In Russia there is a lack of equality, safety, and public health services—and many men have lost status and authority following the collapse of the Communist party structure. Meanwhile, in a number of sub-Saharan African countries, there is serious corruption in government, deficient governance structures, food insecurity, and inadequate public health services.

The conventional assumption, also evident in the WCED report, has been that a health dividend will flow from poverty alleviation. However, it is becoming clear that those anticipated health gains are likely to be lower because of the now-worldwide rise of various non-communicable diseases, including those due to obesity, dietary imbalances, tobacco use, and urban air pollution.[22]

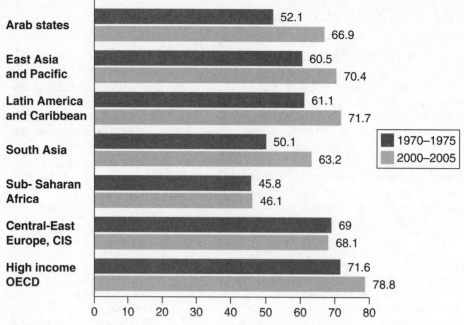

Changes in life expectancy by region, over the past three decades

Note: Differences are marked between regions—especially the lack of gains in sub-Saharan Africa and the central and eastern European (including ex-Soviet) countries.

Source: Based on M. Marmot, "Health in an Unequal World," *Lancet* 368, no. 9552 (2006): 2081–94.

Conclusion

The WCED was commissioned to examine critically the relationship between environmental resource use and sustainable development and to propose solutions for the tensions between environment (including the pressures of population growth and urbanization) and development. A prime task for the commission was to formulate a "global agenda for change" within the frame of ecologically sustainable development, while recognizing the aspirational goals of people and communities everywhere.[23]

During the time that the commission was developing its report, a widely held view, reinforced by the Green Revolution successes of the 1970s and early 1980s, was that continuing population growth need not have adverse environmental impacts. The commission was hesitant to embrace that view, which has recently been re-evaluated,[24] with renewed recognition of the adverse effects of rapid population growth, especially in developing countries, on both social and environmental conditions.[25]

In the 1980s, national governments and multilateral agencies began to see that economic development issues could not be separated from environment issues. Many forms of development erode the environmental resource base (including forests, fertile soils, and coastal zones) necessary for sustained development. And conversely, environmental degradation can jeopardize economic development. The WCED report rightly emphasized the futility of addressing environmental problems without alleviating poverty and international inequality. The report also recognized the needs for stronger social structures and legal processes to deal with tensions over environmental

commons, and for more enlightened public agency structures at the international level to address these issues. It advocated partnerships with the private sector—a sector in which there is now a growing recognition that business-as-usual is no longer an option.

Those formulations remain important and valid, but they are an incomplete basis for future strategic policy. They overlook the fundamental role that sustaining an intact biosphere and its component systems plays in enabling the social and human developmental processes that can reduce poverty, undernutrition, unsafe drinking water, and exposures to endemic and epidemic infectious diseases. The report, if updated today, would seek a better balance between these sets of relationships.

The idea of "ecologically sustainable development" was, in the latter 1980s, ahead of its time. We had, then, neither the evidence nor the insight to know just how fundamental that framework was to achieving the other human goals that would be embraced over the next two decades. Today, the ongoing growth of the global population and—with economic development and rising consumer expectations—the increasingly great environmental impact of that population means that we may be less than one generation away from exhausting much of the biosphere's environmental buffering capacity.[13] Unless we can constrain our excessive demands on the natural world, the demographic and epidemiological transitions (faltering in some regions) will be further affected and human fulfillment will thus be eroded.

Twenty years on from the report of the World Commission on Environment and Development, we can see additional layers to the environment challenge that were little understood in the 1980s. Clearly, some fundamental changes are needed in how we live, generate energy, consume materials, and dispose of wastes. Population arithmetic will impose a further dimension of challenge: 4.8 billion in 1987; 6.7 billion in 2007; perhaps 8 billion by 2027. Beyond that, the numbers and outcomes will be influenced by what current and future "Brundtland reports" formulate, and how seriously and urgently we and our governments take their formulations and recommendations.

Notes

1. World Commission on Environment and Development, *Our Common Future* (Cambridge, UK, and New York: Cambridge University Press, 1987).

2. A. C. Kelley, "The Population Debate in Historical Perspective: Revisionism Revised," in N. Birdsall, A. C. Kelley, and S. W. Sinding, eds., *Population Matters: Demographic Change, Economic Growth, and Poverty in the Developing World* (Oxford, UK: Oxford University Press, 2001), 24–54.

3. P. McMichael, *Development and Social Change: A Global Perspective* (Thousand Oaks, California: Pine Forge Press, 2004).

4. A. J. McMichael, M. McKee, V. Shkolnikov, and T. Valkonen, "Mortality Trends and Setbacks: Global Convergence or Divergence?" *Lancet* 363, no. 9415 (2004): 1155–59; and R. Eckersley, "Is Modern Western Culture a Health Hazard?" *International Journal of Epidemiology* 35, no 5 (2006): 252–58.

5. United Nations, "Process of Preparation of the Environmental Perspective to the Year 2000 and Beyond," General Assembly Resolution 38/161, 19 December 1983.

6. WCED, note 1 above, page 1.

7. G. H. Brundtland, speech given at the launch of the WCED report, Oslo, Norway, 20 March 1987.

8. D. G. Victor, "Recovering Sustainable Development," *Foreign Affairs 85*, no. 1 (January/February 2006): 91–103.

9. WCED, note 1 above, page 98.

10. Intergovernmental Panel on Climate Change, *Climate Change. The IPCC Scientific Assessment* (Cambridge, UK: Cambridge University Press, 1990).

11. Ibid.; and C. M. Wackernagel et al., "Tracking the Ecological Overshoot of the Human Economy," *Proceedings of the National Academy of Sciences* 99, no. 14 (2002): 9266–71.

12. Worldwide Fund for Nature International (WWF), *Living Planet Report 2006* (Gland, Switzerland: WWF, 2006), http://assets.panda.org/dowloads/living_planet_report.pdf (accessed 23 Aug 2007).

13. S. Rahmstorf et al., "Recent Climate Observations Compared to Projections," *Science* 316, no. 5825 (4 May 2007): 709.

14. See R. L. Naylor et al., "The Ripple Effect: Biofuels, Food Security, and the Environment," *Environment* 49, no. 9 (November 2007): 30–43.

15. Millennium Ecosystem Assessment, *Ecosystems and Human Wellbeing. Synthesis* (Washington, DC: Island Press, 2005).

16. UN Department of Economic and Social Affairs, Population Division: http://esa.un.org/unpp/p2k0data.asp (accessed Nov 1, 2007).

17. WCED, note 1 above, page 95.

18. WCED, note 1 above, page 95. This statement has faint resonance with the ideas of the late U.S. economist Julian Simon, whose book *The Ultimate Resource* made the tendentious argument that the more people on Earth the greater the probability of occurrence of important new ideas. J. L. Simon, *The Ultimate Resource* (Princeton, NJ: Princeton University Press, 1981).

19. A. J. McMichael and C. D. Butler, "Emerging Health Issues: The Widening Challenge for Population Health Promotion," *Health Promotion International* 21, no. 1 (2006): 15–24.

20. McMichael, McKee, Shkolnikov, and Valkonen, note 4 above.

21. R. Smith, R. Beaglehole, D. Woodward, and N. Drager, eds., *Global Public Goods for Health* (Oxford: Oxford University Press, 2003).

22. M. Ezzati et al., "Rethinking the 'Diseases of Affluence' Paradigm: Global Patterns of Nutritional Risks in Relation to Economic Development," *Plos Medicine* 2, no. 5 (2005): e133.

23. Brundtland, note 7 above.

24. Kelley, note 2 above.

25. M. Campbell, J. Cleland, A. Ezeh, and N. Prata, "Return of the Population Growth Factor," *Science* 315, no. 5818 (2 February 2007): 1501–2.

ANTHONY J. MCMICHAEL is a professor at the National Centre for Epidemiology and Population Health (NCEPH) at Australia National University in Canberra. From 2001 to 2007, he was director of NCEPH, where he has led the development of a program of epidemiological research on the environmental influences on immune disorders, particularly autoimmune diseases such as multiple sclerosis. Meanwhile, he has continued his pioneering research on the health risks of global climate change, developed in conjunction with his central role in the assessment of health risks for the Intergovernmental Panel on Climate Change. His work on climate and environmental change, along with longstanding interests in social and cultural influences on patterns of health and disease, also underlie his interests in understanding the determinants of the emergence and spread of infectious diseases in this seemingly "renaissant" microbial era. He may be contacted at Tony.McMichael@anu.edu.au.

Protecting Climate Refugees

The Case for a Global Protocol

FRANK BIERMANN AND INGRID BOAS

In August 2006, the government of the Maldives organized a meeting of representatives of governments, environmental and humanitarian organizations, and United Nations agencies on an issue that had until then been largely outside the climate policy debate: the protection and resettlement of "climate refugees."[1] For a small island nation like the Maldives, located only few meters above sea level, this question is surely at the heart of its national security, if not national survival. Such low-lying island nations are likely to be the first to suffer from global climate change, and many atolls may disappear or become uninhabitable over the course of the century.

Yet climate-related migration could also evolve into a larger, global crisis far beyond threats to a few island nations. According to some estimates, more than 200 million people might have to give up their homes due to climate change by 2050.[2] Such estimates have a large margin of error[3] and depend on underlying assumptions about population growth, economic development, temperature increase, or the degree and timing of climate change impacts such as sea-level rise. And yet most scenarios agree on a general trend: in this century, global warming may force millions of people—mainly in Asia and Africa—to leave their homes and migrate to other places.

The Intergovernmental Panel on Climate Change's 2007 assessment indicates that climate change will likely include regional increases in the severity and frequency of extreme weather events.[4] In some worst-case scenarios, by 2080, with a global temperature increase of merely 1–2 degrees, storm surges could affect approximately 103 million people each year.[5] Gradual sea-level rise, another major effect of climate change, will threaten low-lying coasts and further increase the damage caused by storm surges.[6] Thousands of small islands will be at risk, and many possibly flooded.[7] If sea levels rise by 1 meter, storm surges could make island nations such as the Maldives, the Marshall Islands, Kiribati, or Tuvalu largely uninhabitable.[8] In addition, droughts and water

scarcity may increase because of global warming. Some studies predict that even under the lowest growth-rate assumptions, a world 1–2 degrees warmer could lead to water shortages for 700–1,500 million people.[9] Hundreds of millions of people who depend for their water supply on glacier melt could experience severe water stress.[10] For instance, increasing water scarcity may become a grim reality facing the nations that lie downstream from the Himalaya-Hindu Kush mountain ranges—a region that encompasses approximately 50 to 60 percent of the world's population.[11]

Asia, Africa, Latin America, and the small island states have the largest populations at risk of becoming climate refugees. Asia is vulnerable because of its highly populated, low-lying coastal regions[12] and high vulnerability to tropical cyclones.[13] A temperature increase of 2–3 degrees could result in 39–812 million South Asians at risk of water stress.[14] Climate refugees just from Bangladesh might outnumber all current refugees worldwide.[15] Water scarcity and drought will also affect millions of Africans.[16] Fourteen African countries experience water scarcity at present. This may increase to 25 countries by 2030.[17] Africa is also highly vulnerable to sea-level rise, notably in the river deltas of Egypt and Nigeria. In Latin America, thousands of people in Venezuela and Uruguay live in areas where the risk of flooding is high, while millions of Guatemalans and Mexicans may face increasing droughts. Water scarcity due to glacier melts in the South American Andes may affect 37 million people in 2010 and 50 million people in 2050, including larger cities such as Quito, Ecuador; La Paz, Bolivia; and Lima, Peru.[18]

Most climate refugees are expected to remain within their home countries,[19] especially when only parts of the country will be affected by climate change. Yet some studies suggest that climate refugees could potentially also cross international borders. For example, the Development, Concepts and Doctrine Centre Global Strategic Trend Programme of the United Kingdom's Ministry of

Defense foresees large migration flows from sub-Saharan Africa toward the Mediterranean, the Middle East, and Europe between 2007 and 2036.[20] The German Advisory Council on Global Change projects mass migration to the United States from the Caribbean islands and Central America and many migration flows within Central America.[21]

Climate Change and the UN Refugee Regime

In light of this looming climate migration crisis, the current refugee protection regime of the United Nations seems poorly prepared. At present, the United Nations High Commissioner for Refugees (UNHCR) deals with merely 10 million refugees.[22] It is doubtful, without major reforms, whether this institution can protect and support a stream of refugees that is possibly 20 times larger. Moreover, its current mandate covers only individual political refugees who flee their countries because of state-led persecution based on race, religion, political opinion, or ethnicity.[23]

As a result, delegates at the Maldives meeting in 2006 proposed an amendment to the 1951 Geneva Convention Relating to the Status of Refugees that would extend the mandate of the UN refugee regime to include climate refugees.[24] Yet such an amendment does not promise to effectively resolve the emerging climate refugee crisis. Indeed, it is highly uncertain such a proposal is even politically feasible. The UN refugee regime is already under constant pressure from industrialized countries that seek restrictive interpretations of its provisions; it is highly unlikely these governments will agree to extend the same level of protection to a new group 20 times larger than those currently under UN oversight and equal to half the population of the European Union.[25] Moreover, extending the current UN refugee regime to include climate refugees will raise difficult moral issues. It will create unnecessary tensions and tradeoffs between the persons protected today under the Geneva Convention and the new additional streams of climate refugees.[26]

More importantly, the proposal of extending the UN refugee regime misses the core characteristics of the climate refugee crisis. Climate refugees do not have to leave their countries because of a totalitarian government. In principle, they still enjoy the protection of their home country's government. The protection of climate refugees is therefore essentially a development issue that requires large-scale, long-term planned resettlement programs for groups of affected people, mostly within their country. Often this will be in concert with adaptation programs for other people who are not evacuated but can still be protected, for instance, through strengthened coastal

defenses. From this standpoint, then, international agencies such as the UN Development Programme (UNDP) and the World Bank are better equipped than the UNHCR to deal with the emerging problem of climate refugees.

A Role for the UN Security Council?

Scenarios of streams of millions of climate refugees have conjured up the risk of violent conflict, both within affected countries and internationally once refugees try to cross borders.[27] Climate migration could thus turn into a "threat to the peace" and international security, a phrase that is at the center of Article 39 of the United Nations Charter that mandates the Security Council to request all types of measures to respond to such threats, including the use of force.[28] Indeed, in April 2007, the council addressed the impacts of climate change on international peace and security. British Foreign Secretary Margaret Beckett, who chaired the session; Papua New Guinea UN Ambassador Robert G. Aisi, who spoke on behalf of the Pacific Islands Forum; and UN Secretary-General Ban Ki-Moon named climate change–induced mass migration as a possible factor that could lead to major conflicts and instability.[29]

Representatives from most developing countries, however, forcefully maintained that the UN Security Council is the wrong institution to deal with climate policy.[30] One concern is that most climate-related migration will occur in Africa, Asia, and Latin America. Allowing the Security Council to exert a strong mandate will thus extend its sway over the internal affairs of developing nations. Yet the council lacks legitimacy in many developing countries because of the special voting power of its five permanent members (China, France, Russia, the United Kingdom, and the United States)—many of which are, at the same time, the largest emitters of greenhouse gases. Moreover, it is dubious what the Security Council could initiate that could not be done by other institutions such as the UN Framework Convention on Climate Change or intergovernmental agencies such as the UNDP and the UN Environment Programme (UNEP). The core function of the Security Council is the preservation of international peace, mainly through man-dating UN member states to take forceful action against countries whose governments pose a threat to international security and do not comply with international rules and requests from the council. The emerging climate refugee crisis is clearly different in character, so it remains unclear whether a stronger role of the council is needed and what its added benefits would be. And, given that developing countries—including India and China—have clear objections toward any role of the Security Council in climate policy,[31] a stronger involvement seems rather unlikely in any case.

The Case for a Specific Regime on Climate Refugees

For these reasons, dealing with the climate refugee issue calls for a different approach: a separate, independent legal and political regime created under a Protocol on the Recognition, Protection, and Resettlement of Climate Refugees to the United Nations Framework convention on Climate Change. Such a protocol could build on the political support from almost all countries as parties to the climate convention. It could draw on widely agreed principles such as common but differentiated responsibilities and the reimbursement of full incremental costs. It could aid climate refugees by linking their protection with the overall climate regime, including future advances in climate science in defining risks for people in certain regions. Given the increasing pressure from developed nations to integrate advanced developing countries in a global mitigation regime of quantified reduction and limitation objectives, a protocol on the protection of climate refugees could become for developing countries a major bargaining chip in negotiations.

Such an agreement would operate under five principles. First, at the core of the agreement must be the objective of a planned and voluntary resettlement and reintegration of affected populations over periods of many years and decades, as opposed to mere emergency response and disaster relief. Spontaneous flights, often unavoidable during political turmoil or war, can then be prevented for climate change–driven events such as floods.

Second, climate refugees must be seen and treated as permanent immigrants to the regions or countries that accept them. Climate refugees cannot return to their homes as political refugees can (at least in theory).

Third, the climate refugee regime must be tailored not to the needs of individually persecuted people (as in the current UN refugee regime) but of entire groups of people, such as populations of villages, cities, provinces, or even entire nations, as in the case of small island states.

Fourth, an international regime for climate refuges will be targeted less toward the protection of persons outside their states than toward the support of governments, local communities, and national agencies to protect people within their territories. Essentially, the governance challenge of protecting and resettling climate refugees involves international assistance and funding for the domestic support and resettlement programs of affected countries that have requested such support.

Fifth and finally, the protection of climate refugees must be seen as a global problem and a global responsibility. In most cases, climate refugees will be poor, and their own responsibility for the past accumulation of greenhouse gases will be small. By a large measure, the wealthy industrialized countries have caused most past and present greenhouse gas emissions, and it is thus these countries that have the greatest moral, if not legal, responsibility for the victims of global warming. This does not imply transnational migration of 200 million climate refugees into the developed world. Yet it does imply the responsibility of the industrialized countries to do their share in financing, supporting, and facilitating the protection and resettlement of climate refugees.

Regarding terminology, some intergovernmental agencies—such as the International Organization for Migration and the UNHCR—reject the term climate "refugee" because of narrow legal definitions in the post-1945 system. In their view, the term "refugee" should remain limited to an individual recognized under the 1951 Geneva Convention Relating to the Status of Refugees: "a person who is outside his or her country of nationality or habitual residence" and cannot rely on the protection of his or her home state for fear of persecution.[32] As an alternative, some international agencies prefer the notion of "environmentally displaced persons," which is more in line with the UNHCR's "internally displaced persons" designation that carries with it less responsibility on the part of the international community.[33] However, because climate change will cause both transnational and internal flight, the UNHCR's traditional distinction between the two categories of involuntary migration does not seem germane; it is difficult to argue that a global governance mechanism for the protection of people who have lost their homes due to climate change should bestow a different status, and a different term, depending on whether they have crossed a border. Moreover, it does not stand to reason to reserve the stronger term "refugee" for a category of people who earned international attention after 1945 and to invent less appropriate terms—such as "climate-related environmentally displaced persons"—for new categories of people who are forced to leave their homes now, with similar grim consequences. Why should inhabitants of some atolls in the Maldives who require resettlement for reasons of a well-founded fear of being inundated by 2050 receive less protection than others who fear political persecution? Therefore, it seems sensible to continue using the term "climate refugees" and adjust the outdated UN terminology accordingly by allowing for different types of refugees (for instance, political refugees that fall under the 1951 Geneva Convention and climate refugees that fall under the climate refugee protocol proposed here) as well as for different agreements on their protection.

Blueprint of a Protocol on Climate Refugees

How could a protocol on the recognition, protection, and resettlement of climate refugees work in practice?

The Climate Refugee Protocol in Practice: A View from the Future

How would a protocol on the recognition, protection, and resettlement of climate refugees work in practice? Assume a country "Lowtidia" has large population centers in flat river deltas as well as a number of smaller low-lying islands under its jurisdiction. Assume further that by 2050, global warming has raised the sea level and increased the frequency of storm surges in this region. Severe tropical cyclones may have wrecked many of the islands and delta areas of Lowtidia, destroying fields, polluting freshwater resources, and seriously damaging infrastructure and settlements. Many people may have perished in storms that have become more frequent. Eventually, the government of Lowtidia, which is a party to the climate refugee protocol, files a formal request to the executive committee of the protocol, demanding the international recognition of the populations of two coastal provinces and 10 atolls as climate refugees. In addition, Lowtidia requests financial and technical support for the resettlement of the affected populations within its own territory from the Climate Refugee Protection and Resettlement Fund.

The executive committee of the protocol would take immediate action according to the rules of the protocol. First, scientific and technical advice is requested by the relevant advisory bodies, including special working groups of the Intergovernmental Panel on Climate Change and a number of UN agencies. Based on the situation in Lowtidia and expected further climate changes, the executive committee decides that parts of the two river delta provinces can still be protected by increased coastal defenses with financial and technical support through the adaptation fund and related support mechanisms of the UN climate convention.

However, other parts of the river delta provinces, as well as all the islands, are deemed too difficult to protect in the long term. The executive committee therefore decides to recognize all people who are legal residents of these areas as climate refugees under the protocol and lend them the support that the protocol provides. This decision is taken by the simple majorities of the representatives of donor countries and developing countries in the executive committee and later reconfirmed by the conference of the parties to the climate refugee protocol.

As a consequence, a "Lowtidia Working Group" is set up that includes representatives of the Lowtidia government; local governments of the affected provinces and islands; local civil society; and the UN Development Programme, the UN Environment Programme (which may by then have been transformed into a World Environment Organization), a number of other relevant UN agencies, and the World Bank. The Lowtidia Working Group decides on retraining programs; the construction of new infrastructures on the mainland for the fishing fleet of the islanders; emergency assistance for the transition period; and developing a number of specific projects, including the purchase of land on the higher mainland of Lowtidia. A few years after the decision under the climate refugee protocol, the first inhabitants of the islands would break up their settlements and relocate to the mainland to their new villages behind newly erected coastal defenses. All costs of the relocation are borne by a special program budget from the Climate Refugee Protection and Resettlement Fund, which is regularly replenished through international levies on air and maritime transportation.

International List of Affected Populations

The most important governance mechanism would be a list of specified administrative areas (such as villages, islands, or districts) under the jurisdiction of member states with populations that have been determined in need of relocation due to climate change or threatened by having to relocate due to climate change. Any state party to the protocol—and in fact only state parties—would be entitled to propose areas under their jurisdiction for inclusion on the list of affected areas. The protocol would provide for an executive committee on the recognition, protection, and resettlement of climate refugees that would function under the authority of the meeting of the parties (which could meet back to back with the conference of the parties to the climate convention). In line with the sovereignty principle of the United Nations, the executive committee would determine the inclusion of affected areas, as well as the types of support measures, only upon formal proposal from the government of the affected country. (Thus, in

rare cases of governments that reject international assistance, such as the situation in Myanmar in May this year, the proposed new institution would not be able to help.)

Regarding decisionmaking procedures, the executive committee could include an equal number of affected countries and donor countries, and its decisions could require a double-weighted majority; that is, the simple majority of donor countries and the simple majority of affected countries. This rule would allow both the affected developing countries and the donor countries to hold a collective veto right over the future evolution and implementation of the regime.

If certain groups of people from a number of coastal villages (for example) were included in a list of populations in need of relocation due to climate change, they would gain specific rights and would benefit from the support mechanisms under the protocol. This could include financial support; inclusion in voluntary resettlement programs over several years together with the purchase of new land; retraining and integration programs; and, in the special case of small island states, organized international migration (see the box on this page for an illustration on how the protocol might work).

Since wealthier countries will be able to support their own affected populations, the rights under the protocol should be restricted to inhabitants of developing countries (in technical terms: countries that are not listed in Annex I to the climate convention). For example, the climate refugee protocol would not support the hurricane-affected inhabitants of New Orleans, who can rely in principle on the support of their own (wealthy) country and do not require international financial assistance.

Funding Mechanism

Resettlement of millions of people will require additional and, most likely substantial funds. Institutionally, the best governance mechanism would be a separate fund, which might be called the "Climate Refugee Protection and Resettlement Fund."[34] While one could link the operational aspects of this fund with existing financial mechanisms to increase efficiency, the governance of the fund should be independent and stand under the authority of the meeting of the parties to the climate refugee protocol. To generate the funds needed, the Climate Refugee Protection and Resettlement Fund could be coupled with currently proposed, novel income-raising mechanisms, such as an international air-travel levy.[35] A key question for this new facility will be the amount of funding required by the international community and the funding principle underlying the climate refugees' protection. For mitigation programs under the climate convention, industrialized countries have committed to reimburse developing countries the agreed full incremental costs, a concept originally developed in the 1990 London amendments to the Montreal protocol on the protection of the ozone layer.[36] Similar provisions apply to adaptation.[37] In addition, the climate convention obliges industrialized countries to assist the most vulnerable countries in meeting adaptation costs (Article 4.4) and gives special rights to least developed countries (Article 4.9). This suggests applying the principle of reimbursement of full incremental costs to the protection and resettlement of climate refugees, at least in situations where the causal link with climate change—namely sea-level rise—is undisputed. For other situations in which climate change is only one factor to account for environmental degradation—for example, in the case of water scarcity—a principle of additional funding instead of full reimbursement may be more appropriate. In any case, the costs of the voluntary resettlement and reintegration of millions of people who have

to leave their islands, coastal plains, or arid areas will be substantial—probably in the order of billions of euros over the coming decades. Even if novel mechanisms are introduced, the final responsibility for funding will rest with the governments of industrialized countries and possibly wealthier developing countries.

Implementation through Existing UN Agencies

A climate refugee protocol should not create new international bureaucracies; the resettlement of millions of climate refugees over the course of the century should be the task of existing agencies. Given the complexity of climate-related flight, the best model will be to mandate not one single agency but rather a network of agencies as implementing agencies of the protocol. A crucial role lies with the UNDP and the World Bank, both of which could serve as implementing agencies for the climate refugee protocol in the planned voluntary resettlement of affected populations. Although it lacks a strong operational mandate, the UNEP may provide further assistance in terms of scientific research and synthesis, information dissemination, legal and political advice, and other core functions of this program. A small coordinating secretariat to the climate refugee protocol would be needed, possibly as a subdivision of the climate secretariat in Bonn. In addition, although it is unlikely to be the main agency given the special characteristics of the climate refugee crisis, the UNHCR should play a role; its expertise in view of emergencies, as well as its legal and technical expertise in dealing with refugee crises, will be indispensable for the protection of climate refugees.

Conclusion

Scientists predict serious impacts of climate change that could compel millions of people to leave their homes beginning sometime in the next decades. Yet the existing institutions and organizations are not sufficiently equipped to deal with this looming crisis. Reforms toward a system of global adaptation governance as part of a larger program toward comprehensive Earth system governance[38] are thus needed. As stated above, some of the possible reform options—extending the definition of refugees under the 1951 Geneva Convention Relating to the Status of Refugees or giving responsibilities to the UN Security Council—are less promising and might even be counterproductive. A better solution appears to lie with a new legal instrument specifically tailored for the needs of climate refugees—a Protocol on the Recognition, Protection, and Resettlement of Climate Refugees to the United Nations

Framework Convention on Climate Change, supported by a separate funding mechanism, the Climate Refugee Protection and Resettlement Fund.

The broad predictability of climate change impacts requires and allows preparation and planning. It is crucial, then, that this protocol not be framed in terms of emergency response and disaster relief but in planned and organized voluntary resettlement programs. There is no need to wait for extreme weather events to strike and islands and coastal regions to be flooded. All areas that we cannot protect over the long-term through increased coastal defenses, for practical or economic reasons, need to be included early in long-term resettlement and reintegration programs to make the process acceptable and endurable for the affected people. This, however, calls for early action in terms of setting up effective and appropriate governance mechanisms. The planning for a climate refugee protocol and the related institutional settings cannot wait until 2050 when it might be too late for orderly and organized responses. It must begin now.

Notes

1. See Republic of the Maldives Ministry of Environment, Energy and Water, *Report on the First Meeting on Protocol on Environmental Refugees: Recognition of Environmental Refugees in the 1951 Convention and 1967 Protocol Relating to the Status of Refugees* (Male, Maldives, 14–15 August 2006, on file with authors).

2. See, for example, N. Myers, "Environmental Refugees: A Growing Phenomenon of the 21st Century," *Philosophical Transactions: Biological Sciences* 357, no. 1420 (2002): 609 and 611; and N. Myers and J. Kent, *Environmental Exodus: An Emergent Crisis in the Global Arena* (Washington, DC: Climate Institute, 1995), 149. The 2006 Stern Review maintains that the 150–200 million estimate in Myers and Kent (above) "has not been rigorously tested, but it remains in line with the evidence presented throughout this chapter that climate change will lead to hundreds of millions more people without sufficient water or food to survive or threatened by dangerous floods and increased disease." See N. Stern, *The Stern Review on the Economics of Climate Change* (London: UK Government, 2006), http://www.hm-treasury.gov.uk/independent_reviews/stern_review_economics_climate_change/stern_review_report.cfm (accessed 6 September 2008), 77.

3. For criticism of such estimates, see A. Suhrke, "Environmental Degradation and Population Flows," *Journal of International Affairs* 47, no. 2 (1994): 478; S. Castles, *Environmental Change and Forced Migration: Making Sense of the Debate,* New Issues in Refugee Research Working Paper 70 (Geneva: United Nations High Commissioner for Refugees:, 2002), 2–3; and R. Black, "Environmental Refugees: Myth or Reality?" New Issues in Refugee Research Working Paper 34 (Geneva: United Nations High Commissioner for Refugees (UNHCR), 2002), 2–8.

4. For regional impacts in Africa, Asia, Latin America, and the small island states, see Intergovernmental Panel on Climate Change, *Climate Change Impacts, Adaptation and Vulnerability,* Contribution of Working Group II to the Fourth Assessment Report of the Intergovernmental Panel on Climate Change, edited by M. L. Parry, O. F. Canziani, J. P. Palutikof, P. J. van der Linden, and C. E. Hanson (Cambridge, UK: Cambridge University Press, 2007), chapters 9, 10, 13 and 16. For the effects of climate change on sea-level rise, the severity of tropical cyclones, and the severity and frequency of storm surges, see also German Advisory Council on Global Change, *The Future Oceans: Warming Up, Rising High, Turning Sour* (Berlin: German Advisory Council on Global Change, 2006), 38–39 and 40–43.

5. See R. Warren, N. Amell, R. Nicholls, P. Levy, and J. Price, *Understanding the Regional Impacts of Climate Change,* Tyndall Centre Working Paper 90 (Norwich, UK: Tyndall Centre for Climate Change Research, 2006), 67.

6. See R. J. Nicholls, F. M. J. Hoozemans, and M. Marchand, "Increasing Flood Risk and Wetland Losses Due to Global Sea-Level Rise: Regional and Global Analyses," *Global Environmental Change* 9 (1999): 72.

7. Ibid., page 81; and N. W. Arnell et al., "The Consequences of CO2 Stabilization for the Impacts of Climate Change," *Climatic Change* 53 (2002): 432.

8. See German Advisory Council on Global Change, note 4, pages 46 and 50.

9. See Warren, Arnell, Nicholls, Levy, and Price, note 5, page 20.

10. See T. P. Barnett, J. C. Adam, and D. P. Lettenmaier, "Potential Impacts of a Warming Climate on Water Availability in Snow-dominated Regions," *Nature* 438, no. 7066 (17 November 2005): 303–9.

11. Ibid., page 306.

12. See, for example, Nicholls, Hoozemans, and Marchand, note 6, page 80.

13. Munich Re Group, *Megacities—Megarisks: Trends and Challenges for Insurance and Risk Management* (Munich: Münchner Rückversicherungs-Gesellschaft, 2004), 76.

14. Warren, Arnell, Nicholls, Levy, and Price, note 5, page 18.

15. For example, in Myers, note 2, page 611, it was projected that 26 million climate refugees will come from Bangladesh.

16. See, for example, Warren, Arnell, Nicholls, Levy, and Price, note 5, page 18; and Barnett, Adam, and Lettenmaier, note 10, page 306.

17. Tearfund, *Fleeing the Heat* (Teddington, UK: Tearfund, 2006), 12.

18. For estimates on Egypt and Nigeria, see Myers and Kent, note 2, pages 137, 143, 148, and 149; for estimates on Venezuela and Uruguay, see L. Bijlsma et al., "Coastal Zones and Small Islands," in R. T. Watson, M. C. Zinyowera, and R.H. Moss, eds., *Climate Change 1995—Impacts, Adaptations and Mitigation of Climate Change: Scientific-Technical Analyses* (Cambridge, UK: Cambridge University Press, 1996), 289–324 (cited in R. J. Nicholls, "Case Study on Sea-level Rise Impacts," Organization for Economic Co-operation and Development (OECD) Workshop on the Benefits of Climate Policy: Improving Information for Policy Makers (Paris:

OECD, 2003), 16); for estimates on drought and water scarcity in Latin America, see G. J. Nagy et al., *Understanding the Potential Impact of Climate Change and Variability in Latin America and the Caribbean,* report prepared for N. H. Stern et al., *The Stern Review on the Economics of Climate Change* (London: UK Government, 2006), 10 and 20.

19. German Advisory Council on Global Change, *World in Transition: Climate Change as a Security Risk* (Berlin: German Advisory Council on Global Change, 2007), 118; and Christian Aid, *Human Tide: The Real Migration Crisis* (London: Christian Aid, 2007), 6.

20. UK Development, Concepts and Doctrine Centre (DCDC), *The DCDC Global Strategic Trends Programme 2007–2036,* 3rd edition (Swindon, UK: Crown Copyright/MOD, 2007), http://www.mod.uk/NR/rdonlyres/94AIF45E-A830-49DB-B319-DF68C28D561D/0/strat_trends_17mar07.pdf (accessed 6 September 2008), 29.

21. German Advisory Council on Global Change, note 19, pages 151 and 163.

22. UNHCR, *2006 Global Trends: Refugees, Asylumseekers, Returnees, Internally Displaced and Stateless Persons* (Geneva: UNHCR, 2007), 4–5.

23. J. McGregor. "Climate Change and Involuntary Migration: Implications for Food Security," *Food Policy* 19. no. 2 (1994): 126; and D. Keane, "'The Environmental Causes and Consequences of Migration: .A Search for the Meaning of "Environmental Refugess,'" *Georgetown International Environmental Law Review* 16, no. 2 (2004): 214–15.

24. See Republic of the Maldives, note I.

25. See the discussion in Myers and Kent, note 2, pages 151–53: and McGregor, note 23, page 128.

26. See discussion in McGregor, note 23, page 128; and G. Kibreab. "Environmental Causes and Impact of Refugee Movements: A Critique of the Current Debate." *Disasters* 21, no. 1 (1997): 21.

27. German Advisory Council on Global Chang, note 19. page 174; and DCDC, note 20, pages 78–79.

28. United Nations, *Charter of the United Nations* (New York: United Nations. 1945),. http://www.un.org/aboutun/charter/ (accessed 6 September 2008).

29. United Nations Security Council, "Security Council Holds First-Ever Debate on Impact of Climate Change on Peace, Security, Hearing over 50 Speakers." 5,663rd Meeting of 17 April 2007, United Nations Department of Public Information News and Media Division. For a review of the debate, see F. Sindico, "Climate Change: A Security (Council) Issue?" *Climate Change Law Review* 1 (2007): 29–34.

30. See the various statements from developing country representatives in United Nations Security Council, ibid.

31. United Nations Security Council, note 29 above.

32. General Assembly of the United Nations, 1951 Convention Relating to the Status of Refugees, Geneva, Switzerland, 25 July 1951, Article I.

33. See discussion in Keane, note 23, pages 214–17.

34. See also German Advisory Council on Global Change, which proposed an Environmental Migration Fund, note 19, page 211.

35. See B. Müller and C. Hepburn. *IATAL—An Outline Proposal for an International Air Travel Adaptation Levy* (Oxford, UK: Oxford Institute for Energy Studies, 2006).

36. See F. Biermann, "Financing Environmental Policies in the South: Experiences from the Multilateral Ozone Fund," *International Environmental Affairs* 9, no. 3 (1997): 179–218.

37. Article 4, paragraph 3 of the climate convention reads: "The developed country Parties and other developed Parties included in Annex II shall provide new and additional financial resources . . . including for the transfer of technology, needed by the developing country Parties to meet the agreed full incremental costs of implementing measures that are covered by paragraph 1 of [Article 4] and that are agreed between a developing country Party and the international entity or entities referred to in Article 11, in accordance with that Article." Paragraph 1 of Article 4 includes in section (e) the commitment of developing countries to "cooperate in preparing for adaptation to the impacts of climate change and develop and elaborate appropriate and integrated plans for coastal zone management, water resources and agriculture, and for the protection and rehabilitation of areas, particularly in Africa, affected by drought and desertification, as well as floods." United Nations, *United Nations Framework Convention on Climate Change* (New York: United Nations, 1992).

38. On Earth system governance in general, see E Biermann, "'Earth System Governance' as a Cross-cutting Theme of Global Change Research." *Global Environmental Change* 17, 3–4 (2007): 326–37. See also Earth System Government Project, http://www.earthsystemgovernance.org (accessed 6 September 2008).

FRANK BIERMANN is a professor of political science and environmental policy sciences and head of the Department of Environmental Policy Analysis at the Institute for Environmental Studies, Vrije Universiteit Amsterdam, the Netherlands. He is also director of the Netherlands Research School for the Socio-economic and Natural Sciences of the Environment, director of the European research consortium Global Governance Project, and chair of the Earth System Governance Project under the International Human Dimensions Programme on Global Environmental Change. He has held professional or visiting affiliations with Freie Universität Berlin, German Advisory Council on Global Change, Harvard University, Jawaharlal Nehru University, University of Maryland at College Park, Potsdam Institute for Climate Impact Research, Social Science Research Centre Berlin, Stanford University, and The Energy and Resources Institute. His most recent book is the co-edited volume *Managers of Global Change: The Influence of International Environmental Bureaucracies* (MIT Press, forthcoming 2009). He may be reached at frank.biermann@ivm.vu.nl. **INGRID BOAS** is a researcher with the Department of Environmental Policy Analysis at the Institute for Environmental Studies, Universiteit Amsterdam, the Netherlands. She is also a research fellow with the Global Governance Project and coordinator of the Climate Refugee Policy Forum. In addition, she is currently working on a number of research projects on climate governance, Dutch water management, and the application of participatory research methodologies on the energy policies of Curaçao. She may be reached at ingrid.boas@ivm.vu.nl.

This research has been partially funded by the European Commission (Global Change and Ecosystem Priority of the Sixth Framework Research Programme, Integrated Project "Adaptation and Mitigation Strategies. Supporting European Climate Policy," contract no.

018476).All views expressed are of the authors and not necessarily shared by the European Commission. For valuable suggestions and comments, we are grateful to Harro van Asselt, Steffen Bauer, Klaus Dingwerth, Philipp Pattberg, and Fariborz Zelli, as well as the editors of *Environment*. In addition, Frank Biermann wishes to thank The Energy and Resources Institute, New Delhi, for generous hospitality during a research visit in September and October 2007, when most of his research on this article was undertaken.

More information is available at the Climate Refugee Policy Forum (http://www.glogov.org/?pageid=80), a new initiative set up by the Global Governance Project, a joint program of 12 European research institutions.

Reversal of Fortune

Why Preventing Poverty Beats Curing It

ANIRUDH KRISHNA

L ifting people out of poverty has become a mantra for the world's political leaders. The first U.N. Millennium Development Goal is to halve the number of people whose income is less than $1 per day, currently about 1 billion people. And, in the past decade, millions around the world have been pulled out of poverty by economic growth, effective development aid, and sheer hard work.

Four years ago, I set out to discover which countries—and which local communities—were doing the best job of ending poverty. Using a varied sample of more than 25,000 households in 200 diverse communities in India, Kenya, Peru, Uganda, and the U.S. state of North Carolina, my colleagues and I traced which households have emerged from poverty and attempted to explain their success. At first, the data were very encouraging. In 36 Ugandan communities, 370 households (almost 15 percent of the total) moved out of poverty between 1994 and 2004. In Gujarat, India, 10 percent of a sample of several thousand households emerged from poverty between 1980 and 2003. In Kenya, 18 percent of a sample of households rose out of poverty between 1980 and 2004.

Looking at these figures, one could be forgiven for feeling a sense of satisfaction. But pulling people out of impoverishment is only half the story. Our research revealed another, much darker story: In many places, more families are falling into poverty than are being lifted out. In Kenya, for example, more households, 19 percent, fell into poverty than emerged from it. Twenty-five percent of households studied in the KwaZulu-Natal province of eastern South Africa fell into poverty, but fewer than half as many, 10 percent, overcame poverty in the same period. In Bangladesh, Egypt, Peru, and every other country where researchers have conducted similar studies, the results are the same. In many places, newly impoverished citizens constitute the majority of the poor. It's a harsh fact that calls into question current policies for combating poverty.

All sorts of factors—including financial crises and currency collapse—can push people into poverty. But our research indicates that the leading culprit is poor healthcare. Tracking thousands of households in five separate countries, my colleagues and I found that health and healthcare expenses are the leading cause for people's reversal of fortune. The story of a woman from Kikoni village in Uganda is typical. She and her husband lived relatively well for many years. "Then my husband was sick for 10 years before he died, and all the money that we had with us was spent on medical charges," she said. "My children dropped out of school because we could not pay school fees. Then my husband died. I was left with a tiny piece of land. Now I cannot even get enough food to eat."

Among newly poor households in 20 villages of western Kenya, 73 percent cited ill health and high medical costs as the most important cause of their economic decline. Eighty-eight percent of people who fell into poverty in 36 villages in Gujarat placed the blame on healthcare. In Peru, 67 percent of recently impoverished people in two provinces cited ill health, inaccessible medical facilities, and high healthcare costs. When families are hit by a health crisis, it's often hard to recover. In China, one major illness typically reduces family income by 16 percent. Successive illnesses ensure an even faster spiral into lasting poverty. Surveys in several African and Asian countries show that a combination of ill health and indebtedness has sent tens of thousands of households into poverty, including many that were once affluent. The phenomenon exists in the rich world as well; half of all personal bankruptcies in the United States are due to high medical expenses.

Millions of people are living one illness away from financial disaster, and the world's aid efforts are ill-suited to the challenge. An intense focus on stimulating economic growth isn't enough. Healthcare is not automatically better or cheaper where economic growth rates have been high. In Gujarat, a state in India that has achieved high growth rates for more than a decade, affordable healthcare remains a severe problem, and thousands have fallen into poverty as a result. Healthcare in fast growing Gujarat is no better than in other, often poorer, states of India. Indeed, Gujarat ranked fourth from the bottom among 25 states in terms of proportion of state income spent on healthcare. Perversely, rapid economic growth often weakens existing social safety nets and raises the danger of backsliding. In places as diverse as rural India, Kenya, Uganda, and North Carolina, we observed how community and family support crumbles as market-based transactions overtake traditional networks.

As economic growth helps lift people out of poverty, governments must stand ready to prevent backsliding by providing affordable, accessible, and reliable healthcare. Japan's recent history offers hope that enlightened policy can prevail. At 4 percent, Japan's poverty rate is among the lowest in the world. Sustained economic growth undoubtedly helped, but so too did an entirely different set of policies. Quite early in the country's post-World War II recovery, Japanese officials recognized the critical relationship between illness, healthcare services, and poverty creation, and they responded by implementing universal healthcare as early as the 1950s.

Regrettably, that insight hasn't traveled nearly as well as Japan's many other exports. It's well past time that political leaders put as much effort into stopping the slide into poverty as they do easing the climb out of it.

ANIRUDH KRISHNA is assistant professor of public policy and political science at Duke University.

UNIT 6
Women and Development

Unit Selections

Key Points to Consider

- What are the obstacles to ensuring women's rights?

- In what ways does educating girls contribute to development?

- What accounts for lagging school attendance rates for girls?

- What has been the pattern of progress on women's rights in the Middle East?

- Why are women so much more likely to die in childbirth in the developing world?

- How is the global recession affecting women?

Student Website
www.mhcls.com

Internet References

WIDNET: Women in Development NETwork
  http://www.focusintl.com/widnet.htm
Women Watch/Regional and Country Information
  http://www.un.org/womenwatch/

© Thomas Hartwell/2003

There is widespread recognition of the crucial role that women play in the development process. Women are critical to the success of family planning programs, bear much of the responsibility for food production, account for an increasing share of wage labor in developing countries, are acutely aware of the consequences of environmental degradation, and can contribute to the development of a vibrant, civil society and good governance. Despite their important contributions, however, women lag behind men in access to health care, nutrition, and education while continuing to face formidable social, economic, and political barriers. Women's lives in the developing world are invariably difficult. Often female children are valued less than male offspring, resulting in higher female infant and child mortality rates. In extreme cases, this undervaluing leads to female infanticide.

Those females who do survive face lives characterized by poor nutrition and health, multiple pregnancies, hard physical labor, discrimination, and in some cases violence. Clearly, women are central to any successful population policy. Evidence shows that educated women have fewer and healthier children. This connection between education and population indicates that greater emphasis should be placed on educating women. In reality, female school enrollments are lower than those of males because of state priorities, insufficient family resources to educate both boys and girls, female socialization, and cultural factors. Education is probably the largest single contributor to enhancing the status of women and promoting development, but access to education is still limited for many women. Sixty percent of children worldwide not enrolled in schools are girls.

Education for women leads to improved health, better wages, and greater influence in decision making, which benefits not only women but the broader society as well. Educated women contribute more to their families, are less likely to subject their daughters to female genital mutilation, and are three times less likely to contract HIV.

Women make up a significant portion of the agricultural workforce. They are heavily involved in food production right from planting to cultivation, harvesting, and marketing. Despite their agricultural contribution, women frequently do not have adequate access to advances in agricultural technology or the benefits of extension and training programs. They are also discriminated against in land ownership. As a result, important opportunities to improve food production are lost when women are not given access to technology, training, and land ownership commensurate with their agricultural role.

The industrialization that has accompanied the globalized production has meant more employment opportunities for women, but often these are low-tech, low-wage jobs. The lower labor costs in the developing world that attract manufacturing facilities are a mixed blessing for women. Increasingly, women are recruited to fill these production jobs because wage differentials allow employers to pay women less. On the other hand, expanding opportunities for women in these positions contribute to family income. The informal sector, where jobs are small scale, more traditional, and labor-intensive, has also attracted more women. These jobs are often their only employment option, due to family responsibilities or discrimination.

Women also play a critical role in the economic expansion of developing countries. Nevertheless, women are often the first to feel the effects of an economic slowdown. The consequences of the structural adjustment programs that many developing countries have to adopt have also fallen disproportionately on women. When employment opportunities decline because of austerity measures, women lose jobs in the formal sector and face increased competition from males in the informal sector. Cuts in spending on health care and education also affect women, who already receive fewer of these benefits. Currency devaluations further erode the purchasing power of women. The global economic crisis is only going to worsen the plight of working women. Because of the gender division of labor, women are often more aware of the consequences of environmental degradation. Depletion of resources such as forests, soil, and water are much more likely to be felt by women, who are responsible for collecting firewood and water, and who raise most of the crops. As a result, women are an essential component of successful environmental protection policies, but they are often overlooked in planning environmental projects.

Enhancing the status of women has been the primary focus of several international conferences. The 1994 International Conference on Population and Development (ICPD) focused attention on women's health and reproductive rights, and the crucial role that these issues play in controlling population. The 1995 Fourth World Conference on Women held in Beijing, China, proclaimed women's rights to be synonymous with human rights. Along with the Convention on the Elimination of All Forms of Discrimination against Women, these developments represent a turning point in women's struggle for equal rights, and have prompted efforts to pass legislation at the national level to protect women's rights.

There are indications that women have made progress in some regions of the developing world. The election of Ellen John-Sirleaf as president of Liberia and Africa's first female head of state is the most visible indicator of a trend toward greater political involvement of women in Africa. In the Middle East, the 2002 Arab Human Development Report highlighted the extent to which women in the region lagged behind their counterparts in other parts of the world. While there has been some progress in the region recently, it has been uneven. There remains a wide divergence in the status of women worldwide, but the recognition of the valuable contributions they can make to society is increasing the pressure to enhance their status.

Women's Rights as Human Rights
The Promotion of Human Rights as a Counter-Culture

ZEHRA F. KABASAKAL ARAT

Human rights are rights claimed against the State and society by virtue of being a human being. However, the human rights of most people have been continuously violated all around the world. Since all civilizations have been patriarchal,[1] regardless of the overall human rights conditions maintained in a society, women have been subject to more human rights violations than men. Women constitute the poorest and the least powerful segments of their communities. They are denied equal access to education, job training, employment, leisure time, income, property, health care, public office, decision-making power and freedoms, as well as control over their own body and life.[2] Cultural norms, laws and philosophies, including those that are considered progressive and emancipatory, have usually discriminated against women.

Omission of Women

The ancient Stoics' notion of natural rights, that human beings are created with certain inalienable rights, did not encompass women. When the Christian Church leader St. Thomas Aquinas (c.1225–1274) was exposed to ancient Greek philosophy—largely through the writings of the Muslim philosophers Avicenna (Ibn Sina, 980–1037) and Averroes (Ibn Rushd, 1126–1198) who studied ancient Greek philosophy, reconciled reason with faith and championed equality and religious tolerance—he incorporated natural rights theory into his teaching. However, he ignored Averroes' egalitarian approach that opposed the unequal treatment of sexes and considered the reduction of women's value to child-bearing and rearing as detrimental to the economic advancement of society and thus causing poverty.[3] Instead, Aquinas revived Aristotle's misogynous perception of woman as "misbegotten man" and wondered why God would create woman, a defective creature, in the first production of things;[4] while other church leaders later questioned if women had souls, that is, if they were fully human.

In modern times, progressive philosophers, such as Jean-Jacques Rousseau (1712–1778), could promote political freedoms and rights, but reject the notion of equality of the sexes. The revolutionary fervour of the eighteenth century that opposed oppression led to the French Declaration of the Rights of Man and Citizen (1789). However, the articulation of human rights in this document, which continued to inspire people all over the world for centuries, could not escape sexism prevalent at the time and omitted women. Nevertheless, a few elite women, such as French playwright and essayist Olympe de Gouges (1748–1793) and English philosopher Mary Wollstonecraft (1759–1797), raised their objections and defended women's rights by issuing The Declaration of the Rights of Woman (1790) and A Vindication of the Rights of Women (1791), respectively. The collaboration of Harriet Taylor Mill (1807–1858) with her husband John Stuart Mill (1806–1873) resulted in writings that advocated women's rights and political equality.[5]

Yet, gender biases prevailed throughout the twentieth century. Even members of the Commission that drafted the 1948 Universal Declaration of Human Rights were willing to employ the word "man" in reference to the holder of the rights. When the Soviet delegate, Vladimir Koretsky, objected to using the words "all men" as "historical atavism, which preclude us from an understanding that we men are only one half of the human species", the Commission Chair, Eleanor Roosevelt, defended the wording by arguing: [in English] "When we say 'all men are brothers', we mean that all human beings are brothers and we are not differentiating between men and women."[6] Thus, the language was maintained for some time. The final draft mostly employed the gender-neutral terms of "human being", "everyone" and "person", and the Preamble included a specific reference to the "equal rights of men and women", thanks largely to the efforts of two female Commission members, Hansa Mehta of India and Minerva Bernardino of the Dominican Republic.[7]

However, the Universal Declaration and the subsequent human rights documents adopted by the United Nations and other intergovernmental organizations have continued to employ the nominative and possessive pronouns "he" and "his", in line with the established tradition and understanding that male nouns or pronouns would stand for the female ones as well. Despite their clearly and repeatedly stated anti-discrimination clauses, which specify that sex as a characteristic or status cannot be used as grounds for discrimination or for denial of human rights, documents issued by the United Nations fell short of ensuring that human rights are equally applicable to both sexes.[8] Gender gaps were visible even in the United Nations, which did not have women in high office posts, as they were concentrated in clerical and lower-paying jobs, thus maintaining occupational segregation. Starting in the 1970s, however, some significant steps towards addressing gender disparities have been taken by various intergovernmental and non-governmental organizations and government agencies.

The Cedaw: An International Treaty for Women's Rights

A very important stimulus was the UN General Assembly resolution of December 1972, declaring 1975 as the International Women's Year. In 1975, the first UN world conference on women, held in Mexico City, declared 1976 to 1985 as the United Nations Decade for Women. The intensive efforts and actions undertaken during the Decade included organizing more conferences on women, the creation of specialized agencies, such as the United Nations Development Fund for Women (UNIFEM) and the UN International Research and Training Institute for the Advancement of Women (INSTRAW), elevating the Branch of the Advancement of Women to a "Division" status and putting women's rights and concerns on the agenda of other conferences and organizations. Arguably, the most important development that took place during the Decade was the preparation of the Convention on the Elimination of All Forms of Discrimination against Women (CEDAW), which was adopted by the Assembly in 1979.

CEDAW was the culmination of a long process, but was given impetus in 1973 by the UN Commission on the Status of Women (CSW). In its working paper, the Commission stated that neither the Declaration on the Elimination of Discrimination Against Women (1967) nor the legally binding human rights treaties had been effective in advancing the status of women. It also argued for a single comprehensive convention that would legally bind States to eliminate discriminatory laws, as well as de facto discrimination. With 30 articles organized in six parts, CEDAW defines "discrimination against women" in its first article: "For the purposes of the present Convention, the term 'discrimination against women' shall mean any distinction, exclusion or restriction made on the basis of sex, which has the effect or purpose of impairing or nullifying the recognition, enjoyment or exercise by women, irrespective of their marital status, on a basis of equality of men and women, of human rights and fundamental freedoms in the political, economic, social, cultural, civil or any other field."

The subsequent 15 articles of the Convention (Articles 2 to 16) specify the areas of discrimination, such as laws, legal structure, political and public life, education, employment, health care, rural environment, marriage and family, in which States parties should take measures to eliminate discrimination. The last two parts (Articles 17 to 30) refer to the administration of the implementation of the Convention. "For the purpose of considering the progress made in the implementation", Article 17 creates a Committee on the Elimination of Discrimination against Women, which functions as a monitoring and advisory agency. The Committee evaluates the periodic reports submitted by States parties, questions government delegations that present the report, guides and advises States parties in meeting the objectives of the Convention, and issues general recommendations that help interpret the intention and scope of the Convention.

The general recommendations issued by the Committee have been important for elaborating on the provisions of the Convention and for drawing attention to some gender-specific human rights violations and the attitudes and practices that disregard the value of women. By stressing such issues as gender-based violence, unequal pay for work of equal value, undervalued and unremunerated domestic activities of women, polygamy and other marital practices that disadvantage women and violate their dignity, the general recommendations have broadened the scope of CEDAW and made it a living document. In other words, some limitations in the wording of the Convention, such as treating man as a measure by requiring States parties to ensure that women enjoy a series of rights "on equal terms with men", or failing to make explicit references to some violations that are experienced mainly by women, are redressed by CEDAW through the general recommendations.

The popularity of CEDAW, as reflected in its high rate of ratification, has been encouraging. It entered into force on 3 September 1981, less than two years after the General Assembly adopted it on 18 December 1979. According to the Office of the High Commissioner for Human Rights, as of 15 February 2008, 185 countries constituting 96 per cent of UN Member States have become parties to the Convention. However, ratification, accession or succession by 78 countries (42 percent of States parties) involved declarations or reservations, which allow them to limit their treaty obligations.[9] Since more States have placed reservations on this Convention than on any other human rights treaties,[10] CEDAW appears to be "the human rights instrument least respected by its States parties".[11] Reservations can be withdrawn later; so far, 14 States parties have withdrawn their reservations and a similar number withdrew or modified theirs with regard to some provisions. However, reservations justified by the claim that the culture or religion of the country conflicts with the provisions of the Convention are not likely to be withdrawn in the near future. Such broad reservations undermine "the object and purpose" of the treaty and leave it inapplicable for all practical purposes.

Cultural or religious objections to the provisions can be challenged by two interrelated arguments: first, it should be pointed out that the United Nations human rights regime, including regional ones, are essentially counter-culture; and second, although there may be tensions between goals (e.g., the preservation of culture versus the elimination of discriminatory cultural norms) or between two or more human rights (e.g., people's right as opposed to women's rights to self-determination), the international human rights regime requires them to be resolved by upholding the principles of universality and equality in dignity.

Promotion of Human Rights as a Counter-Culture

Although recognition and respect for some rights articulated in the Universal Declaration on Human Rights can be found in the cultural references and religious texts of many communities, the traditional cultural norms and practices also include numerous discriminatory stipulations. The novelty of the Declaration and subsequent human rights documents is not only universalism—the notion that *all* people hold certain rights by virtue of being human—but is also the desire to end *all* forms of violations that have been allowed in existing cultures. In other words, international human rights follow a reactive pattern: as violations are noticed, the rights violated within prevailing cultures are enumerated in declarations and treaties to bring them under protection. In the case of women, many human rights violations and discrimination have been not only culturally permissible, but often encouraged or demanded by cultural norms. That is why CEDAW makes specific references to culture, as well as traditions and customs embodied in cultures, and emphasizes the need to change discriminatory cultural norms, values and practices.

- It stresses that "a change in the *traditional* role of men, as well as the role of women, in society and in the family is needed to achieve full equality between men and women" (Preamble);
- States Parties . . . agree . . . "to take all appropriate measures, including legislation, to modify or abolish existing laws, regulations, *customs and practices* which constitute discrimination against women" (Article 2(f));
- States Parties shall take in all fields, in particular in the political, social, economic and *cultural fields,* all appropriate measures, including legislation, to ensure the full development and advancement of women, for the purpose of guaranteeing them the exercise and enjoyment of human rights and fundamental freedoms on a basis of equality with men (Article 3);
- States Parties shall take all appropriate measures: (a) To modify the *social and cultural patterns of conduct* of men and women, with a view to achieving the elimination of *prejudices and customary and all other practices* which are based on the idea of the inferiority or the superiority of either of the sexes or on *stereotyped roles* for men and women (Article 5). (Emphasis mine.)

Tensions between Competing Rights

The universality of human rights, and especially women's rights, is often challenged by cultural relativists. Relativist arguments, especially when combined with charges of cultural imperialism, pose a major dilemma for the international human rights community. How can peoples' cultures and their right to self-determination be recognized when several aspects of those very cultures systematically violate a number of human rights? This question is particularly important for women's rights. Since all contemporary societies are patriarchies, promoting women's rights inevitably conflicts with patriarchal "cultural" values, religious norms and other hierarchical structures in all countries. Thus, following a strict rule of cultural relativism would keep women's rights "alien" virtually to all societies, and the

emancipatory aspects of the international human rights regime would be undermined and jeopardized in the name of cultural preservation.

With regard to culture and religion, we need to ask the following questions: Who speaks on behalf of the people and religion? Who *defines* the meaning of culture or *interprets* the sources of religion and develops doctrines? Cultures, of course, are neither monolithic nor static, but within each culture there are people who would benefit from making it monolithic and keeping it static. In other words, cultures are based on power structures, and by setting norms and assigning values they also perpetuate those structures. Culturally (and officially) promoted values privilege some members of society and disadvantage others, and the privileged ones would tend to use their power to sustain those values that would justify and preserve their privileged positions. Thus, without any democratization of the interpretation and decision-making processes, cultural relativism and preservation of culture end up serving only as shields protecting the privileged people.

By the same token, all religious texts and oral traditions are received in a cultural context and filtered through and fused with the prevailing cultural norms. Always open to interpretation, their messages can be subverted and mitigated by the existing power structures. Thus, religions can embody contradictory norms, which are selectively used and reinterpreted both by the privileged and those who challenge their understanding of religion and its requirements. It is needless to note that in patriarchal systems, it is the voice of the privileged men that dictates cultural and religious norms, even though women may help in their transmission and perpetuation. Egalitarian and emancipatory interpretations by women and their advocates tend to be disregarded or suppressed.

What Needs to Be Done?

Human rights are closely linked to culture, and the expansion, full recognition and protection of rights would demand the transformation of cultural norms and their material foundations. Thus, compliance with international human rights would require a shift in cultural mores, as well as political commitment. The advocacy of human rights has to involve: (1) analyzing cultural norms in terms of their conformity with human rights principles; (2) acknowledging the diversity of the interpretation of cultures and religious sources; and (3) demanding that States parties to conventions be specific about their reservations, indicating when and how they will remove their reservations.

Universalists usually attempt to advance their arguments against relativist claims by pointing out that several rights embodied in the Universal Declaration and other human rights instruments have existed and have been respected in the cultural and religious traditions of most societies. Although such assertions can be empirically supported, as already noted, the traditional cultural norms and practices also include numerous discriminatory stipulations. Thus, both aspects of cultures (egalitarian-emancipatory and discriminatory-oppressive) should be acknowledged, and all cultures analysed as to where and how they observe the principle of universality. Since human rights are about human dignity, the principle of universality means establishing the dignity of all and calls for equal treatment. Cultures therefore should be examined to identify their contradictions with regard to the principle of equality. Once revealed, the "egalitarian" aspects of cultures can be highlighted and linked to international human rights in terms of principles.[12]

Critical assessment of cultures and egalitarian interpretation of cultural sources already exist, but these alternative voices tend to be repressed at home and ignored in international debates. Nations and other members of the international human rights community have to break away from the habits of tolerating cultural discrimination in the name of respect for differences, attributing violations solely to the culture, equating culture with religion and treating cultures as monolithic and static. While there has been considerable attention on interfaith and inter-communal conflicts and domination, e.g., rights of religious and ethnic minorities, their has been no effort to address *the intra-communal differences and hegemonies.* Acknowledging the diversity within a culture and religious community by States parties and in international forums would provide support to the alternative voices and help democratize the interpretation process.

The relativist arguments and reservations placed on treaties can be countered by pointing out that international human rights norms demand such a change of customs and traditions, and what is presented as religious requirement is open to interpretation. It should be demanded of States parties that make such claims, not only to fully explain and specify their reservations, but also to stipulate a programme that would lead to their removal. The expert committee that oversees the implementation of CEDAW has already taken some action on these lines. For example, it has issued several recommendations to press States parties that placed "blanket reservations", declaring they would implement CEDAW as long as its provisions do not contradict the Islamic law *Shari'a,* to clarify their points of reservation.[13] The Committee also problematized the issue of interpretation: " . . . at its 1987 meeting, the CEDAW Committee adopted a decision requesting that the United Nations and the specialized agencies promote or undertake studies on the status of women under Islamic laws and customs, and in particular on the status and equality of women in the family, on issues such as marriage, divorce, custody and property rights and their participation in public life of the society, taking into consideration the principle of El Ijtihad (interpretation) in Islam."[14]

Not surprisingly, the States parties affected by the decision denounced it as a threat to their religious freedoms and rejected the Committee's recommendation, but the Committee has been persistent in pressing this issue. In 1994, it amended the guidelines for the preparation of reports to provide additional and specific guidelines for States parties that have entered substantial culture-and religion-based reservations. Jane Connors provides a summary:[15] "Such States should report specifically with regard to their reservations, why they consider them to be necessary, their precise effect on national law and policy, and whether they have entered similar reservations to other human rights treaties which guarantee similar rights. Such States are also required to indicate plans they might have to limit the effect of the reservations or withdraw them and, where possible, specify a timetable for withdrawing them. The Committee made particular reference to . . . [some States], indicating that the Committee considers such reservations to be incompatible with the object and purpose of the Convention and requiring a special effort from such countries who are directed to report on the effect and interpretation of their reservations."

In its persistent effort, the Committee should also encourage shadow reports, which not only include the assessments of what has not been done by the reporting State towards implementing the Convention, but which also present alternative interpretations of the culture and religious sources. Inviting such reports would equip the Committee with the information needed to effectively question States parties' justification for their reservations and allow them to recognize the diversity within their society. It would also support women and women's rights advocates by validating their *right to interpret* their cultural and religious sources.

Notes

1. Here, "civilization" is employed as a sociological term in reference to societies that achieve high levels of economic productivity, which lead to specialization of labour, social stratification and institutionalization. A curious case is the Iroquois nations. The extent of power that the Iroquois matrons had over public affairs has led many impressed observers to classify these nations as "matriarchy". Although the Iroquois matrons enjoyed some authority, they could not be chiefs or serve on the Council of Elders—the highest ruling body of the six-nation Iroquois Confederacy. Women mainly maintained a veto power and exercised an indirect influence due to their control of food and other supplies. No matriarchal society—as exact opposites of patriarchy—has been recorded in history. Although some pre-civilized societies have demonstrated more egalitarian gender relations, even in those societies the power balance has been usually tilted in favour of men. See, Rayna R. Reiter, ed., *Toward an Anthropology of Women* (New York: Monthly Review Press, 1975).

2. For current statistical information on the gender gap in many areas, see *Human Development Report 2007/2008.* (New York: Oxford University Press, 2007) tables 28–33.

3. Majid Fakhry, *Averroes: His Life, Work,* (Oxford: Oneworld Publications, 2001).

4. St. Thomas Aquinas found women to be valuable (thus created in the first production) only for their reproductive role (in procreation). See, St. Thomas Aquinas, Summa Theologicae, Question XCII, art. 1, "Whether Woman Should Have Been Made in the First Production of Things", available at http://www.newadvent.org/summa/109201.htm.

5. John Stuart Mill and Harriet Taylor Mill, *Essays on Sex Equality.* Edited with and an introductory essay by Alice S. Rossi (Chicago: University of Chicago Press, 1970).

6. Mary Ann Glendon. *A World Made New* (New York: Random House, 2001), 68.

7. Glendon, (2001): 111–112 and 162.

8. Hilary Charlesworth, "Human Rights as Men's Rights", *Women's Rights Human Rights: International Feminist*

Perspectives. Edited by Julie Peters and Andrea Wolper (New York: Routledge, 1995): 103–113.

9. Article 28 allows the ratification of the Convention with reservations, as long as they are compatible "with the object and purpose" of the Convention. Thus, States may enter reservations or "interpretive declarations" when they sign or ratify the Convention. Although "declarations" are not referred to in the text, they tend to employ a language similar to the one used in reservations and play the same role in limiting State obligations. Thus, for the purposes of this essay, declarations are treated the same as reservations.

10. Henry J. Steiner and Philip Alston, *International Human Rights in Context: Law, Politics, Morals*. Second Edition (Oxford: Oxford University Press, 2000): 180.

11. Belinda Clark, "The Vienna Convention Reservations Regime and the Convention on the Discrimination against Women." *American Journal of International Law*, 85:2 (April 1991): 281–321, 318.

12. Such a study of *The Qur'an*, the sacred text and highest authority in Islam, shows that Muslim women are granted equality with men at the spiritual level, but denied equality at the social level, and argues for the elevation of the spiritual equality recognized in the sacred text to become the standard that would be used in the reformulation of social roles. See, Zehra Arat, "Women's Rights in Islam: Revisiting Qur'anic Rights", *Human Rights: New Perspectives, New Realities*. Edited by Peter Schwab and Adamanta Pollis, eds., (Boulder: Lynne Rienner Publishers, 2000): 69–94.

13. Michele Brandt and Jeffrey A. Kaplan, "The Tension between Women's Rights and Religious Rights: Reservations to CEDAW by Egypt, Bangladesh and Tunisia", *The Journal of Law and Religion* 12:1 (1995–96): 105–142; Connors, 1997; Clark, 1991.

14. UN Doc E/1987/SR 11.

15. Jane Connors. "The Women's Convention in the Muslim World", *Human Rights as General Norms and a State's Right to Opt Out: Reservations and Objections to Human Rights Convention*. Edited by J.P. Gardner (London: British Institute of International and Comparative Law, 1997): 85–103, 99–100.

ZEHRA F. KABASAKAL ARAT is Juanita and Joseph Leff Professor of Political Science at Purchase College of the State University of New York and is Chair of the Human Rights Research Committee of the International Political Science Association. She is the author of *Human Rights Worldwide*. Some of the arguments presented here appeared in her earlier publications.

Educating Girls, Unlocking Development

"Compelling evidence, accumulated over the past 20 years . . . , has led to an almost universal recognition of the importance of focusing on girls' education as part of broader development policy."

RUTH LEVINE

One of the most important public policy goals in the developing world is the expansion and improvement of education for girls. Vital in its own right for the realization of individual capabilities, the education of girls has the potential to transform the life chances of the girls themselves, their future families, and the societies in which they live. Girls with at least a primary school education are healthier and wealthier when they grow up and their future children have much greater opportunities than they otherwise would; even national economic outcomes appear to be positively influenced by expanded girls' education.

Unlike some development outcomes that depend on multiple factors outside the control of policy makers (either in developing countries or among donor nations), significant improvement in girls' education can be achieved through specific government actions. Expansion of basic education, making school infrastructure and curriculum more girl-friendly, and conditional cash transfers and scholarships to overcome household barriers have all been used to improve key outcomes, with demonstrable success. Lessons from regions that have made rapid advances with girls' education, and from programs that have introduced successful financing and teaching innovations, can be applied to accelerate progress.

While public policy can make the difference, policies that ignore important gender-related constraints to education at the primary and, particularly, at the postprimary educational levels can have the opposite effect, reinforcing existing patterns of gender discrimination and exclusion. Those patterns are often deep-seated. Families in many societies traditionally have valued schooling less for girls than for boys. In most households, the domestic workload falls more to females than to males, leaving less time for school. If families are struggling to find income, the demand for girls' help around the house (or in wage labor) may increase. Many parents believe that the return on educational investments varies according to gender—particularly if girls, when they marry, leave their parents' households to join the husbands'.

When girls in developing countries do enroll in school, they frequently encounter gender-based discrimination and inadequate educational resources. Large numbers of girls in sub-Saharan Africa drop out, for example, when they reach puberty and the onset of menstruation simply because schools lack latrines, running water, or privacy. Parental concerns about girls' security outside the home can limit schooling where girls are vulnerable in transit and male teachers are not trusted. And in some countries, cultural aversion to the education of girls lingers. Afghanistan's Taliban insurgents, who believe that girls' education violates Islamic teachings, have succeeded in closing numerous schools, sometimes by beheading teachers. Afghanistan is an extreme case, but a reminder nonetheless of the challenges that remain on the path toward achieving the high payoffs from girls' education.

The Benefits

Why is the schooling of girls so critical? Education in general is among the primary means through which societies reproduce themselves; correspondingly, changing the educational opportunities for particular groups in society—girls and minority groups—is perhaps the single most effective way to achieve lasting transformations. A considerable body of evidence has shown that the benefits of educating a girl are manifested in economic and social outcomes: her lifetime health, labor force participation, and income; her (future) children's health and nutrition; her community's and her nation's productivity. Most important, education can break the intergenerational transmission of poverty.

Female participation in the formal labor market consistently increases with educational attainment, as it does for males. In at least some settings, the returns to education of girls are superior to those for boys. Several studies have shown that primary schooling increases lifetime earnings by as much as 20 percent for girls—higher than for their brothers. If they stay in secondary school, the returns from education are 25 percent or higher.

The inverse relationship between women's education and fertility is perhaps the best studied of all health and demographic phenomena. The relationship generally holds across countries and over time, and is robust even when income is taken into account. Completion of primary school is strongly associated with later age at marriage, later age at first birth, and lower lifetime fertility. A study of eight sub-Saharan countries covering the period from 1987 to 1999 found that girls' educational attainment was the best predictor of whether they would have their first births during adolescence.

Another study examined surveys across the developing world to compare female education and fertility by region. The higher the level of female education, the lower desired family size, and the greater the success in achieving desired family size. Further, each additional year of a mother's schooling cuts the expected infant mortality rate by 5 to 10 percent.

Maternal education is a key determinant of children's attainment. Multiple studies have found that a mother's level of education has a strong positive effect on daughters' enrollment—more than on sons and significantly more than the effect of fathers' education on daughters. Studies from Egypt, Ghana, India, Kenya, Malaysia, Mexico, and Peru all find that mothers with a basic education are substantially more likely to educate their children, especially their daughters.

Children's health also is strongly associated with mothers' education. In general, this relationship holds across countries and time, although the confounding effect of household income has complicated the picture. One study, for instance, compared 17 developing countries, examining the relationship between women's education and their infants' health and nutritional status. It found the existence of an education-related health advantage in most countries, although stronger for postneonatal health than for neonatal health. (In some countries the "education advantage" did appear to be eliminated when controlling for other dimensions of socioeconomic status.)

Other studies have found clear links between women's school attainment and birth and death rates, and between women's years of schooling and infant mortality. A 1997 study for the World Bank, which focused on Morocco, found that a mother's schooling and functional literacy predicted her child's height-for-age, controlling for other socioeconomic factors.

Although the causal links are harder to establish at the macrolevel, some researchers have made the attempt, with interesting results. For example, in a 100-country study, researchers showed that raising the share of women with a secondary education by 1 percent is associated with a 0.3 percent increase in annual per capita income growth. In a 63-country study, more productive farming because of increased female education accounts for 43 percent of the decline in malnutrition achieved between 1970 and 1995.

In short (and with some important nuances set aside), girls' education is a strong contributor to the achievement of multiple key development outcomes: growth of household and national income, health of women and children, and lower and wanted fertility. Compelling evidence, accumulated over the past 20 years using both quantitative and qualitative methods, has led to an almost universal recognition of the importance of focusing on girls' education as part of broader development policy.

The Trends

Given the widespread understanding about the value of girls' education, the international community and national governments have established ambitious goals for increased participation in primary education and progress toward gender parity at all levels. The Millennium Development Goals (MDG), approved by all member states of the United Nations in 2000, call for universal primary education in all countries by 2015, as well as gender parity at all levels by 2015.

There is good news to report. Impressive gains have been made toward higher levels of education enrollment and completion, and girls have been catching up rapidly with their brothers. As primary schooling expands, girls tend to be the main beneficiaries because of their historically disadvantaged position.

The rate of primary school completion also has improved faster for girls than for boys, again in large part because they had more to gain at the margins. Across all developing countries, girls' primary school completion increased by 17 percent, from 65 to 76 percent, between 1990 and 2000. During the same period, boys' primary completion increased by 8 percent, from 79 to 85 percent. Global progress is not matched, however, in every region. In sub-Saharan Africa, girls did only slightly better between 1990 and 2000, with primary completion increasing from 43 to 46 percent. (The primary completion rate for boys went in the opposite direction, from 57 to 56 percent.)

The overall good news about girls' progress must be tempered by realism, and a recognition that the goal is not to have boys' and girls' educational attainment "equally bad." Today, a mere nine years from the MDG deadline, it is clear that the important improvements over the past several decades in the developing world—in many instances, unprecedented rates of increase in primary school enrollment and completion—still leave a large number of poor countries very far from the target. While girls are making up ground rapidly, in many of the poorest countries the achievements on improved gender parity must be seen in the context of overall low levels of primary school completion.

An estimated 104 million to 121 million children of primary school age across the globe are not in school, with the worst shortfalls in Africa and South Asia. Completion of schooling is a significant problem. While enrollment has been increasing, many children drop out before finishing the fifth grade. In Africa, for example, just 51 percent of children (46 percent of girls) complete primary school. In South Asia, 74 percent of children (and just 63 percent of girls) do so.

Low levels of enrollment and completion are concentrated not only in certain regions but also among certain segments of the population. In every country completion rates are lowest for children from poor households. In Western and Central Africa, the median grade completed by the bottom 40 percent of the income distribution is zero, because less than half of poor children complete even the first year of school.

The education income gap also exacerbates gender disparities. In India, for example, the gap between boys and girls from the richest households is 2.5 percent, but the difference for children from the poorest households is 24 percent.

Girls are catching up quickly in most countries, but the level they are catching up to is still quite low.

In some countries the main reason for low educational attainment is that children do not enroll in school. In Bangladesh, Benin, Burkina Faso, Ivory Coast, India, Mali, Morocco, Niger, and Senegal, more than half of children from the bottom 40 percent of the income distribution never even enroll. Elsewhere, particularly in Latin America, enrollment may be almost universal, but high repetition and dropout rates lead to low completion rates. In both cases poor students are much more likely not to complete school.

In many countries the rural/urban education gap is a key factor explaining education differentials. In Mozambique, the rural completion rate is 12 percent, while at the national level 26 percent of children complete school. Burkina Faso, Guinea, Madagascar, Niger, and Togo all demonstrate a similar pattern. In rural areas, the gender gap in completion is pronounced in Africa: in Benin, Burkina Faso, Guinea, Madagascar, Mozambique, and Niger, a mere 15 percent of girls who start primary school make it to the end.

Policy makers increasingly are recognizing the importance of addressing the special needs and vulnerabilities of marginal populations, even in relatively well-off countries with education levels that, on average, look quite good. As my colleagues Maureen Lewis and Marlaine Lockheed at the Center for Global Development highlight in a forthcoming book, girls who are members of marginalized groups—the Roma in Eastern Europe, the indigenous populations in Central America and elsewhere, the underprivileged castes and tribes in India—suffer a double disadvantage. Low educational attainment for girls is an obvious mechanism through which historical disadvantage is perpetuated. In Laos, for example, more than 90 percent of men in the dominant Laotai group are literate, while only 30 percent of the youngest cohort of women belonging to excluded rural ethnic groups can read and write.

Beyond the primary school enrollment and completion trends, a complex problem is the quality of education. Although measurement of learning outcomes is spotty at best, analyses of internationally comparable assessments of learning achievement in mathematics, reading, and science indicate that most developing countries rank far behind the industrialized nations. This is all the more of concern because the tests are taken by the children in school who, in low-enrollment countries, are the equivalent in relative terms to the top performers in the high-enrollment developed nations. The data on national examinations is equally alarming. Student performance on national exams in South Asian and African countries shows major gaps in acquisition of knowledge and skills.

Thus, the picture of progress and gaps is a complex one: rapid improvements relative to historical trends, but far off the ideal mark in the poorest countries. Girls are catching up quickly in most countries, but the level they are catching up to is still quite low. In many nations, the "lowest hanging fruit" has already been reached; for all children, and for girls in particular, the ones now out of school come from the most economically and socially disadvantaged backgrounds, and will be the hardest to reach. Finally, even among those children in school, evidence about poor learning outcomes should be cause for alarm.

The Challenges

The central imperative for improving educational opportunities and outcomes for girls in the low enrollment countries, including in sub-Saharan Africa and parts of South Asia, is to improve overall access and the quality of primary schooling. In doing so, planners and policy makers should ensure that they are not perpetuating barriers to girls' participation.

Getting to universal primary education (either enrollment or the more ambitious goal of completion) in sub-Saharan Africa and South Asia will require large-scale expansion in physical infrastructure, the number of teachers, and teaching/learning materials. Moreover, it will require fundamental improvements in the education institutions: more attention to learning outcomes rather than enrollment numbers, greater incentives for quality teaching, and more responsiveness to parents. This is a huge agenda. The donor and international technical community can support it, but it must be grounded in the political commitment of national and subnational governments.

Secondary to the "more and better education for all" agenda, and of particular relevance in countries that have already made significant progress so that most children go to school, is the need to understand and address the needs of particular disadvantaged groups, where gender differentials are especially pronounced. Beyond the efforts to reach children from poor and rural households, public policy makers need to understand and pay attention to ethnic and linguistic minorities, reaching them with tailored approaches rather than simply an expansion of the types of educational opportunities provided to the majority population. In addressing this challenge, policy makers must accept that reaching these key populations implies higher unit costs, as well as the adoption of potentially controversial measures, such as bilingual curriculum.

Finally, success in moving close to universal primary school enrollment generates its own new challenges. As more children complete primary school, the private benefits, in higher wages, decline (though the social benefits remain high). Private rates of return—perceived and real—cease to be seen as much of a reason for sending children to primary school, unless there is access to postprimary education. In addition, both the expansion of the existing education systems in many developing countries and the "scaling-up" of other public sector functions (such as health services, water management, and general public administration) require a larger cadre of educated and trained workers, the products of postprimary education. For these reasons, attention must be given to expanded opportunities for girls at the secondary level.

While international attention and goal-setting have been directed almost exclusively at the primary level, and the donor community has been persuaded by arguments about greater economic returns from primary education and the potentially regressive effects of investments at the secondary level, a large agenda remains unattended. It is at the secondary level that many of the microeconomic, health, and fertility outcomes of girls' education are fully realized. And common sense alone suggests that the large (and growing) cohort of children moving through primary schooling will create unsustainable pressures for postprimary education opportunities. If those are severely rationed, as they are in much of sub-Saharan Africa, the negative feedback to parents who sacrificed to send their children through primary school may be profound. Sorting out the design, financing, and institutional arrangements for effective secondary schooling—that is also responsive to labor market demand—is an essential part of good policy making today.

The Way Forward

Beyond general expansion of enrollment, governments can get out-of-school children into school by crafting specific interventions to reach them, and by increasing educational opportunities (formal and informal) for girls and women. In designing these initiatives, success depends on understanding and taking into account powerful demand-side influences that may constrain girls' school participation.

Specific interventions have been shown, in some settings, to get hard-to-reach children into school. These include eliminating school fees, instituting conditional cash transfers, using school feeding programs as an incentive to attend school, and implementing school health programs to reduce absenteeism. Several interventions have proved particularly successful where girls' participation is low. These include actions that increase security and privacy for girls (for example, ensuring that sanitation facilities are girl-friendly), as well as those that reduce gender-stereotyping in curriculum and encourage girls to take an active role in their education.

While few rigorous evaluations have been undertaken, many experts suggest that literacy programs for uneducated mothers may help increase school participation by their children. Adult literacy programs may be particularly useful in settings where there are pockets of undereducated women, such as ethnic or indigenous communities.

It is tempting for policy makers to focus on specific programmatic investments. But sustained improvements in education are impossible to achieve without improving the way in which key institutions in the sector function, and without increasing parental involvement in decisions affecting their children's education. Many countries with poorly performing educational systems suffer from institutional weaknesses, including low management capacity, nontransparent resource allocation and accounting practices, and substandard human resources policies and practices. Incentive structures that fail to reward good performance create and reinforce the most deleterious characteristics of weak institutions.

Parents who are well informed of policies and resource allocations in the education sector and who are involved in decisions regarding their children's schooling exert considerable influence and help contribute solutions. Involved communities are able to articulate local school needs, hold officials accountable, and mobilize local resources to fill gaps when the government response is inadequate.

In Benin, Burkina Faso, Guinea, Madagascar, Mozambique, and Niger, a mere 15 percent of girls who start primary school make it to the end.

A Modest Proposal

Donor agencies have been at the leading edge of the dialogue about the importance of girls' education, often providing the financial support, research, and political stimulus that may be lacking in countries that have more than their hands full with the basics of "Education for All." There is a broad consensus in the international donor community about the value of girls' education, and innovations have been introduced through donor-funded programs under the auspices of UNICEF, the World Food Program, the US Agency for International Development, and other key agencies. These have been valuable contributions, and have supported the work of champions at the national and local levels.

The donor community could come together now to accelerate progress in a very particular way. Working with both governments and nongovernmental organizations in countries where specific excluded groups—ethnic and/or linguistic minorities—have much poorer education outcomes, donors could finance the design, introduction, and rigorous evaluation of targeted programs to improve access to appropriate educational opportunities, with a particular emphasis (if warranted by the baseline research) on the needs and characteristics of girls. While different bilateral and multilateral donors could take the lead in funding specific types of programs or working in particular countries on the challenge of the "doubly disadvantaged," a shared learning agenda could be coordinated across agencies to generate much more than the spotty anecdotes and case studies on which we currently depend.

The learning agenda would include three components: first, the enduring questions to be examined—for example, determining the most effective strategies to improve learning outcomes among children who come from households where the language spoken is not the language of instruction; second, the use of methods that permit observed results to be attributed to the program; and third, the features that will ensure maximum credibility of the evaluations, such as independence, dissemination of results (whether the findings are favorable or not), and wide sharing of the data for reanalysis.

Just as education can transform individuals' lives, learning what works can transform the debates in development policy. The beneficiaries in developing countries would include not only girls who receive the education they deserve and need, but also families and communities and future generations thereby lifted over time out of poverty.

RUTH LEVINE is director of programs and a senior fellow at the Center for Global Development.

From *Current History*, March 2006, pp. 127–131. Copyright © 2006 by Current History, Inc. Reprinted by permission.

Education: It's Not Just about the Boys. Get Girls into School

JONATHAN ALTER

Who wants more poor children around the world to go to school? Raise your hand. Yep, everyone's hand is up. Education is the ultimate mom-and-apple-pie (or rice-and-beans) issue. Everyone's for it. But our best efforts to get more impoverished kids into schools aren't always effective. Despite some recent progress in China and India, 73 million children worldwide don't go to primary school. Three times as many never go to secondary school. Though they can sometimes be trained later in life, their shortened time in school is often a major impediment to advancement. These kids are mostly doomed to a life of poverty, and so are their families.

The way out is not just to champion education generally but to focus intently on one subset of the problem: girls, who make up nearly 60 percent of the kids out of school. In parts of sub-Saharan Africa, only one in five girls gets any education at all. Here's where to zero in on the challenge: most of the benefits that accompany increased education are attributable to girls, who use their schooling more productively than boys. Women in the developing world who have had some education share their earnings; men keep a third to a half for themselves.

"The reason so many experts believe educating girls is the most important investment in the world is how much they give back to their families," says Gene Sperling, a former top economic adviser to President Bill Clinton (and currently advising Barack Obama). Sperling's book, "What Works in Girls' Education" (with Barbara Herz), is simultaneously disturbing and encouraging. It's disheartening to think of how far we have to go to get all kids into school—one of the United Nations Millennium Development Goals launched in 2000 to accelerate progress on fighting poverty, disease and other social ills. But it's also hopeful: at least we can focus on a specific solution.

When girls go to school, they marry later and have fewer, healthier children. For instance, if an African mother has five years of education, her child has a 40 percent better chance of living to age 5. A World Health Organization study in Burkina Faso showed that mothers with some education were 40 percent less likely to subject their children to the practice of genital mutilation. When girls get educated, they are three times less likely to contract HIV/AIDS.

Unfortunately, many African parents still don't know that their own lives can be greatly improved if their daughters go to school. They're often uncomfortable when their girls have to travel long distances to school (making them more subject to sexual predators). Girls themselves grow uncomfortable in school when they have no separate latrines. They fear being spied on by boys; their parents agree and withdraw them. This is the kind of everyday impediment to progress that aid organizers notice on the ground but rarely becomes part of the debate.

The biggest barrier to primary and secondary education in the developing world remains the fees that too many countries continue to charge parents for each child in school. Sometimes it's a flat fee; sometimes it's barely disguised as a fee for books or school uniforms. The practical effect is that poor families (disproportionately in rural areas, where school attendance is lightest) send their two oldest, healthiest boys to school with the hope that they will support their parents in their old age. This often deprives girls—the ones actually much more likely to help their families—of the chance to go to school.

The waste of human capital is incalculable. Consider that only 5 percent of children with disabilities get any education at all in the developing world. Countries like Kenya and Uganda, which have abolished fees, have seen a flood of new students, with enrollments surging by 30 percent or more. So why haven't other developing nations followed their example? It's not the loss of fee revenue but the absence of a large-enough education infrastructure to sustain the influx of new students. Five years after abolishing fees, Kenya still needs 40,000 new teachers. Officials there say they can't meet the need without more consistent funding.

Donor nations and NGOs are increasingly reaching a consensus that global education, especially for girls, is the keystone to the arch of development. The Millennium Development Goals of universal primary education with gender equity are among the hottest topics at international conferences. But Sperling calls these "the world's most ambitious and pathetic goals—ambitious because so many countries are not on track to reach them; pathetic because of the idea that five or six years of primary education will suffice when there's no real demonstrable advantage without eight."

The challenge extends beyond funding to changing the culture of the developing world. Fathers must be convinced that if their daughters go to school, they will learn enough math to help them in the market. Mothers must learn that while sending their daughters to school might mean one fewer pair of hands to help around the house, their families will be better off in the long run. "This is not a disease without a known cure," says Sperling. "These things work everywhere." If these become the mom-and-apple-pie values of the developing world, we'll all win.

Women in the Middle East: Progress and Backlash

Throughout the region, recent advances in family planning, women's health, and female education and labor force participation have led to greater and more equal participation by women in national life.

Nikki R. Keddie

Women's groups became involved in the modern politics of the Middle East and North Africa in the late nineteenth and early twentieth centuries. Their initial involvement came primarily through nationalist movements and organizations, some of which had separate women's wings. Early political movements in which women were involved included Iran's Tobacco Revolt against the British in 1891–92, the Iranian "constitutional revolution" of 1906–11, the Egyptian nationalist movement of 1919, and the successful Turkish resistance, after World War I, to the Versailles Treaty's dismemberment of the country.

In the early twentieth century, women's groups importantly began to make efforts to improve the position of women in society. These early efforts, and many later efforts as well, focused on issues such as welfare, health, education, and job training. These goals, though social in nature, were political in their implications, in that they touched on spheres that had previously been controlled by the Muslim *ulema* (religious leaders) and local elites. Conservatives, including members of the ulema, often opposed public activity by women and education of girls outside the home. Such resistance occasionally led to violent struggle (although early opponents of women's employment and girls' education were less extreme in their views and methods than are, say, the Taliban in Afghanistan).

After World War I, women's groups experienced growth in several countries—including the most populous—Egypt, Turkey, and Iran. Some of these groups had close ties to political parties, especially communist, socialist, and nationalist parties. In the 1930s, however, both President Kemal Ataturk in Turkey and Iran's Reza Shah, in different ways, ended the independence of women's organizations and brought all women's groups under central control. In recent decades central organizational control in some form, along with the dissolution of nonconforming women's groups, has been the pattern in a number of Middle Eastern countries, though nongovernmental organizations often enjoy varying amounts of autonomy.

Activists and Islamists

These changes in women's activism have paralleled larger political changes that have occurred in the Middle East and North Africa. In earlier decades nationalism was the dominant political ideology, and communism and socialism were important as well. Recent decades, especially since the 1970s, have seen the growth of Islamist movements, many of which have ideologies that deny women's equality with men.

The growth of Islamism has been in part a reaction to the failures of nationalism and socialism and to Western policies (especially regarding Israel). It is also partly attributable to the growing influence of oil-rich Saudi Arabia and its subsidies abroad, including to religious organizations. This Islamist trend has been largely negative for women's rights (though some women's Islamic groups have begun to reinterpret Islam in a more gender-egalitarian way and sometimes to join in activities helpful to women's rights). Even women's allies—such as nationalist and leftist organizations whose programs include support for women's rights—have often asked women to defer their goals. And nationalist governments have rarely undertaken to change the cultural attitudes that underpin gender inequality (though some educational measures of this type are now beginning in Turkey).

Contributing to the rise of Islamism (here, *Islamism* refers to politics based on appeals to Islam, and can comprise right, center, and leftist groups) have been the recent urbanization and politicization of lower-class and bazaar-class men and women, who in most Muslim countries tend to be resistant to Western or modern ways. As early as the late 1920s, in fact, after the formation of the Muslim Brotherhood in Egypt, Muslim women's organizations began to arise as well, often affiliated with male Islamist groups, and these groups opposed imitation of Western and Christian ways. This phenomenon stands in contrast to the early movements to extend women's rights, which—as in the West and in East Asia—attracted mainly educated, upper-and middle-class women, who modeled many of their demands and practices on Western ones. Recent research suggests that both women's Islamist groups and other women's organizations partly imitated and partly reacted against Christian and other missionaries. These missionaries often pioneered girls' education and health, but their aim of religious conversion was resented locally.

In the early decades of the women's movements in the Middle East, the chief political demand was for the vote. Ataturk granted women's suffrage for municipal elections in 1930 and for national elections in 1934—well before France, Italy, or Switzerland adopted universal suffrage. Today, women have the vote in all Middle Eastern countries except Saudi Arabia. Women's issues expanded from political participation to include health, family planning, and education, as well as the continually fraught issue of family law, which has remained largely based on sharia (the Islamic code) even when other sharia laws were abandoned.

Nearly all countries in the region have made reforms to family law, but the nature of these reforms varies greatly. The earliest and strongest changes to family law were made by nationalist leaders, without much input from women's organizations. Notable among these was Ataturk's replacement of sharia with a code modeled on the Swiss system. In 1957, Tunisian President Habib Bourguiba instituted a personal status code that abolished polygamy and included a large measure of gender equality. Most of the former Ottoman-Arab states retained the Ottoman family law, as reformed and codified in the late nineteenth century. In Afghanistan, gender reform from above—attempted first by kings and then by communists—failed in the face of local and later foreign-backed armed opposition. The leftist prime minister who led the overthrow of Iraq's monarchy in 1958, Abdul Kasem Qasim, significantly reformed that country's family code in 1959. This code as modified remains the basis of Iraqi family law, though it is under attack from Islamists and other conservatives. In recent decades, pressure from women's groups has increasingly influenced family law reform in countries such as Morocco, Egypt, and Iran.

Throughout the region, recent advances in family planning, women's health, and female education and labor force participation have led to greater and more equal participation by women in national life. These advances owe something to the women's organizations that have fought for them. However, no absolute correlation exists between a history of strong women's organizations (as exists in Egypt) and relatively greater success in achieving legal gender equality (as in Turkey and Tunisia). When it comes to gender reform, many factors come into play.

Advances in Morocco

As previously noted, increasing numbers of both men and women in the Middle East have become politicized in recent decades. This is the result of a number of trends such as rapid urbanization, population growth, fast-changing economic circumstances, growth in education and labor force participation (especially for women), as well as a number of international issues that draw widespread attention. This increased politicization has involved secular nationalist groups, socialist groups, and—especially since about 1970—rapidly growing Islamist organizations, whose appeal has often been strongest in small towns and among the newly urbanized and educated.

In North Africa an important factor contributing to Islamization has been a policy of Arabization in instruction and communication, a trend particularly strong in Morocco and Algeria. Both Arabization and the growing use of Islamic laws and norms are resented by the large non-Arab Berber populations of Algeria and Morocco. These groups, for whom the French in earlier times encouraged law codes different from those applicable to Arab Muslims, generally favor laws and practices that are more secular and gender-egalitarian. Indeed Morocco, where both secular and Islamist political participation has grown in recent decades, makes an interesting case study for gender issues because its recent achievements in women's rights have influenced women's politics in Iran, Algeria, and elsewhere.

Once a French protectorate, Morocco gained its independence in 1956. Today it is a parliamentary monarchy that has political parties and holds elections, though the monarch maintains much de facto control. In both Morocco and in Algeria, an ex-French colony, a legal code governing family matters known as the *Mudawwana* retained inegalitarian elements from the sharia, having undergone only minor reforms. For decades Moroccan women's groups aligned with progressive political parties, along with women intellectuals—most famously the sociologist and author Fatima Mernissi—have agitated for reform. At the same time, however, Islamism has grown in strength as it has elsewhere in the Muslim world. Some secularists have adjusted to this. It is instructive to compare Mernissi's first book, *Beyond the Veil,* which supports secularism, with her later works, many of which try to reinterpret Islam in a feminist way. In Morocco as elsewhere, even those who hold basically secular values often come to stress new interpretations of Islam.

Women's groups and their progressive allies in Morocco long struggled to establish egalitarian family laws. In 1992 the innovative One Million Signatures campaign aimed to collect a million signatures to a petition in favor of such laws. The campaign was spearheaded by the important Democratic Association of Moroccan Women, formed in 1985 as the first Moroccan women's organization independent of any political party (though its leaders were affiliated with the leftist Party of Progress and Socialism). Although over 1 million people did sign within a few months, Islamist activists countermobilized at schools and universities and collected 3 million signatures opposing the campaign. Islamist newspapers joined in the opposition and implicitly questioned the Islamic devotion of King Hassan II. The pro-petition women, at the king's urging, ended the campaign and instead addressed their demands to him.

In 1993 Hassan issued some partial reforms. Although this disappointed those hoping for egalitarianism, the king in 1998 brought into his government opposition parties, including socialists, and they drafted a comprehensive plan for the development of women. The plan argued for extensive reform of the Mudawwana, as the One Million Signatures campaign had proposed. Islamists were again angered, but a new king—Mohammad, who acceded to the throne in 1999—included in his reform program the extension of women's rights.

The new government issued a plan to integrate women into the nation's development, a plan that included major egalitarian changes to the law. In March 2000 hundreds of thousands demonstrated in Casablanca against the plan. Somewhat fewer demonstrated in its favor in the capital, Rabat. King Mohammad, in the face of strong opposition, officially dismissed the plan, but he continued to work for it behind the scenes. He abolished the royal harem, married a modern woman, and, after a deadly terrorist bombing, took harsh measures against Islamists. Late in 2003 he issued, and in 2004 the parliament approved, a major change to family law that brought Morocco's law close to Tunisia's almost egalitarian code (though polygamy was still allowed if a judge and the first wife agreed to it, and more power was left with judges in divorce cases). King Mohammad—like Bourguiba in Tunisia but unlike Ataturk—grounded reform in Islam.

Implementation of the reforms remains a problem today, as conservatives and Islamists continue to agitate against the reformers, calling them imperialists and agents of Zionism. All sides now use Islamic language, though only a few, like Mernissi, are engaged in serious reinterpretation of Islam.

A Mixed Picture in Iran

In Iran, women's status has long been affected by the country's adherence to the minority school of Islam, Shiism, to which most Iranians were converted under the Safavid dynasty (1501–1722). Shiism contains some special provisions that affect women—better inheritance rights for daughters who have no brothers but also, more important, the institution of temporary marriage, which legitimizes relationships of any duration and the offspring resulting from them. Iran's Shiite ulema, moreover, have traditionally been more economically and politically powerful, and more independent of the state, than the Sunni ulema in other countries, and this has often affected women's status as well.

Women had important roles in the revolution of 1906–11, which gave Iran a modern constitution, as well as in various twentieth century nationalist and leftist movements. These included the oil nationalization movement under Prime Minister Mohammed Mossadegh. Women's organizations pioneered efforts in girls' education, job training, and health. Clerical and conservative resistance, however, blocked voting and legal reform until women finally got the vote in 1963.

Under Mohammed Reza Shah (who ruled from 1941 to 1979), most women's organizations were centralized under the Women's Organization of Iran (WOI). The WOI backed, and a prominent woman drafted, the reforming Family Protection Law (FPL) of 1967, which was strengthened in 1975. This law widened the grounds on which women could file for divorce,

limited men's divorce rights, limited polygamy, and allowed custody of children to go to either parent, with secular courts making the decisions. In 1975, the minimum marriage age was raised to 18 for women and 20 for men. The FPL did not end the institution of temporary marriage, but was designed to discourage it. The WOI and its director, then–Minister for Women's Affairs Mahnaz Afkhami, often came under criticism from anti-shah leftist and nationalist women, but in retrospect many see their work on the FPL as positive.

The shah's autocracy and his economic and foreign policies provoked increasing opposition, much of which took on an Islamic tone after 1960. The Islamic opposition centered on Ayatollah Ruhollah Khomeini, who was exiled from Iran between 1964 and early 1979. In the 1970s anti-shah secular women often tried to unite with the religious opposition, with some even donning chadors and adopting sex-segregated behaviors to show their solidarity. Forgotten were Khomeini's earlier statements that the FPL was null and void, and indeed in the late 1970s Khomeini, under the influence of young men with a reformist vision of Islam, adopted a more progressive tone. Most secularists thought Khomeini and his clerical followers were incapable of ruling, and each party thought its own group would win out.

Khomeini encouraged massive participation by women in the revolutionary protests of 1978–79 and continued to encourage women's participation in street support after he took power in February 1979. Although in 1962 he may have opposed women's suffrage, he never again spoke of taking away women's votes. However, an early step toward enforced veiling led to a massive women's protest on International Women's Day in 1979—though even larger numbers of pro-Khomeini women counter-demonstrated. The measure was lifted, but gradually reinforced. Since then, the ups and downs of strict veiling have been one measure of change in government policy. But for most activist women fighting discrimination, veiling is the least of issues. More important were economic and social issues, with many women forced out of their jobs in the first revolutionary period, and also legal changes and violence against women.

For most activist women fighting discrimination, veiling is the least of issues.

Family Law and Sharia

Since the revolution, the legal situation of Iranian women has been both complex and controversial. The FPL was denounced immediately after the revolution but it was never formally abrogated, and where no contrary legislation was passed, some of its rules were still observed by the courts. However, courts were now presided over by clerical judges, not secular ones, and their rulings were usually based on sharia. Among sharia-based practices followed after the revolution were unilateral divorce for men but divorce for women only on limited legal grounds and with a court judgment; custody of children, after a very early age, going to the husband or the paternal family; the treatment of women's testimony as only half as valuable as men's; and family compensation for crimes. Stoning was carried out against some married women, or men who slept with married women, not always meeting the strict Koranic evidential provisions for adultery. (Stoning has become very rare, however, and campaigns continue to stop it altogether.)

Many women, as well as some male allies, began to object to the unfairness of the legal environment. Some such women were the wives or daughters of political leaders, and their husbands or fathers often sympathized with them. Campaigns against such rules led to gradual changes. The children of war widows, for example, began to be left with their mothers, not transferred to their paternal relatives. The male dowry, which was often saved until the husband's death (or a divorce), was increased to take account of inflation. The reform provisions of the FPL were after some years reinserted in all marriage contracts—although each provision now had to be individually signed by groom and bride to be considered valid, and little information exists about how often the provisions have been signed or not.

Divorce reforms increased women's economic compensation, but it is unclear how widely these new laws have been enforced. Laws requiring arbitration and certain other procedures before the finalization of male-initiated divorce have resulted in delays of divorces, and have probably prevented the rising divorce rate from rising faster—though if men persist in their efforts to get a divorce, they succeed. Women advisers and recently even limited numbers of female judges have effected improvements in family law outcomes.

The pro-sharia atmosphere in Iran and the heightened role of clerics have allowed an increase in temporary marriage and polygamy. On the other hand, increased urbanization and improved education and health care have caused the average marriage age to rise—the average age is now in the mid-twenties, even though girls can legally marry at 13. More Iranian women than ever before are conscious of, and concerned about, their rights. Many, often with assistance from their natal families, are finding ways to protect those rights and expand them.

> **More Iranian women than ever before are conscious of, and concerned about, their rights.**

New Political Avenues

Since the 1979 revolution, political events in Iran can be summarized according to three trends, which roughly correspond to the three post-revolution decades. All three of these trends have affected women's political activism. First was the rise of Khomeinism in the 1979–1989 period, which involved the suppression of contesting political groups and an appeal to unity and nationalism in the context of the Iran-Iraq War of 1980–88. This period ended with Khomeini's death. The next period, from 1989 to 2001, may be seen as one of reconstruction, realism, and reform. Serving as president during this period were

Ali Akbar Hashemi Rafsanjani (1989–1997) and Mohammad Khatami (1997–2005)—but ultimate power remained with the post-Khomeini leader, Ali Khamenei. In the third period, beginning in 2001, Khamenei encouraged a return to conservatism, and this trend was reinforced with the election of President Mahmoud Ahmadinejad in 2005. (Although the "Islamic left" controlled the parliament for much of the time until 2004, most of that body's reform proposals were rejected by the conservative Council of Guardians.)

During all three periods women played important political roles, despite the suppression of oppositional movements. During the Iran-Iraq War Khomeini stopped discouraging women from working, and even in the first period women entered many new nongovernmental professions. Women relatives of progressive or pragmatic political leaders were important in restoring some women's rights and educational opportunities; these included Zahra Rahnavard, who until Ahmadinejad's 2005 election was president of the women's university al-Zahra; Azam Taleqani, a founder of the Women's Solidarity Association of Iran and editor of a women's newspaper, *Payam-e Hajar;* and Faezeh Hashemi, daughter of ex-President Rafsanjani, who launched the Islamic Women's Sports Committee and edited the women's newspaper *Zan.* These and other progressive Islamists took advantage of a great extension of education (including religious education) for girls and women to develop Islamic approaches to extending women's rights. These included new oral and printed interpretations of the Koran, Traditions, and Islamic law, and the formation of new women's circles to discuss them. These trends were similar to those found in many other Muslim countries.

Secular women also found new ways to be active, especially after 1989, and especially through the printed word. Although nearly all writers have had to support their ideas with Islamic arguments, secularists pushed their arguments the furthest. Such secularists were very active in the women's press, which flourished in the 1990s. Notable was the monthly *Zanan,* launched in 1992 by Shahla Sherkat. The magazine took gender-egalitarian positions, raised forbidden subjects, and included material by authors from the Iranian diaspora and by reformist clerics. The prominent secular attorney Mehrangiz Kar was a frequent contributor. *Zanan* pioneered new interpretations of Islam and helped bring about the gradual reinstatement of women judges. *Zanan*'s writers and others also argued that women could run for president, and several women in 2001 and 2005 presented their candidacies, though the Guardian Council disallowed them. The women's press often features frank discussions of women's problems, and includes reporting on the cases of individual women. Because of Iran's lack of political parties, the press was central in organizing pressure for reform, and until the crackdown on freedoms beginning in 2001 the press was very free. It has continued to enjoy some freedom since the crackdown.

The internet has taken on ever-growing importance, especially since restrictions on the printed press increased. Persian-language sites and their readership are huge in number, and the sites include both personal and political blogs, including some feminist ones that feature writings from among the Iranian diaspora and even some by Western authors. The government has tried technical ways to stifle the internet, but without great success, as people figure out ways to post new pages with new web addresses.

In the 1990s, the importance of women's political participation was demonstrated by the election (and later reelection) of reformist President Khatami, whose candidacy was not favored by Khamenei. Women and young people were the backbone of his huge victories in both elections, and various formal and informal women's groups worked for him. He appointed a woman vice president, encouraged the growth of women's official organizations and NGOs, and relaxed cultural restrictions and censorship. The Guardian Council, however, nullified parliamentary laws benefiting women, except that the minimum age for girls to marry was raised to 13.

An important recognition of Iranian women's struggles came with the award of the 2003 Nobel Peace Prize to the human rights attorney Shirin Ebadi, who has fought courageously in Iran for legal reforms and for the rights of women, children, and dissidents. She has represented several prominent jailed clients and the relatives of some people murdered by "rogue" governmental men. As Ebadi recognizes, some Western reports attribute too much of Iran's human and women's rights activities to her, ignoring the many other brave and intelligent women who are devoted participants in these struggles.

The Conservative Revival

While Iranian women have continued to advance significantly in fields including education (where they have reached 65 percent of university entrants, though the government installed gender quotas this year), health, birth control (the country features probably the world's most successful voluntary program), and entrance into the labor market, women have also faced continuing legal and economic inequalities and a revival of conservative strength, especially since the election of Ahmadinejad. He has appealed especially to widespread economic discontent and has profited from splits among reformers. He represents the social conservatism and religiosity of the lower and bazaar classes, which make up most of the powerful Revolutionary Guard.

At first Ahmadinejad did not increase restrictions on women, and even said women would be allowed to attend soccer games. Clerical reaction forced him to rescind this order. Recently there have been growing restrictions on women, such as increased policing of "bad veiling," makeup, and the "unusual" coiffure and dress found among the new middle and upper classes of the big cities.

The most important governmental attacks were aimed at attempts by women activists to mobilize women in a new way. In 2006 several women activists, inspired in part by the Moroccan example, launched a major campaign to end all legal discrimination against women. This campaign, originally called "One Million Signatures Demanding Changes to Discriminatory Laws," began with a peaceful protest meeting in Tehran in June 2006, which was violently disrupted by the police. The campaign then began to organize visits to homes to both educate and learn from

women in all parts of Iran. It trained hundreds of women and stated, with citations from two ayatollahs, that its aims were not in conflict with Islamic law. In contrast to Morocco, however, the Iranian government strongly opposed this campaign. Government forces have broken up subsequent meetings to promote the campaign and arrested and jailed several of its women leaders, as well as some other women's rights activists. The government has also recently published false accusations against Ebadi and her family and associates, tying them to Zionism and Baha'ism.

Recently Ahmadinejad's government proposed a bill ironically named, like the reform laws of 1967 and 1975, the Family Protection Law. Its provisions would have reinforced polygamy, temporary marriage, and men's privileged position with regard to divorce. On the last day of August 2008 approximately 100 leaders and activists from various women's groups met with members of the parliament and argued against the bill. The worst articles in the bill were removed in early September, and the bill was sent back to the Parliamentary Judicial Committee for further revisions. This was a great victory for women's rights.

The Struggle Goes on

While the campaign for equal laws and rights in Iran continues, many women and men have for now abandoned oppositional activity in view of its dangers. American threats against Iran may have aroused nationalism and strengthened the government's appeals for national unity. On the other hand, Ahmadinejad's failure to fulfill his campaign promises, and the worsening of major economic and other problems, have led to much discontent. Most Iranians are angry and disillusioned because of their severe economic problems. They associate these problems with Ahmadinejad, and such sentiment could lead to continued strikes, economic protests, and perhaps a new president in 2009.

Many women and men have for now abandoned oppositional activity in view of its dangers.

Iran and Morocco, though their histories regarding women's rights have followed different trajectories, demonstrate how the interaction of world and local circumstances—along with the actions of feminists, nationalists, socialists, Islamists, and rulers—can lead both to an expansion of women's rights and status and to resistance to this expansion. Activist women face major challenges but also have major achievements and, along with some male allies, continue to struggle.

NIKKI R. KEDDIE is professor emeritus in the department of history at the University of California, Los Angeles. Her books include *Women in the Middle East: Past and Present* (Princeton University Press, 2007) and *Modern Iran: Roots and Results of Revolution* (Yale University Press, 2006).

Women in Developing Countries 300 Times More Likely to Die in Childbirth

UN report reveals 500,000 women in developing world die each year as a result of pregnancy.

SARAH BOSELEY

Women in the world's least developed countries are 300 times more likely to die during childbirth or because of their pregnancy than those in the UK and other similarly developed countries, a UN report says today.

The death toll is more than half a million women a year, according to Unicef, the UN children's emergency fund. Some 70,000 who die are girls and young women aged 15 to 19. Although it is the subject of one of the millennium development goals, the death toll is not going down.

The reasons are multiple, according to Unicef's annual state of the world's children report on maternal and newborn health. "The root cause may lie in women's disadvantaged position in many countries and cultures and in the lack of attention to, and accountability for, women's rights," it says.

"Saving the lives of mothers and their newborns requires more than just medical intervention," said Ann Veneman, Unicef's executive director. "Educating girls is pivotal to improving maternal and neonatal health and also benefits families and societies."

Women die as a result of infection and of haemorrhage. Some have obstructed labour and cannot get a caesarean section. Others die of preventable complications.

Both mothers and babies are vulnerable in the weeks after birth, the report points out. They need post-natal visits, proper hygiene and counselling about the danger signs for themselves and their baby.

Many developing countries have succeeded in reducing the death rate for children under five, but have failed to make much progress on mothers. Niger and Malawi, for example, cut under-five deaths by nearly half between 1990 and 2007.

In the developing world, a woman has a one-in-76 risk of dying because of pregnancy or childbirth in her lifetime. In developed countries, that risk is only one in 8,000.

Having a child in a developing country is one of the most severe health risks for women. For every woman who dies, another 20 suffer illness or injury, which can be permanent.

The 10 countries with the highest risk of maternal death, says Unicef, are Niger, Afghanistan, Sierra Leone, Chad, Angola, Liberia, Somalia, the Democratic Republic of Congo, Guinea-Bissau and Mali.

Deaths of newborns have also received too little attention, the report says. A child born in one of the least developed countries is nearly 14 times more likely to die within the first 28 days of life than one in an industrialised country such as the UK.

Recession Hits Women in Developing Countries

OLIVIA WARD

In Nepal, destitute parents sell their daughters to traffickers. In Pakistan, marrying off underage daughters relieves a family's financial burden. In parts of Asia and Africa, mothers are forced to choose which of their children they will feed, and which will starve.

Today, International Women's Day, women celebrate the gains made in achieving equal rights and highlight the widespread wrongs that damage the lives of the 3.3 billion females around the world.

But the issue foremost in women's minds is the global recession, which has hit the most vulnerable half of humanity with exceptional force.

Seventy per cent of the poorest people on the planet are women and girls, and even in a wealthy country like Canada they are the majority of the poor.

Although the global downturn began in the financial sector, dominated by men, it is now bearing down on women, most often found in low-wage and part-time jobs.

The recession has plunged from wealthy to developing countries, where women lack safety nets to help them survive.

"As the economy slows, the disaster in the financial institutions is affecting the real economy," says Sylvia Borren, co-chair of the Global Call to Action Against Poverty, a coalition of groups in 100 countries.

"What happens is the informal sector suffers first—the cleaning women, gardeners and people who do the household jobs. They are mostly women."

As worldwide consumer confidence fades, says the International Labour Organization, traditionally female service jobs in cafes and retail stores are also disappearing. It predicts that 22 million of an estimated 51 million to lose their jobs this year will be women.

Adding to the problem is a global food crisis that has caused a spike in the price of dietary staples like rice, narrowing the line between malnutrition and starvation.

"The increase in hunger and economic stress is accelerating fast, and that affects women in a number of different ways," says Borren.

Because women earn less than men even in good times—a 16 per cent global pay gap, according to the International Trade

Struggle in Iraq

The most shattering moment of Bushara's life arrived without warning: "One year ago when I went out to buy breakfast, I saw something written on the wall of our house," she said. "The graffiti told Shiites in the neighbourhood to get out."

Bushara, an Iraqi mother who lived near Abu Ghraib prison, knew there was no time to waste. The death squads were on the march. In bare feet, she fled with her husband and young daughters as the winter winds propelled them from their home. Her story, told to Oxfam International, is typical for Iraqi women, who have suffered loss and destitution since the U.S. overthrow of Saddam Hussein in 2003. Nor has the reported lessening of violence since 2007 improved their lives.

According to an Oxfam survey released last week, "despite fragile security gains and a decline in indiscriminate and sectarian violence over the past months, the day-to-day lives of many women in Iraq remain dire." Questioning 1,700 women in five provinces, Oxfam found:

- More than 40 per cent said their security situation was worse than last year; 22 per cent said it was about the same.
- 55 per cent said they had become victims of violence since the invasion.
- More than 30 per cent had family members who died violently.
- About 69 per cent said access to water was worse; 25 per cent had no daily access to drinking water.
- Two-thirds had electricity less than six hours a day, and one-third less than three hours a day.
- 40 percent said that their children were not attending school.

—Olivia Ward

Union Confederation—they have less to fall back on when times turn bad.

But those at the bottom are also caught in a vicious circle of poverty and abuse. Women who held normal jobs are forced into the "shadow" economy of prostitution, drug smuggling and other criminal activity. Or they are drawn into the nets of vicious international traffickers.

They're also more at risk of domestic violence, when unemployed husbands and fathers take out their frustration at home.

At the same time, cuts in humanitarian aid budgets mean less money to spend on education, the key factor in lifting women out of poverty. Health care suffers, with devastating effects on pregnant women, HIV/AIDs victims, and those in conflict zones where women are targeted for sexual attack.

Some of the worst affected women are migrants, whose numbers grow as life gets harder in their original countries.

"Women and girls are disproportionately affected by the risks of migration because of their vulnerability to exploitation and violence," says Ndioro Ndiaye of the International Organization for Migration. And, he adds, lack of access to health care can have long-term effects for women and their children.

But as the economic storm clouds gather, the horizon is not entirely dark for women, says Borren.

"If you go to local solutions, you see room for hope," she says.

"To help in the food crisis, there's organizing and investing in microcredit so women can have plots of land. Unions are trying to solve the problem of lack of qualified teachers with fast-track training. Small water and electricity projects can work at the household level."

Along with increased risk there is great opportunity for women in the current crisis, Borren says. "We're concentrating on top-down solutions, which have proved unsustainable, and often stupid. Now it's time to put women at the centre, and work from the bottom up."

Test-Your-Knowledge Form

We encourage you to photocopy and use this page as a tool to assess how the articles in *Annual Editions* expand on the information in your textbook. By reflecting on the articles you will gain enhanced text information. You can also access this useful form on a product's book support website at *http://www.mhcls.com*.

NAME:

DATE:

_____

TITLE AND NUMBER OF ARTICLE:

_____

BRIEFLY STATE THE MAIN IDEA OF THIS ARTICLE:

_____

LIST THREE IMPORTANT FACTS THAT THE AUTHOR USES TO SUPPORT THE MAIN IDEA:

_____

WHAT INFORMATION OR IDEAS DISCUSSED IN THIS ARTICLE ARE ALSO DISCUSSED IN YOUR TEXTBOOK OR OTHER READINGS THAT YOU HAVE DONE? LIST THE TEXTBOOK CHAPTERS AND PAGE NUMBERS:

_____

LIST ANY EXAMPLES OF BIAS OR FAULTY REASONING THAT YOU FOUND IN THE ARTICLE:

_____

LIST ANY NEW TERMS/CONCEPTS THAT WERE DISCUSSED IN THE ARTICLE, AND WRITE A SHORT DEFINITION:

We Want Your Advice

ANNUAL EDITIONS revisions depend on two major opinion sources: one is our Advisory Board, listed in the front of this volume, which works with us in scanning the thousands of articles published in the public press each year; the other is you—the person actually using the book. Please help us and the users of the next edition by completing the prepaid article rating form on this page and returning it to us. Thank you for your help!

ANNUAL EDITIONS: Developing World 10/11

ARTICLE RATING FORM

Here is an opportunity for you to have direct input into the next revision of this volume.
We would like you to rate each of the articles listed below, using the following scale:

1. **Excellent: should definitely be retained**
2. **Above average: should probably be retained**
3. **Below average: should probably be deleted**
4. **Poor: should definitely be deleted**

Your ratings will play a vital part in the next revision.
Please mail this prepaid form to us as soon as possible.
Thanks for your help!

RATING	ARTICLE	RATING	ARTICLE
	1. The New Face of Development		28. Asia's Democracy Backlash
	2. How Development Leads to Democracy: What We Know about Modernization		29. India Held Back
			30. Bring Me My Machine Gun
	3. The Ideology of Development		31. Who Will Speak for Islam?
	4. Africa's Village of Dreams		32. Free at Last?
	5. The Case against the West: America and Europe in the Asian Century		33. Iran in Search of Itself
			34. Lula's Brazil: A Rising Power, but Going Where?
	6. Development as Poison: Rethinking the Western Model of Modernity		35. An Empty Revolution: The Unfulfilled Promises of Hugo Chávez
	7. Industrial Revolution 2.0		36. Booms, Busts, and Echoes
	8. The Toxins Trickle Downwards		37. Emerging Water Shortages
	9. The Poor Man's Burden		38. Water Warriors
	10. Social Justice and Global Trade		39. Soot from Third-World Stoves Is New Target in Climate Fight
	11. Cotton: The Huge Moral Issue		
	12. Across Globe, Empty Bellies Bring Rising Anger		40. Population, Human Resources, Health, and the Environment: Getting the Balance Right
	13. The Politics of Hunger		
	14. The New Colonialists		41. Protecting Climate Refugees: The Case for a Global Protocol
	15. Power to the People		
	16. The Micromagic of Microcredit		42. Reversal of Fortune: Why Preventing Poverty Beats Curing It
	17. The Coming Revolution in Africa		
	18. The End of War?		43. Women's Rights as Human Rights: The Promotion of Human Rights as a Counter-Culture
	19. Fixing a Broken World		
	20. The Roots of Failure in Afghanistan		44. Educating Girls, Unlocking Development
	21. Pakistan's Perilous Voyage		45. Education: It's Not Just about the Boys. Get Girls into School
	22. The Shiite "Threat" Revisited		
	23. The Most Dangerous Place in the World		46. Women in the Middle East: Progress and Backlash
	24. Will the Kenyan Settlement Hold?		
	25. Mexico's Drug Wars Get Brutal		47. Women in Developing Countries 300 Times More Likely to Die in Childbirth
	26. Dangerous Liaisons		
	27. Call in the Blue Helmets		48. Recession Hits Women in Developing Countries

BUSINESS REPLY MAIL
FIRST CLASS MAIL PERMIT NO. 551 DUBUQUE IA

POSTAGE WILL BE PAID BY ADDRESSEE

McGraw-Hill Contemporary Learning Series
501 BELL STREET
DUBUQUE, IA 52001

ABOUT YOU

Name

Date

Are you a teacher? ❑ A student? ❑
Your school's name

Department

Address   City   State   Zip

School telephone #

YOUR COMMENTS ARE IMPORTANT TO US!

Please fill in the following information:
For which course did you use this book?

Did you use a text with this ANNUAL EDITION? ❑ yes ❑ no
What was the title of the text?

What are your general reactions to the Annual Editions concept?

Have you read any pertinent articles recently that you think should be included in the next edition? Explain.

Are there any articles that you feel should be replaced in the next edition? Why?

Are there any World Wide Websites that you feel should be included in the next edition? Please annotate.

May we contact you for editorial input? ❑ yes ❑ no
May we quote your comments? ❑ yes ❑ no